MW01205099

Rousseau's Daughters

Becoming Modern: New Nineteenth-Century Studies

SERIES EDITORS

Sarah Sherman
Department of English
University of New Hampshire

Rohan McWilliam
Anglia Ruskin University
Cambridge, England

Janet Aikins Yount
Department of English
University of New Hampshire

Janet Polasky
Department of History
University of New Hampshire

This book series maps the complexity of historical change and assesses the formation of ideas, movements, and institutions crucial to our own time by publishing books that examine the emergence of modernity in North America and Europe. Set primarily but not exclusively in the nineteenth century, the series shifts attention from modernity's twentieth-century forms to its earlier moments of uncertain and often disputed construction. Seeking books of interest to scholars on both sides of the Atlantic, it thereby encourages the expansion of nineteenth-century studies and the exploration of more global patterns of development.

For a complete list of books that are available in this series, see www.upne.com and www .upne.com/series/BMS.html

Jennifer J. Popiel, *Rousseau's Daughters: Domesticity, Education, and Autonomy in Modern France*

Paula Young Lee, editor, *Meat, Modernity, and the Rise of the Slaughterhouse*

Duncan Faherty, *Remodeling the Nation: The Architecture of American Identity, 1776–1858*

Jennifer Hall-Witt, *Fashionable Acts: Opera and Elite Culture in London, 1780–1880*

Scott Malloy, *Trolley Wars: Streetcar Workers on the Line*

William C. Dowling, *Oliver Wendell Holmes in Paris: Medicine, Theology, and the Autocrat of the Breakfast Table*

Betsy Klimasmith, *At Home in the City: Urban Domesticity in American Literature and Culture, 1850–1930*

Sarah Luria, *Capital Speculations: Writing and Building Washington, D.C.*

David L. Richards, *Poland Spring: A Tale of the Gilded Age, 1860–1900*

Angela Sorby, *Schoolroom Poets: Childhood, Performance, and the Place of American Poetry, 1865–1917*

Rousseau's Daughters

Domesticity, Education, and Autonomy in Modern France

Jennifer J. Popiel

University of New Hampshire Press
Durham, New Hampshire

PUBLISHED BY UNIVERSITY PRESS OF NEW ENGLAND
HANOVER AND LONDON

UNIVERSITY OF NEW HAMPSHIRE PRESS
Published by University Press of New England,
One Court Street, Lebanon, NH 03766
www.upne.com
© 2008 by University of New Hampshire Press
Printed in the United States of America
5 4 3 2 1

All rights reserved. No part of this book may be reproduced in any form or by any electronic or mechanical means, including storage and retrieval systems, without permission in writing from the publisher, except by a reviewer, who may quote brief passages in a review. Members of educational institutions and organizations wishing to photocopy any of the work for classroom use, or authors and publishers who would like to obtain permission for any of the material in the work, should contact Permissions, University Press of New England, One Court Street, Lebanon, NH 03766.

Library of Congress Cataloging-in-Publication Data
Popiel, Jennifer J.
    Rousseau's daughters : domesticity, education, and autonomy in modern France / Jennifer J. Popiel.
        p.   cm. — (Becoming modern: new nineteenth-century studies)
    Includes bibliographical references and index.
    ISBN 978-1-58465-732-3 (cloth : alk. paper)
    1. Motherhood—France—History—19th century. 2. Child rearing—France—History—19th century. 3. Sex discrimination against women—France—History—19th century. 4. Rousseau, Jean-Jacques, 1712–1778. I. Title.
    HQ759.P642 2008
    306.874'3094409034—dc22   2008021314

University Press of New England is a member of the Green Press Initiative. The paper used in this book meets their minimum requirement for recycled paper.

To my parents

Contents

Acknowledgments

One of the happiest parts about seeing one's work come to fruition is the fact that there is—at long last—a public forum for recognizing all of the support that has made the book possible. Given both the range of subjects that I cover and the amount of time that has lapsed since I first began work on the project, I have wide-ranging intellectual and personal debts. While a brief mention of the people and institutions that have supported me can hardly begin to adequately convey my thanks, I hope that everyone mentioned will know how thankful I am for their assistance and how much better the book is for their help. If errors remain, they are entirely my own and should not be seen as a reflection upon anyone who has helped me along the way.

In some sense, this book began long before I had any inkling that I might want to be a historian. My first history class at Trinity University, which was, serendipitously, taught by Gary Kates, compelled me. I had no idea that the history of France—indeed, history at all!—could be so fun, so lively, so critical and engaging. Gary has continued to be a mentor and a model in the years that have passed and I appreciate his willingness to take time out of his busy schedule to read the entire manuscript. My dissertation advisor at the University of Pennsylvania, Lynn Hunt, has also been a wonderful mentor as well as a source of encouragement and inspiration. Her advice is always timely and her example has offered me instruction in everything from intellectual engagement with the world to maintaining one's humanity in academia.

I have been fortunate enough to call a number of institutions home while working on this project, including the University of Pennsylvania, the University of California at Los Angeles, the University of Wisconsin, Green Bay, and Saint Louis University. I conducted research at the Bibliothèque Nationale de France, Archives Nationales, Bibliothèque Historique de la Ville de Paris, Institut National de la Recherche Pédagogique, Musée des Arts Décoratifs, Musée de la Mode, and the Musée National de l'Éducation. The librarians, archivists, and historians of all these institutions helped me find the information that I needed and offered their own thoughts and expertise to assist me. I am truly thankful for all their assistance.

Funding for the many stages of this project came from the Department of History at the University of Pennsylvania, the Mellon Foundation, Faculty Research Grants at the University of Wisconsin, Green Bay, and the University of Wisconsin's Center for European Studies. The Provost's Office at St. Louis University provided the final research leave that made completion of the project possible, and a Mellon Faculty Development Grant helped underwrite publication.

Countless people have generously shared their time to read parts of the manuscript. Their insightful questions and thoughtful feedback cannot be overrated. Participants in the Western Society for French History, UCLA European History Colloquium, the Wisconsin French History Group, Society for French Historical Studies, the Western and Midwestern Divisions of the American Society for Eighteenth-Century Studies, and the Eighteenth-Century Interdisciplinary Salon offered me questions and comments and helped me refine my work. Susan Kling read it when it was still a dissertation and has continued to offer thoughts, advice, and friendship. Suzanne Desan carefully read more than one chapter and provided a number of important criticisms that helped me to rethink my argument. Elinor Accampo, Rachel Fuchs, and Jennifer Jones have also read portions of the work; for their helpful evaluations I am extremely grateful. As the book neared completion, the readers for the University Press of New England, especially Jennifer Heuer, provided crucial feedback that allowed me to clarify my argument and contextualize my findings. Phyllis Deutsch, the editor-in-chief for UPNE, suggested the Becoming Modern series as a possible venue for publication long before the work I had completed was really worthy of such hope. She and the series editors have been quick to read and respond and I can count on their comments to be both critical and constructive, a wonderful combination. I hope that all of these people will find that my revisions have done their hard work justice.

My colleagues and friends have also been a source of useful criticism as well as willing lunch-partners, coffee-drinkers, and friends. Ellen Amster, Lauren Clay, Gene Ogle, and many other graduate students at Penn made my time there pleasant. Warren Breckman and Lynn Hollen Lees offered important feedback when the project was "just" a dissertation and helped me to envision the process by which it could become a book. Dena Goodman has been unfailingly cheery, helpful, and kind. I always look forward to conferences when Joelle Neulander and Carolyn Eichner are going to be there. Jeff Horn not only introduced me to the BN and the AN but also shared some of his favorite Paris haunts and can be counted on to make me laugh.

Others, like Greg Aldrete and Joyce Salisbury, were ideal colleagues at the University of Wisconsin, Green Bay. They, as well as Kim Nielson, Andy Kersten, and Harvey Kaye, not only welcomed me with open arms but made UWGB a congenial place to be. While leaving such wonderful historians in Green Bay was hard, I found at St. Louis University countless colleagues who are equally supportive, helpful, and engaged. From the moment that I met her, Elisabeth Perry was willing to discuss, read, and analyze my work. I am thankful for her generous intellect. Dan Schlafly closely read the entire manuscript more than once. If there are split infinitives, they have found their way in despite him! The chairs of SLU's History department, Thomas Madden and Michal Rozbicki, have supported my research and have been extremely accommodating. R. Bentley Anderson, S.J., Mark Ruff, Silvana Siddali, and Damian Smith have been good friends in addition to being excellent colleagues. I appreciate their sense of humor, their ability to bring me down to earth, and their support. Kathy Bonsack, Teresa Harvey, and Chris Pudlowski have provided me with office supplies, assistance, and friendly conversation, all while refraining from commentary on my printing excesses. Research assistants Anne Romine, Julie Forster, and Susan Mokhberi did some legwork that saved me time, money, and embarrassing mistakes.

Annie Smart, my Doppelganger in SLU's French department, has been an incredible resource. She pointed me to Louis-Aimé Martin, deepened my understanding of the literary components of eighteenth- and nineteenth-century domestic ideology, and has been an excellent critic. I still marvel at the ways that our work overlaps and look forward to many more conversations with her.

Parts of some chapters of this book have already been published in other venues. A very early incarnation of chapter 2 was published as "'To Amuse and Instruct': Freedom, Education, and the Molding of the Child in Modern France," in *Childhood and Youth: A Universal Odyssey* (1998). Portions of chapter 3 were published in *The Journal of Family History* 29 (2004), as "Making Mothers: The Maternal Advice Genre and the Domestic Ideal, 1760–1830." Some of chapter 4 can be found in the article "'To Repress the Exuberance of Their Characters': Self-Control and the Definition of Womanhood in Nineteenth-Century France," published in the *Proceedings of the Western Society for French History* 26 (2000). I am grateful for the permission of these editors and publishers to reprint my work as well as the opportunity that they gave to present my thoughts as I was working them out.

On a personal note, this project would not be the same without the support of my friends and my family. Kasey Walker has commiserated with me about the trials of academic life and been a better friend than I could invent, given the opportunity. The "internet moms" in my life have shared my triumphs and trials, encouraged me to push on, and, as women who are smart mothers, have lent a critical eye of a different sort to my work. All of these friends have made sure that I remained rooted in reality and encouraged me not to lose sight of the truly important things in life.

The more than ten years in which I have studied domestic motherhood and education have also been years of marriage to my husband, David Borgmeyer. He has lived with this project from very early on, and his critical readings and encouraging support have not only allowed me to pursue my work but also have made me a clearer thinker and a better writer. His willingness to fully engage with nurturing and domestic fatherhood allows me to be a successful working mother. The fact that our family thrives is a tribute to him, and I hope that our four children recognize it as clearly as I do. I am also grateful to Dave's parents, Elmer and Dorothy Borgmeyer, not only for the virtue they instilled in their son, but also for their willingness to pack boxes, watch children, and generally offer support.

Last, but decidedly not least, my parents, Rod and Arlette Popiel, set the first example of nurturing in my life. I am intellectually, personally, and spiritually indebted to them. In loving thanks, I dedicate this book to them.

Rousseau's Daughters

Enlightening Mothers

Gender and Self-Control in France

The strictness of the relative duties of the two sexes is not and cannot be the same. When woman complains on this score about unjust man-made inequality she is wrong. This inequality is not a human institution—or, at least, it is the work not of prejudice but of reason. It is up to the sex that nature has charged with the bearing of children to be responsible for them to the other sex.   —Jean Jacques Rousseau, *Emile, or On Education* (1762)

Over and over women heard in voices of tradition . . . that they could desire no greater destiny than to glory in their own femininity. Experts told them how to catch a man and keep him, how to breastfeed children and handle their toilet training . . . how to dress, look, and act more feminine and make marriage more exciting . . . A thousand expert voices applauded their femininity, their adjustment, their new maturity. All they had to do was devote their lives from earliest girlhood to finding a husband and bearing children.
—Betty Friedan, *The Feminine Mystique* (1963)

*W*hen I first encountered Jean-Jacques Rousseau, I despised his work. I still have my first copy of the *Letter to d'Alembert on the Theatre*, complete with underlinings, exclamation points, and hostile reactions. The marginalia complain about the sexism, the emphasis on "nature," and the hyperrational exclusion of women, the "banishment to the domestic sphere,"[1] all the ways that his work demonstrated for me what was wrong with Enlightenment thought about the sexes. As I began research on education and domesticity in the eighteenth century and read *Emile*, those thoughts crystallized. I, like Joan Landes, believed that Rousseau "yoked [women] to a conservative and ultimately passive function,"[2] and I agreed with feminist philosophers like Carol Blum and Lydia Lange that Rousseau was the epitome of the "male political philosopher [who was] 'sincere, manly, and quite hysterical' in his preoccupation with women and their proper role."[3] This was, to my mind, a man who, despite prescient criticism of much of contemporary society, reinforced his society's ideals about women, and I believed that Rousseau's "primary 'human' values—equality and freedom—[were] swept aside entirely when he [discussed] the proper place and role of the female sex."[4] After all, Rousseau's work proclaimed that public women unmanned men and calmly declared it self-evident that Sophie was made only to please Emile. While I could see how eighteenth-century men might have found his vision of the world reassuring, I wondered how Rousseau was able to inspire so many eighteenth-century women.[5]

As I read deeper in the literature, I found a second perspective on Rousseau's work. Other scholars, such as Helena Rosenblatt and Lori Jo Marso, moved beyond accusations of misogyny and instead drew finer historical and literary distinctions within Rousseau's work.[6] Taking lessons from them, and incorporating some ideas of my own, I began to realize that Rousseau could be read in a new way, by bringing a multiplicity of sources to bear on the same questions that he introduced. Indeed, since even Rousseau himself had not mastered the problems on which he focused, especially the tension between mastery and self-control, I realized that the field was wide open for alternative readings.

As I approached Rousseau again, something unexpected happened. Rousseau's writing drew me in with its simplicity and strength. I saw the ways in which Rousseau's analysis of a woman's proper role could be understood as his contemporaries read it, as an integral part of his emphasis on the need for virtuous action and the creation of individuals for a new society. I came to read the Discourse on Inequality without cringing at its underlying sexism and bizarre throwaway remarks. Rousseau's work became compelling. I understood why revolutionaries had seized upon his vision of the moral individual. Eventually, I found myself sympathizing with—and even befriending—him. Imagine my amazement on the day when I found myself nodding in agreement with Joseph Reisert's words: "Whenever I read Rousseau, I feel that he is speaking directly to me"![7]

My newfound appreciation for Rousseau's social vision was part of a long process and one that should not be construed as wholeheartedly affirming his gender politics. However, as I examined sources for education, child-rearing, and domesticity in eighteenth- and nineteenth-century France, I came to understand why an eighteenth-century French philosopher, so concerned with the modern condition, could be central to a widespread ideological shift toward domestic nurturing. New genres of literature, new forms of clothing, and new approaches to schooling all arose from the widespread attempt—by men and women alike—to convince eighteenth- and nineteenth-century women that the refashioning of their families, including a new emphasis on gender difference, was essential to any reconstruction of society. From this perspective, Rousseau's demands for self-control, gendered spheres, and a new approach to childhood education come together. The more I examined the broader context of domestic motherhood, the less convincing appeared the interpretation that insisted that any eighteenth-century woman who liked Rousseau was at least mistaken and quite possibly self-hating.[8] Many intelligent and accomplished women in the eighteenth and nineteenth centuries were attracted to Rousseau's vision. Were they really blinded to his politics or responding to "an unconscious temptation to surrender and even to destroy" themselves?[9] Seen in historical context, Rousseau's statements about men's and women's natural roles can be interpreted more positively. If he was not a twenty-first-century feminist, neither was he, by eighteenth-century standards, a complete misogynist.

Cultural History of Gender and Child-Rearing

This book is the result of a struggle—partly personal, but primarily historiographical—to reconcile an increased philosophical emphasis on individuality, including the promotion of modern nurturing approaches to childhood, with demands, such as Rousseau's, for greater self-control and gender differentiation. It examines domesticity and child-rearing in the context of the philosophical, cultural, and educational changes of the eighteenth and nineteenth centuries and argues that an eighteenth-century literature that revolutionized approaches to childhood and domestic motherhood continued to have a great ideological impact in the nineteenth century, not only for child-rearing, but also outside the home, helping shape new approaches to education and new visions of gender and society.[10] In his work on masculinity and the home, John Tosh defines domesticity as "not just a pattern of residence or a web of obligations, but a profound attachment: a state of mind as well as a physical orientation. Its defining attributes are privacy and comfort, separation from the workplace, and the merging of domestic space and family members into a single commanding concept."[11] Certainly, the new emphasis on privacy, separation, and a changing state of mind will also be found in this work. However, the sources from this work indicate it need not be urban nor even a product of the nineteenth century. Domesticity certainly changed the symbolic landscape and broader visions of family life, but in France, domestic ideals—including a new prominence for maternity and child-rearing—were emphasized in multiple contexts even before the French Revolution.

The questions raised here should make it clear that this is not a work of social history or educational theory, but rather of cultural and intellectual history. While eighteenth- and nineteenth-century schooling in France has often been examined from both a theoretical and practical standpoint, the contemporary eighteenth- and nineteenth-century rhetoric about child-rearing and domesticity remains largely unexplored. This book surveys a wide range of topics central to understanding childhood and individuality. The sources reflect themes of both self-control and increasing gender differentiation. They show that axioms that were intended to increase the autonomy and equality of individuals also had important implications for their gender, discipline, and self-control. The ideological tension between social control over education and emotional mastery of self and child also raises fundamental questions regarding nurturing affection, self-control, and gender difference.

In the late eighteenth and early nineteenth centuries, literature and philosophy encouraged French parents to see the family as the new locus of social change. Domestic child-rearing took on new importance. Not only was the ideal mother the moral center and focus of educational literature, but political and moral tracts also claimed that she was the crucial instrument for preparing and disciplining her offspring so that they could face and eventually reshape the world. All children needed to have similar private training because they were all capable of acquiring the same qualities that were fundamental for all autonomous adults, male and female, most notably self-control. Despite an increasing focus on the gender of children, descriptions of, as well as prescriptions for, the proper maternal role were largely the same for boys and girls and could be summarized in a few maxims, beginning with leaving children's bodies unconstrained and free so they would grow up to be healthy and strong. Physical health and strength were not simply goals in and of themselves, however. A sound body was also a necessary prerequisite for eventual autonomy, since the desired values of rationality and self-control could not be divorced from the ability to experience the world physically. Children would learn the way they should relate to the world even as they internalized social expectations from their mothers' examples. These expectations emphasized gender differences, but many, if not most, moral expectations were the same for girls as for boys.

Eighteenth- and Nineteenth-Century Childhood and Domestic Education

Historians often point to the later eighteenth century as the moment of the "invention" of the domestic mother. Before the eighteenth century, childhood was not seen as a distinct stage of life where children needed special nurturing. Educational philosophers often depicted children as

evil or barbarous.[12] Since they were born steeped in original sin, their tendency to greedy self-indulgence and outright iniquity had to be corrected
by parents and educators who would force them to conform to proper
(and adult) ways of behaving. Children betrayed beastly tendencies in a
number of ways, from crawling on the ground like animals to greedily
sucking away their mother's milk. Education could be provided by a wet-
nurse as well as a parent, for the primary task was to prevent children
from acting like animals and to teach them to behave like adult members
of society. The transition from childhood to adulthood meant embracing
one's personal responsibilities in a community formed by God and based
on a hierarchy where the children's status was already determined.
Hence, allowing children freedom to explore, play, and develop "naturally" was out of the question and actively discouraged, as reflected in
treatises and the records of material culture.

From the medieval era until well after 1700, French parents routinely
shipped their newborn boys and girls off to be nursed by complete
strangers, who wrapped the babies in rags and hung them on hooks on
the wall so that the nurses could go about their daily work without the
burden of their charges. Child-rearing manuals of the early eighteenth
century demonstrate that it was the rare mother who visited these children, even when she had the leisure and means to do so. A mother's reproductive duty did not extend far beyond becoming pregnant and giving
birth, so nurturing was not seen as socially relevant in parenting advice.[13]
By the early nineteenth century, the situation had changed dramatically,
however. Tributes to breast-feeding and "natural" mothers declared nurturing *the* priority. Only the "unnatural" mother could give birth to a
child and then place the future and oversight of the child into other
hands. Not surprisingly, mothers who refused to fulfill their God-given
obligations to breast-feed, care for, and educate their children personally
could find themselves subject to censure by husbands, neighbors, or even
legislators who wished to protect the welfare of the future citizens.

Though he was not the only catalyst for these changes, Jean-Jacques
Rousseau's work drove this shift in perception. Rousseau claimed that
children were not by nature beastly but instead were capable of rational
thought and good actions if they were removed from the constraints
placed upon them by society and nurtured by a domestic mother. In
Rousseau's opinion, the existing French system of educating children
stifled many positive and natural impulses, which it replaced with the
artifice of civilization. "Civilizing" children actually meant that they
would grow up to be jealous, acquisitive, and competitive; in a word, they
would become antisocial. Therefore, it was far better to let children discover their true nature at home, away from the prison of social institutions and customs. "In the natural order all men are equal and their com-

mon calling is that of manhood,"[14] so what need was there for excessive control by institutions? As Rousseau claimed in Book One of *Emile*, his treatise on education, "God makes all things good; man meddles with them and they become evil."[15] These ideas spread rapidly. On the eve of the revolution in France, Germaine de Staël claimed, "[e]veryone has adopted Rousseau's physical system of education. A sure system has permitted no disagreement . . . He has succeeded in restoring happiness to childhood."[16] While Staël may have been overly optimistic about the actual degree of implementation, her words indicate how far-reaching Rousseau's ideological influence had become. Rousseauian training, which emphasized physical and mental freedom and assumed that children needed good mothers if they were to become contributing members of society, had, at least ideologically, established domestic nurturing as a high calling.

Civilization, Oppression, and Gender

The questions surrounding Enlightenment ideals, freedom, and social training speak to the heart of two contemporary historiographical debates about the meaning of ideological changes in the modern world. While Staël saw an emphasis on childhood as a positive shift, a different reading of the same process offers the possibility that civilization does not bring anyone, male or female, the progress that the Enlightenment promised but instead led to totalitarianism and unending control. Much of the recent work dealing with modern life argues that changes like those demonstrated by a more intense focus on the care of children and a new veneration of mothers hardly make the modern world more "free." Instead, these emotional changes can be taken as proof that the post-Enlightenment world coerces and constrains us in ways that we can neither recognize nor effectively oppose. After all, in the *Social Contract*, Rousseau also famously wrote that people who would not willingly go along with the general will must be "forced to be free." To our contemporary minds, such phrases incline us not to visions of freedom and human rights, but instead Nazism, Stalinism, and other oppressive ideologies of the twentieth century. In a similar vein, thinkers ranging from Sigmund Freud to Michel Foucault have argued that the modern world forces us to retreat farther and farther from our true selves and our good—or at least natural—inclinations.

The evidence given here contests the post-modern assumption, typified by the work of Foucault, that increasing social control and expectations of self-discipline are inherently opposed to the development of freedom and individuality.[17] Instead, it argues that the new approaches to education, with their increased focus on the self-control and mental training of individuals, promoted liberal ideas of individuality, autonomy, and freedom. In his sociological theory, Norbert Elias has argued in favor of this position, positing that modern self-discipline belies a "diminishment of social inequality between the sexes,"[18] and modern structural changes generally tend toward increased differentiation at the same time as they head toward integration.[19] However, his work gives few concrete examples by which one might judge what impact an increased focus on gender has for the integration of members of the female sex into society as a whole. The cultural history of French child-rearing provides a testing ground for Elias' suppositions even as the sources demonstrate that the rise of gendered and individualized children went hand-in-hand with the creation of institutions designed to guide youth to a proper recognition of their rights and duties.

Additionally, despite the similarities between moral expectations for boys and girls, an emphasis on gender difference places this work in the middle of another historiographical problem. Scholars have long recognized that restricting women to the domestic sphere seems to contradict general notions of individuality and freedom. For example, historian Joan Landes has argued that liberalism was founded on the exclusion of women from the public sphere. She explains that, "unlike her male companion, of whom Rousseau also demands the sublimation of particular interests on behalf of a desire for the public good, woman is barred completely from active participation in the very sphere that gives purpose to her actions."[20] Landes' work claims that public politics became masculine in the nineteenth century and women's lives became private, domestic, and apolitical. Political theorist Carole Pateman joins this refrain, making a case that the social contract, where "freedom becomes obedience and, in exchange, protection is provided," is fundamentally patriarchal.[21] Acceptance of the social contract, she contends, creates a situation where liberalism offers increased opportunities for men at the expense of women, so that men benefit from the new democratic societies, but women suffer. According to this argument, the term "man of virtue" is no accident, for the new freedoms are designed for men alone and come at the price of women's exclusion from public life.

A quick glance at Rousseau's work seems only to confirm the assumption that submission and inequality were central components in the new domesticity as in the new liberal ideal. If Rousseau had a clear vision of the ways in which modern liberal societies needed to educate citizens to seek self-control for the good of the nation, then it is surely significant that his works, such as *Julie, or The New Heloise* and *Emile, or On Education,* also emphasize that women must be relegated to the domestic sphere in order for society to function properly.[22] The link between domesticity, education, and oppression seems explicit; Rousseau openly argues for women's seclusion in a domestic sphere and emphasizes that women should evaluate their personal worth by their ability to raise their children and care for their families. Given the fact that modern liberalism emphasizes the rights of the individual citizen and claims that all citizens, including women, become free and equal in a representative political system, it becomes even more pressing to explain why, as societies became more liberal, they increasingly limited women to a domestic world, confined to the home and removed from direct political participation and, ideally, all outside influences. Landes and Pateman therefore mark the beginning of an active and ongoing debate about the links between liberalism and patriarchy, and a large body of feminist scholarship in the past twenty years has argued that the French Revolution excluded women from political participation and instead confined them to an apolitical domestic sphere. Even if the Enlightenment opened up options for women, the French Revolution soon limited their alternatives. As Suzanne Desan has summarized, "[w]ork coming out of diverse fields—including political theory, literary criticism, philosophy, intellectual and social history—coalesced to support a set of shared assumptions about the centrality of the Revolution in defining public politics as a male domain and domesticity as a female one."[23]

However, as with the increasing nuance in studies of Rousseau, a new generation of scholarship has complicated this vision of separate spheres and explained that an emphasis on family life did not have to be entirely—or even primarily—negative. Work in both French and American contexts has demonstrated that even domestic women, like the ideal mothers of this study, were able to find spaces for agency and created new familial worlds that were explicitly liberating.[24] For example, Desan and other historians have examined family life in the context of revolutionary politics in order to demonstrate that concepts of motherhood, fatherhood, and national citizenship were embedded in revolutionary language and ideals.[25] However, most of these works do not explain how the creation of these separate universes arose at the same time as the impulses that caused women to demand social and political equality.[26] As a result, while this new work convincingly argues that revolutionary politics were more complex than previously assumed, and that women's domesticity was itself contested, many scholars continue to claim that the rhetoric that trumpeted self-control and docility was inimical to egalitarian ideas and generally reinforced ideas about women's inferiority. For example, Desan contrasts "Rousseau's idealization of domestic submission" to republican ideology and insists that a nineteenth-century emphasis on domesticity was opposed to individual liberty and egalitarianism.[27] Though Desan convincingly demonstrates that the French

Revolution did not preclude political roles for women, she continues to see Rousseauian domesticity and its sacrificial rhetoric as necessarily oppressive and exclusionary.

The intellectual and cultural history of Rousseauian domesticity, however, offers ways to examine the rhetoric of self-control and gender difference in order to see its ideological relationship to an increased emphasis on individualism. By examining the cultural and intellectual content of domesticity, we can see if Rousseau's promotion of education for domesticity and self-control is in any way compatible with liberal ideals.[28] Analyzing Rousseau's model in a wide range of sources addresses both the post-modern critique of post-Enlightenment control and the feminist concern with the post-revolutionary exclusion of women. In particular, investigating motherhood and the realms of education and child-rearing using Rousseau's rhetoric of virtue will demonstrate how self-sacrifice and domestic hierarchies actually contributed, long before the French Revolution or Napoleon's rise to power, to a new ideal predicated on the active participation of women in civic life rather than their banishment or silencing. In the end, the demand that girls should be raised with the strength of character to rule over their passions made their education like that of boys, who were also to become autonomous actors. The rhetoric of domestic virtue therefore moved toward a greater ideological integration of women, as individuals, into the emerging liberal societies.

None of this is to argue that women's exclusion from the political sphere was insignificant. During the French Revolution, Olympe de Gouges' *Declaration of the Rights of Woman and Female Citizen* promoted women's political and social equality with its direct challenge to prevailing attitudes that underlined and promoted women's inferior position. Equally radical arguments for women's equality were given voice by thinkers of the eighteenth and nineteenth centuries like the British Mary Wollstonecraft or the Dutch Etta Palm d'Aelders, both of whom set the stage for economic and political demands by later feminists. The arguments of this book in no way intend to undercut their accomplishments or to suggest that they were somehow misguided. Instead, this work emphasizes that domesticity, even when limited, was also profoundly important in promoting the intellectual and cultural value of women's roles. The language that upheld increasingly significant gender distinctions may not have endorsed political or economic equality, but it did note that women, like men, had the crucial civic characteristic of self-control and were thus in a unique position to shape the future. This was not a fallback response created in the late nineteenth century by budding feminists after they had already been inscribed into a separate sphere, but was a central part of domestic rhetoric as early as the final years of the eighteenth century.

"Well-Conditioned" Frenchmen . . . and Women

Rousseau's work provides an ideal place from which to begin the exploration of how and when domestic ideology fit into new ideals of civic life and nurturing individuality. Rousseau was one of the first and most sympathetic proponents of the idea that "progress" could be oppressive. Far ahead of his time, he explained why civilized rationality was not necessarily or even likely to be a state of freedom.[29] However, Rousseau hardly believed that an education in self-control was to blame for the lack of true autonomy in people's lives. In his *Social Contract,* Rousseau began by outlining his theory that absolute rule was a perversion of the original social contract in which men gave up some freedoms and rights in order to guarantee others. If "man is born free, yet everywhere is in chains," this was not due to external forces but to man's own choice to subject himself to others and reject his own judgment in order to gain prestige and affluence. For this reason, Rousseau's other works, such as his *Emile, or On Education,* were fundamental in arguing that the one who internalized the values of the ideal society would be freer than someone who did not. As Joseph Reisert explains, "What Rousseau presents in *Emile* as human virtue is in fact the most important virtue required of citizens in liberal regimes: the Rousseauian man of virtue steadfastly respects the rights of others, even at great cost to himself."[30] Despite the fact that Rousseau was deeply suspicious of modern rational civilization, he saw training in self-control and the internalization of social norms as the central guarantor of freedom and rights, not the source of their destruction. Seen in this light, Rousseau's claim that "Education itself is but habit" takes on new importance for the education provided within the home, where children learned habits of virtue even as they were trained to be autonomous.[31]

This examination of gender, self-control, and autonomy in domestic education uses Rousseau's work as a point of entry in order to explore the ideals and processes that conditioned modern understandings of motherhood and social change. The issues raised by Rousseau and promoted by the expansion of his ideals throughout eighteenth- and nineteenth-century culture thus offer a conceptual framework for reexamining possible relationships between education, gender, and civic life.

French Instruction and Nurturing Education

When introducing her 1824 work on education, Mme Campan wrote, "I have divided my work into a number of parts: the first three deal with maternal education, the last with public education."[32] She went on to apologize for her lack of attention to public schooling and explained that her ability to discuss governmental policy became more limited as the state became more and more involved in education. Almost two hundred years later, I, like Mme Campan, have chosen to focus on the realm of private education to the exclusion of public. This time, however, it is for a different reason, namely that the most fruitful work remains to be done in this area. While there has been considerable research on the history of public education, little has been written on domestic education and child-rearing in this period. Although this book includes substantial discussion of schooling, institutional instruction is always placed into a larger educational, and usually familial, context. This organization is designed to capture the complex nature of education in the late eighteenth and early nineteenth centuries more accurately than studies that focus on educational legislation or activities in locations specifically denoted for learning.[33]

There is already a well-established historiographical conflict over education in the modern era that links nurturing care, individuality, and institutional schooling to changes in French history. The seminal work in family history, Philippe Ariès' *Centuries of Childhood*, provoked a long-running debate after its publication more than forty years ago. While there is little consensus, it is generally agreed that our sentimental notions of what it means to be a child developed late in the early modern period. Ariès' critics recognize that he provided a compelling argument for the importance of understanding the relationship between child, parent, and the surrounding society, but they disagree with his conclusions about the relationship between parental care and normative education. Instead, these critics have provided numerous competing descriptions of what "childhood" entailed; their primary criticisms of Ariès focus on his contention that families became emotionally closer to their children.

Historians who entered the debate over affectionate child-rearing were often convinced, in opposition to Ariès, that greater emotional contact was fundamentally opposed to the control that modern families and societies exerted over their children by sending them to school. David Hunt, one of Ariès' most ardent critics, concurred with those who argued that a major reason for establishing public schools was to provide discipline. He further explained, "It is hard to understand how 'a desire on the part of the parents to watch more closely over their children, to stay nearer to them, to avoid abandoning them temporarily to the care of another family,' should have been translated into a decision to send them off to school."[34] Rather than phrase the question as one of historical change, Hunt rejects Ariès' contention that society as a whole shifted from a focus on the community to one on the individual. Colin Heywood likewise maintains that it is "paradoxical, to say the least, for Ariès to suggest that an increased awareness of the needs of children has produced the disciplined regime in the schools."[35] Both Heywood and Hunt insist that the nurturing ideal and parental desire to see each child as an individual in need of particular care ought not to have resulted in a greater demand for public educational systems in France. Despite these criticisms, however, both historians have left a detailed examination of the relationship between individuality, education, and social control as an incomplete project. Their work on French childhood points to education as the crucial component in understanding the intersection between the individual, familial, and social realms, even as it fails to investigate adequately the implications.[36]

In order to untangle the seeming contradiction between institutional education and nurturing family life, we must note a crucial distinction between "instruction" and "education," with instruction denoting acquisition of a specific skill, like reading, while education entails the development of the whole person. While today we may distinguish between moral education and instruction in "the 3 Rs," we often assume that schooling and education accomplish the same goals or, at the very least, that a desire for education and one for schooling are two complementary trends, one implying the other. In early modern France, this was not true.[37] Education was not synonymous with schooling; people might receive "instruction" at home, at work, or at church. Additionally, many of the children "schooled" under the tutelage of a priest, nun, or brother received an education that focused on moral and religious instruction, perhaps even to the exclusion of other learning. After all, many of these children were never taught to write, and some, mostly females, might never even have learned the rudiments of reading.[38] Education was not primarily a matter of legislation or philosophy but rather a central part of everyday life. It was for this reason that eighteenth-century educational theorists began to look to the domestic education that boys and girls received in their formative years, conducted by a mother within the home, to explain the success or failure of formal schooling outside the home. This distinction was not lost on French revolutionaries, some of whom even contemplated requiring all parents to give custody of their children to the state so that they would be raised appropriately, as republicans.

Over the course of the nineteenth century, as more and more children were publicly educated, historians lost this understanding of the dual nature of education and instead came to see education solely as an outcome of public instruction. As a result, when historians like David Hunt or Colin Heywood argue that changes in institutional schooling, like those that occurred in nineteenth-century France, ran counter to prevailing educational ideals, they often overlook the original situations in which "education" was provided. This book recaptures the familial context for education and argues that if we are to understand either the changing face of gender and family life or explain the trend toward institutional instruction, we must first recognize schooling and domestic life, as contemporaries did, as interrelated parts of a whole.

Contextualizing Rousseau

Using Rousseau's educational work to examine domesticity shows that the figure historians recognize as the "Republican mother"[39] was not, in fact, necessarily related to any particular social or political republic, but rather to the "republic of virtue." She appeared in advice manuals long before France contemplated killing its king, and she continued as a model well after the restoration of Bourbons to the French throne. However, she is often seen as "republican" because, as domesticity and nurturing received more ideological emphasis, mothers necessarily became more important as the primary source of moral education, and the family itself became the cornerstone in the process of developing ideals that are often tied to liberalism, such as autonomy and individuality. Despite the fact that there seems to be an easy elision between domestic mothering and republican virtues, this study emphasizes that an increased focus on child-rearing, individuality, and self-control was already culturally prominent long before the French Revolution emphasized civic education or abolished primogeniture and, indeed, that revolutionary legislation was founded on a general expectation of domestic nurturing. Similarly, the valorization of motherhood and domesticity was widespread long before Napoleonic and Restoration rhetoric emphasized women's removal to private life. Increasingly restrictive social and political expectations may have demanded that women justify their participation in public life, but domestic ideology did not develop in response to that political trend.

Chapter Summary

Each chapter makes the chronological progression of domestic ideology explicit in a new way. My source material, which ranges from philosophical and educational treatises to children's toys, clothes, and books, illustrates how the ideals that crystallized in Rousseauian domesticity eventually drove widespread cultural and intellectual change, resulting in new genres of literature, clothing styles, and demands for education. The analysis of various ideas, products, and institutions demonstrates how ideas about gender, society, and social reform were interrelated and mutually reinforcing. Surprisingly, even as the new philosophies about motherhood and family life emphasized the removal of women from public life, they also had an ideological impact well beyond the home and even promoted women's civic participation. The Rousseauian rhetoric of self-control and autonomy certainly included an emphasis on gender distinctions and gender roles, but it also increasingly conceptualized women as central to the recreation of society and the promulgation of the new civic ideals. In the end, Rousseau's work offers us a lens through which we can examine a wide range of sources in order to see how the emergence of domestic ideology, as well as its incorporation into multiple arenas, changed child-rearing ideals and could even lead to the envisioning of women as central to the integration of politics and family life.

Chapter 1 uses intellectual history to examine philosophical treatises and educational tracts in the pre-revolutionary era. It seeks to establish that the publication of *Emile* in 1762 marked the beginning of a widespread shift toward demands for domestic nurturing, which included an emphasis on self-control, autonomy, and gender difference. Eighteenth-century educational theory proposed sweeping changes to both hierarchy and family life, but the most far-reaching of these theories was found in *Emile,* which centered the new education on individual training and radical removal from society. While Rousseau's work had some similarities to educational proposals by John Locke and many French *philosophes, Emile* went far beyond them in its demands for self-control and individual training. When put into the context of the pre-revolutionary ferment over education and individuality, *Emile* and Rousseauian domesticity help provide a deeper understanding of the analysis of public life found in French educational philosophies of the eighteenth century.

Before the eighteenth century, one's social position largely determined the type of education that one would receive. While gender was not irrelevant, hierarchical position was paramount, and early education was designed to teach children of both sexes how to behave appropriately as adult members of a particular stratum of society. In the eighteenth century, as economic and social realities changed, the foundation of educational theory shifted. Different educational priorities came to the fore, each reflecting a particular view of equality and social change in France. Once children were seen as unique individuals in need of constant care and concern, parents, philosophers, educators, and legislators alike worried about the future implications of early experiences and discussed ways in which parents could provide the best early education possible for children so that they might become moral and productive members of society. For Rousseau in particular, the family became a haven where prerational boys and girls would be raised according to the new approach to the first stages of life, which included less physical coercion, more attention to mental development, and a clear distinction between the duties and abilities of the child and those of the adult.

Despite this potentially universal call for freedom, Enlightenment ideas about schooling certainly did not expect to revolutionize social relations; instead their ideal systems frequently amplified either gender or social discrepancies. Some *philosophes* maintained that schooling was not meant for every person but should be reserved to elite males. Others highlighted gender in ways that had clear implications for the treatment of girls and women. Female children, like Rousseau's Sophie, were not to be given the freedom and latitude that a boy was due, but were instead to remain close to the hearth, learning responsibilities proper to their gender. Rather than pointing the way to more equal duties and expectations, these theories deepened the divide between women and men. In other words, the changing perception of early experiences led to an emphasis on distinctions between male and female at ever younger ages and with ever greater implications for adult women. However, the gender politics of instruction and moral education should not necessarily be construed as implying a conservative social vision. Primary to Rousseau's plan was the training of conscience, which operated "independent of reason." Thus it was precisely the prerational education, outside formal schooling, that created the most sweeping transformation of society and hence was truly radical, with the mother now at the center of a new society, grounded in natural equality.[40] Even if the exigencies of everyday life meant that not all women could implement the nurturing ideal, it was applicable to all, without respect for social class. Since "the attraction of domestic life is the best antidote for bad morals,"[41] child-rearing took on new importance well before the French Revolution, with families and mothers as the loci of social change and the models of autonomous self-control.

Chapter 2 explores how these Enlightenment intellectual shifts, especially debates over individuality and social transformation, led to new standards for child-rearing that became increasingly widespread as the eighteenth and nineteenth centuries progressed. *Emile* and the philosophical and educational currents surrounding nurturing education made it clear that the full development of the child focused on the body just as much as the mind. In the years after 1762, then, philosophers and professionals used the new ideologies, often with specific reference to Rousseau, to attack the physical coercion of children; the swaddling, corsets, and clothing that had restricted children gave way to more freeing designs. As demands for physical freedom for infants and small children became more common, cultural expectations of the appropriate material surrounding family life, that of child-rearing in particular, also changed. The changes in material culture also demonstrate that an increased emphasis on domestic ideology was not coterminous with political changes. The

French Revolution did not create the changing narrative about child-rearing, nor did its changing family law establish new norms. Rather, the ideals found in Rousseauian families increasingly found expression in legal shifts that echoed the already-established trends in material culture.

The sources for this chapter, advice manuals and designs for children's clothing, offer an overview of the changes in material culture from the 1760s to the 1830s, the period when an increasing emphasis on nurturing child-rearing came to the fore in new fashions for children. The cultural production of those years reflected an increasing emphasis on physical freedom, self-control, and gender difference. Conduct manuals used Rousseauian ideas about the individual to encourage parents to condition their children properly, using long walks, recreational play, and new types of amusements that ranged from entertaining games to toys that encouraged physical activity. The life of the child became a focus of concern, and instead of being merely frivolous objects to be left behind as soon as possible, toys and loose clothing were now objects that could help the child's body develop and promote a proper understanding of the surrounding world.

Shifts in material culture confirm that the new styles encouraged greater exploration even as they began to differentiate between boys and girls at ever younger ages. Where all prerational children had been dressed in skirts in the early modern era, now even toddler boys were too masculine to share their sisters' dresses, at least in theory. Toys also enjoyed a new prominence as play and material objects became more important in the life of the child. By 1833, children enjoyed the freedom to move and a variety of playthings that would have been unthinkable in 1750, and a nurturing mother became increasingly emphasized for the care of infants and small children. However, the new fashions and pastimes also meant that the gender and behavior of individual children increased in importance. As children had more ability to make choices and to move and play, literature emphasized their demeanor to ever greater degrees. Enlightenment principles prioritized physical freedom even as they demanded self-control.

It is true that when they stand alone, advice manuals can be problematic sources. While these texts offer an explicit record of ideal practices, they do not leave a clear sense of how much of the rhetoric was descriptive, emphasizing practices that already were widespread, and how much was centered instead on prescription and a desire to reshape the world. Additionally, when they are not combined with other indicators of social standing, important questions remain about who would have had access to these works, let alone responded to their imperatives. While the question of practical implementation is of less concern in a cultural and intellectual history than in a social history, this chapter still attempts to limit the problems with the sources by looking at their recommendations in the perspective of contemporary emphases on similar texts. The shifts in rhetoric are matched to similar shifts in high intellectual culture, so that Rousseau's work, explicitly referred to in many of the conduct manuals, serves as one clear impetus for change, if an ideal one. In another way, this chapter takes a lesson from literary scholarship and recognizes that texts always present multiple meanings. While some parents, already convinced of the need for looser clothing, may have read these works as confirmation of their beliefs, others may have been influenced by the importance of the rhetoric of domesticity and nurturing that they encountered. In either case, the clothes and books, no matter how ideal or practical, offer us a discourse of domesticity that was rising to prominence.

The study of eighteenth- and nineteenth-century material objects and their cultural implications also contextualizes who exactly was likely to be reading these manuals and thinking about the relationship between motherhood and the new objects. Women's journals told stories of objects that their readers had purchased and pointed to the locations where such fashions could be found. While some recent historical works have emphasized attempts on the part of the bourgeoisie to set themselves apart from both aristocratic and working-class ideals, women's advice manuals and material objects point to the expansion of domestic ideology within a broader spectrum.[42] Not only was a domestic mother supposed to be the ideal for all families, but discussion of names, titles, and social position within the works also makes it clear that the intended audience for the objects ranged from the ambitious bourgeoisie, anxious to have the right clothing and behavior, to those who already had social influence and political power.

The examination of material culture, put into the environment of advice for the ideal mother, is also particularly helpful for understanding how different ideas about hierarchy, equality, and cultural change might relate to a changing emphasis on gender distinction, independence, and self-control. As Jennifer Jones has explained for adult dress:

Eighteenth-century French men and women were concerned about the ways in which identities were constructed by clothing, by the ways in which one's gender and social identity were marked and constructed, by what one wore in an emerging "society of taste." More than other commodities, clothing became the problematic emblem of modernity . . . A culture that was increasingly obsessed by the private realm of the family and the public realm of politics focused on and debated the meaning of clothing, that middle ground between private and public . . .[43]

In that sense, clothing, which is often seen as frivolous and without real historical importance, occupied a liminal position that makes it particularly useful for the investigation of cultural standards linking public and private. Children's fashions in particular, though they have merited even less historical attention than adult fashions, demonstrate important ways in which the meanings of social roles changed dramatically in this period.[44] Child-rearing was the responsibility of the "private realm of the family," and yet, the intellectual and educational currents make it clear that it was of critical importance for the "public realm of politics" as well. Accordingly, this chapter's examination of children's material culture, juxtaposed with conduct manuals that reflect the same trends, demonstrates how ideas about economy and society also influenced suppositions about the nature of individuality and equality, as well as the future of society.

Given that Rousseau's and Locke's emphasis on early physical training looked remarkably similar, parents who had been inspired by the *philosophes*' visions for society, or more likely, had read the theories on childcare that had been influenced by their writings, could, if they wished, attempt to refashion the world starting with a new focus on the physical care of their prerational children. As a result, clothing that was designed to fulfill the new principles provides not only evidence of the shifting cultural meaning of childhood, but also the possibility of a changing relationship of adults to their children. Modifications in the production and meaning of material objects in the eighteenth and nineteenth centuries reflect the rise of new ideas about individuals and their roles in the surrounding environment. While we do not have exact numbers on how many parents adopted the new styles, the change over time, the disappearance of the old fashions, an increasing prevalence of the new designs, and the relationship of these changes to the advice being meted out in manuals, demonstrates the breadth of the impact of the new child-rearing ideals by the 1830s.

Chapter 3 examines how acceptance of ideas about childhood and the new mother changed the appearance of the ideal family in very definite ways. According to the new domestic ideals, children who were individuals now needed a parent who would devote herself to their care, not simply as an overseer, but instead as someone whose life was centered on raising her children so that they might become moral and productive adults who were fully integrated into society. Advice manuals produced in the years after the publication of *Emile* intended to develop the ideal domestic mother who could take care of the newly free child and, at the same time, provide the all-important first impressions. The literature directed at women, while prescriptive in nature, demonstrates the many ways in which the later eighteenth century witnessed the selflessly nurturing and domestic mother displace the distant and controlling father as the new ideal parent for early childhood. Now that children were supposed to be physically free, they needed the emotional and physical attention of caretakers to keep them safe and train them to behave in the absence of external constraint. Women, unlike men, were seen as uniquely capable of giving young children the love and care that they would need to become moral adults, but women themselves also needed to develop the qualities enabling them to be nurturing and self-controlled from a relatively young age.

Though the new mother owed much in inspiration to Rousseau, and her mothering was supposed to be "natural," the advice genre itself belies that notion. As one treatise admitted, "Life is a wild land / The seed of happiness does not grow randomly / Child of nature, he asks for a bit of artfulness."[45] In order to cultivate their gardens properly, women were expected to refer to advice from those who knew best: either women who were already experienced mothers or men who, by virtue of their professions or social positions, could claim authority. Mothers with the leisure to adopt the new ideals found assistance for their task in many ways. Advice manuals taught them about their children's minds and bodies, giving them a "proper" approach to the sundry tasks that awaited them. Fashion journals and the periodical press offered women useful advice and provided them with models by which they could judge their mothering. Even children's books, such as the *Magasin des enfans,* had much to offer the mothers who read them with their children. As one contemporary put it, "the stories are written to amuse and instruct children, the dialogues to instruct and teach the mothers."[46] Even if the ideal mother never truly existed, she certainly was made real in the cultural discourse that surrounded the domestic mother.

A number of authors have studied the changing figure of the mother in eighteenth- and nineteenth-century France, describing the increasing power behind the image of the angel in the house, our model for today's "traditional" mother. All agree that motherhood found its highest praise in centuries as the ideal of domesticity rose to prominence. Some of these studies have focused on the evolution of motherhood throughout the ages,[47] while others ignore the family structure almost entirely, developing a picture of the mother in the later nineteenth century and focusing especially on her social role as a domestic consumer.[48] Even studies that place the mother's role in the context of changes in power and family structures tend to miss the crucial intersection between affectionate childrearing, domestic mothering, and self-control.[49] Most important, none of them attempt to provide an analysis of the literature, much of it produced long before the French Revolution, that surrounded these women and communicated the ideology under consideration. As a result, even the studies that see domesticity as providing a unique sphere of liberation miss the particular contexts that made a prescriptive and gender-loaded language seem generally applicable to civic life and cultural formation. A unique rhetoric valorizing the maternal ideal developed long before the

Napoleonic Code limited women to their homes and, in fact, even appeared in advance of the legal shifts that intersected to create an ideal revolutionary family. The domestic mother who established the new family was a creation not, first and foremost, of nineteenth-century politics but of eighteenth-century culture.

As with the preceding chapter, the conduct manuals and fashion journals also reveal the existence of a new narrative about child-rearing, one in which elite mothers took an increasingly prominent role. Women of leisure, both bourgeois and aristocratic, were to remove themselves from the world and care for their young children. However, because domestic ideologies developed in conjunction with changing perspectives on childhood, neither concept could stand alone. Philosophically, the wife remained incomplete as long as she was not also a mother, but boys and girls who did not have devoted and nurturing mothers were themselves deficient and seen at a distinct disadvantage, because the radical reconstruction of society relied on the existence of an appropriate model for each child. Advice manuals for mothers expanded on the ideas found in Rousseau's work and taught women how to demonstrate proper behavior for prerational girls and boys by being concerned with social norms and focused on their duties, just as all children would eventually be. Only if they themselves embodied appropriate adult behavior, most notably self-control, would they be able to shape future citizens properly. While this changed image of ideal motherhood demanded considerable sacrifices on the part of women, advice literature, often written by women, also told a new story about the ways in which mothers could use their positions as founders of a new society to shape a world that would be to their own and their sons' and daughters' advantages.

A mother was actually being asked to make two decisions. The most obvious choice was made for her children, since the rhetoric made it clear that a woman's child-rearing philosophy served as the framework by which her offspring would respond to the world around them. The second and only slightly more hidden agenda revolved around women's roles as wives and mothers, that is, where they would wield power and find value. The primary difference between the ideal wife of earlier years and the devoted mother of the later eighteenth and early nineteenth century was her sentimental attachment to children and family. More than simply obedient, the new mother obeyed the dictates of her heart, or at least those of the literature that surrounded her, finding fulfillment in her home. The completion of her task would result in a child who had greater physical freedom and more emotional expectations than in years past. Mothers found an independence of esteem and sentiment and could make their own claims to the exercise of civic virtue even as their children received nurturing and physically freeing educations.

Chapter 4 demonstrates that mothers were not the only targets of advice literature in France. Once the maternal ideal had been well inculcated, an explosion in the publication of children's books and stories responded to the perceived need of mothers for help in teaching their young children proper social behaviors. For that reason, the beginning of the nineteenth century witnessed the development of new literary genres and educational forms for children. As historians of children's literature have noted, though children's literature had been nonexistent as a genre before the mid-eighteenth century, from the 1760s forward, generally acclaimed writers of talent such as Mme de Genlis and Arnaud Berquin began to direct all or most of their efforts toward children.[50] The trickle of production became a flood after the turn of the century, with publishing houses developing books on education and story after didactic story designed to respond to changing educational goals as well as to the political desire to reassert control after the upheaval of the revolutionary years.

While greater literacy and increasing amounts of disposable income certainly meant that more parents had become a better "market" for these goods, the particular format and lessons of these works also demonstrate the ways in which the growing philosophical and intellectual interest in individuality and education had a decisive impact on the design of objects for children. The new educational theories had clearly influenced the form and content of children's books, which, like Rousseau's works and women's advice manuals, emphasized self-control and often featured a domestic mother or tutor as the central pedagogue. These books were often particularly concerned with helping boys and girls make the transition from "private" life inside the home, whether that meant domestic or public education, to life in society.[51]

Most specifically, a new didactic genre, which intended to serve as a transition from early childhood to autonomous civic life, sought to teach older children self-control and proper social behaviors ranging from table manners to charitable giving. Chapter 4 demonstrates the ways in which children's literature changed to incorporate the new gender distinctions and expectations for childhood as ideas about children's education developed. Unlike literature designed for adults, books intended for youth not only offered advice but also used ABC primers, fables, and didactic stories to develop children's moral conscience and social understanding. As the distance increased between "childish" and "adult" behaviors, different types of literature designed specifically for children became a new way of transmitting the new values more effectively to young readers. By the early nineteenth century, these new values, like those held up for women, assumed that children would develop virtuous self-control in addition to intellect. With proper maternal affection and use of the new methods for the transmission of values, these properly educated children would become the rational individuals that society expected. Self-control would allow children, like their mothers, to enter adult society and transform the world around them, preferably in an orderly and rational fashion.

The themes and norms of children's literature make it clear that adults' goals and expectations for their children were at a crucial juncture in the late eighteenth and early nineteenth centuries, as society moved from earlier notions of childhood development and training to ones now recognizably "modern." Children's stories and primers began to emphasize the process of human mental development, which allowed writers to articulate what qualities made one adult, that is, a fully formed person capable of making autonomous rational decisions. In that context, literature designed specifically for children provided a location for adults to enunciate the moral and social values that they desired to pass on to the coming generation, especially self-control. These books, written by members of the upper and middle classes, demonstrate the ways in which "[b]ecoming civilized, a preoccupation of the nineteenth century middle class, meant more education, more polite behavior, more understanding, and helping others to follow suit."[52] And yet, while the stories were often set in locations of affluence and leisure, such as a provincial chateau, the target audience was not only the wealthy elite, for stories also featured characters who came from artisanal families, and numerous prefaces appealed to all women to implement the new educational ideals. Because the function of children's literature was explicitly pedagogical, the evolution of this genre and its explicit application to a broad spectrum of society provides another lens by which we can observe the developing perspective on self-control, gender, and social change.

Taken together, the first four chapters demonstrate some of the ways in which domestic narratives, broadly construed, increased in importance and prominence over the course of the eighteenth and nineteenth centuries. By the 1830s, an elite—but by no means solely bourgeois—ideal that prioritized nurturing at home meant an increasing emphasis on a domestic mother who would use her training, as well as material objects like new books and items of clothing, in order to cherish each of her children and teach them to exercise self-control. This model was not, however, intended to keep children entirely within the confines of the family but instead prepared them to enter society through their own rational choices. Domestic nurturing and affection were a foundation for developing the whole person, but not the entire stage on which the person would act. For that reason, all of these changes in child-rearing and domesticity demanded not only new forms of literary and material culture, but also new forms of schooling and ways of entering modern society.

Chapter 5 analyzes some of the ways in which ideas about nineteenth-century schooling pointed the way to modern institutional change in its emphasis on self-control and moral education within the family. It offers a new analytical focus for explicitly political texts dealing with schooling. Unlike most educational histories, it begins well before the common focus on institutional change after the compulsory instruction of the Ferry Laws. By centering on instruction after the Enlightenment, it challenges the existence of any *a priori* division between domestic education and public instruction, with public instruction being more central or important. Instead, it demonstrates how, from the French Revolution forward, legislative debates about public instruction showed a continuity that was surprising given the level of political upheaval. When, in 1833, Prime Minister Guizot demanded that every commune have a public school, his plan reinforced the notion that familial education had a relationship to pedagogy in the world at large.

While the ideal domestic education existed apart from society and allowed children to develop without early corruption from external forces, not even its most radical proponent had intended for the children involved to remain removed from society for their entire lives. As Mira Morgenstern has explained, Rousseau's ideology formed the basis for expectations that "[a]t a relatively early age—certainly by school age—children [were] no longer to confine their most intense feelings to the intimacy of the closed family circle. Rather, they should widen the extent of their emotional engagement to include the entire State, but without sacrificing any of that feeling's intensity."[53] As advice manuals, clothing, and children's literature demonstrate, mothers were supposed to be preparing the new individuals for eventual integration into society, where their virtue, self-control, and rationality would operate for the general good.

The sources for this chapter parallel the sources for the preceding chapters insofar as they involve prescriptions for schooling and rarely deal with the "actual" practices within the schools. However, the projects for schooling provide an important context for understanding the reception and promulgation of ideas about domestic child-rearing. While domestic literature lauded the importance of the mother and individualized family life, it is noteworthy that legislators also took domestic rhetoric for granted and employed it time and again in their discussions of how to shape their world. While, in the eighteenth century, neither technical instruction nor moral education was the particular domain of a public educational system, by the middle of the nineteenth century, there was a pervasive political belief that general access to public schooling was crucial for a healthy society. No longer were specific skills, which might range from reading and writing to accounting or bread-making, supposed to be taught when and where they were needed. Instead, the increased importance of both moral and physical education meant that more and more parents desired to train their children, first through domestic education and then through public instruction.[54] The same types of literature that used Rousseau's rhetoric to drive early private education were also part of a political trend that demanded new forms of public schooling to continue where domestic education had left off and provide for the greater socialization of the child in order to meet the needs of all. Public instruction, legislators believed, had to begin from an already-established base, that of nurturing domesticity.

Education became a central part of political discourse; debates on instructional policy allowed public men to demonstrate a continuing emphasis on the shaping of the civic individual, which presupposed a coherent adoption of domestic ideology. By 1833, every commune was required to have a public school for its children, not to take away the power of maternal influence, but rather, because people like Guizot presupposed its existence. Unlike the domestic texts, which were directed at women and self-referential, these legislative visions took the narrative of nurturing maternity and self-control out into the world and demonstrated the ways in which not just ideal mothers but also politicians had been affected by Rousseauian rhetoric in the years between 1787 and 1833. With respect to schooling, the "blank slate" approach of Locke had disappeared, replaced by new projects of public education that took molded individuals out of domestic families and integrated them into the new social frameworks.

The book's conclusion uses the insights of the preceding chapters, the rhetoric of a nineteenth-century proto-feminist, and an image from the nineteenth century in order to demonstrate concretely how Rousseauian domesticity and maternal education could be integrated into larger visions of change in nineteenth-century France. It seeks to explain how the rhetoric of self-control and virtue operated alongside liberal ideas that emphasized the autonomy and equality of individuals even as they increasingly focused on the gender, discipline, and self-control of individuals. This book evaluates the cultural and intellectual history of child-rearing in order to demonstrate that the rhetoric of domesticity and virtue offered the opportunity for social transformation based not on egotism—Rousseau's *amour propre*—but instead on devotion to virtuous action. The existence of these new possibilities and of rhetoric about social transformation through disinterested virtue also provided a common ground where modern discourses about autonomy and gender intersected. Not only men, but also women, discovered that they belonged to a society where individual qualities, not position in a social hierarchy, helped to determine one's worth. The evidence here thus demonstrates that a literature focused on the gendered child and domestic mother could go hand in hand with the liberal rhetoric that valued autonomous individuality on the part of all men and women, both inside and outside the home.

Self-Control and Modern Life

Recent historiography clearly suggests that demands for self-control and an emphasis on gender are likely to represent insidious forms of repression, and not freedom. If this is true, it would seem that Rousseau's system freed neither girls nor boys, and that the new educational plans, far from equalizing children or removing them from the community to guarantee their goodness, demanded that society have a role equivalent to that of the family in raising gendered and self-controlled children. By the early nineteenth century, the ideal family, run by a nurturing mother, was supposed to be the location where prerational children learned both universal and gender-specific lessons so that they could contribute to the formation of a new society. However, the evolution of domesticity from *Emile* to Guizot's law of 1833 also demonstrates that accompanying demands for changes in child-rearing were the basis for a new social conception of even the prerational individual as deserving of nurturing and particular rights, and at a very early age. Once we understand how rhetoric that emphasized the importance of modern child-rearing and domestic motherhood did not necessarily contradict equality and civic participation but could instead foster autonomy and individuality, we are forced to rethink many current historical perspectives. In domestic culture, a greater emphasis on self-control and gender difference did not always imply oppression but might provide an ideological space for demands for inclusion in society. Instead of being merely coercive, the new ideas paved the way for individuals to think of themselves as unique beings with personal needs and the ability to make a special contribution to society. In that sense, the feminine ideal became not only the source of "the problem that has no name," but also of literature that was based on the concrete expectation that society's transformation depended as much on women's participation as on men's.[55]

CHAPTER ONE

Lessons from Rousseau

Self-Control, Sexual Difference, and Changing Ideals

Men's happiness or misery is most part of their own making. He whose mind directs not wisely, will never take the right way; and he whose body is crazy and feeble will never be able to advance in it.
—John Locke, *Some Thoughts Concerning Education* (1693)

What is the first part of politics? Education. The second? Education. And the third? Education.   —Jules Michelet, *The People* (1846)

Emile, *Politics, and Family Life*

*O*n June 8, 1762, the *parlement* of Paris condemned *Emile* and ordered the arrest of its author. Fortunately, Rousseau had been warned the night before and fled the city for the apparent safety of Switzerland. Parisian authorities had to be satisfied with burning the book. Still, Rousseau was far from safe, for just over a week later, Genevan officials condemned both *Emile* and the *Social Contract,* adding a warning to Rousseau that he would be arrested if he dared set foot in Geneva. Why all the uproar over an educational treatise in the guise of a novel? Historians and political theorists alike have often claimed that the "principles formulated in *Emile* are precursors to the principles of legislation laid out in the Contract,"[1] both of which subverted the current political order. According to this formulation, Rousseau's *Emile* was controversial not as an educational treatise, but rather because it was a thinly disguised political allegory. To prove this point further, historian Lucio Colletti argues that "[p]olitics is presented as the solution (the only possible solution) to the problems of human existence . . . Evil is 'inequality,' social injustice. The ethical task of the triumph of good over evil is therefore necessarily identified with the political task of the transformation of society."[2] Others continue this line of reasoning, arguing that *Emile*'s discussion of the inadequacies of contemporary society is tantamount to a call for reform along the lines of the *Contract*. "While *Emile* is devoted to the education of the individual in the 'old' society, the true education offered to the new citizen of the *Contract* lies in participation in public life itself."[3] In other words, by teaching the citizen how best to lead a moral life in a corrupt society, *Emile* would also teach him how to transform the society in which he lived.

While historians and political theorists find the political explanation appealing, it is an insufficient explanation for the uproar that surrounded the book. In no location save Geneva did the the the *Social Contract,* a much more explicitly political work, provoke the same wave of criticism as *Emile*. The latter struck a chord that was not simply a result of its political aspirations. If, in general, the public was willing to let the political analysis of the *Contract* stand, what did they find disturbing about *Emile?* If Rousseau's ideas were threatening, did they not pose the same threat in any shape? In fact, it seems that they did not. Rousseau recognized the particular power inherent in the format of *Emile*. As Rousseau said when being persecuted, "It mattered little that a band of children should not act out their tawdry comedy, but it mattered greatly that what I have said should be said. Thank heaven, my task is done. I shall have no more anxiety on that score."[4] Rousseau was relieved to have this work finally in print, seeing it "from first to last as his 'most useful, best' and 'most important' work, the one 'most worthy of himself by comparison with which all his other works are mere pamphlets.'"[5] Rousseau believed that his work would resonate with and inspire men and women in its demands for radical change and educational and familial, not political, reform as the solution to social and civic problems. No less a thinker than Immanuel Kant agreed with Rousseau's evaluation. Kant not only wrote that Rousseau's work outlined the problem of "restoring the rights of mankind" but also went so far as to argue that *Emile*'s publication was as historically significant as the French Revolution.[6]

Few contemporary scholars have agreed with Kant in seeing *Emile* as central for understanding Rousseau or later reactions to his ideas. Political theorists such as John Rawls and Andrew Levine have focused on the *Social Contract* in order to formulate questions of political right and social change. Literary scholars have been more concerned with Rousseau's nonpedagogical novels or the political arguments in the *Discourse on Inequality* and *Social Contract.*[7] One exception is political scientist Mira Morgenstern, who has attempted to correct what she sees as a modern overemphasis on politics, explaining that, from her perspective, Rousseau's central argument—developed clearly in *Emile*—is that the family is the necessary foundation of radical change.[8] However, the overwhelming emphasis of the canon has been on Rousseau's political works. Kant may have read *Emile* as Rousseau's most significant writing, but it is most often relegated to secondary status within Rousseau's oeuvre, precisely because it does not easily fit into a political critique of the world. For that reason, Allan Bloom has noted that of "Rousseau's major works [*Emile*] is the one least studied or commented on,"[9] with perhaps the exception of pedagogues who read it for "the harangues against swaddling and in favor of breast feeding and the learning of a trade."[10]

Even if many later theorists have lost sight of the radical nature of this work, Rousseau's contemporary readers, whether favorably inclined or not, often understood that *Emile* held the key to revolutionary change not because of its concrete childcare recommendations but rather because of the way it argued for the creation of fundamentally different individuals.[11] As Morgenstern explains, in Rousseau's work, "the family as it has developed throughout history is responsible for the cognitive misperception of life. The negative repercussions arising from these ill-founded notions explain what Rousseau claims is modern man's inability to ask the proper questions and thus to elucidate effective solutions for the ills plaguing him."[12] In other words, the family, not a new political system, would have to be the source of true reform. *Emile* was threatening and radical, not because of its political agenda, but because of the challenge that it posed to family life and traditional understandings of the self. Accordingly, this chapter will focus on rereading *Emile* in order to demonstrate how eighteenth- and nineteenth-century readers could see the work not as part of a concrete political agenda, but as a challenge to become autonomous through a new type of family life.

In order to discover the truly radical nature of this work, one must understand, as many contemporaries did, that Rousseau was recreating society, not reforming it. We should see the significance of *Emile* not, as is usually done, in conjunction with Rousseau's analysis of the social contract or demands for the recreation of a politically free man.[13] Instead, we should respect Rousseau's own claims that this novel was his masterpiece because it told the story of the quest for the creation of a radically new individual. This individual was not a political being so much as a man who, because of his rearing by an affectionate mother and a virtuous tutor, had become an autonomous being. What was ground-breaking about the character *Emile*, raised as part of a new family, was that he was a "moral man," by which Rousseau meant a man who set himself apart from the corrupting influence of institutions and remained unconcerned for the petty advantage to be gained in class hierarchy. Since they would choose the common good instead of promoting a personal agenda, Rousseau's creations would be authentic beings, not slavishly dependent on others. This freedom was based on the proper balance between a physical and moral upbringing, one where all individuals were properly educated and learned to be self-controlled and self-sufficient in order to be able truly to judge the worth of things. Modern theorists who cast Rousseau's importance in the context of the *Social Contract* or *Discourse on Inequality* therefore miss the ideological centrality of family life and education as found in *Emile*.

Rousseauian Education and Gender Oppression

One exception to the tendency to downplay the importance of *Emile* can be found in much feminist criticism of Rousseau. While traditional historians and political theorists may misunderstand Rousseau's philosophical goals, feminist historians, political scientists, and literary critics often point to the omnipresent gender distinctions, central to *Emile,* as the most troubling portion of Rousseau's work. They emphasize the fact that Rousseau's use of the term "man" was no accident, and they argue that the author of *Emile* not only demanded extraordinary change but also postulated as a central component of his theory the creation of male and female social beings. *Emile*'s educational plan provides a central demonstration of Rousseau's misogyny and can be faulted particularly for the gendering of educational spheres that is the foundation for the oppression of women and the limitation of their opportunities. Historian Mary Hilton explains, "[i]n Rousseau's model, the male child would grow to use his reason in the service of the state," while the female child's influence would be relegated to the home.[14] According to Victor Wexler, this means that, while "Emile was to be a critical, self-reliant citizen," Sophie would be merely a wife and mother.[15] Even historian Linda Kerber, whose work has offered a nuanced view on domestic ideology, argues that, "[a]lthough much that Rousseau wrote implied sharp criticism of contemporary society and envisaged drastic change, what he said about women usually reinforced the existing order."[16] It is here that the assertion that Rousseau wished to create a new political man bears the most tainted fruit, at least for historians of gender. After all, combining the politics of *The Social Contract* with the gendered spheres of *Emile* seems to leave us with an example where the new political vision was fully predicated on the exclusion of women, or at least their continued oppression.

If Rousseau's highest philosophical priority was a new political agenda that emphasized participation in public life, critics would be right to claim that Rousseau's social vision failed to live up to his political ideals. However, women's exclusion from political debate may not be as significant as it seems. *Emile* was Rousseau's most important work because it avoided politics and instead stressed the theme of social recreation and demonstrated the ways in which all beings, whether male or female, were created outside contemporary society and complemented one another in order to re-form properly the natural individual. Rousseau's goal was to encourage radical social change that existed apart from politics and was centered not on politics but on the family, and in his view, men and women were revolutionary, not by virtue of their political service, but rather because they would remake society in their own image. Hence, it remains unclear how much the gendering of social roles was based on a philosophical desire to exclude women from autonomous decision-making and participation in civil society. Distinctions between public and private, well established in much nineteenth-century historiography, and often traced back to Rousseau, therefore merit particular exploration in the context of eighteenth-century demands for reform.

Enlightenment Alternatives to Rousseau

Philosophers, historians, and educational theorists may misunderstand the radical centrality of Rousseau's educational philosophy because *Emile* seems to be just another part of a flourishing eighteenth-century debate about education and ideal training for the individual. In the last half of the eighteenth century, there was widespread demand for change in France's educational system, and in that context Rousseau was not alone, or even necessarily ground-breaking, in his agitation for change. Enlightenment *philosophes* united in a call for progress and improvement through new forms of schooling. Almost all of these thinkers, Rousseau not excepted, based their ideas about education and social change on John Locke's theories of education and the formation of civic individuals. Prominent thinkers who believed in the perfectibility of the individual, such as Denis Diderot and the Baron d'Holbach, decried the ignorance they saw around them and railed against the inability of the educational systems of the day to remedy it. Even Voltaire, who had misgivings about the education of the *menu peuple,* agreed that reason needed to supplant superstition in the minds of all people before civilization could truly advance.[17]

As the first treatise to focus on the importance of sense experience and physical influences on children, Locke's *Some Thoughts Concerning Education* (1693) linked its descriptions of human development to reason and nature when it argued that children's minds were blank slates, gaining knowledge through experience and reflection. According to Locke, every bit of material that found its way into children's hands was crucial for their future growth as individuals. This understanding of the origins and development of knowledge in all children broke new ground and accorded well with Enlightenment ideas about the universality of rationality and human nature. As historians such as Peter Gay have demonstrated, Locke and his followers also set the foundation for Enlightenment ideas about individuality when they openly challenged the philosophical theory that children were naturally evil, with bad impulses that had to be trained out of them.[18] Training children from earliest youth in the proper ways to behave seemed to guarantee that they would need very little correction as they progressed farther on the path to adulthood. Though Locke abandoned neither God nor hierarchy, devoting considerable attention to religious instruction and intending his pupil to be a gentleman's son, he posited that all children were naturally "not capable of Great Vices"[19] and that adults were just as likely to teach children "Vanity, *Lying* and Equivocations . . . *Intemperance*"[20] and other vices as they were to teach them virtues and correct behavior. Locke even demanded:

I desire to know what Vice can be named, which parents, and those about Children, do not season them with, and drop into them the Seeds of, as soon as they are capable to receive them? . . . I desire parents soberly to consider, what Irregularity or Vice there is, which Children are not visibly taught; and whether it be not their Duty and Wisdom to provide them other Instructions.[21]

If children came into the world with no knowledge, bad habits and evil tendencies could not be innate but had to be learned from the world instead.[22] Since the world provided knowledge, experiences of all sorts were educational and vitally important for leading children to rationality and virtuous behavior from a very young age. Accordingly, Locke charged parents and educators with the responsibility of teaching children self-discipline and the proper use of reason, rather than mere obedience. Beating and berating children were to be avoided, as was an excessive focus on rules.[23] According to Locke, no good could come of forcing children to learn unpleasant lessons simply because adults wished to teach them. In his view, "Children have as much a Mind to shew that they are free, that their own good Actions come from themselves, that they are absolute and independent, as any of the proudest of you grown Men."[24] Once the implications of the *tabula rasa,* that all children were naturally capable of rationality and good actions, were accepted, the ideal education became less a matter of forcing each child into a mold and more a matter of searching out the best subjects and methods to encourage a child along an appropriate path of learning.[25] Historians such as James Axtell and Peter Shouls have quite reasonably pointed to this work as beginning a new emphasis on both freedom and individualized education.[26]

Locke's educational vision included mental freedom as only one component in the ideal training. After all, long before the child would be able to react to the world around him as a thinking being, he would exist as a physical being. If "A Sound Mind in a sound Body, is a short, but full Description of a Happy State in this World," then "he, whose Body is crazy and feeble, will never be able to advance in it."[27] Care for the child's body, or physical education, provided a necessary base for moral education. Without it, children might never grow to become adults. Certainly, Locke believed that the force typical of contemporary education, such as rote memorization and threats of corporal punishment, could create a negative attitude about learning for the rest of one's life. However, swaddling a baby, then later dressing him in tight corsets and forcing him to sit, nearly immobile, for hours on end, would, in Locke's opinion, have even more disastrous results, destroying the child's health and perhaps even ending his life.

A Lockean education, then, consisted of two stages, physical and mental, both of which seemed gender-neutral and were crucial to the total development of the child.[28] First the body would be freed, which would develop the mental faculties and pave the way for education that focused on a rational mind. For that reason, things earlier regarded as frivolous, such as the time spent taking long walks, playing with toys, or inventing games with friends, were cast in a new light. Walks provided an ideal location to teach natural science and to fortify the child's body, while games of all sorts allowed the young mind to relax and opened new pathways for thought. Locke's training of the individual demonstrated why child-rearing had assumed such importance: physical training would help prepare the bodies and minds of the reasoning individual.

Locke's use of experience made it clear that his young man's education was fundamentally different in nature from previous forms, as it would provide a secular training in a rationality and virtue that was universal in its applicability.[29] As Locke explained in his preface, "The well Educating of their Children is so much the Duty and Concern of Parents, and the Welfare and Prosperity of the Nation so much depends on it," that "if those of [the Gentleman's] rank are by their Education once set right, they will quickly bring all the rest into order."[30] In Locke's thought, if society was to have moral and social citizens, capable of exercising their rights in a virtuous manner, wealthy parents would have to mold their children in a rational and disciplined fashion.

Locke's Influence on Changing Ideals

From the vantage point of gender distinctions, Rousseau looks less radical than John Locke, who wrote more than half a century before Rousseau. After all Locke, unlike Rousseau, used universal concepts such as the *tabula rasa* without qualification and developed an educational theory potentially remarkably ungendered in its application. Linda Kerber has noted that in its attack on patriarchy, Locke's *Two Treatises of Government* directly considered the role of women in the public order, and though he did not make a place for women within the power structure, Locke did integrate women into his social theory.[31] John Locke's work thus seems to offer a contemporary analysis of social change that was more egalitarian than Rousseau's domestic model. Though his work was based on a series of letters that offered advice and education on the rearing of a privileged boy, Locke's central concepts implied that both male and female children could benefit from the new approaches to education.

However, despite the fact that ideas like the *tabula rasa* and freer physical education were universal concepts, Locke's work took contemporary social distinctions for granted. His work emphasized physical fitness as a prerequisite for learning, not as a prelude to an egalitarian society. Indeed, after his education was complete, Locke's ideal student would take his place in the social hierarchy, not to refashion society, but to perfect it. While Locke's thought went beyond the negative injunction to educate carefully, avoiding bad influences lest society deteriorate, it did not go further than a demand for the improvement of contemporary society and the continued protection of property.[32] The goal of the vigorous and virtuous male child, in contrast to the weak and often vice-ridden boys that were the products of traditional educational practice, hardly entailed revolution or egalitarianism. The Lockean use of the *tabula rasa* therefore fit perfectly into eighteenth-century desires to improve, but not remake, society.

Many Enlightenment *philosophes,* following Locke, seized upon education and promoted both the idea of the child as innocent and the need for a rational and secular training in virtue. Claude-Adrien Helvétius, for example, took the idea of the *tabula rasa* even further than Locke had. He claimed that people are formed entirely by external influences, leading him to conclude, in *Of Man,* that "education can do anything."[33] The authors of the *Encyclopédie* had a more moderate view of education than Helvétius, but they also argued for the importance and social utility of public instruction as a force for improvement. For example, the article "Collège," written by D'Alembert, attacked the "useless" curriculum generally followed in schools and decried its corruption of the morals of young men. At the same time, D'Alembert's curricular targets of rhetoric, Latin, and philosophy echoed Locke's reasons for distaste with public education, stated nearly seventy years earlier.[34] In the end, almost all Enlightenment writers could agree that empirical education was closely tied to civic virtue and that the present system did not train its young men properly for public utility.[35] While the "unenlightened" system primarily intended to train children to be good Christians and to shape their consciences to respect accepted moral standards, the new education ought to be based on the assumption that creating rational male citizens was equally, if not more, important than forming Christians.[36] As the authors of the *Encyclopédie* explained:

> Children . . . must form the society in which they will one day have to live. Their education is therefore the most interesting object: first of all, for them, because their education should be such that they will be useful to the same society in which they find their well-being; secondly, for their faculties, which they should sustain and exercise; thirdly, for the State itself, which should gather the fruits of the good education that the citizens who comprise it have received.[37]

Enlightenment theorists thus emphasized the ways in which education as a whole, but especially practical secondary training, was essential in preparing children for their earthly future.[38] Society, and each individual child, would recapture the educational investment, resulting in a more prosperous nation. Children were being prepared for a substantial earthly reward in addition to their heavenly one, and schooling was no longer intended merely to cultivate the mind of the child but also to be of service to the nation. This nation was not a new creation, however, but a deliberate restructuring of the old one. Even if education could, as some theorists said, "do anything," its primary function was to ensure that children grew into rational and useful adults, for the benefit of the state.

Enlightenment and Moral Education

Despite the limitations of this educational thought and its replication of social distinctions even when the educational theory itself did not demand them, this new conception of children's roles had a remarkable impact on a broad range of literature about child-rearing. Even though much eighteenth-century educational philosophy focused on secondary training of the well-to-do, more and more works came to apply the new concepts that dealt with the secular role of children to the training of both sexes and all ages and stations in life. New theories of human nature provided alternative ways of conceptualizing the life of children and, indeed, formed a basis for thinking about childhood in ways previously impossible. If individuals determined the path of, and even created, societies, then each child had the potential to change the world, either for good or for bad. Education could nurture and encourage rationality, science, and progress in all classes or it could continue to foster superstition and hinder the advancement of society. In order for children to grow as rational beings and, in turn, to foster the emergence of a rational society, they would all have to become properly enlightened. By the later eighteenth century, treatises on education often tied early moral education and later schooling together.[39]

The last half of the eighteenth century highlighted the *philosophes'* concern with moral education and its relationship to schooling.[40] At the beginning of the 1760s, various French *parlements* (law courts) reviewed the constitutions of the religious orders established in their areas. The reports dealing with the Jesuits provided considerable justification for their abolition, especially that of the *Parlement* of Rennes, which was submitted by Louis-René Caradeuc de la Chalotais.[41] In the process of attacking the Jesuits, La Chalotais argued that their educational work was divisive and only proved that education ought to be controlled by the State and not the Church. Though he made some positive mention of other teaching orders, especially the Oratorians, the main point of his work was that students should be raised so that their first loyalty was to France, not to a particular religious authority or order. La Chalotais' *Overview of the Jesuit Constitutions* (1761) was only the first step in the promotion of a much larger plan. In response to the Jesuits' expulsion (1762) and the subsequent need to replace their influence in the schools they had formerly controlled, La Chalotais published his *Essay on National Education or Plan of Study for Youth* (1763). Following the principles he had outlined in the *Overview,* La Chalotais made a positive outline of reforms that could and must be attempted now that the Jesuits' control of the educational system had been broken. Arguing that the Jesuits were unfit to educate students by virtue of their allegiance to the Society and the papacy, La Chalotais advocated a national education that would prepare advanced students for citizenship in France, not simply membership in a church or life in a religious order. Along the same lines, La Chalotais also promoted a practical curriculum based on an appeal to the senses. Like Locke, he prescribed the reading of fables, long walks, and play activities.[42] He wanted to replace the Latin classics with French ones and increase the focus on the natural sciences. Education was intended to be, above all, constructive, concrete, and national, not individual or individualized.[43] These Enlightenment thinkers saw children as a part of society as a whole and hoped to modify both the environment and individuals at the same time. While none of them envisioned girls as participants in this education, one can readily see how a national education might have incorporated young women as well as young men, for a universal education might well extend to anyone who would contribute to the new society.

The basis of La Chalotais' work was clearly philosophical and incorporated his predecessors' educational theories, for despite their differences, Helvétius, Diderot, D'Alembert, La Chalotais, and others like them all sought a form of national public education that would reform mankind. Where Locke's examples focused on the education of one gentleman and how he might be encouraged to free himself from the unreasonable bonds of education in order to embrace learning more fully, the *philosophes* now emphasized how a new approach to instructing children might change their role in the world. Unlike Locke, these later philosophers were concerned with children collectively, including their secondary public instruction, rather than with the individual child. Instead of looking at how the child's own inclinations might allow him to be freer, they wished to use the child to set society free. Both, however, thought of child and society as imperfect and needing reform, but not a complete refashioning.

Rousseau Recreates Education

Studies of educational philosophy have often focused on the *tabula rasa* and physical education in order to emphasize the similarities between Rousseau and Locke.[44] While these connections do exist, the fact that Locke and Rousseau ended with radically different conclusions should encourage us to see them as opposed in important ways. Jean-Jacques Rousseau, like Locke, did begin with the assumption that humanity was perfectible and innately good. However, unlike La Chalotais, Diderot, and other philosophical contemporaries, Rousseau wanted to go beyond instructing a valuable and practical citizen in the current system. Instead, Rousseau sought the development of a truly autonomous individual, a moral man instead of a political one. Certainly, Rousseau and the other *philosophes* had both been influenced by Locke in their vision of the proper mode of physical training, as they were all united in their opposition to swaddling infants and their advocacy of free movement, including educational walks and long periods of recreation. However, Rousseau was far more radical than his contemporaries because he managed to combine Locke's child-centered focus with the *philosophes'* demands for social change, not by looking to higher education for a small elite, but by promoting citizenship through early education that was, at least in theory, accessible to all children. Rousseau's perspective on moral education, not instruction in a technical sense, thus restored Locke's individualist focus to eighteenth-century educational ideas while it continued to explore the role of the individual within the world.

In his *Emile, or On Education* (1762), Rousseau demanded the creation of a new man, one who would exist outside society and would be able to make decisions freely. As Rousseau explained in the preface to *Emile,* one could not reform existing society to make it more equal and, indeed, even to try would be to corrupt oneself beyond redemption. "I would rather follow exactly the established method than adopt a better method by halves," he said. "There would be fewer contradictions in the man; he cannot aim at one and the same time at two different objects."[45] Rather than be like Diderot or Helvétius and suggest small improvements in men's relations, Rousseau argued that happiness would come only from educating children, beginning at a very early age, to see through society's false attractions so that they could discern what was true and good on their own. As a result, *Emile* directly rejected the recommendations of other philosophers to modify existing methods of instruction. He instead advocated raising even very young children outside society in order to avoid all corrupting influences. According to Rousseau, this was necessary because contemporary man had strayed from his true nature and learned to live a false and selfish life, instead of one centered on the common good.[46] With Emile's education, Rousseau intended to work out what he saw as an unresolved tension between natural and social man. For that reason, "*Emile* closes with the founding by Emile and Sophie of a New Family that is supposed to serve as the exemplar of the authentic personal life . . . "[47] The novel attempted to describe the process by which man, already removed from his natural condition, could effect a return to the best qualities of his character.[48] The following pages will demonstrate how this ideological problem and not the issue of political reform was the basis of Rousseau's demand for a new education.

A Revolution in the Human Condition

In the famous words of the *Social Contract,* Rousseau would fashion a man who was "forced to be free." Unlike the citizens of his society, who lived in slavish dependence, Emile would be independent. He would know his own mind, would not be subject to the concerns of others, and would, above all, be master of himself. Emile's tutor would accomplish this, not by moralizing, lecturing, or sending his child off to school, but by taking a child who had been emotionally nurtured and then guiding the child through his early experiences. A Lockean belief in the innate capacity of each child for good was central to the success of Emile's education. Since Emile, like all children, was naturally good and spoiled only by improper example, his tutor would only have to remove Emile from society, so that he would not be corrupted by social practices, and instead expose him to the proper formative influences.

The first half of the new education, which focused on family life as the source for emotional health and physical fitness, was the prerequisite for individual self-control and ethical development that stood outside established norms. Morgenstern explains that "Rousseau does look to the family . . . as the harbinger of the revolution that would restore authenticity to its rightful place as the cornerstone of the human condition. This is evident particularly in Rousseau's emphasis on breast-feeding at the beginning of *Emile,* which is actually his attempt to reestablish the family on an emotionally honest basis."[49] Malleable children, represented by Emile and his future spouse, Sophie, would be shaped by mothers and then personal educators before they joined together in a marriage based on loving consent. Then they, in a continuation of the process, would themselves reconstitute the new society, with Emile as the revolutionary individual entering into new conditions of social responsibility and Sophie as the genetrix of the new society, a mother who would create the conditions necessary to form new radical individuals. Both Sophie and Emile had their proper places in the physical and moral orders, but their political roles were clearly secondary to their familial ones. Differing from the Lockean view of the world, where all minds and bodies deserved equal treatment initially, but social change remained limited, and also from the demand for practical changes to the existing system evidenced by the *philosophes, Emile* made a case for deeper transformations that were, in the end, founded on autonomy, domesticity, and family life. These were far more revolutionary and all-encompassing than mere political or instructional change.

As Rousseau explained in Book One of *Emile,* "The natural man lives for himself; he is the unit, the whole, dependent only on himself and on his like. The citizen is but the numerator of a fraction, whose value depends on its denominator; his value depends upon the whole, that is, on the community."[50] Rousseau's work, unlike Locke's, was explicitly concerned with reconciling these two visions, making an autonomous and independent man who recognized his obligations to the whole, or creating a new society through the remaking of men. Rousseau's new man, Emile, was neither a citizen nor a savage but instead lived in a way that combined "all the advantages of the natural state" with "those of the civil state."[51] It was this assertion that both brought *Emile* under fire and gained it praise from revolutionaries and later reformers. This could hardly be read as echoing the views of d'Alembert and La Chalotais, for instead of arguing for a modification of a rational child's environment and his relationship to society, Rousseau argued that both self and society needed a complete regeneration, a result that was neither savage nor civilized and was different for boys than for girls. If persons were fundamentally equal and basically good, with experience providing the basis for their future thought and actions, then children, as much as or even more than adults, deserved radically individual and personal treatment.

Self-Control and Self-Sufficiency

If "true happiness consists in decreasing the difference between our desires and our powers, in establishing a perfect equilibrium between the power and the will,"[52] then Emile would be happy, not when he was actively trying to change society, but when he realized that society could not contribute to his happiness. Rousseau gave his reader a clear ratio for happiness: decrease desires until they equal powers. Self-control was the crucial characteristic for decreasing desires; self-sufficiency would increase one's powers so that the equation would balance. Since Emile could not guarantee that others would be as honest as he, Emile would only find balance once he controlled his desires in order to lead a self-sufficient public life, not one that attempted to change others, over whom he had no control, to his way of thinking. Penny Weiss has noted that an education for freedom would offer the "development of one's power and restriction of one's desires to the realm of that which can be obtained without becoming a master or a slave."[53] An education in self-sufficiency and self-control would thus create an independent person, free from external constraints, even as it emphasized internal consent and social obligations. *Emile* was both revolutionary and unthinkable because of its promotion of an entirely new vision of modern moral man.

Self-control, the individual's need to "decrease his desires" with respect to society, was the first half of Rousseau's educational theory. It was also the primary tenet missing from other contemporary educational theory. In his criticisms of duplicity and insistence on uncontaminated experience, Rousseau rejected both contemporary society and public education. The problem with contemporary society was that people believed "[o]ur heads are not good enough as God made them, they must be molded outside by the nurse and inside by the philosopher."[54] Instead of training his student in rationality, which could mislead, the tutor would provide a training of the heart and body. As Rousseau says, the education in self-control will "make him patient, steady, resigned, calm, even when he has not got what he wanted,"[55] a characteristic that Emile will achieve before he is rational, though it will certainly be of great use once he is a rational being as well. Rousseauian freedom avoided unnatural molding by focusing on self-control, or wishing to behave as one ought.

In this work, Rousseau offered a lesson in how to accept the inevitable, not only with regard to physical reality, but also other people's prefer-ences, or social constructs. As a prerational child, unable to reason, Emile would be exposed to nature and the stimulation of his senses, so that he might recognize physical necessity, especially in the realms of force, dominance, and self-interest. Once the child assimilated the facts of these experiences, he would eventually tie his rational understanding to his emotional and physical experience, which would allow him to extrapolate this awareness to other situations and even, eventually, to treat other men as he would wish to be treated. All of this would not rely on moral lectures or esoteric concepts such as duty and responsibility, but would be taught naturally, by normal, if sometimes orchestrated, episodes in his life.

The second half of the equation, increasing one's powers, indicates that Rousseau had as a fundamental maxim the idea that liberty was also found in a practical and radical self-sufficiency, not only of material conditions, but also of mental imagination.[56] In Rousseau's scheme, the individual should be as physically independent as possible. Unlike Locke, for whom physical training and creating a healthy body were important primarily because they allowed for the development of a healthy mind, Rousseau's "education of nature" was itself an indispensable educational stage, not a precursor to "real" education.[57] Emile, for example, was raised to be healthy in body, trained in manual labor, and competent in gardening. In this way, he could live, as much as possible, within his own means, without being dependent on the good will of others.[58]

Economic independence was an adult corollary to physical fitness. When discussing the necessity and utility of trades, Rousseau wrote, "[n]ow of all the pursuits by which a man may earn his living, the nearest to a state of nature is manual labor."[59] Rousseau added a new claim when he explained that "of all stations that of the artisan is least dependent on Fortune."[60] Not only should man avoid susceptibility to the flattery of others and practice an art of "real utility," but his source of income should also remain, as much as possible, free from the constraints that might require him to please others. Since this was not possible in the falseness of contemporary society, but was theoretically accessible to any who cared to try, Emile's path was predetermined. "Remember, I demand no talent, only a trade, a genuine trade, a mere mechanical art, in which the hands work harder than the head, a trade which does not lead to fortune but makes you independent of her."[61] Manual labor thus was a response to the charlatanism and illusion of society. It was useful, independent, and close to the state of nature. That is why "agriculture is the earliest, the most honest of trades, and more useful than all the rest, and therefore more honorable for those who practice it,"[62] and "only idle or useless trades were excluded [from consideration by Emile], such as that of the wigmaker who is never necessary, and may any day cease to be required, so long as nature does not get tired of providing us with hair."[63]

Emile, unlike many of the useless and deceived members of society, would never be taught "so many useless things, while the art of doing is never touched upon!" He would truly be "fit . . . for society, and [not] taught as if [he] were to live a life of contemplation in a solitary cell, or to discuss theories with persons whom they did not concern."[64] This education would raise Emile to be a self-controlled and self-sufficient person who could be of real benefit when he reentered society. While, given the limitations of physical development, complete independence was not something that was possible for any child, Rousseau emphasized providing more freedom for children than had before existed, because he intended for them to be mentally, physically, and economically independent.

Rousseau began the treatise by claiming, "[t]o my mind those of us who can best endure the good and evil of life are the best educated,"[65] and even before discussing Emile's future profession, he described how the world's esteem of such professions differed from his. First, he explained, "[w]e can do nothing simply, not even for our children. Toys of silver, gold, coral, cut crystal, rattles of every price and kind; what vain and useless appliances."[66] Then he underscored what such pointless baubles cost and what message that would send to a less discerning individual than Emile. "What idea will they form of the true worth of the arts and the real value of things when they see, on the one hand, a fancy price and, on the other, the price of real utility, and that the more a thing costs the less it is worth?"[67] Rousseau eventually took the diatribe against luxury one step further to make a point about power relationships between people. Since those who had the most social power were the most deeply ensnared by false social relationships, the value attached to power was in truth, if not in human perception, illusory. "Power itself is servile when it depends upon public opinion . . . Those who approach you need only contrive to sway the opinions of those you rule, or of the favorite by whom you are ruled, of those of your own family or theirs,"[68] and you will be at their mercy, and hence not only unproductive, but also dependent. This does not mean that the powerful would ever perceive this. They were used to getting the things they wanted, no matter how little actual value they had. "The *artificial education of the rich* never fails to make them politely imperious, by teaching them the words to use so that no one will dare to resist them."[69] However, Emile would recognize this trap for what it was. You could "expect nothing from him but the plain, simple truth, without addition or ornament and without vanity . . . he will use speech with all the simplicity of its first beginnings."[70] Emile, taught by the method that saw words for what they were, would not only be useful but also truly polite. He would not fall victim to the false experiences of society, for perhaps "the worst effect of artificial politeness is that it teaches us how to dispense with the virtues it imitates. If our education teaches us kindness and humanity, we shall be polite, or we shall have no need of politeness."[71] The tutor would take him from physical fitness to manual trades and total honesty in all relationships in a few easy steps.

Unlike Locke and Rousseau's contemporaries, Rousseau promoted an education that began before the child was rational and was radical in its demands for self-control and independent mental judgment. The format of *Emile* proves that Rousseau, at least, thought that the theoretical element of his education was more crucial than the practical method of instruction. Rather than providing a historical study that pointed out the flaws of current society, he offered a fable of education that hinted at the necessary change in virtue. Rousseau, in his author's preface, explained: "It is not to this study [of educational theory] that I have chiefly devoted myself, so that if my method is fanciful and unsound, my observations may still be of service. I may be greatly mistaken as to what ought to be done, but I think I have clearly perceived the material which is to be worked upon."[72] Instead of asking man to live in the world and modify his behavior based on an understanding of society's needs, Rousseau's story demanded that men learn to discern what was true and good so that they could live independent of the values and expectations of society. *Emile* was "not to be taken for historical truth, but merely as hypothetical and conditional reasoning,"[73] all the better as a means for overturning the false society—existing in reality, though not in truth.

The Art of Being Ignorant

The difference that Rousseau described between mere obedience and actual independence provides one clear example of the tension between freedom and self-control. As Rousseau insisted, "[t]he man who is truly free only desires what he is capable of doing and only does what pleases him."[74] Rousseau was describing something much more fundamental than physical freedom or individualized treatment, so the child had to begin training before schooling or practical education could itself really begin. The pupil had to be educated such that he would always be free, would do what his own heart dictated and what his circumstances permitted. As many others have observed, this combination seems disingenuous: the child learned not only to do his tutor's will but also, it appears, merely to be content with what was possible and not strive for the impossible.[75] While these criticisms of duplicity on the part of the tutor certainly have an element of truth, Rousseau's corpus demonstrates how he believed that his type of training in rationality and virtue might develop independent-thinking adults. Additionally, the wide-ranging attempts to fashion a new, Rousseauian, society during the French Revolution indicate that followers believed that the "merely possible" reached beyond contemporary descriptions of the probable. In both his own work and its broader implications, Rousseau's demands went far beyond mere obedience.[76] Additionally, Rousseau's invective against "illusion," a running theme in much of his work, finds its logical culmination in the format of *Emile*, making the point, by both argument and design, that the needs of public life were less "real" than the self-control that allowed distance from society's frauds. Emile was a private man not because he existed outside society, but because his primary existence was within the limits of his mind.

Emile proved this point by its very structure. Rousseau's examples of social corruption covered nearly every possible permutation of society, from kings to philosophers and priests. Clearly, this was a cumulative attack on the influence of social institutions. "Reverse the usual practice and you will almost always do right"[77] is not simply a reference to the pedagogy of the day, but a widespread revolt against prevailing social practices. When describing the extent of corruption with reference to illusion and charlatanism, Rousseau used formulas that would have been familiar to readers of his earlier works.[78] Nevertheless, the format of *Emile* makes this point even more striking, pairing examples of social fictions with moral teachings about discernment of good and evil. Though the form of this work follows the precedent firmly established in Rousseau's earlier works, that of "laying aside [historical] facts, for they do not affect the question,"[79] in order appropriately to "illustrate the nature of things"[80] apart from the exigencies of society as it has developed, it went significantly farther than his previous "pamphlets." In the completed form of *Emile,* Rousseau made himself "better understood by everyone" by saying "fewer things with more words,"[81] words not limited by political and social possibilities. The presentation of *Emile* as a literary work made a more forceful and dangerous point than a mere treatise could provide because it fully outlined the relationship of men not only to society but also to their creation of self through the operation of self-control.

Accordingly, while this book was a strong indictment of public institutions, one would be quite wrong to understand this as equivalent to a call for political change. Most discussion of *Emile* fails to understand, however, that it is not a call for concrete political reform of any kind, least of all in the educational sphere; otherwise, it would be no different than what came before. Indeed, it had to propose a more radical and deepseated change in order to be seen in its proper role as a "true" myth. Rousseau writes, "[i]f he is always directed by the opinion of the author, he is only seeing through the eyes of another person, and when those eyes are no longer at his disposal he can see nothing."[82] The "he" to whom

Rousseau refers is not only Emile, but also any reader who has a clear enough vision to evaluate modern society. If "only a few men are freed by knowledge, determination, and courage,"[83] Rousseau intends that Emile and a few other "ordinary people" will be these men who will "serve as a pattern for the education of their fellows."[84] Through the rhetoric of illusion and sham, Rousseau makes one point over and over again; that is, that society is fatally flawed, false to the core, and that happiness comes in recognizing the different ways in which this manifests itself. In much the same manner as the fables that he describes, Rousseau uses a story to illustrate social corruption, then transforms it into a moralistic tale that teaches the reader to discern good from evil. His fable, however, unlike those designed for children, will not corrupt but only edify. Instead of putting into the hands of others "the means of deceiving you, of depriving you of knowledge of their real character, of answering you and others with empty words when they have the chance,"[85] he teaches his pupils how to live lives that help them to avoid the kinds of society where such things might happen. Instead of "teaching them how to make another drop his cheese rather than how to keep their own,"[86] he will teach them how to live apart from such dangers.

This was a direct attack on previous forms of knowledge and authority, including those promoted by Rousseau's contemporaries. Man alone, properly educated and self-controlled, was the only judge of good and evil. That is why the tutor must "[f]irst teach him things as they really are, then afterwards teach him how they appear to us. He will then be able to make a comparison between popular ideas and truth . . . I am therefore convinced that to make a young man judge rightly, you must form his judgment rather than teach him your own."[87] Truth and reality are the same the world over, but each man must form his own judgments about them so that he can avoid the prejudices of others. "Let us therefore seek honestly after truth; let us yield nothing to the claims of birth, to the authority of parents and pastors, but let us summon to the bar of conscience and of reason all that they have taught us from childhood."[88] The obligation was clear and required a response from each individual, regardless of hierarchy. "For all their humility, Rousseau and his priest retained the right to decide for themselves exactly what they would and would not believe."[89] If "[o]nly men, I repeat, can learn from fables,"[90] it also went without saying that these men who recognized the truth of that statement also had a duty to fulfill. The juxtaposition of Rousseau's judgments on society with discussion of Emile's education told readers that a properly educated man's conscience and reason provided all the judgments he needed, and that the guidance of the church, the state, and perhaps even most especially even the philosophers would only misguide him.

Rousseau is at his most powerful when he applies these specific truths about fakery in society to philosophy and its understanding of the good and the true. "Locke would have us begin with the study of spirits and go on to that of bodies. That is the method of superstition, prejudice, and error; it is not the method of nature, nor even that of well-ordered reason; it is to learn to see by shutting our eyes."[91] Instead, Rousseau provided "true," if fictional, examples of good and evil in order to demonstrate that truth could not be gained solely through our physical experience in the world. "To judge and to feel are not the same,"[92] and the tutor's fable will teach us to know the difference. After all, in the world as it is,

[i]f the philosophers were in a position to declare the truth, which of them would care to do so? Every one of them knows that his own system rests on no surer foundations than the rest, but he maintains it because it is his own. There is not one of them who, if he chanced to discover the difference between truth and falsehood, would not prefer his own lie to the truth which another had discovered.[93]

Certainly Rousseau would not have us look to rationality or to the philosophers to teach us the true and the real, the difference between good and evil. Through the use of such examples, Rousseau instead taught his "pupil an art the acquirement of which demands much time and trouble, an art which your scholars certainly do not possess; it is the art of being ignorant, for the knowledge of any one who only thinks he knows, what he really does know is a very small matter."[94] Rather than preferring his own system, it is enough for the student of truth to be where he is. He and Rousseau speak in one voice, saying, "[f]or myself, I am not pledged to the support of any system. I am a plain and honest man, one who is not carried away by party spirit, one who has no ambition to be head of a sect; *I am content with the place where God has set me.*"[95] Compare that with the philosophers who, more concerned with systems than actions, cannot even tell us what it is to be useful. "This word makes no impression on [them] because . . . other people always undertake to supply their needs so that they never require to think for themselves, and do not know what utility is."[96] In fact, so far are they from actually understanding the importance of things that, at a dinner party, "[t]he [properly-educated] child is philosophizing, while philosophers, excited by wine or perhaps by female society, are babbling like children."[97] The child, unlike the philosophers, the kings, and the lovers of luxury, has understood the truth behind the appearances. He knows that "[t]o limit our desires comes to the same thing, therefore, as to increase our strength. When we can do more than we want, we have strength enough and to spare, we are really strong."[98] Once the student has applied that truth to himself, he will have restricted the world of imagination and also restricted "all the sufferings which really make us miserable," for they "arise from the difference between the real and the imaginary."[99] He will not be taken in by the charlatans that he sees around him. Truly free to make his own decisions, he would be able to make them correctly.

Through the descriptive power of his words, Rousseau enunciated most clearly that "it is in education that the link between the construction of the inner person and the construction of society occurs. This is why *Emile* is Rousseau's most profoundly and fundamentally radical work."[100] In the end, Rousseau's ideas demonstrated, not a particular political ideology or a demand for public instruction, but rather the reconstruction of society outside the realm of rationality and politics, beginning with the education of self-sufficient and self-controlled young men. This was not a call for political change but a rewriting of the terms of the debate, with new fields of discussion, such as those surrounding child-rearing and family life, adopted because of Rousseau's insistence that minor changes would never accomplish truly radical goals.

Sophie and Civil Society

Despite his primary emphasis on the creation of a new male, Rousseau recognized that women were central to both child-rearing and education and that family life and proper education within the family were the true sources of civil society. Hence, Rousseau was also vitally concerned with explaining women's social roles. Lydia Lange writes that, although many political philosophers had views about the ideal place of women, "Rousseau devoted a remarkably high proportion of his work to questions concerning women and the family and insisted that his thought on these matters was crucial to his whole political vision."[101] It is for this reason, among others, that the modern focus on Rousseau's exclusion of women from the "public sphere" may not illuminate the impact of Rousseau's gender politics on the new individualist ideal. For, while it is true that Rousseau's work offers us no shortage of demands for the submissiveness and passivity of women, to emphasize those demands is to ignore the complexity of Rousseau's arguments and their appeal to his readers. If the argument of Rousseau's *Emile* was merely that, for the good of society, women should be passive and desire to submit their wills to those of their husbands, Rousseau would have offered the eighteenth century little new concerning women's ideal roles. Instead, his insistence on the foundational importance of creating radically free individuals within the domestic rather than the political sphere—a point seized on and expanded by later writers—simultaneously reconceptualized the meaning and purpose of the politically active individual and reached a new understanding of women as a central part of this genesis. For that reason, in addition to inquiring into the meaning and location of women's particular roles, we must also understand the role of women in creating politically active and independent individuals.

Although Rousseau explicitly excluded women from public life, the fifth book of *Emile* included substantial discussion of "Sophie, or the Woman." Sophie would, like Emile, receive an education of the heart, and she "is a pupil of nature just as Emile is."[102] In the last book of *Emile,* Rousseau used sexual difference to link popular sovereignty and the general will, ideas he had already developed, to the specific interests of private individuals. Sophie, as a female individual, received an education that prepared her, not to be the active participant in a new moral society, but to be the observer and shaper of male activity, or "the woman of the man."[103] And yet, despite Rousseau's description of what seems an entirely private and passive role, in which women are "shut up in their houses" and have "limited all their cares to their households and their families,"[104] Sophie had an equal role in forming the new society, both in her control over her husband and in her ability to produce children and provide their first education. Rousseau's good mother would need to "remove the young tree from the highway and shield it from the crushing force of social conventions" and "from the outset raise a wall round [her] child's soul,"[105] whether that child was male or female. Sophie thereby demonstrated the same self-control expected of Emile, and she was promised that she would "reign over [Emile] when she reigns over herself."[106] In fact, one gets the impression that the book itself, addressed to "a good mother who knows how to think,"[107] was addressed to women who themselves desired to be Sophie and who could, like Emile, make the active choice to remove themselves from civilized society. As the book explains, the partnership of Emile and Sophie "produces a moral person of which the woman is the eye and the man is the arm."[108] In this description, the combination of the two individuals results in only one new creation. Sophie, as half of the new person, guides Emile and has authority over his heart, which is, according to Rousseau, the most important part.[109] Without his companion, Emile could not be the complete moral man of Rousseau's creation. Sophie might have been an observer, but she was far from being a mere bystander. Without Sophie, there could be no new society. The private and domestic sphere was not, for Rousseau, set up in opposition to the political sphere but instead in opposition to the artificiality of public life. Sophie may have been private, but that in no way implied that she was not civic.

Additionally, while to us "Rousseau's Sophie . . . seems completely out of place in the late twentieth century . . . more a plaything than a partner,"[110] seeing her as fundamentally unequal to Emile is to forget the role of self-control in the ideal education. If happiness consists in establishing an equilibrium between desire and power, Sophie's education emphasizes the same characteristics as Emile's. Feminist philosopher Denise Schaeffer has explained the ways in which Sophie remains an independent thinker and, because the eye drives Emile's actions, Sophie is the controlling force behind the family dynamic.[111] Sophie sets the relationship in motion and keeps it going, with even greater self-awareness than Emile, because she understands the true demands of society and acts to create the new family. In order to support Emile's idea that he chooses freely what Sophie knows he ought to choose, she dissembles. In terms of self-control and self-sufficiency, this makes Sophie even more powerful, just as the tutor may dissemble for the sake of Emile's ultimate training. "In order to maintain the illusion, Sophie must not be fooled by the illusion,"[112] nor must the reader, whose education "would then resemble Sophie's more than Emile's."[113] Sophie is not only civic, but also, because of her self-control, the governor of the new society and, ultimately, the arbiter of her own happiness.[114]

Early Education Revised

Readers who understood Rousseau's focus on education as a demand for a new society and radically new male and female individuals often perceived Rousseau, perhaps not entirely incorrectly, as a lunatic who wanted to destroy society and social roles.[115] Many of these saw potential flaws in the current methods for the moral and social upbringing of children but could not believe that so drastic a solution as complete removal from society could be either warranted or efficacious. Some apologists for the current system argued that boys could be trained to be good citizens within the current system and side-stepped Rousseau's arguments about gender or social corruption altogether.[116] But even those who opposed Rousseau's educational and philosophical scheme did agree with him that civic virtue and political change were in fact tied to education and child-rearing. These thinkers, no matter how contradictory their political leanings, now recognized that either conserving or remaking the world involved shaping the minds of the young from their earliest days.

Within a few years of the publication of *Emile*, the scope of commentary changed. Eventually, instead of a wholesale attack on Rousseau's ideas, critics of the novel limited their disapproval to its treatment of religious questions or its call for the isolation of the child from corrupting factors. Even critics often praised Rousseau's suggestions for improving physical care of children and his emphasis on a nurturing mother.[117] Unlike Rousseau, these authors called for educational change that would reform social mores but not simultaneously remake society. "Education is construed as vitally important" in these works, "but proposals for reform rarely contain the subversive implications of *Emile*."[118] Rousseau's recommendations on physical education were the most easily employed, least controversial, and most derivative component of *Emile* and remained popular for years. In fact, most critics compared this limited set of Rousseau's suggestions to Locke's and argued that they were entirely reasonable. For example, Alphonse Serre de La Tour claimed, "I advise every rational mother to read Locke in his entirety, & the first Section of *Emile*. One might even believe that I inscribe this last Work at the beginning of mine, & that what is mine, is made to indicate the ways in which I think differently from M. Rousseau."[119] In other words, Rousseau's educational prestige in the pre-Revolutionary period and his reputation as an educationist were primarily due to his "innovations" for physical childcare, not his basic theory or his ideas for the refashioning of moral individuals, concepts that generally continued to be misunderstood or half-digested.[120]

Before the turn of the century, then, Rousseau's influence was primarily limited to the elements of his maternal and domestic education that focused on the physical needs of the child, while the general Enlightenment response continued to see instruction as a public matter and therefore remained unconcerned with issues of hierarchy, self-control, and radical individualism. To be sure, Enlightenment theorists offered thoughts on the necessity for a national education, in which children would be raised with the proper allegiance to France. In their plans, education would advance the needs of society, with students educated to be moral citizens. "All wanted to produce more useful members of society," writes Jean Bloch, "a doubtless perennial aim of schooling, which in this case meant to be more abreast of modern knowledge, proficient and reliable in one's vocation, and a good *citoyen* for *la nation* and *la patrie*."[121] However, the primary issues for these theorists were a curriculum that was more practical and nationalistic and teachers who could implement such a curriculum without forcing their religious agenda to the fore.[122] In practical terms, this was often reduced to a call for state-run education with less emphasis on philosophy, rhetoric, and Latin and more teaching of French literature and the methods of scientific inquiry. Education was important for the vitality of the nation, but calls for change remained, by and large, limited to reform in public schooling.[123] Emile's domestic and private education, on the other hand, had—unacceptably, it seemed—implied the removal of all children from society and rejected a focus on later public education in favor of a reformed family life and widespread training in civic responsibility.

Despite these differences in approach and intent, French revolutionar-

ies saw Rousseau as a—perhaps *the*—source for remaking the school system with the state as the active agent. Still later, educational theorists saw
him as the founder of both democratic thought and the modern system of
education.[124] How could the creator of Emile and Sophie, both trained
outside any institutional system, also be a foundational theorist for modern public education? The answer to that question lies in a peculiar combination of the appeal of Rousseau's radical demands for autonomy and
social reordering and his similarity to other educational theorists of his
era in the realm of physical education. Despite the fact that "he is original enough to be properly called revolutionary, [Rousseau was] so familiar with his predecessors as to offer hardly an idea that he had not read
in one or more of them."[125] This combination of similarity and radical
change allowed Rousseau's contemporaries and, later, legislators, to
adapt what they thought were Rousseau's ideas to modern education
without a sense of paradox. Instead of looking at Rousseau as a critic of
contemporary instruction, most revolutionary practitioners were concerned instead with individual education and followed very closely in the
footsteps of Locke's and Rousseau's contemporaries, who had described
the physical needs of the child only as part of the larger question of social
fitness. In this way, Locke's work provided a foundation for the reception
of the entire Enlightenment ferment over education, including Rousseau's
demands for complete social change, and guaranteed that limited institutional reform would exist alongside social change stemming from the refashioning of family life.[126] At least initially, Rousseau was read primarily, as de La Tour had advised, for his advice on maternal and domestic
education, which, as we shall see in the following chapters, was "popu-
larized in children's books, sentimental novels, and medical manuals."[127]
And yet, once the emphasis on maternal education became widespread,
the more radical implications of a nurturing domesticity had additional
cultural currency. In the end, Rousseau's recommendations for the physical upbringing of children were widely publicized and put into the context of the formation of a new civic being by a loving mother.

Although public instruction remained hierarchical and exclusive, the
profoundly gendered and, to our eyes, sexist, enunciation of Sophie's social roles had a widespread impact on debates over women's inherent
worth and potential contribution to society. Public instruction remained
out of the reach of most girls, but a new rhetoric arose in which the good
mother independently raised her children to be healthy adults and therefore healthy citizens. This mother contributed to the moral well-being of
the nation as much as any male citizen. Bad mothers failed to raise their
children properly, which resulted in the death or illness of the children,
and, by extension, the malaise of the nation.[128] Though schooling and
public instruction continued to emphasize rationality and limited social

change, parents, and especially mothers, came to be valued for their unique role as the shapers of the physical health and moral judgment of their children, especially in their rearing of self-controlled and autonomous children. As Lydia Lange has noted, while Rousseau's philosophy emphasized "sexual, domestic, and familial matters," he raised "the banner that the character and role of women, and the character of the family over all, [was] crucially important for a good civil state . . ."[129] In the end, as the Rousseauian rhetoric valorizing women as domestic mothers increased in prominence, it also became increasingly clear that virtues that Rousseau construed as masculine, especially autonomy and self-control, also applied to domestic women in his system. Eventually, when demands for social change collided with calls for the recreation of society though public instruction, Rousseau's framing of regeneration through early moral education was waiting in the wings to influence the social understandings of domesticity and individuality.

Even if Enlightenment theorists made only limited attempts to reshape society and tended to promote the distinctions of the eighteenth century in their focus on public instruction, we should note that this was as likely to come from the conservatism of Locke and the *philosophes* as from the particular radicalism of Rousseau. After all, as distinct from the limited instruction of the *philosophes* that was intended to protect property and hierarchy,[130] Rousseau's solution saw the family as the source of political regeneration, where changes in nurturing and child-rearing would affect society in general through autonomous individuals. Additionally, despite the fact that Rousseau believed virtue and self-sufficiency to be different for men than for women, he admitted that "good sense belongs to both sexes alike."[131] When he claimed that "[w]oman is worth more as a woman and less as a man" and explained that "when she makes a good use of her own rights, she has the best of it,"[132] he also promoted acceptance of the idea that woman had a natural, even decisive, part to play in the physical and moral order.[133] If, as Rousseau believed, only the rational, self-controlled, and independent individual would be prepared to be of real service to society, a space was opened into which nineteenth-century maternal and domestic education of both sexes could easily enter.

CHAPTER TWO

Freeing the Body, Educating the Mind
Childhood in Clothing and Toys

A Sound Mind in a sound Body, is a short, but full Description of a Happy State in this World. He, whose Body is crazy and feeble, will never be able to advance in it. —John Locke, *Some Thoughts Concerning Education* (1693)

All mothers know what usefulness one can draw from the game of the doll: the practice of creating clothing, the first use of the needle, taste, games develop all of these qualities that are so precious in our sex. The fact that children are disposed to imitate the practices of their parents can also be observed in this type of recreation. If the small girl has a mother that is too occupied with her toilette, one will see the girl using her mornings to calculate the taste and the effect of her ornaments, she will torment everything around her until she has ribbons, plumes, new feathers, flowers, and the ability to change her doll's decorations continually. —Madame Campan, *On Education* (1824)

Physical Freedom, Material Culture, and Philosophical Change

As the last chapter has demonstrated, Rousseau's new analysis of the social role of the modern individual was indicative of ways in which demands for radical autonomy and social change could, perhaps paradoxically, be accompanied by a greater emphasis on gender and the reimagination of the domestic world. And yet, while Rousseau's *Emile* also suggested new educational forms, only the general Enlightenment emphasis on early childhood freedom first became widespread. Even if they disagreed about the nature of political right or social change, both Locke and Rousseau were part of a growing cultural consensus about childhood's importance, especially insofar as an emphasis on healthy bodies, early physical training, and recreation were concerned. New books not only offered parents advice on how to follow Locke and Rousseau but also spelled out ways to conform to the ideal. The focus on healthy bodies emphasized maternal care, as opposed to wet-nursing, and recommended letting children exercise their limbs free of swaddling bands or tight clothing. Thus as the new philosophies became more influential, ideal forms of clothing became less restrictive, demonstrating in yet another way the impact of the new theories about children's physical and emotional needs.

The new ideal meant that French children of the nineteenth century were supposed to be cared for at home and clothed less restrictively. When this actually occurred, it would have meant that the children required greater individual attention and care than the swaddled babies of earlier years, a turn of events that reinforced demands for a nurturing mother to be in the home to care for the children. However, even as new forms of clothing became freer, they, like Rousseau's theories, also increasingly emphasized gender distinctions and self-controlled behavior. As parents, philosophers, and educators changed their minds about the necessary material goods for infants and children, they expressed the concepts that underlay the new ideas of nurturing. Fashions reflected an attempt to be "natural" as clothing became looser and less restrictive. A growing emphasis on toys pointed to the new importance of play and relaxation as necessary activities for children. Accessories ranging from small pets to ribbons also demonstrated the growing role of consumption as fundamentally important for children and the adults intent on raising them in the proper French styles.

Long before political revolution reared its head, children's clothing underwent a revolution of its own. Before the middle of the eighteenth century, children's clothing was not a fashion concern, as is clearly evidenced by the complete disregard of it in fashion magazines, tailoring manuals, and that eighteenth-century compendium of knowledge, the *Encyclopédie*. But by the end of the eighteenth century, children's clothing had become a substantial part of the luxury and tailoring industries. Children's fashions demonstrate the paradoxes inherent in the extension of freedoms; even as more and more children could have clothing that was physically less constraining than adult fashions, a more precise focus on gender, order, and self-control accompanied the new designs.[1]

By the middle of the nineteenth century, children's clothing also helped parents to define the changing "necessities" of the early stages of life. As one contemporary theorist explained, "[c]lothing influences health and manners and morals more than one might think. It is without doubt for this reason that the Writers who have dealt with education have prescribed certain rules on the manner in which one dresses children."[2] Now that childhood was the crucial moment for determining future accomplishments and behavior, fashion illustrations and child-rearing manuals encouraged parents who wanted their children to grow up healthy and moral to buy goods to prepare their children's minds in addition to their

bodies. More often than not, the fabrics and styles reflected adult fashions and concerns even as they incorporated the new thinking about the
nature of children. Additionally, these illustrations and manuals were intended for parents who had enough income that they could afford to purchase unique clothes, which would soon be outgrown, for their children
rather than cutting an old woman's dress down to size. As a result, much
as today, parents of the nineteenth century could choose particular fashions not only because the parents wished to raise healthy and productive
children who would contribute to society but also because they intended
to demonstrate their status by dressing their offspring according to the
latest fashions. These different meanings for clothing help us to see the
cultural shift to modern individualized and self-controlled children. As
the new fashions were promulgated and implemented, children's clothing
became, like adult clothing, both artistic and style-driven. It therefore
reflects not only historical impulses but also a personal vision of self and,
in the case of children, the future. Fashion, intensely fickle and subject to
momentary whims, reflects the changing ideas surrounding children's
bodies in ways that few other things can.

Changes in material culture also mark the period from 1760 to 1830 as
an especially critical time in the development of distinctions in taste and
behavior for French people in general and children in particular. Before the
middle of the eighteenth century, children's clothing did not differentiate
particularly by gender and served to physically control both boys and girls:
infants were swaddled and corseted, then dressed in long petticoats that
did not allow them to creep or crawl. Since all children, like women, were
subordinate, all young children dressed in long skirts. Though these
clothes could be quite opulent when the family's wealth allowed, children's
fashions changed little and seemed unworthy of public attention. By the
century's end, however, social hierarchies had been supplanted by increasingly gendered ones; at least in an ideal world, little boys and girls were
supposed to have distinctive costumes that emphasized the gender of the
wearer even as they allowed children greater freedom of movement.

Certainly, the change in children's fashion mimicked the increasing sartorial differentiation between men and women.[3] Philippe Perrot has noted
that, within the bourgeoisie, masculine and feminine difference were ever
more clearly expressed in clothing, with men of business wearing solemn
suits and women wearing frivolous clothing designed to reflect their role
in the home.[4] This was, however, not just a bourgeois phenomenon. Napoleonic images demonstrate that the King of Rome was dressed according to the new norms, and portraiture and engravings demonstrate the
prevalence of the ideal across class lines. The changes in fashion thus demonstrate the ways in which new ideas about individuality and gender difference affected childhood across a reasonably broad spectrum. Wealthy

boys were not to remain dressed in the subordinate clothing of women as they would have been a hundred years before. Instead, as hierarchy became less important than individual characteristics, gender came to the forefront, even in designs for very young children. New clothing styles emphasized pants instead of skirts even for very young boys, to clearly differentiate them from their sisters and mothers. Changing fashions also played to different markets: one way of demonstrating wealth or accessorizing an adult was to focus attention on the dress and behavior of an accompanying child. While children who wore the new styles were no longer constrained by their clothes, their relationships to the adult world had become even more closely regulated in the areas of gender and self-control.

The changes in children's clothing had begun even earlier in Britain, during the early eighteenth century. For example, the French called the trend of dressing children lightly and in loose garments fashion *à la anglaise*. However, despite the fact that textile production changed in Britain first and that clothing patterns offered the youth of Britain comfortable clothing years before French children, changes in French fashions provide an excellent reflection of larger cultural changes in the status of childhood and perceptions of individuality. Dress and other leisure industries occupied a central place in French society and were considered an appropriate focus of concern, in part because French culture explicitly linked current philosophical thought to changes in art and fashion. As Susan Sontag has commented, "[t]he French have never shared the Anglo-American conviction that makes the fashionable the opposite of the serious."[5] While it is true that the French fashion industry may have lagged behind its British counterpart in offering comfortable new clothes for their children, when children *did* become a focus of concern, fashionable parents in France were more likely, for philosophical, social, and cultural reasons, to insist that their children have the proper types of garments. Additionally, Daniel Roche has argued that early modern France's "culture of appearances" changed over the course of the eighteenth century to meet new distinctions as society shifted from a focus on hierarchical position to individual characteristics.[6] An examination of French children's clothing in the eighteenth and nineteenth centuries therefore demonstrates the ways that new ideas about society related to changing cultural constructs of gender and individuality.

Physical Control and Caretaker Indifference in Early-Modern Clothing

Before 1750 in France, children's clothing did not have any particular "fashion" but took only two general forms: Infants and toddlers were dressed more or less like adult women, in corsets, petticoats, and skirts. Older children, judging by images from the era, found themselves in clothes that were virtually identical to those of adults of the same sex. Of course, for girls, this still meant corsets and long skirts, while boys graduated to trousers and coats. Especially for young children, little attention was paid to the specific characteristics and needs of the child. Age rather than gender was the crucial characteristic defining what clothing a child would wear. Babies were swaddled and clothed in dresses that ended well below the feet. Toddlers' outfits had leading strings and shorter skirts than infants, to allow for walking. Both little boys and girls below the age of reason wore smaller versions of adult female dress, or a reasonable facsimile. It was not until roughly seven, the age of reason, that male and female children were dressed differently, distinguished by clothing that indicated gender as well as social position.

All infants were swaddled until roughly eight months of age. For practical reasons, even older babies might remain in swaddling clothes throughout the winter and advance to corsets and skirts once the weather got warmer. Though nurses from different regions often had their own particular methods of wrapping, the process was fairly consistent across time and place, and the end results looked remarkably similar (see figures 1 and 2). Immediately after birth, the elaborate swaddling process began. First, babies were washed with a special concoction to clean their bodies

Figure 1. Swaddling a newborn after birth, circa 1700. Bibliothèque nationale de France

of any remaining vernix and "protect" their skin. These solutions ranged from a salt scrub to watered-down lye, wine and water, or even a mixture of honey and milk. Once a child was clean, the head was the first target for shaping. After a nurse pressed and pushed the head into as circular a shape as possible, a leather hat with a round cushion (shaped like a doughnut) was put onto the child's head. Another cap was placed over that, and then a cloth or large ribbon was wrapped around the entire contraption.[7] This was intended to protect the child's head from drops or falls, and accordingly, the leather doughnut often remained until the child was a toddler and a steady walker. This was also intended to avoid the misshapen skull that sometimes came from leaving swaddled children, unable to move, in the same position, day in and day out.

Not forgotten, the body was next. The child's legs were pulled straight and bound together. In order to defend against rickets and ensure the straightness of the body, a piece of padding or pieces of cloth were often placed in between the legs before they were wrapped together. The arms were held out to the sides and the baby's body was encased in bands as well. Finally, the arms were brought alongside the body and bound.[8] The child

Figure 2. Swaddling a newborn, detail of figure 1.
Bibliothèque nationale de France

now looked like a compact, rectangular parcel and would remain in this form for months. The arms would be freed before the rest of the body, allowing the child to bring things to his mouth while preventing him from getting into trouble, but at all stages of swaddling, the baby was severely constrained. Swaddling served multiple purposes: those who cared for the child could focus on other duties, carry the child easily from place to place, and even hang the swaddled bundle on a nail to keep the baby out of harm's way and off the dirty floor. Contemporaries believed that swaddling would also protect the baby from his own too-vigorous movements and properly shape the child's arms and legs. As one early critic of the widespread use of swaddling was careful to explain, "[i]n any case, one should not believe that it is our intention to forbid completely the use of swaddling. We agree that it is necessary in the first period [of life] to keep the child in a secure situation, for fear that when he turns from one side to another, he will hurt himself."[9] The deformities due to rickets, they believed, were also caused by improper shaping of the newborn.[10] By pulling the arms and legs straight, the nurses intended to provide for not only the portability and easy compliance of their charges but also their health and comeliness.

Perhaps most important, however, the elongation of the child through swaddling guaranteed a package that was immediately comprehensible and attractive to adults. In a world dominated by hierarchy, infants occupied a suspect position. Humanity was the highest of the earthly creations because of its ability to walk upright and reason. Babies could do neither. As their children were incapable of demonstrating rational thought, parents were not about to allow them to demonstrate actively animalistic tendencies by creeping or crawling on the ground. They were to look and act like humans and not beasts, which meant looking and acting like adults insofar as it was possible. At a few months of age, a child might have the hands unswaddled and then be allowed to reach for objects but would certainly not be able to kick, creep, or crawl. This revulsion toward children's creeping and crawling was not merely aesthetic. In addition to inhibiting the types of behavior that seemed animalistic, swaddling promoted upright posture. The newborn could be held upright, tricking the eye into believing that infants were able to hold up their heads and even stand. "As for the stiffness of the swaddled child's body, its final purpose was not simply to make carrying the child easier; it was the fruit of an old rational vision of humanity as the ultimate state that was always threatened with bestial behavior: to force the correct position with a tight bandaging was to hasten a process of development, to humanize correctly."[11] Children were swaddled so that they would not look or act notably different from adults, despite their immaturity. Early-modern theorists were convinced that children who were allowed to behave like beasts might be so influenced by their early behavior that they would never develop into reasoning human beings. The idea that children should not be allowed to creep and crawl on the ground was similar to that of shaping the head and body, for both assumed that children would have to be physically molded and controlled in order to become reasonable and attractive adults.

Engravings of the period demonstrate that swaddled children could even be laced into their cradles. This common practice not only kept the children from falling out onto the floor or into a fire, but it also gave infants some protection from the overzealous rocking of nurses, a hazard alluded to in childcare manuals from the seventeenth to the nineteenth centuries.[12] Conveniently, it also allowed nurses and parents to leave children unattended for long periods of time while they went about their business. Today, we know that it is likely that swaddled children also cried less than nonswaddled ones. Since they were wrapped tightly enough to compress their chests, babies could draw only shallow breaths, which slowed bodily functions (they urinated and defecated less frequently) and discouraged screaming. Even as infants were wrapped so that they might look more like adults, they were likely to be physically controlled in ways that allowed adults to devote their time to other pursuits. One could almost forget that the newborn in the cradle was not yet a self-sufficient being.

Though the babies might have seemed more human, this was hardly humane. In the twenty-first century, this appears as egregious child abuse. It is true that in the eighteenth century, swaddling not only prevented children from wandering into fires or crawling in filth, but also kept babies from being trampled by animals around the house. These practices almost certainly kept the children warm in badly heated homes. However, doctors recommended that the bands be replaced at least once or twice a day and this injunction makes it clear that the period between changes was generally longer.[13] Slowed body functions or not, children were likely left in filthy rags for hours on end. As one opponent of swaddling noted, "[o]ne presses on the knees and the legs straighten; one seizes this instant to enclose him entirely in the wrapping, and with him, all the excrement that he can make."[14] It ought to come as no surprise that diaper rash remedies and discussions of various types of open sores were a common topic of advice manuals, with mothers being urged to take care of wounds before they began to fester. As if this were not enough, manuals also mentioned how the straight pins that held the bands in place were known to stick the children, leading to, at best, fussy children, and at worst, seizures and other serious traumas.[15] Perhaps worst of all, swaddled babies were often set or hung in one location and left there for hours, until the person responsible for the child had the time or inclination to pay some bit of personal attention to the infant. While a swaddled infant did certainly need to be kept out of harm's way, manuals and illustrations make it clear that these infants were often kept out of everyone's way so that they could be entirely ignored except for the occasional feeding or changing. Containment was at least as important a part of the design as protection.

The situation did not improve drastically even after the first few months of life. Much as women found their freedom of movement inhibited by hoops, corsets, and long skirts, the child who moved to dresses saw little improvement in physical mobility or attention from caregivers. Birth took the child from one form of constraint to another and swaddling immediately gave way to tight clothing and long skirts that prevented crawling. Once the swaddling bands were discarded, they were replaced by a cotton chemise and a corset, meant to ensure that the child sat up straight and continued to look like an adult, both in comportment and demeanor. It is important to remember that the corset did not make the child look like the adult of today but like the woman of yesteryear. "This garment [took] the form of a cone, where the base is on top, and the point is on the bottom, a shape diametrically opposed to that of the chest, which is flared at the bottom and narrow on top."[16] The waist was drawn in quite tightly, especially for little girls (see, for example, figures 3 and 4). In other words, from the time that swaddling was abandoned

Figure 3. Wet-nurse with her charge, circa 1700.
Bibliothèque nationale de France

Figure 4. The *promeneuse* of the Duke de Bourgogne, circa 1700. Bibliothèque nationale de France

altogether until the child reached the age of reason, historically defined as seven, but often earlier, both boys and girls dressed in costumes similar to those of grown women, long dresses with petticoats underneath. Just as women's long skirts and wide collars symbolized dependence, so too did the long skirts and wide collars of children signal their subordinate place in the hierarchy.[17] From a very early age, adults used this kind of shaping and these types of sartorial signs to force the child's body into adult positions and postures, both physically and mentally. Because the skirts linked children to a woman's world and reminded them of their dependence, they promoted a vision of the world in which dependence was more important than gender. The primary message of the skirts was rank and subordinance in a hierarchical world.

For very young children, the skirts of the dresses fell far below the feet, inhibiting any attempt to creep or crawl and ensuring that the child could be left in one place with ease. Even when carried or held, children looked like miniature adults, fully capable of walking. Older children, both boys and girls, strengthened their legs in two ways. Toddlers learned to walk with the use of leading-strings. These were ribbons or ropes attached to the back of a child's garment or wrapped around the chest and attached to the shoulders. A nurse or governess or, more rarely, a parent would walk behind the child, leading him or her with the ribbons, much like a puppet. This prevented children from falling to all fours like a beast, allowed the caregiver to determine when the child would walk (and where!), and gave children practice until they were steady enough to walk on their own (see figure 4). Parents and nurses also could put children into walking or standing stools. Much like today's walkers but without any seat or other support, these allowed children to work their legs without permitting them to sit or crawl on the ground. As one might imagine, these were often abused. Children were left in walking stools for hours on end, with no way to rest. They were also dangerous: children could walk into open fires or fall down staircases. However, they served their purpose insofar as they kept young children upright and allowed them to learn to walk without letting them resort to crawling or taking up valuable caretaker time to ensure their safety. The priorities in early modern childhood remained the same: make sure that the child fit into the natural hierarchy by looking like an adult, while demanding as little personal attention as possible.

Underneath the long skirts, boys and girls shared another component of adult women's clothing: the corset. François Boucher notes that "boys themselves wore whalebone corsets that differed from those of girls only in that they were rounded . . . there was even a special model for the boy who had received his first pants"[18] and accordingly needed a corset with a higher waist. Even as swaddling served an objective purpose of protection, to some degree, so too were the corsets that underlay the skirts designed with some of the child's needs in mind. Swaddling allowed parents and other caretakers to put children safely out of harm's way; corsets were believed not only to shape but also to protect young developing bodies. Proponents of these garments argued that children would grow straighter if they wore corsets that trained them to do so. Makers of corsets also explained that small children, who might become tired out with the effort of sitting, could count on their corsets to support them, requiring them to expend less effort and yet keep the most "healthy" posture. Older and more active children who ran the risk of falling or suffering accidents would be protected by the firm garment, in much the same manner as a rind protected an orange. Much like swaddling, however, the corset was fundamentally restrictive rather than protective and intended to shape children into the physical appearance of an adult at a very early age. And, while the corset was more hygienic than infrequently changed bands, it still allowed little freedom and flexibility to the body of the growing child.[19]

In retrospect, these claims that parents and doctors made for safety or better health may seem misguided. Later theorists certainly argued that caregiver convenience and shaping children to adult models were the only motivating factors. Yet, the writings from the eighteenth century certainly indicate that children's health was of real concern to parents and caretakers; they detail diaper rash remedies, emphasize the need to change soiled clothing, and often warn against vigorous rocking of babies and inattention around hazardous objects. Even if we could claim that such exchanges are primarily disingenuous, mere lip service to cover for and justify inattentive and lax parenting, the claims of increased safety and vitality that corset-makers and defenders of swaddling made prove that children's health was of some concern before the older trends came under widespread attack. These claims, then, demonstrate that parents were not indifferent to the health and welfare of their children. While they did not give primacy to attention or nurturing, the methods that seem so coercive today did not arise out of carelessness or apathy. The apparent lack of differentiation between adult and child and the attempts on the part of parents and nurses to make children appear like miniature adults was not an accident; adults took this model for granted and therefore actively sought to mold their offspring into miniature versions of themselves.

Shaping the Mind, Not the Body

The traditional approach toward molding children and demonstrating their hierarchical position was virtually unopposed until the mid-eighteenth century. By then, as debate over the proper ways to train a child's mind flourished, many theorists argued that a new attention to the physical and emotional well-being of the small child was as important as the growing concern with curriculum. Though Enlightenment *philosophes*, many of whom were interested in pedagogy, had embraced Locke's distaste for swaddling bands and physical shaping, it was not until after the publication of Rousseau's *Emile* that the previous norms for the physical and emotional treatment of children came under widespread attack. New fashions, which followed Rousseau's philosophical lead, were based on the idea that childhood had its own virtues, distinct from those of adulthood. Primary among them was an assumed "naturalness" and innocence, a distance from and a corresponding lack of corruption by society. Children were natural and innocent before they were tainted by culture, and an appropriate focus on clothing and education could ensure that they remained so, at least inasmuch as it was humanly possible.

By the 1770s, fascination with the freer English fashions and new theories of childhood and parenting combined with concerns about public health to encourage new forms of dress for children. This was especially true for boys, who might find themselves in pants well before the age of reason so that they could frolic and strengthen their legs. Even as gender assumed a more prominent role, designs offered more freedom to both boys and girls. Standing stools, leading-strings, and corsets fell into ill repute, and parents with the time and income to spend on their children could purchase numerous treatises describing new approaches to the physical and mental upbringing of children. These objects and garments experienced no fleeting unpopularity; nor did they later find new defenders. The change in perception was permanent; literature about children increasingly demanded that parents respond to their children's emotional needs and clothe their children in ways that were specifically appropriate to age, gender, and temperament. Gone were the days when any truly fashionable child could wear a cut-down version of his or her mother's oldest dress. Given the loosening of restrictions and controls, the new forms of clothing also meant that parents and nurses who obeyed the new imperatives found themselves interacting with young children more and more. No longer could a "responsible" nurse hang her young swaddled charge on a hook and go about her own business. Instead, the care of the child became her primary business and, if Rousseau's vision became reality, the mother would become the ideal nurse, dispensing love and affection along with her breast-milk.

Even if the assumption that children were naive and innocent rather than sinful and animalistic played a major role in demands for children's physical freedom, the literature of the period still emphasized shaping children. Once children were no longer directly shaped into adult appearance and behavior through physical means but were instead formed, with permanent repercussions, through the example of adults, early adult contact with children took on new significance. The mother became increasingly important because physical molding gave way to emotional guidance. While Rousseau had emphasized children's natural goodness, even he advocated a constant vigilance on the part of those who would train a child's emotions. Childhood might be important, valuable, and necessary, but it was also, in the end, an irresponsible and emotionally volatile stage, with characteristics that could not be allowed to continue through to adulthood despite the idealization of infancy. As a result, even as the *philosophes* described children positively as untainted by social convention that still meant that they could be described negatively as imperfect despite their innocence. Unlike adults, who had learned how to be self-controlled, to put the needs of others and the expectations of society ahead of their own frivolous wants, children could be gluttonous, impulsive, and cruel, and a mother needed to shape the "first impressions" of her children so that they would not give in to selfish desires.

The Move Toward Nurturing Individuals

If physical shaping was no longer enough to help children become rational adults, that did not mean that children were hierarchically inferior to adults. Instead, descriptions of physical and mental training emphasized that all people began from the same position, and that children, if trained properly, could acquire self-control. Parents or caretakers could provide the necessary influences using love, physical education, and objects from the new material culture. Physical education was important not only because the possible physical imperfections inherent in childhood were even more obvious than moral ones but also because Rousseau had so clearly emphasized physical development as the most important precursor to moral development. As Rousseau had explained, it was already clear to the most dull-witted observer that infants developed into children who, in turn, became adults. However, what many adults missed was that the primary goal of early education should be to raise children in such a manner that they would become morally and physically healthy adults who desired to work for the good of society. Whether they focused on freedom or control, innocence or responsibility, most theorists could agree that the development of children's bodies and emotions needed careful consideration if society was to have the best use of all its members. As one forward-thinking theorist argued:

Childhood is not, as one might believe, surrounded with tears; only guide childhood on the path that has been traced by nature, and joyfulness will always accompany it; leave the newborn child in liberty and after a few days his eyes and lips will announce that his spirit is open to pleasure; he smiles at his mother and already his tender hands lift to caress her.[20]

Body and spirit were inseparably linked, and leading the child's body toward adulthood inevitably involved leading his soul along the same path. In order to accomplish the new goals, clothing and physical education should be designed not to force physical mortification but instead to feed children's spirits with love and affection in order to inspire them to new levels of emotional sacrifice. The new society was founded on the physical freedom and emotional well-being of children.

Parents learned similar lessons from the authors of the later eighteenth and early nineteenth centuries, most of whom did not stray very far from the theorists that had inspired them. As one treatise "on the necessity and the advantages of Education, etc." explained, "[m]an is born without understanding and subject to vice and error. If one would perfect his spirit, it is necessary to begin when he is still in the cradle."[21] Childhood had advantages, to be sure, but the crucial task was for parents to use their love and authority in order to help their children to retain childlike qualities even as they encouraged the child to be a properly focused and self-controlled member of society. To this end, body and soul were to be cultivated in unison. Writers outlined the physical needs of the child and the ways in which contemporary French society corrupted him from birth, ruining his physical and mental abilities. Since the writers often followed Rousseau's developmental focus, swaddling was the first target, then the use of leading-strings and corseting. Long walks were recommended for slightly older children, and the transition to forms of play and leisure paved the way for discussions of mental education.[22] It is not surprising that swaddling, so recently under attack in *Emile*, was the first practice to be challenged. Far from seeing swaddling as protective armor for the defenseless baby, they claimed, "[s]waddling arrests the development of the child."[23] "Contrary to the laws and intentions of nature, [the moment that the child searching for greater freedom, manages to be born,] fashion dictates . . . that one stretch out his body and his limbs, wrap him up, prevent him from moving, and form an immobile package."[24] Swaddling came under attack for the most obvious of reasons: the children were left to fester in dirty rags. Most of the time, they were virtually ignored and unable to move their limbs and exercise in the necessary manner. In their attempt to mold the perfect child, it was argued that nurses and parents risked destroying their offspring altogether. However, other, equally important, objections were also raised.

That the child, at the time of this procedure, has his head in a good or bad position is of no concern: [swaddling] is not for him, but for others; it is for that reason that one, without distinguishing if we are in the month of August or December, has the gentle graciousness either to roll him in a third diaper or a small wool covering that passes over the head in the shape of a hood, which keeps this part so straight and so controlled that he cannot move it.[25]

Swaddling interfered with the physical liberty of the child, but it also offended new sensibilities because it refused to acknowledge the child as a special and individual being with emotional and physical needs: the need to be cool in heat, to be free to move around, to be attended to and to be made comfortable. Something much more important than mere physical containment was the target of these objections. As individuals, children had rights that corresponded to their needs. Just as Rousseau's natural man had different needs than man in society, so children had different requirements than full-grown adults. To subordinate the demands of infants to the conveniences of adults was tyranny of the worst kind; not only did it endanger the health of the child, but it also embittered rather than inspired and thus risked the future of society. In more than one instance, "[m]ercenary wet-nurses have adopted swaddling for their convenience," so that "they could subordinate the children to their business, whether it was inside or outside, without worrying that their indifference would put the child's life in danger."[26] Of course, as Leroy and others insisted, this was to ignore the fact that the child's life *was* being put in danger. His health and, by extension, the health of a future society, suffered because parents and nurses ignored the child's needs, both emotional and physical.

The suggestion that children had emotional rights in addition to their physical needs may not have borne immediate fruit, but by 1780, Sebastien Mercier wrote of all children, in his *Tableau de Paris,* that "[they] are raised much better than before. One washes them often, though in cold water; we have the happy habit of clothing them lightly and without restraint."[27] He may have been a bit too hopeful in the case of little girls and corsets, but his own words demonstrate one way in which the outcry against constrictive clothing and the calls for physical liberty were increasingly widespread. Before the popularization of these ideas, even the most liberal of theorists had highly recommended corsets for children. Small children might have lighter corsets, not too tightly laced, made out of stiffly embroidered fabric instead of whalebone, but the general assumption had been that children needed physical shaping to attain the proper form and to keep them from harm.[28] By 1786, Monsieur Bailly, a tailor, had seen the changing ideas about children's clothing make enough of an economic impact that he decided to publish a treatise, at his own expense, in order to defend the use of corsets for young children. Though he explicitly cast his treatise in opposition to the misinformation of Rousseau (who was, of course, not an expert in clothing like himself), Bailly also admitted that physical freedom was a necessary component of childhood life. He then justified the use of fitted corsets by explaining that, though, in an ideal world, children would run free, the children of Paris, constrained as they were by city living, needed the physical support of corsets so that they might grow properly and be healthy as adults.[29] His approach recommended well-fitted corsets that supported the child but did not constrain and were changed frequently in size as the child grew. It is significant that even a corset-maker accepted that the typical assumptions about children's needs had changed and, in order to protect his livelihood, justified the old clothing and methods by the new affectionate social standards. While we do not know what impact Bailly's defense had on the purchasing decisions of parents, his essay demonstrates that new philosophies about physical liberty and the emotional needs of children were becoming widespread enough to affect some parents' consumption patterns.

By the very first years of the nineteenth century, doctors made it clear that children's clothing had changed substantially when they noted that it was no longer the general usage to swaddle infants.[30] By the 1820s, writers of advice manuals for mothers, instead of spending pages on the dangers of swaddling bands and corsets, as they might have done at the end of the eighteenth century, simply recommended loose clothing for babies and warned against the possibility that domestic servants might attempt to follow the old traditions, risking the child's health and moral development in the process.[31] There had been a sea change in the perception of infancy. Babies and very small children now deserved clothing that was appropriate to their needs, and only "backward" and impersonal caretakers would fail to give infants the new forms of physical and emotional care that they so obviously required.

Before Napoleon crowned himself Emperor, the reading public had already accepted that infancy was a unique and vulnerable stage with both physical and emotional needs. Now theorists began to focus their attentions on the next developmental phase of childhood. The new targets of these authors were not constrictive clothing so much as restrictive behaviors, or the traditions controlling children's attempts to walk and limiting their ability to move and behave like children. Inveighing against leading-strings in all cases, not just when the children were visibly inconvenienced, with their faces turning red or purple, experts listed potential harms ranging from shoulder displacement to chest compression, asthma, and constipation. Far better to let children creep and crawl, for

[these methods] do not hinder the body, like the bad habit of holding them up with leading-strings, which, attached under the armpits, lift up their shoulders together with the weight of the body, to the point that their head is pulled back as well. This position is tiresome and unpleasant to watch, destroying the figure and hindering circulation; that much one can see every day with swelling and redness in the face and upper extremities where they are suspended in this fashion. And if one attempts to remedy the previously described problems by attaching the ribbons to the middle of the body . . . this manner is even more dangerous than the other. It compresses the chest, the stomach, and prevents the organs from functioning as they ought . . .[32]

Walking would come naturally, writers argued, and while crawling might keep the children from walking as soon, they would be stronger, healthier, and better able to explore when they did choose to walk.[33] Rather than being troubled by the bestial implications of allowing children to roll around on the ground, these authors condemned the old methods. Crawling was not inhuman and unattractive; instead, reliance on the old methods was what was ugly and inhumane. As the previous description of the problems with leading-strings evidences, children were no longer expected to look and behave just like adults, and crawling no longer made children's place in the natural hierarchy subject to question. Children were definitely not bestial, and if they required a great deal of individual attention, this was in some sense only proof of their humanity. Instead of helping society regress into a group of beasts, eliminating the older practices would actually strengthen the general population and produce healthy and responsible adults.

While the concern with creating physically healthy individuals was not new, the link between emotional and physical health led to a broader agenda than ever before. In the new understanding of the world, physical health, accented by looser clothing, did two things. First of all, it provided for healthy bodies that would give children the stamina and capacity to learn. Unlike constrained children, free infants and toddlers would grow strong. Once they were uncorseted and unswaddled, their lungs would be able to expand for deep cleansing breaths and their legs would grow straight. Most important, physical freedom meant not only that children might later have the stamina and capacity to learn, but also that they could positively interact with the world around them from infancy. Freeing the child's body was a necessary prerequisite to training the child's mind. Children who could crawl on their own would find things of interest at all stages and would not have to wait until adults took the time to free them from their bonds or standing stools and parade them about. Allowing children to explore at all stages, from infancy to adolescence, promoted emotional health, intellectual curiosity, and individual development.

Individuality and Gender Differentiation

As with Rousseau's vision of the ideal society, an accent on the relationship between physical freedom and intellectual development resulted in an increased emphasis on gender. While the literature insisted that all infants should be unswaddled, the freeing changes in children's clothing were, at least initially, extended only to male children. Despite the seemingly universal applicability of the new ideas about childhood, French boys' costumes were the first to experience radical change. In this instance, as in many to follow, girls' and boys' clothing helped the different sexes meet different criteria. As one childhood theorist explained:

The man's temperament must be prepared for grand works, to great fatigue; the woman's to more frequent sufferings. Exercises must cultivate strength in one, and develop grace in the other . . . In the man, who has greater hazards to face, physical courage must be daring and audacious. In the woman, who must suffer difficulties rather than braving them, this courage must be quiet and patient.[34]

Most theorists saw no overwhelming need for girls to exercise their minds and instead envisioned the new exploratory education as a young boy's experience. Therefore, even as boys' fashions underwent revision long before the French Revolution, girls' apparel did not immediately evolve into looser clothing that permitted freedom of movement.[35] The difference between male and female clothing demonstrates how closely mind and a gendered body had come to be linked in the general consciousness. Little girls did manage to avoid the hoops that had been their lot fifty years before, but long skirts and corsets were still the fashion, and perfectly acceptable for a "quiet and patient" young woman-in-training (figures 5 and 6).

Gender distinctions, inscribed in the forms and approaches of moral education for hundreds of years, now found physical signification in clothing designs at ever younger ages.[36] Attire for boys, destined to move farther into the realm of public life, incorporated them into male society at ever younger ages. While as a rule their sisters still dressed in the inferior and nearly ageless signifier of women's skirts, different pants outfits were designed for boys that denoted both their gender and their age. Even as children became more important and more individualized, this greater individuality meant more differentiation, not greater similarity. By the 1780s, little boys quickly graduated from skirts to trousers. Though toddlers of both sexes still wore skirts, little boys moved to short pants well before the age of reason. French boys wore the *matelot*, or sailor suit, an outfit with short pants, a jacket and a broad collar that signified the wearer was young.[37] Unlike the dresses, which were a modification of women's clothing, the *matelot* was a particularly masculine outfit, military in origin, and if it did not indicate that the little boys were men, it did signal a transition away from women's skirts even as it created an increased focus on the gender of the child.

Fashion journals document the path of these changes. In the late 1780s, the *Closet of Fashions* offered a few plates depicting the fashionable styles of dress for children (figures 5 and 6). Even as the boys were dressed in the newer fashions, wearing skeleton suits with accompanying sashes and broad collars, the girls that appeared on the facing pages might have been lifted directly from paintings of the seventeenth century. While the boys were not directly engaged in playful activity, one can well believe that they might be about to march, to chase birds, or throw balls, and their accessories supported this conclusion. The girls, on the other hand, were not only stationary, but also holding a flower, a fan, or a bird cage. In images, female children were given ornamental details instead of active ones. In clothes resembling those of adult women, there was little possibility that a girl might be tempted to run after a bird or engage in other vigorous movement. Her body was still corseted and her waist tightly cinched. The skirts of the fashionable outfits were full and trimmed with lace. The fabrics of

Figure 5. Girl with bird cage, boy in matelot with bird. *Closet of Fashions, 1786. Bibliothèque nationale de France*

Figure 6. Boy with ball and hat, girl with fan. *Closet of Fashions, 1787.* Bibliothèque nationale de France

the girls' outfits were of taffeta or silk, though the underskirts were of muslin. These were not play clothes. The boys' pants, on the other hand, allowed them to run and jump, to play more actively with hoops and jump ropes (then considered a boys' game). Additionally, these outfits were often made of fabrics such as linen and muslin that, unlike silk, could be washed when children got dirty. Boys could now explore with less fear of being punished for ruining an expensive outfit.[38]

Initially, children's fashion magazines of the late eighteenth century were also far more interested in young boys' clothing than that of young girls. For instance, at the same time that the *Closet of Fashions* began publishing occasional engraved plates that focused on children's styles, it also asserted, "[s]mall girls almost always follow women's fashions, but small boys, those that one dresses in a sailor suit, have particular styles."[39] As another fashion magazine, the *Journal of Women and Fashion*, explained: "[t]hough the costume of children is less subject to change than that of women and even that of men, there are some variations . . . The sailor suit has been replaced by Turkish pants . . ."[40] The same magazine later praised the new style for boys, claiming that

[n]othing is more adorable than a little boy dressed in the modern Greek costume. The vast muslin trousers . . . give ease to his movements, a childish grace that one doesn't find in the feminine dress, nor with the narrow and bothersome sailor suit. And so fashion, which covers all the ages under her rule, prescribes this commodious and distinguished clothing for [male] children.[41]

While an uncorseted boy in a muslin skirt might have found as much—or more—freedom of movement as a one in a stiffly cut sailor suit, male children were not only in need of loose clothing but also outfits that clearly indicated their gender to the public at large. For very young boys, "distinguished," or at least distinguishing, was every bit as important as "commodious" clothing. Toddlers' outfits make this exceptionally clear. As the outfits of young boys became differentiated from those of adult women, a transitional outfit for male toddlers found a great deal of favor (figure 7). This outfit combined both male and female dress, with pants that signified the masculine gender of the wearer and skirts that denoted the hierarchical placement of the infant in a position well below that of adult males. At the beginning of the eighteenth century, all children were relatively unimportant and completely subordinate, and thus dressed in women's skirts. By the advent of the French Revolution, however, children were already increasingly individualized, and this distinction effected the extension of adult gender distinctions to a younger group. All children were assumed to be human, whether they walked or crawled, and even very young boys were too masculine to be dressed in the same way as women.

Figure 7. Straw hat. Dress and trousers
of percale. *Journal of Women and Fashion,*
1816. Bibliothèque nationale de France

Girls' costumes also eventually saw change as a result of the new ideas about childhood physical and mental development. By the turn of the nineteenth century, little girls' dresses were often designed entirely in muslin, which was both lighter and more washable than taffeta or silk. Little girls who wore clothes made of the new materials could, like their brothers, run and play with less fear of damaging an expensive outfit and explore further afield in order to exercise their minds. While these changes intersected with concerns about children's needs for physical exercise, it is important to understand that women's fashions were becoming looser, and the outfits of little girls, like those of babies, were following suit (figure 8). During the French Revolution and under the Napoleonic Empire, women's fashions lost their corsets and became less fitted. Freer girls' clothing also came about at the turn of the century and seems to have initially developed in conjunction with freer clothing patterns for all women. Despite the striking change in children's clothing as a whole, the changes in girls' clothing were initially driven more by the general changes in women's and children's fashion than by evident concern with the physical stature of little girls.

Figure 8. Bonnet imitating ancient
hairstyles. Borders of lozenges. *Journal
of Women and Fashion,* An 8 (1801).
Bibliothèque nationale de France

Since young girls had always been dressed like their mothers, one
could argue that the initial changes in girls' clothing are not particularly
significant to any cultural history of domesticity or family life but merely
followed the same trajectory as the changes in women's clothing. As
Nicole Pellegrin points out:

The general abandonment of the corset, promoted since 1750 by doctors, was
temporarily achieved under the Revolution; less the result of their active propaganda than the sign of a collective desire for liberty and perhaps equality: the regenerated French nation no longer had need of political tutors and go-betweens,
constituent bodies and corseted bodies. A recent author has commented: "The fall
of the corset has become the sartorial equivalent of the taking of the Bastille."[42]

In other words, women experienced more physical freedom because the
concept of liberty was taking hold everywhere, so the changes in girls'
clothing should not necessarily be attributed to changing theories of
childhood but rather to heightened demands for liberty. And yet, though

women's clothing may have become more freeing, making it easier for children's clothing also to become free, the change itself was significant, for once young girls lost their corsets and tight waists, girls' fashions developed on a trajectory of their own, separate from the women's fashions that had initially encouraged the change.

Unlike women's styles, which experienced a brief respite from corsets and extremely fitted fashions under the Directory and then returned to the constrictive types of the Old Regime during the Restoration, ideas about children's fashion were changed forever. The revolution in clothing was not coterminous with political revolution. Though the French Revolution was important for enunciating and circulating ideas about clothing, individuality, and gender, it did not create the crucial change in beliefs, which began long before political appeals for freedom.[43] Additionally, under the Restoration, girls' styles, unlike adult women's, remained more freeing than the fashions of the eighteenth century. The tightly cinched waists, whalebone corsets, and expensive fabrics were now things of the past for preadolescent girls. By the middle of the nineteenth century, fashions increasingly demonstrated how all children were unique individuals who would be dressed with regard for their age and gender.

One example in particular, that of the pantalette, serves to illuminate the process by which girls' clothing became separate from women's clothing. As we saw, male toddlers had a transitional outfit that combined both male and female dress. For a short time after girls' clothing became freer, this gender-mixed design was allowed to young girls as well. By the Restoration, the new fashions for young girls (ages three to twelve, roughly) involved shorter skirts and pantalettes, even as very young boys (toddlers) wore much the same thing (figures 7, 9, and 10). The short skirt and pants underline the fact that clothing for young girls was finding its own equilibrium, independent of women's styles. Despite the fact that trousers were clearly masculine, wearing trousers underneath a skirt was temporarily deemed to be appropriate for young girls so that they might enjoy active recreation without sacrificing modesty. The pantalettes demonstrate two important things. First, young girls began to have styles that were no longer exactly the same as those of their mothers and, second, clothing for girls could reflect the demand for freedom of movement and individuality for female children even as it maintained many of the old gender premises.

The similarity between the male toddler outfit and the outfit of the older female child confused gender roles less than it might seem. For girls, the trousers were not originally intended to be on display, but "were probably adopted partly to provide necessary warmth under thin muslin dresses, partly because such flimsy, blow-away skirts made some kind of modest underwear necessary for active little girls."[44] As hemlines rose, the pants eventually became part of the outfit. In their initial impulses, these pants

Figure 9. Hairstyle in Leontyne
fashion. Dress of pilgrimage canvas,
decorated with ruffles and a small strop
of tulle. Percale trousers. Ercu gloves
and slippers. *Journal of Women and
Fashion,* 1821. Bibliothèque nationale
de France

likely had more in common with the tights worn by fashionable women of
the seventeenth century than with men's trousers.[45] Frequently, the pantalettes were not even pants but rather tubes that began at the knees and
prevented the legs of the young girl from being exposed to general view.
Girls' fashions, even when they allowed freedom of movement, remained
closer to women's fashions than to men's. After all, a girl, even when wearing pants under her dress, still was dressed in styles that looked remarkably
similar to those of her mother (figure 10). Despite a surface similarity and
an increased amount of freedom, the outfit of the eight-year-old girl had
less in common with the three-year-old boy than one might think.

By the middle of the nineteenth century, fashion differentiated children
both by age and by gender: young girls in clothes that imitated their
mothers' styles but with particular concessions to their stage of life, toddler boys in skirts and pants, and young boys in *matelots,* hussars, skele-

Figure 10. Straw grass hat decorated with lilacs.
Frock coat of rough Oriental cloth. Bonnet of
rough Neopolitan cloth. Gingham dress. Apron
of coarse Neopolitan cloth garnished with hives.
Journal of Women and Fashion, 1831. Bibliothèque
nationale de France

ton suits, or some form of pants outfit that marked them as both male and
young. While some designs toyed briefly with the idea of pants for young
girls, society as a whole came down on the side of discrete children's costumes, one for each sex, with no gender confusion. As one man wrote,
"[c]onsult your mirror, listen to a very sensible vanity, and contemplate
[the fact] that in losing your dresses you lose your graces . . ."[46] Little
girls could be more active than before, but their clothing still underlined
their gender, and with even more emphasis now that all boys past infancy
were supposed to wear pants. The differences that had been noted only at
the age of reason were now inherent, automatic, and prerational.

Recreation and Physical Education

Given the emphasis on the interrelationship between emotional and physical shaping, it is logical that formerly adult characteristics were trans-

ferred to ever younger groups by methods other than clothing. Before the
eighteenth century, educational theorists had seen rationality as the domain of adult males; after mid-century, advocates of educational entertainment placed great importance on the ability of the child to reason,
and on the obligation of adults to encourage this ability through play.[47]
At the turn of the century, time spent in recreation was no longer suspect,
and children were encouraged to use their bodies to run, jump, and make
use of the looser clothing as a means to freeing their minds. In a modern
society, the exercise of judgment and self-control required freedom. For
this reason, not only physical constraint but also mental compulsion was
to be avoided; creative thought could only come from free minds and
bodies. In order to condition children properly in the use of their senses,
parenting manuals encouraged adults to provide their children with long
walks and games outside. If a lack of time or inclement weather failed to
allow this, there were plenty of suggestions for amusement indoors, ranging from toys to word games. The end result was a child who would be
able to understand and engage with the world, whether by way of speci-
mens of natural history or a bubble wand. Childhood was still a time of
apprenticeship, but in reasoning instead of specific skills and trades. The
new values prioritized "training" in freedom for both body and mind.
Only individuals who had been allowed freedom could have a properly
developed understanding of the world around them, not to mention well-
trained minds and healthy bodies.

The new importance of toys, games, and abstract reasoning found expression in commodities. Once physical freedom was tied to moral education, it became a duty to play with one's children, to respond to them
in the manner that would best allow their minds to develop, and even to
purchase the objects that could train them best. Toys and play were first
advocated, and then advertised, as the obligation to amuse became more
widely promoted. As one theorist explained:

Children's recreation and playthings also enjoyed an unprecedented
level of approval. Though they had been seen simply as frivolous objects
to be discarded as soon as possible, toys now took a place of prominence,
and advice manuals claimed that toys and games "possessed an ethical as
well as an aesthetic quotient. They could be interpreted as rehearsals, either for good or ill, of future adult activity."[48] Play also developed the
body and could even teach important lessons about the physical world.
Spinning a top, for example, might help a child to understand the laws of
physics. And in any case, as one manual explained, "[b]alls, racquets, the
hoop, the jump rope, all of these are games that require a certain level of
skill, and strengthen children. They can be usefully employed for girls and
boys."[49] If all children needed free bodies, then all children also needed
play and exercise.

It is necessary to amuse Children. The art of Mothers, of Nurses, and of those called *femme d'enfant,* is marked by carrying a child in their arms, and when he is disturbed and cries, to walk him from place to place, to distract him and sing some lullabies. None of this is what the child wants, nor what invites him. He demands to be entertained, and no one hears him, no one wants to hear him. Sit at a table with the child on your knees, put on this table the least trifle, the smallest toy, and show it to the child. He will take this toy, will handle it in every sense, and will pass whole hours with a satisfaction, a joy, of which his manner allows no doubt.[50]

A good mother would nurture her child by truly listening to the child's desires, which were for interaction with the world around him. As prints of the period made clear, while bad mothers ignored or beat their children, good mothers would have children in their laps *and* toys at their feet (figures 11 and 12). Though books had proclaimed themselves "amusing and instructive" long before *Emile,* material culture and child-rearing manuals demonstrated the ways in which physical education, affection, and emotional development connected.

Figure 11. The Good Mother and the Dear Child,
circa 1810. Bibliothèque nationale de France

Figure 12. The fashionable mother/The mother as all should be (before 1804). "Bonsoir ma petite amie je vais au bal" / "Je vous souhaite autant de plasir qu'à moi." Bibliothèque nationale de France

Boys, Girls, and Toys

After reading such theories and seeing such depictions of motherhood, some argued that play was not necessary, or that it would ruin children for education. On the contrary, advocates protested, toys and play fortified the body, and letting children play would "satisfy their natural curiosity [so that] one will be astonished about the multiplied opportunities that one will have to teach them good habits, and give them exact ideas about an infinite number of things."[51] Exercise and liberty were the key links between the mind and body, between physical and moral education, allowing children to explore on their own and to encounter the world, emotionally and practically. Giving children not only physical comfort but also play and enjoyment was fundamental to the development of their minds. Allowing them to act childish, to be children, first by crawling and later by frolicking, set them on a path of development that would educate them by appealing to their natural desires and tendencies and allowing them enough freedom to practice self-control when control was not forced upon them by external means. Though seemingly superficial, toys helped children to form their characters and their minds because they allowed children to engage willingly with the world. Girls who played with dolls and lavished affection on their "babies" would practice being proper young women; boys who rode hobby-horses and played with bows and arrows learned about being young men. As Mme Campan explained: "One notices in children's games their constant attempts to imitate everything that they see grown-ups do; they love the little households in which all the rooms are like those of their parents: a stick is transformed into one of their parents' horses; they are delighted to make a whip crack like a jockey and to water like the gardener . . ."[52] Some toys were obviously more appropriate for boys than for girls: drums, a bow and arrow, or a sword. Others, most especially dolls, were intended for girls. However, once it had been established that girls could benefit from physical exercise in much the same manner as boys, girls often played with the same kinds of toys. The following story from the *Journal of Women and Fashion* makes the point humorously clear:

At fifteen, boys become the servants of women, but at seven or eight, they are only rivals. This rivalry is felt at the Tuileries [Gardens] more than anywhere else. Hardly have little gentlemen obtained their hoops than the little girls seize them. These fashionably jump rope, those begin to jump there the following day. A few days ago, two pretty boys . . . presented themselves armed with bows and arrows, already triumphant, but the young ladies claimed to be afraid of being blinded and made them discard their new toys.[53]

Though gender had some role to play concerning which toys were allowed to whom, as toys became more acceptable for all children, the lines between the sexes became more fluid than one might expect. Girls played with hoops and jumped rope even as boys did (figures 9, 10, 13), though some claimed that girls jumped and ran and threw with less strength and more grace, as was appropriate for their sex.[54] Another game that involved tossing and catching a large wooden top was also a source of entertainment for all children. In 1812, one could read that "[c]urrently, everyone knows the fashionable toy called 'the devil' . . . This is the subject of the work and most intensive study of our young people of both sexes."[55] The pantalettes that young girls wore, the stories they read, and the toys that they played with demonstrate that gender distinctions did not result in absolute separation between the sexes, nor did they ensure that girls and boys lived in separate universes.

However, gender lines remained even when playthings or social roles looked remarkably similar. For toys, the difference between the sexes was not necessarily who played with what, but for how long. An extended period of childhood, with special toys, clothing, and hairstyles, was far more likely to be allowed to boys than to girls. While boys of eleven or twelve were still allowed to play and considered to be children, with

Figure 13. Straw Hat. Outfit of sheeting.
Collar of silk. *Journal of Women and Fashion,*
1821. Bibliothèque nationale de France

outfits that responded to a child's need for activity, young girls of the
same age fell into a different category. While the hemline of a twelve-year-
old girl was slightly higher than that of an older girl, her dress was remarkably similar to that of her adult counterparts. Her hair would not
generally be dressed in an extraordinarily ornate fashion, but she might
be allowed to wear ribbons or flowers in it, and it would likely be put up
for all important events. Too old for dolls, her gifts might include tools
for drawing, painting, or sewing—necessary accomplishments for a well-
to-do woman. That is, of course, when they were not items meant to in-
duct her into adulthood: gloves, shawls, hats, or hair accessories.[56]

Little girls were not only closer to their mothers in fashion, but also
simply closer to adulthood. Compare the plate of the *very young person*
with that of the *child of 11 to 12 years old* (figures 14 and 15). These de-
pict children of the same age, as the girl was probably about twelve, the
age at which she would be considered a *young person* instead of a *little girl.*
While the boy was dressed in long pants and relatively adult dress, he was
also pictured with toys and his clothing was not particularly form-fitting.

Figure 14. Outfit of a very young person. Coiffure without ornament: braid tied with a satin ribbon. Dress of percale, in the virgin style. Belt of gauze. Gloves of ecru cambric. Italian straw hat. *Journal of Women and Fashion*, 1820. Bibliothèque nationale de France

The girl's accessories were not playthings, but her hat, handkerchief, and the jewelry around her neck. She was no longer wearing pantalettes, for she was not expected to be running and playing in a fashion that would encourage her to show her undergarments. Her shoes were constrictive and her dress increasingly elaborate, especially when compared to that of the boy. Unlike the boy, the young girl was no longer a "child" but a "person," subject to the call of the adult world. Not only would she be allowed to attend grown-up balls and other adult events, but as a member of an elite social class, she might even be married off soon, with a household and children of her own. Very young women were already seen as rational and capable of entering into self-controlled adult life at an age when young boys were still too immature to be trusted with responsibilities.

This was not indicative of a difference in rationality, but in physical and intellectual capabilities, based on gender differences. Contemporaries ar-

Figure 15. Outfit of a child of eleven to
twelve years. *Journal of Women and Fashion,*
1820. Bibliothèque nationale de France

gued that boys *needed* an extended period of childhood. "To be a man, it
is necessary to be a child for a long time: the early fruits are dried up when
the season comes: the tree that grows before the proper time does not have
any more sap when it comes time to produce."[57] Young boys, who would
move into public positions of responsibility, needed extra time to develop
their bodies and minds. In the long run, only an extended childhood could
guarantee a healthy male adult. The comparison of twelve-year-olds
demonstrates that the early distinctions of clothing produced more than
pantalettes or sailor-suits, for these distinctions emphasized even more
markedly the social expectations of particular genders. Girls' minds and
bodies were readied for a maternal future while boys were slowly inducted
into life outside the home. The age at which girls and boys moved into
adult clothing, and, by extension, adult roles, took note of this fact.

Of course, many children of this period never wore the new types of
clothing. For a time, the new fashions existed side-by-side with the older
ones. Not all people, even somewhat affluent families, could afford or

were immediately persuaded by the new styles for children. However, since clothing of all types had always served as an indicator of wealth and social status, it should come as little surprise that plates depicting new styles would not only encourage new dress and accessories for children, but also use children themselves as accessories. After all, a child well dressed in the modern fashion demonstrated the parents' financial status. A little boy dressed in *matelot,* with the latest improvisation (often the placement or styling of buttons), or a little girl in a loose Empire-waist dress with sleeves *à la enfant* proved that not only could the family afford to invest in clothing designed for a very specific age, but also that they had purchased the latest styles. The fashion plates in which children accompanied an adult figure attest to this fact. In the earlier issues of the *Closet of Fashions,* the engravings of children's dress were few and far between and often sandwiched between those of scarves, hats, or other ornamentation. Though one early fashion engraving from the *Journal of Women and Fashion* (1800) depicted a group of children, it did so without comment on their dress or actions. The next decade-and-a-half confirmed this lack of interest in that children only appeared in the plates when accompanying an adult. While the dress of the adults was described in detail, that of the child was ignored. Initially, children were like the books, musical instruments, fireplaces, or horses that also appeared in these engravings: ornaments to show off the clothing, not themselves items of focus.

For the *Journal of Women and Fashion,* this perspective changed after 1815, when there began to be engravings that portrayed children alone or in tandem with an adult. In those that had both a child and an adult, the label on the engraving read "Parisian Outfits" instead of "Parisian Outfit," as it had read for the earlier groupings. Information on the clothier or haberdasher was also included for the children's dress in the later issues, which marked a change from previous years. While such a small sample cannot be construed as representative, the trend matches that seen in other areas and described by other scholars.[58] There was a change over time, from children being relatively unimportant in fashion discussions to children having a fashion of their own. In the mid-eighteenth century, children were often treated as decorations, not individuals in their own right; this had changed by the end of the period under consideration.

The Charm of Good Conduct

However, even as children came to be seen as increasingly distinct from adults and even children of the opposite sex, their behavior came to be as important as their external appearance. A new focus on demeanor had already been hinted at in justifications for changing dress codes. As Rousseau and others had explained, training was no longer physical shaping. Instead, children needed freedom in order to develop healthy bodies and to accustom themselves to proper behavior in the adult world. Given the connections noted between future behavior and current dress, as well as the clear distinctions drawn between girls' behavior and that of boys, at least part of the justification for this intense focus on comportment was already clear. Girls and boys had different patterns of expected behavior, and they should be trained in appropriate behaviors from very early ages. Without freedom of action in a context of emotional nurturing, children would be mentally stunted. While children might physically develop into adults, they would not have grown into the proper emotional role. These children would not only be unhealthy but also feeble and lacking in the determination that would allow them to shape their own society. Physical freedom was not a self-sufficient rationale but a basis for self-control and the ability to carry out actions in accord with one's own judgment. Independent action as evidenced by behavior was the best way to know if children were growing into well-conditioned adults.

A second rationale underlay the increased emphasis on children's behavior. When clothing controlled children, their behavior was rarely of great concern. In an earlier era, it was enough for them to resemble adults physically. However, as clothing became freer, children's behavior became one more basis for placing the child into society. As biological and social difference were demonstrated by children's clothing, so too could behavior help observers make social judgments about the quality of an individual once children were allowed to make decisions on their own. A comparison of how fashion magazines treated children, accessories, and social distinctions will help illuminate this process of change. The *Closet of Fashions,* an early fashion magazine, addressed the following words to women:

Ladies, admit it; when your children are small, you make a glory of showing them . . . then you want them to be dressed elegantly, with taste, fashionable even; you find that they honor you in this way . . . But you do not wish to show off your slightly older children because they don't have the same animation, the vivacity and chatter that attracts another's notice.[59]

The *Closet of Fashions* met with ridicule the idea that a parent would attempt to attract attention through the personality of one's child. Such an attempt marked the parent as shallow and self-serving. However, this quotation also demonstrates that the personality of the child was more appealing when the children were younger and more easily controlled by the parent. By contrast, as early as the first part of the nineteenth century, an older child's disposition and social behavior had become an important test of a parent's quality. No longer did only shallow parents seek to show

off their children, and young children were no longer the focus. In one example given in the *Journal of Women and Fashion,* a young woman (Julie
de Bonneval) was prepared to lead off a dance at a ball when told that she
must let the daughter of the hostess (Mlle de Merval) take her place. She
sat out the dance while speaking with her mother, then congratulated her
rival on a job well done.

This action enchanted all present and was noticed by an old friend of M. de Merval.
The friend spoke to his son, a conversation in which the conduct and the beauty of
Julie figured large, and eight days after that, father and son went to ask for her hand
in marriage. M. de Merval [who had held out hopes for *his* daughter], was rather
put out . . . but the friend simply answered, "I believe that girls who leave [your
daughter's] school dance the *gavotte* well; Mlle Merval is the proof of that: but I believe that a young lady raised by her mother adds to the graces of the dance the
charm of good conduct and a good education, and so I married Mlle Bonneval."[60]

The "charm of good conduct" that mothers would give to their daughters
through maternal domestic education would win a young woman a husband and bring honor to her parents. Love, nurturing, and physical freedom resulted in proper behavior, the most valuable characteristic of all.
   This was not an isolated idea. In another story, the protagonist was
Justine, a young woman who knew how to dance, sing, and play the tam-
bourine, but very little else. "Not only had Justine learned how to be lazy
and proud, but she had completely forgotten the art of making herself
useful. Her soft and tender hands could no longer support the lighting of
a fire or the pressure of a needle, and she had so perfected her legs that
she no longer knew how to hold the feather pen in her hand." Her family, knowing that this did not look good for them or for Justine, gave her
a new domestic education, in which she "had to learn to become bourgeoise again."[61] To her credit (and her family's), she learned her lesson
well, finding a good husband from Paris and prospering. With stories like
this, fashion magazines described the behavior of both boys and girls in
detail, with good mothers and fathers taking pride in the discipline of
their children and proving to society how a proper domestic education
could produce young women who were self-controlled and useful. While
Justine's breeding was attributed to being a good *bourgeoise,* the proper
lessons were in fact clear to any elite parent who read these articles. Girls
of leisure who exhibited not only breeding and artistic address but also
socially useful virtues were more likely to catch a husband and to make
their mothers and fathers look good in the process. Little boys who were
given plenty of time to play and raised with care and concern would grow
to be thoughtful and studious young men who wouldn't dissipate their
lives. How could any parent want more?

The advice manuals and fashion magazines of the nineteenth century thus show us an attention to the behaviorial side of youthfulness not in evidence in the first decades of the eighteenth. Advances in the physical treatment of children allowed succeeding generations to grow up treated as individuals and unencumbered by hoops, whalebone corsets, swaddling bands, and other instruments of confinement. And yet, this increasing interest in the individual meant that the physical barriers gave way to new contextual distinctions erected on the basis of gender, age, and self-control. As Aileen Ribeiro has noted, these changes were grounded on something more closely resembling "the claim of the individual to be important in his own right, and not to be judged on outward appearance only."[62] It is true that outward appearances still mattered, but the criteria for judgment had been redefined. By the mid-nineteenth century, children had become less restricted and physically controlled, but it was even truer that their appearance and behavior could determine their social standing.

That is not to say that we move from a time of "real" freedom to a period in which people are constrained without ever knowing it. Children's clothing, even when ornate and bejeweled or a copy of adult fashions, always betrayed a concern with power and control—control over the smallest bodies, those who were arguably also the most difficult to manage. What is interesting then is not that we move from a time of relatively little control to a time of much greater focus on children's bodies or behaviors, but that the questions surrounding the training and government of children, growing from similar impulses of control, changed to a rhetoric that emphasized physical freedom and self-control even as it focused on individual differences. The role of parents in promoting this evolution changed throughout the period under consideration and moved, broadly put, from literally molding children physically in the earlier period to letting children develop with less physical but more emotional intervention in the later period, especially for behavior conditioned with respect to gender roles. Material culture also demonstrates the trend away from traditional hierarchies and toward increasing gender distinctions. No longer were physical shaping and placement into the social ladder the most important goals of childhood. Instead, the training of modern, rational, and gendered individuals in self-control offered a new vision of the world.

CHAPTER THREE

"You will reign by means of love"
Advice Manuals and Domestic Motherhood

It thus seems to me that parents, or, if necessary, teachers, must cultivate the spirit of the young ladies who are under their direction, to improve their reason and also to carry them as far as their nature allows while always being carefully certain to prefer that which is necessary to that which is merely advantageous.
> —Antoinette LeGroing-LaMaisonneuve, *Essay on the Type of Instruction That is Most Suitable for the Purpose of Women* (1801)[1]

An eloquent philosopher excited maternal enthusiasm, but I believe that a philosophical doctor must direct it.
> —Alphonse Leroy, *Maternal Medicine* (1803)

Physical Freedom and Maternal Affection

We have seen that Enlightenment educational theorists rarely followed Rousseau's demand for the radical reshaping of mankind in their approach to schooling, even when they were attracted to Rousseau's ideas about education. That is not to say that only minor changes took place, however. As the revolution in fashion demonstrates, even when schooling and instruction saw little of Rousseau's influence, the theories behind domestic education underwent a dramatic metamorphosis. The new ideals demanded that children be cared for at home, with a mother providing the nurturing affection and individual attention that would properly form her children as they matured. Childhood came to assume an exalted position over the course of the eighteenth and nineteenth centuries; the new emphasis on physical freedom and nurturing increased the demand for education provided by a domestic wife and mother, much like Rousseau's Sophie.

Despite the fact that Rousseau's proposals did not see widespread political or legislative implementation in the eighteenth century, his formulation of the problem of education framed modern notions of family life. This fit well with Rousseau's own agenda. After all, Rousseau had explained in the preface to *Emile* that his intent was not particularly to direct the pragmatic details of an education that would regenerate the nation but to help "a good mother who knows how to think" in her "art of forming men."[2] Parents and theorists alike joined Rousseau in his focus on family life as the source for self-knowledge and self-control and linked, as Rousseau had, ethical and social development to individual physical and mental fitness.[3]

A procession of expert voices encouraged women to offer their children physical freedom and training in self-control. This same literature also related those ideas to family life and the "necessary" characteristics of gender difference, such as those between Sophie and Emile. *Emile*'s format and Rousseau's writing thus fit into the growing desire to help mothers use individual qualities, rather than tradition or social hierarchy, to determine social roles. Lydia Lange notes that, in this way, Rousseau introduced "new fields of discussion . . . concerning the meaning of gender difference, the relations between family and civil state, and the potential positive contributions of the roles or functions of women, as women, to the development of a liberated polity."[4] Though legislative and social change eventually explicitly limited women's political roles, women's cultural influence grew. As a result, even Rousseau's highly gendered thought may have promoted women's civic power and influence to a greater degree than the "universal" thought of Locke and the *philosophes,* which remained limited in intent and application. This chapter examines the formation of the new ideal mother of the early nineteenth century in order to explain how a sacrificing and loving mother, like Rousseau's Sophie, came to replace a powerful and distant father as the archetypal parent for the emotional formation of citizens.

As the rhetoric of emotional concern demonstrates, parenting of this sort was not a temporary necessity, to be passed off to anyone who happened along. Rather, this was a feminine calling of the highest order and carried its own rewards. No longer was the well-being of the family the responsibility of the breadwinner and official head of the household.

Carole Duncan's work demonstrates that, different from previous centuries, where the power of the father reigned supreme, in this period, "[t]he unifying element of the new family was the wife-mother. From her primarily was to flow that warmth and tranquility that Enlightenment bachelors like Diderot so ardently eulogized as the central attraction of family life . . . Pretty, modest, and blushing, her happiness consists in making her husband happy and in serving the needs of her children."[5] However, Rousseau established an even broader agenda for the wife and mother than Diderot and the other Enlightenment *philosophes* had.

Rousseau's mother's formation of family life would itself be civic in nature and, instead of mere "warmth and tranquility," she would demonstrate and develop the self-control that was central to the creation of independent and politically active individuals. Even as Rousseau himself recognized that "the laws . . . do not give enough authority to mothers,"[6] he claimed that their position would be secured by a new emphasis on nurturing.

While the laws continued to offer men authority over women, Rousseau certainly was right to point to ideological changes as indicating a shift in the source of women's status. In the early eighteenth century, women could easily justify sending their children far from home, no matter what their social class, but nurturing's new civic role meant that, by the turn of the nineteenth century, a woman would find herself vilified for her "unnatural tendencies" if she danced the night away at a ball while a nurse watched over the child in the family home (see figure 12).[7] Aristocratic women like the Countess of Rémusat, revolutionary mothers, and bourgeois writers during the Restoration all promoted an ideal from which any nurturing mother could benefit. Additionally, the advantages that a woman of any class could reap from this new ideology, and the reasons that she might seize on it as her own, desiring to become Sophie or the good mother, become clear when we look at domestic advice manuals from this period. While the representation of Sophie as "an angel from heaven"[8] is hardly liberating in a twenty-first century context, it is not, in the end, a clear example of a controlling discourse. While the images that surrounded the domestic mother tended to focus on difference, with the woman inside and the man outside, or the bad mother outside and the good mother inside, in the context of Rousseau's demands for radical social change, these very contrasts helped promote the idea of women as men's equals in the new society.

Natural mothering was a crucial part of newly affectionate child-rearing because the meaning of childhood had shifted not only emotionally but also logistically. The task of raising children, seen as a nearly lifelong project in the earlier part of the century, now centered on the development of self-control in the crucial first years, in accordance with developmental and educational philosophies. As Rousseau had explained in 1762, "[t]he first education is the most important, and this first education belongs incontestably to women."[9] In order for children to be trained in accordance with the new philosophical ideals, mothers had to occupy a new place in the family, one that they could not or would not refuse. This was supported by and itself supported the new domestic ideologies. Children were to have a focused period of nurturing development, with more time at home before being trained to make their way in the world, all so that they might become rational, moral, and self-controlled adults. Women who exhibited the self-control and sacrifice of devoted wives and mothers would not only ensure the proper development of their offspring but would also model the intended outcomes of their education. Children's blank slates would be filled not only with word but also deed.

The New Mother Rises

Like Julie and Sophie, the paradigmatic mother was devoted, oversaw her children's physical and moral education, and of course, nursed her own infants. This was more than a simple literary device; it was affirmed by the medical literature as well. The reasoning behind the obligation to nourish babies with their mother's milk crystallized many of the issues surrounding child-rearing and ideal motherhood. As Mme le Rebours affirmed in her *Advice to Mothers who want to nurse their children,* "[t]he children nursed by their mothers can gain as much for their characters as for their health, especially if it is true that milk influences the character. At the very least, the [natural] mother can gain a great advantage in the knowledge that she has of her child for its first education."[10] Ostensibly, when mothers knew their children well, they could satisfy the needs that arose from true want and refuse the screams that arose from mere frustration. Biological mothers, unlike mercenary nurses, were assumed to have the best interests of the child at heart, which included moral and intellectual training as well as physical nourishment. Best of all, an informed and devoted mother could not only ensure the well-being of her children, but also educate them in the practice of virtuous and unselfish behavior from the cradle. When a mother was able to respond to a child's real needs and ignore less important demands, she would be training the child to recognize the difference between important and unimportant concerns, just as Rousseau had envisioned in *Emile.*

The mother's centrality to this enterprise meant that she would, at least culturally, come into her own years before the French Revolution opened up political opportunities. It was not only Rousseau who devoted pages and pages of his books to the virtues of the good wife and mother. Doctors dedicated volumes of their works to the women who would implement the new pediatric science, and women themselves argued that there was no greater blessing than to be a mother.[11] In an entirely new development, women could choose from multiple books that would offer them advice on home economics and child-rearing.[12] While today the eighteenth- and nineteenth-century paeans to mothers may seem trite and even condescending, this veneration of motherhood was a breath of fresh air. After centuries in which women were judged to have little worth and authority *as women,* motherhood and domesticity provided a space in which women's work reigned supreme. Early childhood became the exclusive bastion of females. Children, a captive audience for the first years of their lives, learned all the ideals that their mothers could impart, giving women the power to make their offspring virtuous and healthy, self-controlled and productive.[13] The mother who consecrated her life to her family gained honor and power by virtue of her centrality to the development of the family.

This focus on the devoted and virtuous mother as necessary for the proper nurturing of offspring marked a definite shift from the previous period. Previously, the exemplar for parenting was a strict father who oversaw his children's social and moral development. While he might not always have been physically present, he was exacting, and the punishment that he meted out ensured that his children would grow up to know right from wrong and fruitfully contribute to the family and society as a whole. A child's refusal to obey his father was a serious offense and could be met with equally serious consequences. For instance, *lettres de cachet* could ensure the imprisonment of children who threatened their parents' authority or, more drastically, fathers could have their children who "had fallen into conduct that might endanger the honor and tranquility of their family" deported to the colonies.[14] Before the middle of the eighteenth century, mothers and fathers who had sent their children far away, whether to wet-nurses or the French Antilles, could still be considered good parents. This is not surprising, given that a father's value was defined by how well he could bend the will of his offspring to the demands of family and the world, and affection and continuous care were not seen as crucial for control. Children would learn, by force if necessary, how they fit into the forms that society provided. Mothers, whether near or far, were comparatively unimportant in accomplishing this task. As one of the older advice manuals under consideration explained, not only discipline but also education should be especially the father's domain, "because he is a man who has himself almost all the knowledge that one acquires in a course of study."[15] In fact, a mother's most important duty was to produce the heirs, not shape them. However, domineering and control gave way to persuasion and affection over the course of the eighteenth century. As that transition took place, Shari Thurer notes, "Dad's importance in the family waned as mom's waxed. The specifically maternal duties of child care, once defined haphazardly by her round of daily tasks, became a self-conscious enterprise, one that was assigned exclusively to mother, complicated and time-consuming."[16]

At first glance, women's rise to power within the household seems contradictory, for the authority of men over their children was parallel to that of a husband's power over his wife. Seen as inferior to men in both intellectual capacity and virtue, women were also expected to obey the dictates of the man of the house.[17] There was no question: fathers not only had the right to direct their entire household, but they also had the moral obligation to do so. If the king was God's representative on earth, the father was His mouthpiece in the household. Even after 1762—and especially after 1804—men still held sway. Legally, wives remained subject to their husbands. Women who had children without the protection of marriage often found themselves without a job, food, or shelter as well. But these social realities notwithstanding, the cultural perceptions of women and children shifted to allow room for women's authority within the home, overseeing the education of their children. While most women might be unable to carry out business transactions in their own name, the domestic wife fashioned a world in which she reigned supreme.[18] While men directed the family from outside, their return to the family did not bring order so much as reveal it. When the father came home, it was to a domestic haven already in existence.

The father's exclusion from the creation and sustenance of this world was confirmed by his absence as a power within the interior of the home.[19] While men came to play an increasingly important role outside the home, they were no longer the target of the advice genre. Men were providers, disciplinarians, and doctors, but they were not caretakers or homemakers, and it was the role of homemaker that was crucial for the formative years of children. The treatises under consideration generally accepted and even expanded upon these distinctions. The forewords and dedications explained that these works would "limit their Instruction so that [women's] attention would not [have to] cover an overly extended topic,"[20] or that the author "had stripped his style of all scientific devices" because he was writing for mothers and not "doctors, and sensed that, to be truly useful, he had to make himself understood by those to whom his work was addressed."[21] After all, though there were many medical treatises that might be helpful for doctors, "[i]t is doubtful if the best books of this kind have ever been useful for the women to whom they were intended, while it is certain that they have all done a great wrong to society."[22] Even Locke and Rousseau wrote for men of philosophical minds and were not seen as appropriate reading for mothers looking for advice on how to raise their children.[23]

Women were not doctors or philosophers and, therefore, those who wrote for them did not consider them capable of understanding medical jargon or of gleaning the most important bits of information from the midst of philosophy, yet believed that they could and would independently care for their families, given the chance. Operating on this assumption, the professionals who knew what was best for these women offered advice on their terms. "An association with a distinguished doctor, and there are many right now, would be very helpful for the mother of a family. His conversation, listened to with practical interest, would keep her from a number of errors and even dangers that she might follow in ignorance. She would instruct herself for the health of everything that surrounds her."[24] While men might use technical or scientific terms among themselves, someone who wrote advice for wives and mothers, in the words of one such writer, "had to take a simple style, so that I will be better heard by those that I desire to instruct and so that they will be in a position to try what I say to do, without being forced to go and ask for an explanation of a word before taking care of the issue."[25] In short, women who read these treatises were supposed to take the information and act on it themselves, without having to ask their brothers, fathers, or husbands to explain. A woman might need the guidance of men outside the household in order to run her family well, but men were not the ones in charge of domestic education, nor were they supposed to be.[26] Women were autonomous within the home.

A feminine domestic world was only imaginable once home life and child-rearing became so valuable and necessary that women could assume power in their households as a result of their reproductive work. Mothering had to be seen as vitally necessary, as much so or more than any other productive opportunity available to women. This was accomplished, not when industrial patterns changed work habits in the nineteenth century, but as early as the years before the French Revolution, for it was at that point that philosophical and cultural assumptions about education and family linked mothering to the new focus on the necessity for physical freedom for children to the critical role of early childhood. If education, not schooling, was "[t]he art of preserving, strengthening, and perfecting the physical and moral faculties that man received from nature when he was born,"[27] then as educators, mothers' obligations were worked out in relation to these new perceptions of children's needs and parents' "natural" roles.

The link between mothers and primary education was obvious: they controlled the physical well-being of their children while carrying them for nine months, then nursed, clothed, or otherwise raised them after their birth. A number of treatises described in great detail how women might best guarantee strong limbs, healthy bodies, and the proper physical conformation of their children. In these, advice on physical liberty tended to follow the themes advanced by Rousseau: fewer restraints and more attention to exercise, fresh air, and clothing would result in a healthier, happier child. The physical aspect of mothering was far less than half the picture, however. Just as Mme le Rebours, like Rousseau, argued that wet-nursing led to spoiled and unhealthy children, the women's advice manuals tied physical development to emotional well-being and the long-term health of a society.[28] Attention to physical health was important primarily because of its ability to shape mental and moral development. As one typical example explained, "the constitution of a child, his health, his future strength, and his moral character depend much more than one might think on [the mother's] manner of living during her pregnancy."[29] Education began in the cradle, or even the womb, and any reasonable mother "would not want her children to receive their nourishment at the breast of a stranger, would not want their first ideas, so enduring, to be developed in them by a woman without education: after having been the nurse, she will be the governess of these children," since "the errors of education are not correctable, they carry too much weight."[30]

Moral Instruction and Cultural Change

Women were crucial for primary education not only because they carried the child to term or because their milk would provide the first nutrients and guarantee the extension of life. Women's virtue and emotional availability to their children was important because "the mother was no longer only genetrix but also the guarantee of future society."[31] Though physical and moral tasks were linked, mothers were to be particularly concerned with the moral development of their children. As a republican wife and mother insisted, rather than seeking public honor like that sought by men who would defend their country or mount the forum, "[women's] share is in more soft and less vivid virtues: it is by their sustained exercise that you will give heroes to the world: do not doubt that men owe everything they are to you; their vices and their virtues are your work."[32] Mme Gacon-Dufour, one of the foremost home economists of the Restoration, also explained, "[p]rimary education is that which is the most important, and this first education belongs incontestably to women."[33] While Mme Gacon-Dufour claimed that this was due to women's physical education of children, her underlying concern was with moral development:

The tenderness that [mothers] carry for these small little interesting beings, which makes them aware of their least movements, helps them guess from their plaintive cries what [the children] may need and that which they cannot yet express. This attention prevents children from giving themselves over to the impatience and anger that they will [otherwise] feel all their lives. I am convinced that a child nourished by his mother does not have this bitterness of character that one sometimes notices in children fed far from their parents, those that come back to the paternal house, two or three years [after their birth] or even later.[34]

Tenderness, love, and proper devotion could prevent a world of ills. At the same time that mothers were advised to free the child's body from both artificial and natural constraints, they were also warned that to neglect their duties with respect to their offspring's reason could result in disaster. "The greatest Philosophers and the most famous Legislators have always considered the education of Youth to be a certain source of rest and happiness, not only for Families, but even for the State and for Empires."[35] "The first childhood impressions hardly ever fade away. How much more essential it is then to only offer [children] things that are made to develop and nourish in them honest, noble, and elevated sentiments!"[36] The future of, not only the woman's own family, but also of her society depended on proper nurturing.

The importance of a mother's education of her children was stressed again and again, in very specific ways. While the majority of Enlightenment philosophical treatises did not directly link moral instincts and emotional attachment and instead focused on general thoughts about schooling or instruction, when it came to exhorting women in their duties for domestic education, advice manuals followed Rousseau's example. They were direct and to the point.[37] One began by telling his female readers:

If one could ever forget that children are the hope of the society in which they are born, one cannot, without crime, neglect to take the necessary means to render them useful members of society one day, be it by their useful knowledge, be it by their use of their minds, by the qualities of their heart, or finally, by that which is most valuable, by the treasure of their morals.[38]

Women's role as primary educators might not provide useful knowledge or philosophical training, but it could determine morality and, by extension, civic health. In this way, the attention of a mother not only guaranteed a stronger or healthier child, but it also had the most important personal and social repercussions. Theorists explained the relationship between conscience, reason, and primary education in simple and concrete terms. Far more than simply helping their children to exercise their freedom, mothers had to train them in personal restraint as well. As the Countess of Rémusat explained:

The more one gives latitude in the exercise of her children's liberty, leaving to the children the choice of good or bad in order to teach them one or the other by experience, the more important it is to ensure that they develop early on this notion of just and unjust that we all carry inside of us . . . The understanding of obligations follows the use of reason, for it only grows little by little; but it is useful that a child know early on that every creature on the earth has duties to fulfill; and the feeling of moral obligation that education finds and does not give, will shortly provide for the child a clear and applicable knowledge.[39]

The imperatives that women read in this literature were simple and clear: "Is not the duty of education to transform this [inborn sense of good and evil] into reasoned knowledge?"[40] Another explained, "[e]ducation is, properly speaking, the art of handling and shaping minds. It is of all the Sciences, the most difficult, the rarest, and at the same time, the most important."[41] Another writer explained, "[r]ationality is the faculty that demands all the efforts of a teacher or a parent . . . Children do not yet have enough acquired ideas; they have too few objects to compare, their intelligence is contracted into too narrow limits, and their moral sense is too marked."[42] No reasonable mother could misinterpret this message; her duty was to mold her children into adults who were both reasoning and reasonable, willing to behave according to their duties. The object of this education was "to open, to enlighten, to instruct, and to regulate the spirit of children."[43] A mother's love would help fashion a body that was less constrained than before, both by convention and illness, but this freedom demanded greater attention on the part of the mother in order to result in increased self-control on the part of the child.

Even when conflicting political agendas used reason and obedience in different ways, the rhetoric surrounding primary education and women's duties remained much the same. During the Revolution, mothers were told that virtue was "the base of a republican government, by which peoples recovered and preserved their liberty." Accordingly, it was "to this regenerating and conserving virtue that you, mothers of families, should form the young hearts that nature has given to your care."[44] Under the Restoration, when "true liberty [was] founded on the fear of God," rather than the virtue of men, they learned that "[i]n any country and any condition that one may be, one is very free so long as one fears the gods, and one only fears them. In a word, the truly free man is the one that, free of all fear and all desire, submits only to the gods and to reason."[45] Whether instilling religious obedience or the virtue of men, women's family obligations looked much the same. As autonomous individuals, they were to teach their children both reason and obedience, because liberty and self-control went hand-in-hand.

An Ungendered Virtue?

Children's virtue and moral obligation, it should be noted, were not gendered at this point, even if their clothing was. Since both boys and girls were to spend their formative years (roughly until age six or seven) in the parental home, mothers were expected to shape the moral judgment and self-control of boys and girls equally. In the fashion of Rousseau, "[u]ntil the age of six, [mothers were to make] no difference in the manner of raising both sexes."[46] While, in adolescence, boys had different obligations and expectations, the years before the age of reason (often marked by the celebration of a First Communion) looked quite similar for either gender.[47] Advice manuals generally made no distinctions by sex for this age, referring to "the child" or "the student." Mothers were the ideal reader for these books, and the advice that they would be given, "important secrets . . . to guide them in uncertain steps" was for all the boys and girls that they would raise. "All that will be useful for you to know, and possible to learn for your conservation and that of your children, I will tell you," they were told.[48] When gender distinctions were made, usually in advice manuals designed to teach women how to educate their daughters, it was to insist that "[g]irls as well as boys, have a heart that must be formed to virtue, this unique principle of our happiness."[49] Domestic education was the basis that would make any child virtuous and therefore socially useful.

After the age of reason, mothers were expected to place their sons into the hands of either fathers or other male educators. At that point, "the austerity of studies, the violence of games and of exercises, in the end, everything that is necessary in the education of men to strengthen their spirit, would come to strike constantly at a mother's charming sensitivity."[50] However, the children under discussion were too young to be trained as their gender demanded, in part because they were not yet rational enough for such training. As Rollin explained, "[c]are for the education of children [under seven] is principally [a woman's] responsibility, and is part of this domestic empire that Providence has assigned especially to them."[51] The mother's task was to develop self-control and the moral conscience as she brought her children to the age of reason, and then she could teach the girls while men would take over the training of the boys.

The fact that the children under discussion were prerational is central to understanding both the mother's role and the actual process of education. Instead of treating children as if they were already reasoning, mothers were to accustom their children to obedience slowly. One author claimed that the solution was "especially to have patience, never to order, to be severe or rigorous, for that puts the child's heart in a state of siege and perpetual defense; always [use] the language of nature and goodness."[52] Another agreed in principle but disagreed in practice, claiming that orders should be given in every situation, especially for enjoyable things like walks. "In this way, the idea of constraint will be separated from that of obedience, but in all cases, agreeable or not, the order will be irrevocable."[53] With or without orders, the idea was the same: children were not yet rational or capable of exercising correct judgment, so mothers would have to model the proper behavior for them and let them learn by example. Then, when the time came for them to make their own decisions, they would, like Emile and Sophie, already have internalized the appropriate demeanor.

As with Rousseau's *Emile,* this literature recognized that one might see a tension between teaching the habit of obedience and learning individual self-control. As one female writer put it: "To raise a child correctly in the moral sense is to make him acquire the taste and the habit of a virtuous will. But is this to give him reason? Should education dictate the formula of all his duties in advance, or put his spirit in a state by which he can discern them, to know them and to want them, given the opportunity?"[54] The authors of these treatises were not ignorant of the problem of obedience but believed that moral education would itself resolve the conflict between demands for obedience and preparation of the child to make free, rational, and individual choices. Self-control and maternal examples were the crucial components. A proper education, given by a loving mother who herself demonstrated the ability to regulate her own behavior during her children's prerational years, would enable children to know their duties and to act on them correctly. Children's blank slates would be written on with more than a set of rules and regulations that dictated duties in advance. Instead, as mothers behaved morally and reasonably, children would themselves learn moral and rational behavior and, once they had become thinking beings, the children would be able to act in a similar fashion, not because of constraint, but as their freely chosen preference. The adoption of an empirical model for all children held fast, even in women's advice manuals.

Because mothers would model the proper outcomes in addition to shaping their children in an understanding of their duties, mothers were advised to speak rationally to their children, even as they were reminded not to expect their children to behave like grown adults. The theorists sounded Rousseau's alarms, explaining that "[o]ne must never forget the weakness of this age. Too often, it happens that we judge children as if they were men, as if they had our strength, our faculties, our experience."[55] Instead of using corporal punishment for discipline, mothers were to talk to their child calmly and clearly. This would accustom the child to obey and behave correctly. Then, as they began to reason, children would not only continue the desired actions, but would understand and attempt them on their own. Reason would win out over force and ensure each child's ability to choose obedience, even when tempted to misbehave.

Separation and Self-Control

Since the mother's behavior was central to teaching her children self-control, these treatises were as concerned with the mother's conduct as with the intended actions of her children. As described in the introduction to Mme Campan's *De l'éducation:* "An *attentive, hard-working, and patient* mother always receives the price of her labors. She has reason to also note that [her] conduct must always be in accord with her lesson . . . A word, a gesture, a look, nothing escapes [her children]; they will quickly note if a distinction exists between what she says and what she does."[56] The particular characteristics of the mother's personality were vital: they were transferred from mother to child in the milk, by the mother's treatment and upbringing of her children, and also in the children's observance of their mother's actions. The virtues that one wished to pass on to one's children had to be qualities demonstrated by the mother as well. As one advice manual explained: "My daughter will be temperate because I will give her the example of this virtue . . . [s]he will be courageous, because I won't let myself be defeated by physical or moral pain; she will know early that illness and grief are inseparable from man's condition, and that one would rebel in vain against the intrinsic elements of ourselves."[57] An ideal mother had to be perfect in nearly every way if she expected her pupils also to become perfect models. Then the child would also "be wise and modest, because it is impossible that a young person raised with the principles that I have listed would not be."[58] A mother always had to be on her best behavior lest her children stumble.

Though the domestic wife's role became culturally central during the eighteenth and nineteenth centuries, many of the qualities of perfect motherhood were closely related to ideas about the paradigmatic woman that carried over from an earlier period. Some of the qualities described could have been lifted from almost any period's discussion of model femininity. A woman's virtue should not be in question; she should be obedient, modest, and faithful. The claim that, "[w]hile a man can show off his advantages, a woman must make hers more valued by her modesty,"[59] could have come straight out of a seventeenth-century advice manual. But exactly what it meant to be a demure woman of the eighteenth and nineteenth centuries differed from the previous years in a new emphasis on two attributes: woman's removal from outside influence ("interiorization") and the recognition that women would need to make an active choice to model self-control.[60]

Much of the literature addressed to women either advised them to avoid the outside world or told them how to raise daughters who were themselves content to remain removed from the world. Since women were to teach by example, advice about how properly to train adolescent—rational—daughters also demonstrated what the mothers themselves ought to be. As Citoyenne Guerin-Albert explained, "[m]y daughter will be accustomed to taking care of small feminine tasks, and while she works I will read to her from useful publications. It is not enough to be ruled by the laws that govern us, it is also necessary to love them."[61] The "small tasks" that every girl should learn to love included housekeeping and the establishment of a pleasant atmosphere for her family. To this end, mothers could also read Antoine Caillot's dictum that, "[i]t is important then, in order to respond to the demands of nature and of society, to contract the habit of domestic work at a young age,"[62] with its subsequent explanation of why inattention to this particular detail would result in a lazy and untrained daughter. No woman could escape from these domestic expectations, as home economists believed them to be not only ingrained, but also natural to all women. "All mistresses of households have beyond doubt a plan of administration. There is no young woman entering a household who does not herself form a plan of conduct, who doesn't say to herself: I will run my house in such a manner; if I have the happiness to be a mother, I will supervise such an education; I will direct my interior; I will establish my servants on this kind of footing."[63] This literature expected that wives and mothers would sincerely desire to follow their advice because of a woman's natural desire to manage her household wisely. All of these authors also indicate that these are civic obligations, with an implication for social formation. Women who managed their households well would help to create children who also related properly to society.

Feminine and domestic work were only part of a complete understanding of a woman's role. Any woman wishing to raise her daughter as a boon to her family and future husband would of course have to herself be diligent and hardworking. However, she was also expected to remain entirely in the home, focused on the household needs of her husband and children. This was a "natural" duty, one with which any admirable woman would be familiar. Mme Campan declared, "[w]omen are destined to the sedentary life: it is in their own home that they find true happiness."[64] The Countess of Rémusat agreed, giving her mother as an example of a woman who had found meaning, not in society or external things, but in private life. "My mother knew the world, the court, private life . . . As her life continued, it brought her to the full and pure convictions that one customarily abandons . . . with the enthusiasm of an imprudent youth. The more she knew society, the more she retreated into herself . . . she left life and the truth seized her."[65] Mature and reasoning women could not fail to come to the same conclusion, for "[e]very virtuous French woman feels this exclusive attraction that a woman must have for her residence, and tears herself away with even more difficulty than the English ladies leave their *dear home*."[66] Domesticity now meant that the ideal mother belonged at home and entirely at home, where she could properly care for her husband and children without social influences other than her own good inclinations. While a woman of the seventeenth century might have sewing and household chores to do but also find herself socializing with friends in the neighborhood as she completed her tasks, the new understanding of "nature" limited a woman's proper social outlets to her home. As one proverb went, "God did not place limits beyond which a man cannot explore, but He has determined those of the woman to be the walls of her house."[67] Just in case a mother might be tempted to believe that she could be a public being in addition to a mother, she only had to read more carefully. "Duties of society are of a nature that is opposed to that of a mother who wishes to raise her girls. *Les Veillées du Château, Les Enfans du Vieux Château*, these titles of esteemed works prove that the authors of maternal plans of education, in order to avoid having to fight the entrapments of the world, instead chose to escape them."[68] Mothers were expected to focus on their families, not spend time and emotional energy on social events that were unrelated to family obligations.

The denigration of social outlets beyond the family makes it evident that the directive to stay home extended beyond a constant physical presence in the home to a ceaseless emotional attachment as well. Women were warned to be the best friends, and caretakers, of their husbands, not of other women.

Your friends, even the most dear, should not be the confidantes of the small aggravations that are unavoidable in a household: too often a small sting festers by the pernicious advice of strangers and becomes a deep injury that nothing can heal! Mistrust people who justify you and wrong your husband; which under the glib pretext of sympathizing with you, exaggerate his shortcomings, and will portray his behavior towards you as not deserving your affection.[69]

Women did not need the bad advice of friends, which might undermine the nuclear family and the affectionate relationship between husband and wife, the first model of political life. Women were to focus on family life rather than corrupt themselves with worldly concerns and advice that might lead them to seek the esteem of others rather than their own good judgment. For household advice, women had these treatises for reference, and for companionship, they had their husband and children. "One of the things that contributes most to the happiness of a woman, in the interior of her home, is her conduct with respect to her husband: I mean by this her manners, the cares that she takes for him, etc."[70]

For those women who might not find enough companionship in their relationship with their spouse, children could and should fill the emotional gap. "In her youth, a woman must be the companion and friend of the one who gave her life; later, her activities should know no other object than the happiness of her husband and the education of her children." Whether child or adult, the feminine role remained within the family home. "All the duties of girl, wife, and mother, are contained in the family's limited and fortunate circle."[71] This advice told women in myriad ways that for their own happiness and the good of society, they should remain physically and emotionally within the confines of the home. When women spent their time taking care of family obligations instead of gossiping on the street, or even in the parlor, with their friends, they would gain the esteem of their husbands and the companionship of their children. This friendship would be all the more valuable because of the type of adolescents that their children would become, thanks to their mother's guiding example. In this way, "[i]t is certainly permitted to be lovable in order to be happy, and to acquire love and esteem at the same time. The respect of those around her is [a mother's] most gentle reward; all the more dear as the most constant and the most honorable work of her life is to raise daughters who resemble her."[72]

If the phrasing of the obligation is carefully noted, this was not a lesson merely for the mother's protection or benefit. Unlike Rousseau's Sophie, who could remain outside the home with ease *until* she became a wife and mother, the escape from civilization described in these manuals was intended to help all offspring avoid the entrapments of the world as well, further adding to their ability to truly judge things, becoming self-controlled and self-sufficient within the family home. Instead of offering women obligations that would remove them from a greater civic role, their seclusion was what would create the new family and children who would truly judge the worth of things.

As one can imagine when reading these directives, secluded domesticity, whether "natural" or not, demanded great exercise of self-control on the part of the wife and mother. Though the treatises agreed that "[a] woman throws off more light when she passes her life in greater obscurity,"[73] and that a wife and mother would find herself happier and more loved because of her devotion to her family, any acclaim came as a result of the sacrifices that mothers were expected to make. Even if "[e]ducation should equally form both sexes to a good temperament," instead of men's "great works and great risks," women were expected to endure "more frequent sufferings," such that their "courage must be quiet and patient . . . Moral courage, between them, also relies on the same distinctions: while firmness and pride are the man's share, entreaties and resignation suit the woman."[74] The power of women's pleas was founded on personal self-control. "Reserve is the shield of women . . . It is for the woman above all, as Madame de Lambert has said, that *the primary prudence consists in challenging oneself more than others. Their real modesty consists in the respect that they have for themselves. It is necessary to live respectfully with oneself.*"[75] Women were to exercise great moral judgment and personal control, not only so that they would live as a good example to their children, but also because their sacrifices were crucial to the smooth functioning of society as a whole.

The emphasis on domesticity and a completely separate private sphere might seem to confirm the modern treatment of separate spheres that assumes that demands for self-controlled domestic life were about confirming inequality.[76] However, women's placement into a passive moral sphere instead of an active political one did not mean that women were weak or lesser than men. On the contrary, this literature portrayed women as stronger and more capable because of the importance of their role in the home and their ability to control themselves for the good of others.[77] Unlike men who operated by force, women used persuasion of others and control over their own desires to wield power within the home and to become the moral governors of all, a position that took precedence to political governance in Rousseauian ideals. Rather than dismiss this as mere rhetoric, one should recall that Rousseau's construct of Sophie portrayed her as self-conscious in a way that Emile was not and in a way that was the foundation of civic life for both men and women.[78] Women controlled their families and commanded respect not only because of their authority over early education but equally because only they influenced the family's physical and emotional well-being and freely chose to embrace the duty of shaping society by exerting self-control. Instead of allowing people outside the home to affect the harmony of the domestic circle, the constantly attentive and private mother guaranteed, through the sacrifice of her own needs, the comfort and happiness of her family—and by extension, the wholeness of the nation—or so this literature claimed.

The Bad Mother

When reading these snippets of counsel, there were two possible ways that a serious reader could respond. Either she could agree wholeheartedly, examining her own domesticity and coming to the conclusion that early training would be central to her children's imitation of her life and their ability to create a new world, or she could disagree. If she did not agree with the "demands of nature and society" as established by Caillot and others like him, however, she found herself indicted as unnatural and as one of the lazy and improperly trained women who became bad mothers. A bad mother was the antithesis of a good mother: selfish, unnatural, undisciplined, and externalized, and her children and their society paid the price for her selfishness. This was not only true when children got "bad milk" that corrupted their morals, but also when children were sent to wet-nurses and never made it back alive, or were crippled because of their mother's inattention within the home. In order to make it clear that women's self-control was central to happiness writ large, these treatises made frequent reference to bad mothers.[79] As might be expected, given the inveighing of philosophers against wet-nursing, mothers who sent their children away for the first few years of their young lives were seen as one of the clearest examples of bad mothers.[80] According to these manuals, a mother who placed her selfish wants above her children's needs by using a wet-nurse was even worse than a beast, for she sacrificed the "life and health of her children to a contemptible interest, of which [she] rarely makes good use."[81]

One does not see savages give their children to be nursed by other savages; it is only in civilization that luxury and the depravity of morals lead mothers to not want to nurse their own children: some to avoid the annoyance and care, which is nothing in comparison to the advantages and happiness of motherhood, others to very frivolous and transitory qualities.[82]

Only women with the hardest of hearts could be so cruel as to send their newborn children away to be raised by someone else, knowing that they risked their offspring's very lives by doing so. The abandoning mother further reinforced the importance of the "natural" family obligations of affection and concern that mothers ought to have for their children. Of course, since philosophers and doctors had condemned wet-nursing for years, the treatises that attacked mothers who were a part of this institution found themselves already well within a trend toward greater care of mothers for their children.[83]

In fact, the assault on wet-nursing was in many ways less important than the recognition that women could keep their children at home and still be bad mothers who focused more on public life than their nuclear family, spending their time in a search for esteem and frivolous rewards. If "the cares that a good mother takes for her children are a true proof of her love for them," then women who "leave their young children to the care of governesses . . . who themselves leave the child alone to go talk with the porter and meet with their lovers . . . are not worthy of the name of mother. What cruel pains for the unhappy children who have been the object of first a criminal negligence and then an unpardonable indifference!"[84] Others who neither sent their children away nor gave them to the care of a governess could also be culpable. As the naturalist Georges-Louis Buffon explained, women who left their children for hours in a cradle or standing stool were as unnatural as women who sent their children away. Though the children had their natural mother, she was unfortunately "cruel enough not to be touched by [the child's] moaning, and then these small unfortunate persons fall into a kind of despair; they make all the exertions of which they are capable, crying with all their force, finally making themselves sick with the effort."[85] Mothers who kept their children at home but failed to pay sufficient attention to them were also bad mothers. The advice manuals provided numerous examples of this kind of improper mothering. Some women were too preoccupied with social duties truly to love their children and as a result were unable to return the affections that the children gave.[86] Others were not loving and punished too severely; they were so harsh that, from terror, their children would lie to hide faults. Still others never disciplined and were so lax that the children could do anything to get attention whenever they wanted it.[87] And some were not cruel but capricious, first punishing severely and then not at all, so that their children never knew what to expect.[88]

Of course, there was also such a thing as too much attention. Mothers, much more than fathers, were seen as capable of becoming too fond of their children and spoiling them instead of raising them to be self-reliant and disciplined. Mothers who were worried about the effect that too much discipline might have, failed to be necessarily strict, while others who did not want to tax the brain of the child unduly failed to educate him properly.[89] Their sons and daughters were not physically or morally healthy because their mothers had not provided them with proper exercise and they were, in the end, unprepared for civic life. The product of one such upbringing "therefore entered the world as his weak mother had formed him: absolute in his will, capricious, unsociable, ignorant, full of shortcomings; in a word, as a spoiled child will always enter, if providence does not come to halt him on the edge of the abyss where his parents pushed him."[90] In all these cases, mothers who were weak and lacking in self-control resulted in children who were also unable to contribute to the reform of society. Since all of these bad mothers failed to exert self-control in some way, the message was clear: children, like husbands, deserved the complete emotional attachment and care of their mothers, but the women under consideration were not always willing or able to provide it.

If mothering was "natural," why did some women fail to understand the nature of their duties? On this point, most treatises agreed that the problem was not only emotional. While some mothers were lacking in affection and concern for their children, most, those who clearly had not been raised by a mother who gave the proper example of self-control, simply needed better information to help them judge right from wrong and support them in making the right decisions.

Why have the efforts of philosophers and of numerous great doctors failed to achieve happy results? The primary blame is due to the lack of education of a great number of women, the laziness or carelessness of others, the habitual routine of others. But there is also another more powerful reason . . . the works of philosophers or physicians . . . are not presented in the proper form or appropriate style to provide a clear and familiar instruction.[91]

The argument that women needed more appropriate advice makes it clear that the examples of bad or negligent mothering were even more important to the genre than that of the mother who abandoned her children. In their indictment of women who followed the older methods of parenting and who failed to exert control over themselves, these treatises articulated the new affectionate standards *and* justified the advice genre. The argument for the continued existence of bad mothers was particularly clever: women who were selfish or uncaring did not generally harm their children out of willful intent but simply had not yet learned how important it was to become a self-controlled mother. After all, if even savages acted correctly toward their children, would not appropriately educated mothers? If education was to make children into proper adults, it would have to start with assisting women as they became proper mothers.

The Benefits of "Natural" Mothering

Education could form women into being properly domestic and self-controlled parents for two reasons: mothering was a "natural" instinct and, more important, domesticity held its own advantages for women. Not only would women find esteem from their husbands and society as a whole when they fit into the domestic model, but adherence to the standards in these treatises would, in and of itself, fulfill these women and make them a part of society as a whole. Discussions of both good and bad mothers made the rewards of parenting clear: mothers who abandoned, ignored, or failed to educate their children denied themselves some of the best experiences in life and contributed to the downfall of their society. By refusing to nurse and raise their children, mothers missed out on physical, sentimental, and social benefits that accrued to the mother, not the child.[92] Women who sent their children away, first to a nurse and then as soon as possible to a governess or *collège*, were not simply risking the morality and health of their children, but also making themselves strangers to the little beings who would otherwise care so deeply about them. The babies "scarcely know the authors of their days: the parents and children are only united by etiquette, and the soft sentiments of filial piety and paternal tenderness are hardly known by them, except as something that they have heard or read about."[93] And for what? "For such vain motives, she will sacrifice the pleasure, always so pure, of clasping her child in her arms each day, of making his true life run in his veins, of helping with the successive development of his body, of receiving his first smile and being the first to hear the tones of his filial voice!"[94] Women who refused to care for their children could never have the joy that domestic mothers would have.[95]

The importance of such a guarantee was not merely emotional plea-sure at feeling the child's proper affection for his parent. This was also a promise of adequate care for oneself in the future. As one author ex-plained, "[d]o then, oh mothers, all that is possible so that your child will receive your services as kindnesses. Let him learn, let him know about you that you yourself are the author of his days, are his first and best friend, then he will understand that you must never be his slave![96] In ad-dition to being independent in her rearing of the child, such a mother, who took care of her own children, would be the sole recipient of the love and affection that was due her. Her children would recognize a debt of obligation to their mother and act accordingly, venerating and support-ing her instead of merely taking whatever they could and eventually de-serting her. Not only could women have a free reign in their homes, the sentimental pleasure of child-rearing, and the guarantee of future support, but mothers could also ensure greater health for themselves. Though pregnancy could take a toll on a woman's body, these treatises believed that nursing one's own baby could reestablish the body's equilibrium and result in greater health than before. "Some women say that they are too delicate. Oh, well! They should nurse in order to reestablish their health. It is the best remedy that they could employ; the child will be their doc-tor."[97] A woman's constitution was not the only beneficiary, but also her disposition. "The cares that Mothers who nurse take for their children make their character more lovable: the interest that one naturally takes for their presevation becomes more general, and their Father himself will be more concerned with them; in giving more, you Mothers also make all hearts more human."[98] As one of the most popular authors exclaimed, "[t]he good mother, the reasonable mother will listen with careful inter-est, I am sure, to the voice of one who wants to teach her the means of preserving her own health, guaranteeing the constant affection of the hus-band who is dear to her, and of raising beautiful, healthy, and robust chil-dren."[99] A woman would gain a free hand within the home, her health, the love of her husband for taking care of his children and heirs, as well as the love of the children themselves for the support that they had re-ceived.[100] How could any rational woman refuse such promises?

These were advantages that a public life could not provide. No won-der some women found these ideas appealing and even liberating. "It is in family life that women obtain the advantage that they lose in the world; it is there that they are what they should be."[101] While the advice manuals demanded that women give much, becoming like Rousseau's So-phie by devoting their attention, time, and emotions to the interior life of the family, in return they were promised affection, good health, and con-trol over their lives. These women were surrounded by a professional lit-erature that offered freedom and rewards for compliance. Additionally, the advice manuals contextualized women's sacrifices as part of a social reconstruction that indicated how, through domestic motherhood, women could not only personally control their futures but also reshape their entire society.

The treatises under consideration held up domestic education as the key to the future and promised to help mothers raise their children to be obedient and self-controlled, virtues that were expected of all adults, both men and women. Women's ability to reign over their own emotions for the good of their children and society as a whole linked them to the regeneration of society, and men's relegation to professional advice-givers, one step removed from domestic duties, guaranteed women more autonomy than ever within the domestic interior as well as a civic role that was all their own. To be sure, women were themselves expected to be virtuous in order to accomplish their intended tasks, but in return for proper behavior, they received more freedom of action, concrete rewards, and increased social status. Philosophically, the wives who created a nurturing domestic life were much closer to Rousseau's radical reformulation of self and society than were their husbands, who remained tainted by public life and social expectations. As good mothers, they had removed their children and themselves from "the crushing force of social conventions."[102] Equally important, in daily practice, the women addressed by these treatises were not expected to be particularly self-abnegating or generous. If "[t]he man who is truly free only desires what he is capable of doing and only does what pleases him,"[103] the advice genre demonstrated some ways in which these women could do what best pleased them and still reap the benefits of their behavior.

Compliance with the new domestic ideologies was not only to a man's but also a woman's advantage. When women found a new place within the home, their constraints increased in ways that were not negligible but they also gained new forms of independence and respect and new ways to influence the world. When looking at domesticity, American historians like Linda Kerber argue that Republican motherhood "offered an ironic compromise, one that merged Rousseau and Condorcet. It represented both an elaboration of the image of Sophie and a response to attacks like Rousseau's on the mental capacity of women. In this, as in so many other cases, Rousseau provided his own oxymoron."[104] However, the French context demonstrates that Rousseau's own work and the domestic mother's response did not necessarily involve internal contradiction. Women could seize Rousseau's ideal—with no reference to Condorcet or the *philosophes*—because they believed that their nurturing influence was the key that would allow them autonomy and personal happiness as well as a point of entry into civic life. In this sense, the adoption of gendered social roles was exactly what gave them influence and control. As one contemporary declared, "Rousseau gave so much to women that one should not be annoyed because of that which he refused them."[105] While this is not a bargain that has great appeal in the early twenty-first century, we should find it of interest for two reasons: first of all, that the readers of these advice manuals could have practical motives in adopting this ideology as their own and, second, that the enunciation of a seemingly repressive refrain of "separate but equal" was grounded in a vision of the world where self-control was not ideologically separating but unifying, a virtue for any autonomous being, male or female.

CHAPTER FOUR

"To Amuse and Instruct"

Self-Control, Adult Expectations, and Children's Literature

There are still very few books intended specifically for the instruction of young people. Attentive parents are in search of these types of works and are especially pleased when writers enrich this valuable part of their library.
—*The Friend of Young Citizens* (1795)

I have seen little girls that were no sooner rid of their lesson than they threw the book somewhere and could not remember where when it was time to resume studying. These little girls put their mothers in a bad mood every day. Caroline, on the other hand, is a charming child and will become an admirable woman: she has accustomed herself to order and to work, that is to say, to the two qualities that will assure her happiness.
—*The Little Ladies' ABC Primer* (1811)

Self-Control, Social Change, and Children's Literature

Like the advice manual's ideal mother, mentors in children's stories helped the child develop physically and then turned to moral instruction. The books, which were designed for children past the initial stages of education, took up where women's advice manuals had left off. For this reason, children's books tended to summarize the physical component of education if they dealt with it at all. Instead, they focused on stories for moral instruction, with both positive and negative examples of childish behavior demonstrating the proper ways to grow in rationality and moral judgment. The books intended to provide instruction for young children, those able to read but still under a mother's care. Since many young boys and girls below the age of seven were expected to remain at home and under the care of their mothers, these books offered stories for both male and female children. Many of the positive attributes that the books attempted to inculcate into youth were the same across gender lines. For example, stories demonstrated ways in which charity, rationality, and usefulness were prized in all children. However, other attributes, such as modesty and chastity, were identified as womanly characteristics and thus lessons for girls to learn, while boys' lessons focused on bravery and strength. No matter the gender of the reader, the mind and behavior of the child were always a common target. By the way in which the works were structured and the timing of their production, the new genre of children's literature demonstrated the growing belief that only a good, nurturing, and reasonable mother could provide the first physical and moral education that would promote self-control and other civilized behaviors.

After the first steps of maternal education were complete, children being trained at home in the new fashion would need additional molding in order to enter the adult world of rationality and self-control. The authors of children's books believed that the education provided by stories would help children to make a transition from a life directed and controlled by a mother to a life in the wider society. As Rebecca Rogers has noted, "the main objective of these stories is to help young women learn their place, not just within the family, but also within society . . ."[1] Parents and educators used these books to bridge the transition from the earliest years of "prerational" childhood to later childhood; they intended to teach children the outlines of social practices in addition to the shapes of letters. Like advice manuals, these forms of children's literature "show precisely what we are seeking—namely, the standard of habits and behavior to which society at a given time sought to accustom the individual. These [works] are themselves direct instruments of "conditioning" or "fashioning," of the adaptation of the individual to those modes of behavior which the structure and situation of his society make necessary."[2] These works served to initiate children into the mysteries of adulthood and the expectations of the world around them and emphasized in a particular way the rewards that children could expect when they internalized appropriate values and became productive members of society.

As *"Childhood"* Changes, Books Evolve

The evolving status and production of three types of children's books (ABC primers, collections of fables, and didactic stories) demonstrates in a particular way the changing ideas about childhood, individuality, and ideal education. Primers, fables, and didactic tales were all "children's literature" in this transitional period, but each of them demonstrates in a different way a transition from general platitudes and abstract lessons to concrete and gendered explanations of social behavior that were designed to integrate children into society.[3] The format and purpose of these different works thus points to the evolution of new thinking about gender distinctions, self-control, and autonomy.

ABC primers and books of fables, which were older genres, and had been produced before any ideological shift in childhood, were adapted in order to meet the needs of children as demand for educational literature grew. As a result, though fables and primers demonstrate some influence of changing opinions about childhood instruction and were in this period intended for a childish audience, their form and content remained quite similar to earlier examples directed to the adult population. Thus, primers and fables, even when published with children in mind, failed to integrate fully within their pages the new ways of thinking about childhood, gender, and individuality. While a reader of the nineteenth century might have assumed that primers were "children's books" in a way that someone in the seventeenth century would not, both readers could have agreed upon the primary purpose of a primer or collection of fables. Accordingly, the analysis of these sources will indicate which values and standards persisted through time even as they demonstrate adaptation in response to the new ideals.

Didactic tales, on the other hand, were developed in the nineteenth century in France and were the first example of the new genre of children's literature. These stories consolidated and reflected the new view, found in philosophical treatises and advice manuals, of the child as a developing, and gendered, individual, capable of self-control and rational thought, which were often two shoots from the same branch. Each story was only a few pages long and could be found in inexpensive and small books that offered brief reflections on particular virtues and vices.[4] The collections of tales were intended for young children, not yet of school age, either to read by themselves or with their mothers as read-alouds. The titles were explicit about the lesson the reader should draw, as children were introduced by image and word to examples such as "Cheri, or the Little Glutton," "Amy, the Girl who was Lazy and Inattentive," and "Francis, the Hard-Working Boy."

Despite providing a more "modern" perspective, the titles and content of these works are often jarring to modern ears. Didactic moralizing does little to hide its agenda and does not sound like a particularly freeing development in the history of childhood. Literary scholar Geoffrey Summerfield has claimed that didactic tales carry "an unmistakable whiff of sadistic gratification,"[5] while Paul Hazard insists that that the clear moral program of these stories demonstrates the increasing oppression of children.[6] However, as with the contextualization of Rousseau or women's advice manuals, the existence of the didactic genre offers us a clearer understanding of cultural and intellectual change in this historical period. These newest stories, written especially with children and the new educational philosophies in mind, help us to understand how demands for autonomy might exist alongside an increasing emphasis on gender and demands for self-control.

In order to understand the meanings of childhood and gender evidenced by this literature in a context where it was embraced and enjoyed, we must read both didactic stories and their precursors, primers and fables, in much the same way as we read changes in material culture or the advice genre. Like advice manuals, these forms of children's literature show us how society attempted to persuade the individual to behave "properly" and led, in the end, to a social vision of a "naturally" autonomous and self-controlled child. This means that our evaluation of children's works must put them in context, not primarily in comparison to our standards of behavior or our expectations, but as products of the situations where they were produced and as part of demands for a new social order.[7] When we read these works from the perspective of the eighteenth and nineteenth centuries, their messages begin to sound far less unbalanced and may even offer explanations for how an increased emphasis on gender could still lead to greater demands for autonomy. Children's books, whether intended to be gendered or universal, demonstrate in a concrete fashion the roles that gender differentiation did and did not play in the development of modern thought about equality and self-control.

Isabelle Havelange's analysis of didactic literature has demonstrated that women were often prolific writers and producers of these works. For reasons of both production and topic, didactic literature is often recognized as a "feminine" genre, and yet historical and literary studies of children's stories generally fail to deal with the broader implications of this insight.[8] As Elaine Showalter has noted, "'Parents' still means fathers, 'children' still means sons, and even when documenting a decline in patriarchal authority, critics fail to connect their topic to the 'increased authority of mothers,'"[9] even though this authority is evident from the most cursory glance at books written in this period.[10] An examination of children's literature affirms that the French didactic tale, often written by and for women, promoted both self-control and autonomy in its focus on the moral and social education of children. Didactic stories may have taught that feminine virtues were passive, with self-control as one of the highest ideals, but within this message both mothers and children gained new spaces to form moral identity, increase their agency, and to join the society in which they lived. In this sense at least, increased differentiation also promised new forms of autonomy that were related to the new universal ideals of behavior.

The Particular Meaning of French Children's Literature

Though an examination of children's literature promises both to demonstrate and to explain the social attitudes surrounding childhood and gender, the development of the genre is routinely ignored in discussions of the cultural history of the modern era, in large part because children's culture is often seen as insignificant or unimportant. For France, the neglect is twofold. Not only do general histories and examinations of the literature of the early nineteenth century gloss over contributions to this growing field, but even literary histories that center on the development of children's material generally focus on the English-speaking world, leaving France as a footnote, an unsuccessful sidebar to the amazing publishing industry begun in the 1740s by Samuel Newbery in England.[11] Many of France's earliest and most prolific children's writers, such as Mme Leprince de Beaumont, remain virtually unknown, and others, such as Mme de Genlis, have attracted attention primarily because of their ties to illustrious persons in the adult world. It is true that children's literature was not the commercial force in France that it was in England and the United States. However, France's late arrival on the scene, owing in part to her later industrialization and the upheaval during the revolutionary years, did not mean that French writing was merely derivative of the available British and American literature, nor can one assume that all children's literature grew out of the successes of the Epinal press after 1840. Though they were not commercial enterprises on the same scale as the Epinal or Newbery presses, particular publishers recur again and again when one looks at books published for French boys and girls before 1840. Clearly, these presses, such as Ancelle, Pierre Blanchard, Louis Janet, F. Louis, and Veuve Hérissant, found a significant part of their business in publishing books for children and had some degree of success in this field. Writers such as Berquin, Genlis, and Leprince de Beaumont, also found fame with their contemporaries as authors of children's books and frequently justified writing and publishing new volumes in spite of the fact that "[t]here are already a great number of moral works for children."[12] Most of these books were written in French and reflected specifically French concerns, though some of the Newbery classics and didactic tales were adapted, translated, and sent across the Channel as well.[13]

French writers brought their own perspectives to interests that crossed national boundaries. An overwhelming focus on rationality, concern with children's self-control, and demands for respect of and obedience to authority were common features in all of the children's tales.[14] Distaste for fantasy was also a common thread and one area in which the English followed the pattern set by the French, insofar as hostility to fairy tales and magical stories was justified in English literature by reference to Mme de

Genlis, whose educational program for the Orléans children was heavily rational. However, where British literature attempted to entice children into learning and analogously developed stories that focused on children's amusement, French literature was much more likely, even when attempting to be engaging, to focus on maintaining order and preparing children for their future participation in society. Anglophone books, even those of the didactic school, often featured amusing characters—such as talking mice or robins—and promised material rewards, such as a coach and six to every child who learned his lessons well. French authors, even when they appealed to the playful side of childhood and addressed the material benefits of good behavior, tended to focus equally on the punishment of neglectful children, defined as those children who did not work to the best of their abilities and insisted on having their own way rather than obeying their parents.[15] As a result, French didactic tales provide particular insight into the development of the rhetoric of self-control and particularized gender expectations as they related to the construction of a new society.

Book publication was directed at French parents with disposable income, who, by the late eighteenth and early nineteenth centuries, could choose from a wide selection of children's books. As Mme de Campan complained, "I have read a number of works written for youth; almost all of them deal with the education of children who belong to the leisure class."[16] Both in their social expectations and their choice of examples, the greater part of this growing literary industry seems to have been directed at aristocratic and bourgeois children. Yet, despite an emphasis on privileged children in particular, the writers of moralistic tales also claimed that their stories were applicable to all children. Didactic writers made no attempt to hide the fact that their tales were a crucial feature in the attempt to control all of the youngest members of society, beginning at a very early age.

The authors of these works frequently reminded children of their obligations to their elders, who were not only wiser, but also more powerful. Written in a simple form and honest about their intent to shape readers according to an approved model, the themes and characters in these stories conveyed adults' hopes, fears, and expectations in one of the most transparent forms possible. Most tales made no attempt to hide their controlling face, using rewards and punishment to cajole and frighten children into submission.[17] This overt mission to transmit cultural values is one of the qualities that makes children's literature a valuable historical source. While it is not always true that children internalized the message or that the stories achieved their intended results, these books contained what adults believed children could and ought to understand.[18] Adults were present at every stage of literary production, as writers, then editors, publishers, and generally purchasers. The opinions and intentions of adults, not of children, were, and still are, the determining factors in a book's success. As William Carnochan explains, "[l]iterature written specifically *for* children and pedagogic manuals about the upbringing of children imply distance: they give what amounts to a prospect view of childhood."[19] With a focus that adult literature of this period was seldom able to achieve, literature for children surveyed the range of possibilities and responded by reducing multiple potential outcomes to a binary system: good or bad, vice or virtue.[20] Like a two-dimensional map, children's literature charts adults' desired outcomes in black and white, and also demonstrates how the themes of self-control and education had particular importance as the idea of the domestic mother began to expand.

Order, Affection, and ABCs

The moral clarity and focus found in nineteenth-century children's literature were, however, relatively new developments. Before the mid-eighteenth century, books on manners, educational texts, and tracts were directed at the entire literate population. Of these, folk-tales and fables were some of the most popular works, though books on manners and *abécédaires* were also common.[21] Often, the *abécédaire* formed a part of the *bibliothèque bleue*'s general market as well, serving not only as a book for learning the alphabet, but also as a simple catechism, Mass book, or psalm-book.[22] It might include the Our Father, Hail Mary, Apostles' Creed, and other common prayers, usually in Latin. If the book or pamphlet had illustrations, they would not be ornate, but simple woodblock prints. There was little attempt made to be amusing or enticing, to draw in the reader. People who wanted to learn how to read and write or memorize Psalms and prayers would do so whether or not there were funny rhymes or cute animals engraved with elaborate plates.[23]

In the eighteenth century, an increasing number of adults could afford much more expensive versions of religious literature and had little need of such simplicity. As book production and purchasing increased, ABCs became the first and clearest form of children's literature, and by the turn of the century, it was widely assumed that this type of book was only for the young, not for all ages. Primers also changed from simple prayer books to luxurious examples such as the *Playful Abécédaire, contained in an elegantly fashioned case, [with] an alphabet and a toy for the child's recreation after reading*, and *The Alphabet Made into a Game*.[24] These types of *abécédaires* included engravings, games, and simple stories for the enjoyment of children. These works were "intended to instruct Children while amusing them,"[25] and their ornate format betrays the classes of children for which they were intended.

Of course, all the versions of these books, whether expensive or cheap, amusing or simply instructive, did more than simply teach the shape of letters and their function within the language. They also served as rudimentary guides to conduct, especially in France. In Britain, Evangelical influences on alphabet learning often were based on a religious insistence on personal understanding and therefore an ability to read the Bible; in Catholic France, the aim of literacy education was more mixed, with a religious tradition that was predicated much more strongly on hierarchy and obedience to the interpretation and direction of one's religious superiors. As a result, though French alphabet books focused on simple lessons that would teach one to read, they were also intended to teach classification, naming, and morals. The titles and content of these works indicate that the emphasis on social order could be found across the political spectrum. There were republican primers such as *"Elements for a Young Republican . . . in accordance with the National Convention's Decree, to Honor the Supreme Being and Celebrate the Republican Virtues and Feasts."*[26] There were royalist primers, like the *ABC Primer of the History of France, containing, in 70 lessons, excerpts from the reign of France's Kings.*[27] Whether by the words and sentences they chose, such as the Revolutionary "Ad-mi-re the jus-tice and the good-ness of the Sup-reme-Be-ing,"[28] or the Restoration "Ad-ju-di-ca-tion, Be-a-ti-fi-ca-tion, and Fla-gel-la-tion,"[29] the prayers they included, or the illustrations that often accompanied the text, children learned how their society functioned and what their eventual place in the demonstrated order would be.

The process of learning the elementary lessons of ABC primers was equated with learning other social lessons. A popular French proverb expressed this admirably. When one said of someone, "He doesn't know his A, B, C," it could easily be construed as meaning that:

After having received, while young, the elements that no one should ignore, he has been careless or thoughtless enough to forget them completely. For that reason, one has a low opinion of him and says, "He will have to be sent back to A,B,C." This reproach is humiliating, because one doesn't go to school voluntarily when one is young; it is really too late to go there when the time of childhood has passed.[30]

In this contemporary explanation of the role of basic instruction, there was little mention of grammatical knowledge or the obvious components of "schooling," but instead a stress on "education," or proper individual choice and rationality. The interpretation of the proverb also emphasized the difference between adult autonomy or liberty and childhood compulsion. Adults were those who had internalized social mores. Those who had learned primary lessons well functioned freely within their society, and those who had not acted inappropriately. Those who had not developed the proper social behaviors were seen as children, without proper self-control and requiring external control rather than being able to control their own destinies. Thus both children's culture and adult expectations were expressed in French *abécédaires*.[31]

However, since parents were the ones purchasing and using these books to teach their children how to read, the genre's portrayal of education and parental involvement also provides modern readers with as much insight into these parents' intentions and views of the family as it does into what the children actually took away from these lessons. The *Abécédaire Nouveau* provides a typical example. Like much of the genre, this book was dedicated "to tender mothers" and focused on the centrality of maternal involvement in the educational formation of the young.[32] Though alphabets sometimes achieved an authoritative stance when they claimed, "written by a father of a family," men were noticeably absent within the alphabet primer's text. In a Rousseauian fashion, women took their unique authority and close relationship to their children and used it to encourage their offspring to learn their letters while they were still clinging to their mother's skirts.

Love and affection were the catalysts for all good children to motivate themselves to learn the proper social forms. For this reason, primers not only were dedicated to mothers but also presented mothers in pictures, in texts, and in moral lessons that reminded children how central these women were to their very existence. Repayment for this love was expected to come in the form of hard work at one's lessons. Boys and girls who failed to work diligently also failed in their filial duties. As one pedagogue explained, "[t]he course of education . . . only asks, for the schoolchild's part, that he make use of the attachment that he ought to have . . . and [have] a common enough attention to listen to what is said."[33] Obedience was a key indication of a child's devotion to his parents. Parents loved their children enough to take care of them and to give them the lessons that would prepare them to take their place in society. In return for this care, children were to be willing to go where expected, to learn their lessons well, and thereby demonstrate their reciprocal love. This agenda was not hidden. In one engraving, as a young boy held his arms out to his mother, he said, "[m]y little Mama, give your son a hug, he will be very good." She replied, "being good isn't everything; [i]t is still necessary to learn to read."[34] A mother's love might not be wholly predicated on a child's attention to work, but her affections certainly could be, and those affections were central to encouraging children to do their duty and apply themselves with diligence to learning their lessons.

In the cases where these ideals saw actual implementation, the model of a nurturing mother supervising her children's education from their first moments likely belonged to the wealthy elite. Not only were the authors from the aristocracy and the haute bourgeoisie, but it is also clear that such maternal oversight was generally not possible for the lower classes. Additionally, the plan for formation required the mother to have enough education to provide the rudiments of reading, writing, and grammar to her children, which would not have been possible in most working-class families. Even so, similar moral obligations were also proposed in primers intended for use in the public primary schools. In these instances, children were told that they owed the same diligence and attention to their instructors that they would owe to their parents. The moral obligation was the same, though one might imagine that the parents of less privileged children had slightly different educational goals than did the elite mother.

No matter what the class, however, this constant call to duty did not mean that the entire process was intended to be painful or something simply to be endured. Rather, many works, proclaiming themselves as *"Méthode amusante"* or "Amusing and Instructive," betrayed their Enlightenment influences as they assumed, in line with current educational theory, that the child's mind was a blank slate, gaining knowledge through experience and reflection. The argument that children's minds were entirely malleable was picked up by parents and educators and widely disseminated. Parents were encouraged to provide their prerational children with interesting stimuli, helping them learn about society by virtue of their natural desires and filling their minds with things they already recognized, including the qualities necessary for proper adult behavior. In this way, as each child slowly increased in rationality, he would already, by virtue of his mother's diligence and affection, be prepared to become a valuable member of society.

Since mothers used love and good books to shape their children into good citizens, there was an intense focus on the types of literature that might profitably accomplish the dual goals of entertainment and instruction, preparing children for the day when they would make decisions on their own.[35] *Abécédaires* responded to an increasing call for material that would entice children into developing their mental faculties.[36] As one book explained, "[o]f all the *Abécédaires* and *Syllabaires,* the most useful and agreeable for children is, without contradiction, that which offers to their eyes the idea of some existing object."[37] Many included such diverse ingredients as "fables, riddles, poems, maxims, alphabets, moral stories, jokes, and games."[38] Others were structured instead by theme, using such diverse subjects as the professions or natural history to appeal to children's interests. A Revolutionary, promoting the educational ideals of the National Convention, composed one of many republican alphabets, which, much as later royalist compositions, was organized along the following guidelines: "To facilitate my pupil's progress, I simplified all my expressions, particularized all my ideas, gave, in the most short and lucid man-

ner, all necessary definitions, in order to amuse and instruct him."[39] No
matter what political or social agenda one finds in these alphabets, the
varied formats attempted to ensure that all children could find something
to their liking and still learn the lessons that adults, especially mothers,
wished to teach.

All these primers, much as future forms of children's literature, relied
on both punishment and reward to convince children of the need to follow the wisdom of adults and work hard at necessary tasks, the first of
which was the acquisition of enough education to advance to the next
stage of labor, be it more schooling or work in the adult world. ABC
games, rewards for good learning, and a varied format were some of the
carrots. Reminding children of the pitfalls that lay in their path and the
penalties that awaited them if they strayed were just two of the sticks,
present in different proportions for different audiences. With these elements in the literature of the day, children were provided with the material that they needed to learn in order to live successfully in society. Paul
Hazard has argued that this is disingenuous, as if the authors believe that
"to safeguard the sensation of pleasure, to which children are susceptible,
all that is needed is never to pronounce the word 'study.'"[40] However,
even well-to-do children were much closer to the adult world than are
children today. While maxims that urged children to work hard at their
chosen profession or fables that warned them of potential trickery may
seem overly "grown-up" to our modern ears, they were completely appropriate for children that would soon take their place in the real world.
One should not perceive this literature as less appropriate for children or
somehow badly designed because it recognized the exigencies of everyday
life. Rather, we should see these characteristics as precisely where the
strength of this transitional literature lay.

In addition to providing maxims that overtly communicated social values and expectations, the focus and arrangement of *abécédaires* were also
designed to initiate boys and girls into public life. Understanding the social order, as much as obedience, was a primary goal of this education,
and the primer was a perfect place to convey this message. Letters came
from an alphabet, always proceeding in the same order, in both tables and
words. Syllables formed words that could be sounded out and linked together. All these rules were demonstrated with reference to elements of
the physical world; zoology, botany, and geography could all be explored
if a child learned the first lessons well. Pithy adages explained the rules by
which the secular world operated. Children began to learn how to think
rationally and to follow adult paths safely past a variety of pitfalls so that
they might eventually chart their own courses. To this end, ABC primers,
full of maxims and concrete examples, taught little abstraction. Rules existed for the natural world just as they existed for spelling and pronunci-

ation. Though memorizing these rules—no different from following the wishes of one's parents—was the first step to rational behavior, it demonstrated obedience to the wisdom of another and not rational thought of one's own.

Fables and Rational Self-Interest

Though similar to the primer in its encouragement of both order and obedience, the fable explored territory a bit farther from home. Collections of fables became far more than just one of the possible components in the varied primer and were used as beginning books and school texts in their own right. Unlike primers, fables told a story, directing the reader to the proper social and moral interpretation. This allowed more intellectual and personal freedom than simply spelling out the moral message, and yet the lessons were structured in such a way that it was difficult to come to the wrong conclusion. Locke had recommended fables as one of the few truly appropriate forms for the entertainment of a child and the instruction of a future adult,[41] and in France, this inspired the publication of countless editions of *La Fontaine,* not to mention the writing of new fables that would painlessly shape young men and women into the sorts of adults that France needed. Mothers introduced children who had already learned the fundamentals of reading and writing to fables in a much more focused way than before, when children might have encountered an occasional fable in a primer. Now, children even played games with fables to practice their newfound reading and writing skills. Reading fables also provided students with an opportunity to develop and elaborate on the new moral ideas that had been initiated in the *abécédaires.*[42] As one version of Abbé Gaultier's *Amusing and Instructive Conversations for Children,* reprinted in many forms throughout this period, explained:

The merit of this volume of juvenile literature may justly be said to consist in the particular skill with which amusement is made to assist real instruction . . . Whenever the play-learning of infancy is laid aside, for the solid instruction and grounding (as it is not unaptly called) of youth, a wide and fearful leap is found, after all, between the story-book and the grammar; and so absolutely is the work of instruction to begin anew, that, the advantages supposed to be gained by all the previous lessons, at the expense of many cares and sorrows, may be fairly questioned.[43]

Fables provided a middle ground, a transitional area in which children could be taught to discern right from wrong, but within a very limited context. "At the first reading, [the child] may not understand everything right away . . . it is a work for the mind of the child to unravel. One must provide a basic explanation."[44] To that end, the morals of the stories were clear and easy to understand, often provided as an adage at the end of the story. This very clarity meant that children could be led to the proper interpretations essentially on their own. Fables provided a step toward educational autonomy. A step beyond primers, fables allowed children to use their understanding of the world, provided in large part by their earlier experience with primers, to come to the appropriate conclusions about the society and their role in it.

Though fables were rational and thus seen as more immediately appropriate for children than fairy tales, even the fable's educational value came into question. Locke's educational theory, the background for much of the thought behind the explosion of publishing for children, had done more than simply encourage parents to find entertaining subject matter for their children; it also demanded that parents consider the future implications of literature that might be easy enough for children to understand but not proper for their formation.[45] Since sensationalist psychology was founded on the notion of the *tabula rasa,* every bit of material that found its way into children's hands was crucial for their future development. Using this theory, Rousseau turned Locke on his head, attacking the very existence of books for children and asking:

How can people be so blind as to call fables the child's system of morals, without considering that the child is not only amused by the apologue but misled by it? He is attracted by what is false and he misses the truth, and the means adopted to make the teaching pleasant prevent him profiting by it. Men may be taught by fables; children require the naked truth.[46]

Directed abstraction, the very thing that made fables so appealing and appropriate for this stage of life, was the source of Rousseau's complaints. Using popular favorites such as "The Fox and the Crow," and "The Ant and Grasshopper," he explained his belief that children would place themselves in the position of the powerful characters and thus miss the point their parents and tutors wished to teach, learning instead how to be immoral. For example, in the story of the proud crow tricked by the greedy fox into dropping his cheese, Rousseau claimed that children would wish to be the fox, so that they might gain the cheese, thus learning "the basest flattery" instead of humility. In another attack, Rousseau focused on the grasshopper that played and sang while the ant worked, and who died in the winter cold when the ant refused his request for shelter. Rousseau protested, "But what a dreadful lesson for children! There could be no monster more detestable than a harsh and avaricious child, who realized what he was asked to give and refused. The ant does more; she teaches him not merely to refuse but to revile."[47] In the end, Rousseau decided that it was "just as well that they do not understand, for the morality of the fables is so mixed and so unsuitable for their age that it would be more likely to incline them to vice than to virtue."[48] That is why his Emile would be exposed to no books until his moral character was already more fully formed and able to withstand these pernicious influences. In Rousseau's plan, once the child could read, he would be limited to *Robinson Crusoe*, a perfect tale for demonstrating autonomous behavior. Rousseau was not opposed to allowing freedom to young children, but he did not believe that the fable was an appropriate tool for guiding them toward virtuous autonomy.

Though Rousseau's *Emile* had great influence in many ways, his success in convincing children's writers of the danger inherent in fables and other reading material was rather limited. Not a single author or editor of fables replied to the issue at the heart of Rousseau's criticisms, and they continued to publish in great numbers fables intended for children. And how could they have changed their course? The slightly more abstract fable was a useful step in forming young minds that were able to discern the good from the bad and to draw proper lessons from a well-directed tale. As one author explained in his preface, fables had always been looked upon as a system of morality, adapted to the capacity of children. If Plato had recommended Aesop's fables be consumed along with mother's milk, who was he to countermand that authority?[49] While Rousseau's tutor could lead his pupil into well-chosen examples of virtue and vice— fables in action—and guide him to make the proper response, mothers found it more practical to use Aesop and *La Fontaine* to provide moral guidance apart from domestic life.

The fact that parents and writers continued to value fables should not be taken as a sign that they were unaware of Rousseau's critique of the genre, for the collections included explicit responses to the particular vices that Rousseau had singled out for comment in his attacks on fables. Often the editorial response meant leaving the specific offenders, such as "The Fox and the Crow," out of later compilations, though "The Ant and the Grasshopper" remained, with the text unchanged.[50] Editors had their own ways of coming to terms with Rousseau's criticisms, depending on their personal views. The more conservative response, as one can easily imagine, defended the moral of this fable by excusing the ant's behavior. After all, the grasshopper's lack of self-control was something to be condemned explicitly! Along these lines, with Abbé Gaultier's *Jeu de Fables*, in which children won tokens for the proper responses, parents and tutors learned how to teach children the proper responses to Rousseauian criticisms of the ant's behavior, for a grand total of three counters, the most possible for any one response. The proper sequence of questions and answers was as follows:

Q. To whom can one compare this grasshopper?
A. Those who prefer the pleasure of the moment to their happiness to come. (1 token)
Q. To whom can one compare the ant?
A. To the farsighted people that take all measures to avoid ever falling into indigence. (2 tokens)
Q. Do you excuse the uncharitable refusal of this ant?
A. Yes, because one does not provide help gladly to those that have encountered misfortune through their own mistakes. (3 tokens.)[51]

On the other hand, by way of concession, the revolutionary *Fablier des Enfans* included an author's note that urged charity: "The author, though finishing with this moral: ['you sang . . . now dance!'], has as the only goal of his fable to prove the necessity of work; In reading the other fables, one will become convinced that it is far from his intention to insult poor persons, even if the indigence follows as a result of their idleness."[52] Similarly, Laurent de Jussieu's collection included a newly written fable in which the ant who rejected the grasshopper's pleas received a reprimand for her behavior. In this new version, a pheasant destroyed the anthill and all of its inhabitants, forcing the ant to ask for shelter from a bee, who responded, "What would you do, I beg you, if, like you, today I was insensible and proud; if I were to invite you to walk or to sing? But reassure yourself, my dear; come in, eat at your leisure, use my things as your own. And above all, in the future, learn to sympathize with the miseries of others."[53] In this way, the forward-thinking ant was given an instructive lesson: that one can never know what help one may need or who might provide it, so it would pay to be prudent. All of these collections, no matter when they were published or what their social biases were, left the fable of "The Ant and the Grasshopper" untouched. Some, depending on their particular focus, encouraged charitable behavior, but none of them was willing to discount the importance of work and self-control, both of which were central themes.

While Rousseau might use his personal tutor to inculcate self-control, parents continued to believe that these stories would help their children to grow in virtue, especially the autonomous practice of self-control. Fables from many different authors used other animals and things from the natural world to convey the absolute necessity of dominating one's impulses. Mice that enjoyed rich feasts but failed to provide for scarcity starved to death, a gorilla that was unwilling to work at opening a nut did not get to enjoy its tasty center, and favored and lazy pigs became bacon. The morals of these fables help to explain why most authors felt free to bypass Rousseau's criticism of abstraction. In practice, the fable was far more concrete than conceptual. Instead of relying on the force of parents and other adults for punishment, nature herself provided examples of virtue rewarded (or at the very least, vice punished). And if animals with human characteristics failed to make the point clear enough, lazy, prideful, and otherwise vice-ridden children and adults were also targeted. Boys who chose golden oranges tasted their bitter, unripe fruit, girls who tried to catch bees for honey got stung, and adults who preferred flowers to food crops starved to death.

In at least one sense, then, Rousseau was right; the fables did not encourage children to think virtuously but instead appealed to their self-interest and practical desires for survival. In these fables, material gain accompanied virtuous action and unearned riches were the quickest path to a prideful fall. Children were taught, again and again, that good behavior was not its own reward but instead the surest direction for worldly success. If they failed to see this point in the fables themselves, the *jeux de fables* would make the point more overtly. When a child correctly interpreted the moral of the story, he could win one token—more, if the moral was particularly complex or important. The counters were themselves tied to a reward system: words of praise, titles of importance (the winner for the day was the leader—"President"—for the next session), and small trinkets were all possible rewards for the child who had best internalized the social lessons inherent in the story of the day. What were these social lessons? As we have already seen, one of the primary lessons throughout the period was self-discipline, especially the importance of overcoming one's natural desires and instead behaving according to what would be best in the long term. In the fables, those who worked ended up happiest. Tortoises with families had to labor to find food for their young but were provided for in their old age, while the lone cuckoo that sang all day found itself alone at the end. The pig who, unlike all of the other farm animals, had no work to do other than eat, ended up as slabs of meat in the farmer's shed. If even the animals, whether dead or alive, could measure their worth in terms of social utility, how much more necessary was labor for humans!

In the revolutionary period, fables also taught lessons of social equality. For example, in a fable from Year VIII, Fanfan, son of wealthy parents, spent his first few years raised as milk brother to Colas, the son of Perette, his wet-nurse. After Fanfan returned home, Colas came to visit.

After Fanfan had played for a time, Colas said, "It is my turn." But Fanfan was no longer his brother; Fanfan found him presumptuous. Fanfan repulsed him with a proud and·mutinous air. Then Perette took Colas by the hand. "See," she said sadly, "Fanfan has become a great lord. Come, my son, you did not please his heart. Friendship disappears where equality ends."[54]

To make the moral clearer, the author provided a sequel to the fable. Fan-fan's mother, seeing that he was becoming proud and haughty, told him that there had been a mistake and that he was actually Perette's son while Colas was hers. She dressed Fanfan in rough clothes, called him by Colas's name and pretended to send him away. She said,

> Colas, you despised my son and your mother;
> You treated those in misery harshly,
> To subsist, to be obliged to serve:
> You are going to learn to pity them.
> You see that at the breast of happiness,
> Returns of fate are to be feared . . .[55]

Fables like these taught lessons about class position. Not only was there overt sympathy for those of lesser means, but also implicit criticism of a system in which birth provided the sole determination of future social standing. Perhaps most important, when Fanfan's mother called Colas her son and Perette the mother of her natural son, she placed the wet-nurse on a par with herself not only socially but also morally. Fanfan was crit-icized because he allowed himself to feel superior and ignored his obliga-tion to society as a whole. In this fable, the mother recognized her child's faults and acted to correct them. She, like the woman who refused to hug her son until he worked hard, refused to mother a child who had not yet internalized lessons in the new social order. Despite the fact that she was wealthy, Fanfan's mother guaranteed that Fanfan would not be corrupted and that he would instead become a full participant in the new society.

Other fables by other authors offered stories with a similar perspective on social roles. In one, a boy looked out from the top of a bell tower and felt pride at seeing everything so small beneath him. His teacher, seeing him so proud at being up high, gave him advice. "If fortune ever places you in an elevated station, remember the small accident that saved you."[56] If experience was the key to development, these fables would reshape chil-dren's perspectives on hierarchy, equality, and social position. The fable that best reflected this vision of equality told a story of canaries and a goldfinch. Much like the ugly duckling, the goldfinch was raised by a fam-ily of canaries. Unlike the swan that grew into a beauty, however, the goldfinch remained plain and out of place in the canary family. Despite that, the canaries accepted him as one of their own. When a jealous goldfinch tried to tell him that he didn't belong and pointed out his dif-ferences, the adopted bird simply claimed allegiance to his new family and explained that his origins were less important than the role that the canaries played in his life. Accidents of birth could never be as important as the bond of brothers.

It is not surprising that revolutionary fables reminding children of the value of freedom accompanied those that focused on equality. It was far better to live a humble life alone than to live in a palace as a slave to another, the fables taught. Escaped birds refused to return to their gilded cages, children's parents explained the cruelty of keeping animals captive for human pleasures, and everywhere there was rejoicing that the French had realized that men's worth was not a condition of their birth and that no person could have absolute power over another. In a note to one of La-Fontaine's fables featuring a slave, the editor rejoiced, "[i]n France, we do not know this unhappy condition that puts a man under the absolute power of another man."[57]

Of course, the emphasis on freedom and equality, celebrated during the revolutionary years, was tempered under the Restoration. With an ambiguity that remained in collections throughout the early part of the nineteenth century, fables reminded children that self-interest often was not served by social advancement. While the morals of fables still decried the futility of taking pride in one's social position, children were told that, accident or not, one's station in life was fixed, and success was not synonymous with a higher or more leisurely position. The dog who left certain prey to chase a shadow, the blue jay who decorated himself with peacock feathers, and the donkey pretending to be a lion, all were examples of those who tried to rise above their station and abilities and ended up less fortunate than they would have been if they had remained where they were. If the squirrel, happy and self-sufficient before he was tempted to enter the farmer's home and taste new delicacies, died in a trap, how equally unhappy would artisans and bourgeois be who climbed above their station in life? Self-interest was acceptable; social climbing was not. If the squirrel fable was not a clear enough analogy, one could read on to learn about the very different lives of two horses. The first worked hard all his life for a farmer and was eventually retired out to a beautiful pasture. The second was purchased by a prince. It first lived a life of luxury, but soon broke its leg while high stepping in a parade and died a painful death. The lesson made it clear that it was better to have a profitable and menial position than to lose everything in an attempt at glory. However, messages of equality remained present in children's literature and conflicted with the reinforcement of hierarchy, making it difficult for children to come away with a clear picture of anything except the ambiguous position of social roles in the Restoration. During the Revolution, fables encouraged children to think of themselves as free and equal, with clear obligations to society as a whole. Under the Restoration, the same types of stories taught that, while social rank was, in and of itself, nothing of importance, one should be happy with one's lot in life. In much the same manner as their fathers might claim political autonomy while supporting the Charter, Restoration children could recognize that their social rank did not determine their personal worth but was still a fixed entity.

The seeming contradictions between Revolutionary and Restoration messages about social standing underscore the importance of fables for teaching children how to live in their societies. The messages provided by the different fables met prevailing needs and expectations, allowing children to develop their own—socially sanctioned—understanding of the world that surrounded them. Fables were important because they allowed children to internalize important civic lessons and use their new knowledge to make increasingly autonomous decisions of which society would approve. And, across the board, even when they wanted to be selfish, childish readers learned that they would be happiest when they acted in accordance with social expectations. Like women who learned that virtuous childcare would also benefit the mother, children learned that free choices could be self-controlled and self-interested at the same time.

Didactic Tales Offer Order in Context

As the ideologies surrounding childhood changed, even the specific lessons of fables came to be insufficient for educating children to adulthood. In the nineteenth century, more and more girls learned how to read, and the education of both sexes became a rising focus of attention. As the audience for children's books came to include an ever-larger contingent of girls, writers began to respond to the need for appropriate general texts that would not only encourage self-control and social awareness but also emphasize the gender distinctions increasingly central to existing in an adult world. Unlike fables and ABC primers, which had long existed in various forms for adults as well as children, these new books were directed toward children from the beginning, and aimed at moral instruction that began where the fables left off: with duty, self-control, and moral development. If the ABC primer taught children simple lessons and introduced them to order, and the fable, when appropriate, taught them how to use their acquired knowledge to extrapolate to general social concerns, didactic tales gave them "real life" situations in which they could see the pitfalls and possibilities that awaited them and how they could best respond in order to succeed.

Like fables, these tales strayed from the philosophical outline of Rousseau's education for Emile. Their moral schemes relied on providing books for children as young as five or six, much younger than Rousseau's ideal. Even so, one can still see Rousseau's influence throughout, not only in a frequent description of the child as naturally good and spoiled only through improper adult intervention, but also in the very program of the

French didactic authors. They, like Rousseau, were striving for "well-conditioned liberty," and though books took the place of tutors, the stories they provided attempted to maintain discipline through natural consequences, and rather than simply prohibiting behavior, they tried to show the negative impacts of following the wrong path so that children would make good choices on their own. Even more clearly than with fables and *abécédaires*, the popular moralistic stories portrayed naughty children and nice children, all of whom naturally received the appropriate payment for their actions. Bette Goldstone explains, "[t]hrough the characters and plot, the child reader learned about the ramifications of one's actions. He not only was taught the expected mores and behavior of his society, but the reason why it was so important to adhere and conform to these rules. These lessons were taught very directly; not through the homilies of the adults, but through the child characters' own words and deeds."[58] Readers of the didactic tales were to internalize the protagonist's experiences as if they were their own. The moral tale thus fit into the type of education advocated for mothers in advice manuals, as the examples of the stories would help alleviate the tension between demanding obedience and forming a child into a rational and free being.

In addition to being written by women and intended for women's use with their children, moral tales were particularly appropriate reading material for girls. In Sophie Renneville's *Correspondence of Two Little Girls* (1811), the thirteen-year-old protagonist, Caroline Lamercier, told her parents that Madame Hortense, echoing Rousseau, "does not want to let us learn the Fables of *La Fontaine;* she says that this reading is more appropriate to grown-ups, and that children should not hear them at all."[59] Since Mme Hortense was the Lemerciers' choice to reform their inattentive and otherwise wayward daughter, this was not offered as a criticism of Mme Hortense's educational method and was in fact accepted without comment in any of the answering letters. Mme Hortense could not have been a complete Rousseauian insofar as reading material was concerned, for she did permit other books to Caroline and the girls, with sections of Racine appearing in the same letter as the anti–*La Fontaine* message. Making the author's stance on fables seem even more ambiguous, at the same time that Caroline was reading Racine in lieu of *La Fontaine,* another member of the Lamercier family, Caroline's younger brother, Charles, had spent his study time at home memorizing fables. He wrote her to "tell you that I love you and that I am going to become scholarly. I already know by heart a few fables of [the Roman fabulist] Phaedrus."[60] Thus, the *Correspondence of Two Little Girls* offered its readers a moral tale in which fables were decried as inappropriate for the education of girls but perfect for a "scholarly" boy.

Indeed, if he wanted to succeed academically, there was no better place for Charles to start than with fables, since this form of literature was still a staple of classical education. In another didactic story, Raphaël Servas, son of a bourgeois woman fallen on hard times, was taught fables when he obtained a scholarship to study at Louis-le-Grand, and by 1830, newly prosperous artisans who aspired to be well-rounded might well have memorized a few of these stories.[61] The difference between the education of Caroline and that of Charles had far more to do with the social expectations related to gender than with the fables themselves. Most fables, no matter who authored or edited them, were not expressly designed to teach girls how to influence their families and the world, and thus they were not entirely appropriate and, in certain contexts, even provided cause for some concern. Fables and other "masculine" stories could do Charles no harm. If he ended up being a scholar, an attorney, a business-man, or even an artisan, the fables would provide him with a secular moral guide that encouraged him to work hard, behave scrupulously, and look after his own interests. Charles, like Raphaël Servas, would enter so-ciety, and the fables could both amuse and instruct to that eventual end. The guidance of the moral tale could also provide direction as the boys made their own way in the world.

However, Caroline was sent away to school so that she might become more obedient and of greater service to her mother in the domestic realm. As she explained to a friend, "You know why I am here; it is not to my credit: if I had been gentle and wise like you, mama would have kept me close to her at home."[62] Because of her inability to follow her mother's di-rections and to curb her impulsive actions, Caroline was sent away to school to learn self-control. The Lemerciers expected that once Caroline was removed from her family surroundings, she would work harder at being the responsible young woman that they expected her to be. She would then be allowed to return home, never again forced to leave the family where she ultimately belonged. Caroline's education was designed to prepare her for domestic life, by making her into an autonomous woman who could exercise control of herself without relying on social disapproval for a consequence.

Separation from family and society as a whole was not an uncommon method for curing girls whose parents could not persuade them to re-form. In *Little Stories and Tales for My Little Girl and My Little Boy* (1821), Elvira, "the young bluestocking," constantly interrupted adults and corrected them. Eventually, her fault became so well known that friends of her parents told her they would never accept another social in-vitation or come back to the house because she was so abrasive. They even added that, if they met her in public, they would excuse themselves from her presence. Finally, her parents, realizing that they could not have a daughter who was so odious, sent Elvira off to the country to live with only a stuttering, half-deaf maid until she corrected this fault. Elvira soon recognized the error of her ways. As if the reader could miss the point, the narrator explained that "[i]t was necessary to obey and to correct herself, unless she wished to expose herself to the possibility of passing all her life in seclusion. Elvira converted herself in the following manner: First by necessity, then by benefitting from her mother's advice, the reading of good books, and experience."[63] Protagonists like Elvira and Caroline were sent away to reform, with only other women and good didactic stories for company. While going off to school was an indicator of advancement for young boys, this was not the case for girls. While boys might be naturally disciplined by the ridicule of their classmates or the misadventures that befell them, girls were corrected in ways that underlined how important it was for them to learn autonomous self-control.

These differences underline the female need for and desire to return to the family surroundings, but they also make it clear that female society was not "separate" from public life in the way that is so often imagined. Girls were punished by removal from the sphere where they could have autonomy. In this way, women's "natural" place might have been in private life, but as Rebecca Rogers would have it, these stories demonstrate the ways "this vocabulary represented something different for these women than for us today: when they redefined women's place within private life, they located political, social, and cultural influence within families that defined the characteristics of public life."[64] Elvira and Caroline were *punished* with seclusion and isolation; separation from all public life was clearly unnatural for girls as well as boys. Only girls who were unable to be properly sociable were removed from society entirely, and this was clearly not their "natural" place in life. In fact, the very emphasis on a girl's separation from others as a punishment reveals a dynamic in which women were expected to play a social role, because the means of reform was removal from human society, as represented by the girls' families.

The stories demonstrate that the question driving these educational works was not whom women would influence but how they would choose the proper moral direction. Girls, even when sent away, did not belong in public life, but in the bosom of their families, where they could be instructed until they were adult enough to assume responsibility for themselves and to influence their own families positively, as mothers. That did not necessarily mean that, in general, girls should have no education at all, but it did mean that the education they received and the books they read ought to be tailored to their future roles as wives and mothers. As Hubert Wandelaincourt, a pedagogue from the early nineteenth century, explained, an improper education would leave girls unable to "contribute to the reformation of manners, to the happiness and the glory of families. We should instead provide the proper aids to perfect themselves, those

necessary to their happiness and ours. If we abandoned them to themselves, could we complain of the bad result, following inevitably from this
abandonment?"[65] For a feminine education, moralistic plays, stories, and
devotional literature were clearly most appropriate, as they provided the
best examples of women's ideal role: domestic and freely self-controlling.
As one of her friend's mothers wrote to Caroline, "[i]t is not natural that
you should do as you wish at your [advanced] age, with a strong will such
as you have, and at the homes of people who have been directed to supervise your actions and to repress the exuberance of your character."[66]

Feminine self-control was emphasized in the stories that featured girls.
As Alphonsine, who tended to fly into a fury at the least provocation, was
told in "Alphonsine, the Angry Young Girl," "[w]omen, my niece, are
only interesting, loved, and respected insofar as their actions, their words,
and their gestures are in harmony with the gentleness of their features and
the natural sweetness of their sex. Women who have been raised well
should never abandon the shyness and modesty that is their seductive
lot."[67] Once Uncle held up a mirror and Alphonsine could see how dis-
figuring her anger made her, she quickly reformed, vowing to never again
lose control of her temper. Alphonsine, Elvira, Caroline, and the countless others like them were guilty of the fault of not adequately controlling
their passions. Only when they heeded the words of the adults around
them (usually mothers and mother figures) and chose to sacrifice their interests and desires did they become characters worthy of emulation. One
author remarked, "[t]he outcome of this Tale only serves morality, by the
pleasure or pain that the heros and/or heroines . . . feel, depending on
whether or not they have obeyed or disobeyed their parents!"[68] With
statements like this, it will likely come as no shock to discover that all of
these stories were full of rather one-dimensional characters: naughty children and nice children, with bad girls disobeying parents, coveting the
treasures of their friends, or falling prey to greedy whims. Good girls
stayed close to their mothers, sewed clothing for the poor, and generally
prepared for the day when they would run homes of their own. Punishment and reward were quite prominent in the lessons, with bad children
who failed to change their ways soon meeting a bad end of their own
making.[69] Greedy girls stuck their hands in boiling jam and got severely
burned or fell deathly ill from overindulgence. Vain daughters contracted
smallpox, losing both beauty and suitors in the process. If the fruits of
such disobedience did not kill, they generally converted the child to good
behavior ever after.

On the other hand, as with the women's advice manuals and Rousseau's advice to Emile, this literature recognized that a free choice to exercise self-control might also work toward one's self-interest. Doing
what society expected could involve more than emotional pleasure, for

there was often a material reward for the girls who did what was expected and met their responsibilities. Well-behaved girls found good matches and, if poor, were often rescued from their distress by someone sympathetic to their plight. As the popular didactic author Sophie Renneville explained: "I tried to prove, by this *draft* on education, that the misleading entertainments of pride are not happiness, and that prudence alone, which avoids [such amusements], can attract the esteem of good people and fix one's fortune."[70] Boys, women, and girls would all benefit from choosing the right thing, even if it took self-control to make the right decisions in the face of temptation. In short, didactic tales taught girls to suppress their own passions and desires so that they might become autonomous within the sphere of their own home, in order to shape the generations to come and to themselves prosper. Rather than a potentially ambiguous moral instruction, such stories provided concrete examples to guide children along the path to adulthood and linked proper choices to social success.

The important role that the properly educated and educating woman could play in the development of her family, and by extension, in her autonomous entry into society, is one of the salient characteristics of moral literature in this period. Girls, unlike boys, were expected to remain in the realm of the family and under the tutelage of adults. However, once girls learned the appropriate lessons, they replicated their mothers' accomplishments, moving into adulthood and the public eye in ways not immediately expected of the boys their age still playing in the schoolyard and relying on their schoolmates for reminders of improper behavior. Like Sophie, who became the governor of Emile, girls who mastered their passions and desires were in fact more adult than the boys their age because they had already learned how to control themselves for the good of others—and for their own benefit, too.

Learning to read and write, memorizing facts and figures, as boys did, was not without its place, but girls who understood the necessity of caring for others could do more than transform themselves; they could change the people around them. As Claudine Coeurderoy, a mother, explained in the year X, if she had to choose between domestic education and school learning, it would be no choice:

My child, schooling is useful, I have no doubt of it; but that which it does best for women is to occupy them in their private time; it is truly rare for [schooling] to help us in society; it is only in intimate settings that we can make it appear; however, gentleness, this agreeable and touching virtue that makes us avoid hurting people, either by our words or our actions, helps us to endure the moral and physical shortcomings of others; and by that, makes us loved in society. What a difference, my child![71]

Girls were asked to make a choice between concern for their immediate pleasure or the long-term welfare of society, including themselves. They were promised autonomy and success—including love—if they made the proper decisions. This quotation makes it explicitly clear that schooling or instruction for women was primarily applicable to the individual and private life, but a woman's moral education would allow her to enter onto the civic stage. Because women had the ability to transform children and to guide families, they played an independent role by which their influence extended far beyond the family.

And, just as there was a difference between male and female sociability in the didactic novels, so too, it was expected that men and women would play different social roles. Properly educated women would raise a generation of virtuous boys and girls, transforming their society even as they trained their children. This message clearly followed the same line of reasoning as Rousseau's work, which argued that all virtuous citizens should be independent of "public" expectations in order to develop their virtue. As in *Emile,* didactic novels described the ways in which women had the central responsibility for forming society. Once a girl accepted her role in the family, she was initiated into that society, learning how to cook, clean, and support her mother (or direct servants) in the myriad daily tasks around the house. Only mothers who themselves understood the importance of self-control and selflessness would be able to teach their children the importance of those qualities in adult life. As Sophie Renneville explained, didactic tales thus gave a lesson to mothers as well: "Control your morals; your girls will be virtuous; shape their characters to yours; know the power of example."[72] Mothers who stayed close to home and supervised the raising of their children would be rewarded not only by the esteem of others and their own success but also by the moral behavior of their offspring. As one writer explained, echoing the book of Proverbs, a virtuous woman "forms the mind of her children to accept wisdom, and her example ensures the proper morality. Her speech is the law of their youth; one look from her is an order for their obedience."[73] Women might be expected to control their passions, but by doing so, they could also exert considerable influence over their children and their futures, and that message was delivered time and again in didactic tales.

One might think, then, that these books were not appropriate for boys, since their primary messages often seemed directed at girls. However, this was not true. Though authors claimed that fables were inappropriate for girls and some collections of didactic stories were also designed specifically for girls, most didactic tales were intended for children of both sexes, since all children needed to develop autonomous self-control. Collections of moral tales bore such titles as *Stories and Advice to My Young Children, Appropriate to the First Childhood of Both Sexes,* or *The*

Evenings of Adolescence, or Funny Adventures, Told by a Group of Young Children of Two Sexes. If Amy was lazy, Cherie was a glutton, and Césarine was vain, then César was a coward and George played instead of studying. Like girls, boys also had faults that should be corrected and merits that could be emulated. Amédée, who was overly proud of his royal heritage and complained about being called by his first name by his social inferiors, received a stern talking-to from the officials at his school. Since he respected their opinion, he realized the error of his ways and worked to gain the friendship of all those he had spurned.[74] Prosper, like Caroline, lacked discipline. Because he did not like to work and frequently skipped school, his father threatened to beat him, so Prosper ran away. But as he had no money and no skills, he almost starved and was nearly killed by dishonest travelers on his way to his uncle in Paris. The narrow escape from death reformed him and he devoted himself to hard work and honest behavior for the rest of his life.[75]

Didactic stories even offered themselves as the instruments of salvation. One man, in his attempt to save a little boy who was going bad, explained that, "[i]n spite of a terrible education, I learned to read, to write and even to count a bit. I read a number of moral stories, where, by lively and natural examples, the author proved that in spite of all sorts of impediments, one can always make himself happy with patience, courage, and confidence in God. It is probably these good readings that sustained me in all the tests of my life."[76] The fact that didactic stories were far more self-referential than fables or primers demonstrates in a concrete way the increasing trend toward autonomy. Though ideally all children would have mothers to serve as moral examples, even those children with a "terrible education" might be able, with the help of "good readings," to learn self-control. Even didactic stories, with their clear morals and their ability to help children make the transition to adult life, could provide enough guidance for children to become productive members of society. Even if it was not the ideal, it clearly points toward the increasing emphasis on independent thought as children progressed toward adulthood.

Because moral stories had saved him, this man, the Père Lajeunesse, in turn saved both a boy and a girl. "The little boy became an attorney like his father; the young lady married M. de Vesselmond, a rich and well-respected magistrate."[77] Both the girl and boy became successes in symptomatic ways; the boy became an upstanding member of society and the girl became the wife of someone like her brother. That is not to say that girls' qualities were only relative to those of their spouses. Whether a boy or a girl was the central character, some values remained constant throughout. Self-discipline was featured such that truthful, obedient, and good-natured children were always rewarded, and both sexes provided examples of lying, spiteful, or selfish children.[78] Still, good boys were not obliging and gentle but courageous and prudent; bad boys were not vain or frivolous but prideful, lazy, or selfish. Perhaps most important, unlike the girls in didactic tales, boys often found themselves corrected when classmates mocked their actions or made them see the error of their ways. While girls were intended for a life where they would exercise influence from inside the family and accordingly learned their lessons from parental chastisement or the natural results of their actions, boys were to be concerned additionally with the esteem of people outside their homes, and these stories reflected that difference.

This did not mean that books had to be marketed to different audiences. While some books were specifically sold "for the education of girls," many more were intended for both boys and girls, because any child could read a story and learn appropriate values from it. Even when the story centered on a value that was "gendered," such as vanity (typically considered to be a feminine fault), both male and female children could learn from the story because it contextualized gendered behavior in addition to universal concerns. Unlike primers and fables, which made general appeals not only to order and obedience but also to self-interest, didactic stories helped children to mold themselves and their behavior according to the proper social context. Boys and girls each had both universal and gender-specific virtues and responsibilities, and learning about the education of the other would only reinforce proper ideas of hierarchy and order.

To a modern eye, the morals taught in the didactic tales often differ little from those in the fables. Punishment and reward were still prominent in the lessons, with bad children who failed to change their ways soon meeting a bad end of their own making. Frugality and hard work were prized, and lack of charity and thrift remained traits of a wayward child who refused to exhibit self-control. However, unlike the more diffuse lessons of the primer and the fable, didactic stories taught their lessons in context. Children learned that obedient girls sewed and embroidered and became mothers, while naughty boys were lazy and gluttonous and disobedient. The first group prospered, finding favor with their mamas and papas and recognition within the story. The latter group either repented or found themselves duly punished as a result of their bad actions. The education of children, like that of mothers, emphasized difference even as it promised rewards for its universal demands of self-control and expected that women would contribute to the transformation of society. Certainly, since grown-ups were expected to be self-disciplined, part of the process of becoming an adult was learning the boundaries of polite social behavior. Self-controlled boys and girls could become men and women who were not only free but also poised to change the world.

Didactic Stories, Domesticity, and Childhood

Didactic stories did more than increase the emphasis on gender. Their format and message also bore the imprint of new ideas about parenting and the nature of the individual, as they demonstrated new assumptions about childhood. Parents and educators adjusted the existing methods of value transmission in childhood education. Now, rather than a potentially ambiguous moral instruction, parents chose concrete exemplars to guide their children along their gendered paths to adulthood. When the mother offered an ideal beginning by providing the affection and nurturing that would inspire the emulation of virtue, the didactic tale offered an intermediate step, as Rousseau's tutor provided in later childhood, a step toward independent rationality. After affection and physical freedom had set the stage for independent mental judgment, literature directed the children's learning by demonstrating appropriate social roles for newly rational children and leading them to proper conclusions and behavior on their own.

As children made the transition from secluded home lives to lives with a greater social impact, be it as "public" males or "private" females, the new forms continued to shape young men and women. And yet, despite the fact that girls' educations were, according to this form, explicitly limited to the bounds of the family, the same rhetoric of affection and control made them the center of the new society and expected independent behavior from each of them as well. Just as clothing offered young children physical freedom and affectionate nurturing paved the way for early engagement with the world, the didactic tale encouraged older children to learn on their own and explore territory a bit farther afield from the nuclear family. Now that affection and physical freedom had laid the groundwork, boys and girls were ready to become responsible and civic adults through their own demonstrations of self-control.

CHAPTER FIVE

Education and Politics

Schooling, Revolution, and Rousseau

Public education is a duty of society to its citizens.   —Condorcet (1791)

Education, not God, is the source of grace.
                                —J. A. Passmore, *The Perfectibility of Man* (1970)

Public Instruction and Maternal Authority

*D*espite Enlightenment philosophers' widespread concern with education writ large, in France, eighteenth-century cultural changes remained
within the purview of the domestic sphere. Though Enlightenment
thinkers like Diderot, d'Alembert, and Voltaire disagreed with both
Church and State on the methods of instruction, with few exceptions,
philosophical ideas about schooling remained heavily theoretical and
could not be implemented within the existing educational system. Certainly, nurturing concern became a higher priority for mothers. However,
neither philosophers nor members of the government implemented instructional change on a national level, and as we saw in previous chapters, only the ideas about physical and maternal education of children had
a widespread intellectual and cultural impact.[1] Schooling from the Revolution onward, however, saw a break with this trend. During the French
Revolution, philosophical musings on education took an ever more practical turn, with legislative plans of all sorts proposed for the edification of
children and the advancement of all. The Revolutionary agenda, unlike
the Enlightenment one, often focused on legislating public instruction
precisely because revolutionaries, following the *philosophes*, argued that
the proper education of a citizenry was necessary for a republican state

and that new forms of instruction should be a central component in raising children. Though Rousseau's tutor in *Emile* would have been heartily opposed to an increase in governmental control of education, his assertion that social reform could not be founded on institutional changes seemed to be a minority view. The government continued to emphasize public instruction and, by 1833, Prime Minister François Guizot even persuaded the government to pass a law requiring every commune to have a public school. As more and more people accepted the idea that education could have radically transformative properties that would be extended into society, they also came to believe that schooling young children was a prerequisite for an educated citizenry.

It might seem that this increasing emphasis on public instruction was intended to replace the domestic mother's authority or remove her even further from influencing public life. Certainly, the literature on increasing demands for elementary schooling during and after the Revolution has seen the emphasis on public education as the primary means of building civic character and changing the nation.[2] And yet, historians have missed the fact that both educational literature and legislative debates emphasizing instruction and schooling continued to be premised on the importance of domestic women and a mother's role as the moral educator of her very young children.[3] "In the *Social Contract*," Mira Morgenstern writes, "Rousseau calls the family 'the first model of political societies.'"[4] Mothers were central to public life and, except in the most radical revolutionary plans, were not supposed to be displaced by public instruction but were to provide the moral foundation for children to enter the schoolroom for practical and continued civic education. As Louis-Aimé Martin, a disciple of Rousseau who taught at the Ecole Polytechnique, explained in the 1830s:

Good teachers make good scholars, but it is only mothers that form men; this constitutes all the difference of their mission; it follows that the care of educating the child belongs altogether to the mother, and that if it has been usurped by men, it is because education has been confused with instruction—things essentially different, and between which it is important to make the distinction, for instruction may be interrupted, and pass without danger into other hands; but education should be continued by the same person.[5]

Maternal education remained a necessary foundation for children's development and was not to be displaced by schooling.

It is true that mothers were not to instruct their children in public life, but they had not, after all, been the primary instructors of their children in the eighteenth century, either. Although public instruction provided training in civic virtue, basic moral and physical instruction were now, in variance from previous centuries, the almost-undisputed domain of the mother. As a result, the shift to an increasing emphasis on public instruction should be seen on a trajectory similar to the advice surrounding swaddling. Once adoption of the new domestic ideal became—at least theoretically—commonplace, there was far less need to continue to emphasize demands for change. In this context, Lynn Hunt's criticism that, "[f]or all their supposed interest in education, officials said little about how the psychology or personality of children figured in the republican order, imagining them as entirely malleable material,"[6] makes more sense. Educational theorists and legislators said little about the children themselves in the context of the school because mothers were already to have done the work of writing on the blank slates. Once mothers changed the hearts of children, then instructors would need only to change their methods in order to continue the perfection of the nation. It was not that domestic life stood apart from the demands for a modern society or could be shunted aside in favor of schooling but instead that the nurturing domestic mother existed as the foundation for public instruction.

While the French revolutionaries often claimed to follow Rousseau's lead and could be found citing the *Social Contract* or the *Discourse on the Origins of Inequality, Emile* was a less frequent presence in their political language. As a result, some readers may question the claim that Rousseau's civic imagination, and the eventual demand for public instruction that arose from his vision, was characteristic of an intellectual and cultural ideal premised on a nurturing domestic education. Others may find it implausible that legislators and theorists who wished to effect political change based their changes on domestic ideologies that existed, at least theoretically, entirely apart from the political world they inhabited. I do not wish to argue that *Emile* was the sole or primary source of Revolutionary proposals, educational or otherwise. However, this chapter demonstrates some concrete ways that increasing political demands for public instruction dovetailed with cultural and intellectual trends emphasizing domestic education, and highlighted women's influence rather than limiting it.

Decentralized Education Shifts to Public Instruction

In a very general way, French kings had concerned themselves with the state of schooling in France long before the revolution. For example, there had been *Déclarations du Roi* in 1698 and 1724 that required children to attend Catholic schools until the age of fourteen. Despite this official requirement, no state monies were provided to make the requirement become a reality, and local resources were often sadly lacking. With no enforcement and little funding, it seems that the *déclarations* were intended to serve as a defense of the Catholic faith and were not serious attempts by the state to direct or control education.[7] Additionally, the Enlightenment saw much discussion of education and schooling, like those outlined in chapter 1, but very few demands for or attempts at concrete action. Public schooling was neither in widespread demand nor of great interest to the state before this era; the Revolutionary period marked one of the first concerted efforts by the French state to intervene in schooling. While the educational plans, treatises, and proposals from 1789 to 1799 had such varying agendas and qualities that it is difficult to generalize about them, a few observations may be made. First of all, the very quantity of concrete educational plans proposed in this period indicates a growing politicization of the issue of instruction. Much pre-Revolutionary thought dealt with the importance of training citizens, but even where theory went beyond existing practice, reform did not take place on any grand scale. With the beginning of political reform in the Revolution, education and reeducation became tied to the Revolutionary agenda and were expected to effect a general transformation of society in ways previously unimaginable.[8] Though this should not be taken as evidence that practical instruction before the Revolution was haphazard or nonexistent, it does indicate a shift in emphasis, so that "the virtue that [the Revolution] hoped to inculcate was primarily social, or even political, where earlier educators had aimed more at developing individual character."[9] Enlightenment thinkers had presented education as the hope of the future, a means of peaceful and gradual change that could be, at the same time, revolutionary in its implications. Now, however, mothers were to develop individual character and train their children in self-control, which meant that schools could take on the civic and public role of socializing children to fit more properly within the new institutions.

Though philosophers had heavily criticized church control of education before the revolution, few proposed any concrete changes to the educational system until social and political reforms provided the impetus and ability to do so. Once the revolution made change to the existing system possible and allowed for the refashioning of public education's goals, representatives attempted to adjust the educational framework in such a way as to promote the training of both youth and adults in the new *civisme*. Soon, Revolutionary ideology relied on public education and practical training as its key components. By September of 1791, an article had even been inserted into the constitution that demanded the creation of free and general schooling, organized by the departments.[10] Primary education was a central component of this training. Since children provided the key to the future, their instruction would necessarily encompass skills such as reading and writing and also training in republican virtue. Legislators argued that the *ancien régime* system of education was corrupt and fundamentally opposed to the new goals; as a result, representatives decided to abolish the pre-Revolutionary system. Wiping the slate clean would allow true social change, producing free children who understood love and allegiance, and would, as a result, create a free society like that envisioned by Rousseau in the *Social Contract*.

A desire to do away with the old forms of public education did not, however, mean that the relatively new domestic ideal was also to be eliminated as part and parcel of the old regime. Instead, the nurturing education that had increased in prominence throughout the century was recognized as a fundamental component of any training in the new values and thus a necessary foundation for a properly civic instruction outside the home. As Jean Verdier, one philosopher who encouraged legislators to think concretely, argued: "The Nation herself must write a *National Plan* into legislation. *The domestic and regimented educations must blend, to lead all the students of the nation toward the individual and common good.* However, their confusion, their imperfection, their vices and their opposition have, to this point, produced little more than wild fruits, few in number and often poisoned."[11] Domestic education had become the obvious basis on which a national or public education could build, and politicians were its proponents as well as the targets of its rhetoric. Legislators already believed that civic mothers would mold their children's virtue and individual character, preparing their children for instruction outside the home; domestic life was the obvious foundation for civic life. The Rousseauian emphasis on character building was not, as some have argued, in tension with public life, which was based on "encyclopedic faith in the physical sciences,"[12] but instead was harmonized with it by the work of the domestic mother. As Rousseau had noted, "[a]long with his mother's milk, every true republican sucks the love of his country, that is, of the laws and liberty."[13]

A closer look at some plans from throughout the Revolutionary period makes the legislative connection between individual virtue, home and state training, and social change clearer. Charles Talleyrand-Périgord delivered the first major proposal concerning public schooling to the Constituent Assembly in the fall of 1791. As the Assembly debated the ideal form and content of a constitution for France, Talleyrand spoke to the entire body. As he spoke on behalf of the newly created Committee on Public Instruction, he argued that the constitution would need to recognize that the old methods of instruction, unenlightened and irrational as they were, needed to be replaced by a new system based on reason. As he explained, though changes in the law would provide some insurance of fundamental rights, education would be the most secure guarantor of rights, and political language would have to incorporate this understanding. Only when every citizen could understand the constitution and put his rights into practice would the gains of the revolution be secure.[14] For this reason, the state had a duty to provide some form of civic education.

Talleyrand's plan divided schools into three phases in order to achieve his goals. All children were to have the first stage of education, some would enter the second phase, and only a select number would be allowed the final step of education. The understanding was that these divisions would not only provide the necessary instruction, but would also ensure the proper distribution of talents in society. In this plan, schooling received both a concrete form and a secular mission, making the issue of training in the crucial formative years of utmost priority. Though reforms of secondary and higher education were important, many children would not need advanced training but would instead complete their education at the primary level. Talleyrand's plan also noted that girls might possibly be publicly educated with boys until the age of eight (two years from the projected beginning of cantonal schooling at the age of six), but they should then retire to the home and learn domestic tasks that would be useful to the nation, including child-rearing. Since girls were not intended to remain in society, a widespread or far-reaching training of them for public life was superfluous.[15] Though Talleyrand recognized that women provided half the productive capacity of society, he agreed with Rousseau and earlier philosophers that most of their training should take place in the home.

This was not to denigrate women's civic importance, however, for the plan was based on the assumption that moral education, as delivered by women, was the foundation for future schooling provided by the state. Despite the fact that the rhetoric of the proposed legislation claimed that local primary schools were "the only guarantee of civil liberty," the most generally applicable stage of education did not teach moral virtue but was intended only to teach practical skills in a rational fashion, in order to promote the goals of national unity and usefulness to the state. As proponents of the law explained, reading and writing in French would encourage both national unity and social and political equality. Elementary arithmetic, geography, and history would make the child useful in society and help him to recognize the importance of the rights guaranteed by the constitution.[16] Last but not least, physical instruction would continue the work of the mother in a concrete way, strengthening the body of the child and accustoming him to work so that he might become a productive member of society. Instruction would no longer rely on the goodwill of the Church, for instead of priests, brothers, and nuns, secular educators would train children in public schools. However, training in self-control and other prerational virtues was not the primary concern of these educators but would be provided at an earlier stage by mothers as the "natural" teachers of their children. The focus of the law demonstrates that Talleyrand and other legislators accepted Rousseau's distinctions and saw practical education's "mission" as fundamentally about social utility and civic indoctrination upon entering the secular world, not about the provision of moral education, which would already have been provided by nurturing and domestic mothers.

Despite the fact that Talleyrand's plan had been submitted in response to a widespread desire to reconfigure society through schooling, the Constituent Assembly took no action on this plan, nor did it pay special attention to it or any other type of educational reform. It was not that the plan failed to meet prevailing expectations for schooling. In fact, the proposed legislation offers a careful outline of how education could create children who would be revolutionary beings who would enter into the new gender constructs of society. However, politically, the Assembly was preoccupied with debates over the king's acceptance of the Constitution and nearly ready to dissolve itself after the completion of the Constitution, so it referred Talleyrand's report to its successor, the Legislative Assembly. Direct action on the matter of the reconstruction of secular and universal primary education had to wait.

In December 1792, over a year after Talleyrand presented his report to the Constituent Assembly, a new education plan finally came to the floor of the Legislative Assembly. The former marquis of Condorcet, Marie Jean Antoine Nicolas Caritat, had chaired the Committee of Public Instruction for the past year and eventually spearheaded the charge to reform education. As a result, the plan that the Committee on Public Instruction presented bore his name. The Condorcet plan had been in the making for longer than a few months. Condorcet himself had been interested in public education long before the Revolution, and though he had not published his educational ideas before the Revolution, the Condorcet plan demonstrated the influence of earlier educational theorists, including Rousseau and Diderot.[17]

Condorcet's plan had many similarities to that of Talleyrand. Both men directed their advice to fellow politicians and believed that a national system of education was a necessary prerequisite to lasting freedom and equality. Citizens, they both argued, could only secure their natural rights and fulfill their duties to the state when they were properly indoctrinated in social obligations in order to understand the meaning of the political equality granted by the new laws. As Condorcet explained, if the state failed in its goal of universal primary education, its citizens would rise up against it and say: "The law guaranteed me complete equality of rights, but they refuse to provide me the means by which I might know them. I should depend on the law alone, but my ignorance leaves me dependent on everything that surrounds me."[18] It is important to note that this plan also operated on the assumption that public or social education relied on a basis of education within the home. For, immediately after saying that citizens would blame their dependence on the state's failure to provide public instruction, Condorcet explained that they would say: "In my early childhood, I was taught everything that I needed to know but, forced to work in order to live, these first notions faded away, and all that remains is the pain of feeling in my ignorance, not the will of nature, but the injustice of society."[19] Domestic education would teach children "everything that they needed to know," in terms of self-control and liberty, but their training could not end there. Once they left home, their reason would have to be instructed so that they might become publicly useful and fruitful members of society.

While Condorcet's plan, like Talleyrand's, did not extend all levels of education to all children, the organization of Condorcet's system encompassed a broader section of society than Talleyrand's plan. Condorcet claimed that practical and rational instruction was necessary for all ages, so that everyone could develop his or her capacities to the best of his or her abilities. For this reason, the primary and secondary school teachers would not only teach both boys and girls from ages four to six, but also would be obliged to hold sessions on Sunday that would be designed for all citizens.[20] Rather than three subdivisions, each more restricted than the first, Condorcet proposed five degrees of instruction. While the outlines of primary instruction were very similar under both plans, Condorcet's secondary schools were open to a greater percentage of the population (almost any child who could be spared from work for a long enough period of time) and paid for at the expense of the state, allowing more children to take advantage of this education. The plan also set up *lycées* and institutes for the study of practical sciences such as agriculture, military technology, and medicine. These were also free, though more limited in enrollment than the previous two degrees. The final stage of Condorcet's plan involved a *Société Nationale des Sciences et des Arts* that would concern itself with the direction of the entire system so that the people as a whole could be instructed and perfected.[21]

Perhaps most astonishing in comparison to most contemporary plans, Condorcet's plan would have educated girls in the same fashion as boys. Taking Enlightenment suppositions about reason, rights, and human nature to their logical conclusion, Condorcet argued that all women who had the capacity to continue studies past the primary level ought to be encouraged, not hindered.[22] Women might even, he claimed, have more proficiency in certain areas, such as the development of texts for children. Their special areas of expertise should be thus encouraged and harnessed for the good of the nation, and they had the right to public instruction just as men did. Furthermore, this equality would produce more domestic tranquility because women and men would be able to share interests within their homes. Perhaps most important was the recognition that domestic education was necessary across all social boundaries, since:

one may note that in poorer families, the domestic education of children is almost always left to their mothers; that if one reflects on the fact that, of twenty-five families devoted to agriculture, to trade, to arts, at least one has a widow at its head, one will understand how important this portion of the task which has been entrusted to us is, not only for the common good, but also for the general progress of enlightenment.[23]

General revolutionary tenets accepted that children might have gendered roles, but schooling could serve both men and women as they fulfilled their national duties. While Condorcet's plan, like Talleyrand's, was never enacted into legislation, the underlying arguments of both plans strengthened the connection between widespread practical needs of the state and the early social training of the child. As Jean Vignery demonstrates, "[t]he function of the teacher was to instruct students in facts and to provide them with techniques for separating truth from error, not to inculcate religious and political doctrines."[24] Fact and reason were the realms of the school; moral education was left to families.

Condorcet's and Talleyrand's plans thus combined the practical emphasis of the majority of the *philosophes* with the domestic education found in Rousseau's *Emile*. Their educational plans demonstrated the widespread belief that early education in self-control would prepare each individual to enter onto the public stage and be trained to participate fully in an increasingly gendered society. For both Condorcet and Talleyrand, public instruction, unlike early domestic education, assumed that children were ready to translate their knowledge of virtue into reasoned action. While Condorcet's plan integrated women into schooling to a far greater degree than Talleyrand's, both proposed training that relied on a gendered and familial foundation.

If both schooling and public education were intentionally gendered, this did not indicate an intentional exclusion of women from civic roles. The foundation for schooling and civic virtue was laid by the mother. As the theory behind domestic education made clear throughout this same era, without the basis of obedience and the virtuous habits taught by mothers, no education could ever be successful, for children were not born as rational beings or even beings who were ready for a training in rationality. Mothers would prepare the child to be instructed; it would be their moral training that would help children reach the point where they might begin to use reason appropriately. As a result, even when legislators focused on public instruction, they operated on the assumption that domestic education was a natural precursor to schooling, for mothers would complete the necessary tasks of writing on the blank slates by raising children who were cognizant of their social roles and their obligations to humanity. If, as domestic education had demonstrated, mothers were the best people to train children to be obedient and thoughtful, then they were also the ones to provide the basis for future instruction. Once these children were ready to enter society, they could commence public education that, unlike domestic education, would be practical and based on reason. The rationality central to this instruction would compel citizens by the clear truth of its maxims, rather than by the demands for rote obedience and adherence to "superstition" that had been such common schooling techniques under the Old Regime.

Reason, trained in public schools after the acquisition of moral understanding in the home, was the best guarantor, not only of rights, but also of national virtue.[25] Citizens educated in rationality would confirm the gains of the revolution even as they contributed to the perfection of the people.[26] This was true of both sexes, whether or not women were educated alongside men. For if all education of a higher order was to be specialized to allow each individual to best fulfill his potential and function in society, women's education might take a different path and still forcefully contribute to the freedom and perfection of the nation.[27] Just as men's courage and training in military matters would protect the state and allow liberty to flourish, women's special talents in domestic science and the raising of children would provide future citizens with the necessary foundation for their future contributions to society.

The Revolution — and Education — Radicalize

Why, with such strong ties to contemporary currents of thought, was no plan like that of Condorcet or Talleyrand never adopted? After all, the existing system was in desperate need of a practical fix. Schools had relied on Church funds and personnel for their daily operations, and, with religious orders banned from teaching and the Church tithes revoked, the schools were in dire straits.[28] If schooling was as central to the mission of the revolution as the potential legislation suggested, it was high time to take concrete action.[29] The debates surrounding this particular educational plan suggest that the inaction was not because the revolution was uninterested in education but, on the contrary, because the revolution had also taken a leap forward in its conceptualization of public instruction and was looking to provide far more than Condorcet's plan could offer.[30] Girondin plans like Talleyrand's and Condorcet's, which had provided for different stages of schooling, came under attack as elitist and likely to foster division, as well as out of touch with the needs of the nation. Despite pressing questions of war and legislative struggles against the king, education took an ever more central role in republican ideology, and was itself a battleground in the ideological struggle between factions. Rather than being content with the "seeds of a movement for vocational training in the elementary schools,"[31] Jacobin revolutionaries came to argue for more comprehensive national education that would regenerate the souls of all Frenchmen equally. National festivals and physical exercises allowed no differences and promoted unity and, as such, were a necessary component of every educational scheme.[32] Unity might not mean completely equal schooling by age or gender, but it did demand equal public attention. Education had become fundamental to political understanding of the nation, and one's educational commitments were a litmus test for one's revolutionary status.

While much historical discussion has noted the ways in which uniformity was increasingly emphasized and "elitism" decried, fewer historians of education have noted that education and instruction drew closer and closer together.[33] Public exercises and affirmations of belief such as marches, festivals, and other forms of spectacle were not only more egalitarian in nature but also expressed the broader forms of indoctrination that revolutionaries sought. Since the king was no longer on the throne and opposition to the revolution had become increasingly evident, new approaches to schooling moved away from practical instruction and toward moral education in revolutionary values. Revolutionaries now wished to do more than impart useful skills for citizens; they intended to inculcate morality. Talleyrand and Condorcet now seemed hopelessly conservative, since they had provided plans centered on instructing the minds of children, with an assumption that children who were enlightened and accustomed to rational thought would provide the foundation for a regenerated society.

Opponents of Condorcet's plan—his political opponents on far more than education—now argued that, among other flaws, this plan seriously neglected general moral and civic training.[34] Though Condorcet claimed to provide education for all members of society, subject to their choices and abilities, Jacobin deputies to the Legislative Assembly explained that there were not enough civic festivals or a broad enough focus on general education. Leaving moral training in the hands of families could, these legislators feared, undermine efforts to transform the nation. Some revolutionaries seemed to think that a simple education in rationality was no longer an adequate guarantor of revolutionary gains. Now, in order to facilitate the advancement of society, children and adults needed social education, provided by the state, that would replace aristocratic and superstitious beliefs with egalitarian and rational ones. After all, intellectual exercises were only one small part of a general moral and physical education.

At least initially, the new focus on unity as demonstrated through *fêtes* and marches was central to a political struggle, not part and parcel of an attempt to wrest education entirely from the hands of parents. Given the real problems with taking control of schooling away from clerics and enforcing edicts even in the nonrebellious provinces, the desire for public demonstrations of support for the revolution were primarily an attack on the forces of counterrevolution and not on the rights or abilities of parents. Some legislators, like Girondin Claude-Louis Masuyer, criticized what they saw as overly intellectual plans but, in addition to promoting revolutionary *fêtes* or state schooling, continued to emphasize a healthy family's role in reshaping society. Masuyer, like his colleagues François-Xavier Lanthenas and Durand de Maillane, wished to use state power to reinforce the family's unique obligation to provide moral education, not to displace it. In the early years of the revolution, few deputies argued that parents were unable to provide a proper upbringing or that state interests were so overwhelming as to justify the removal of children from the home altogether.[35] Political interests did not override the need for domestic education, directed by a good mother.

Like much other legislation during the Jacobin ascendancy, debates surrounding education became increasingly wide-ranging in 1793. Once the legislature convicted and executed the king, it returned to its most pressing issues: war, money, and public instruction. In a context like this, it should hardly be surprising that educational proposals became increasingly radical. As the Jacobins came to power in 1793, new calls for an increase in civic activities began to assume that moral and physical education ought to be promoted by the state, in a public atmosphere. These plans eventually attempted to displace the domestic mother as the "natural" provider of moral education and argued that primary schools should treat practical skills as secondary to physical and moral education, which ought not to be left to the discretion of potentially unreliable parents. For example, Gilbert Romme explicitly accepted the distinction between "education" and "instruction" but insisted that education was not a family affair but rather a public obligation. Practical skills like literacy and numeracy were no more important than republication regeneration directed by the state.[36] The Jacobin André Jeanbon Saint-André seems to have been the first to make the transition from Rousseau's individualist focus to state-run *éducation* when he claimed that the government needed to step in and develop individual character.[37] Jacobins like Saint-André increasingly used Rousseau's ideas but placed the state in the ideological role that the nurturing parent had possessed.

Drafts of proposals began to deal with public and moral instruction to a degree previously thought unnecessary, and some even suggested that parents ought to relinquish control of their children to the state. Instead of being a necessary supplement to the moral and physical education that parents would provide, elementary education was now intended to replace it, at least partially, ensuring that children would be raised in the ways that the state saw fit.[38] Before much longer, Robespierre and others used educational proposals to explicitly outline the ways in which the state ought to provide both education and instruction, seizing control not only of rational instruction but also of prerational domestic education. The formation of children's sentiments and their early integration into public life was no longer to be left to mothers within the home.

In 1793, for example, a special planning commission argued for adoption of the Lepeletier plan, named for the assassinated deputy who was its original author. This plan, promoted by Robespierre, argued that schools could and must condition citizens in a way that one family could not. While it included practical instruction like that proposed by Condorcet or Talleyrand, it also included substantial focus on education by establishing state dormitories in addition to the typical schools. While basic instruction for literacy and numeracy was kept at a relatively high level, Lepeletier's plan made time for the reformation of each child's character, not by eliminating instruction, but by demanding that all children be reared by the state after they had passed the first stage of infancy. In an all-encompassing approach that built on the moral and political education that Romme had proposed, Lepeletier planned for all children to be put into "homes of equality" at the age of five. The communal living he envisioned would guarantee that children's "home" life would be their social life as well, effectively collapsing distinctions between private and public virtue. As the rhetoric of the plan explained, "[t]he whole being of the child belongs to us . . . Everything which belongs to the Republic should be cast in a republican mold."[39] Under this proposal, all parents who refused to educate their children publicly would not only pay a double education tax but also forfeit their civic rights.[40] This plan claimed to ask no more of parents than the *levée en masse* required of male citizens. In times of trouble, all Frenchmen were expected to defend the liberty of the country, and primary schooling, like military service, was another obligation of a free people.

In a practical sense, the Lepeletier plan was not only controversial but completely unrealistic. The nation could hardly afford to continue to wage war, let alone find the finances and manpower to raise thousands of children, even if parents were willingly to give their children over to the state for rearing in communal boarding schools, which was hardly more likely. And yet, widespread approval for this plan, including its backing by Robespierre, indicates how the idea of education as a civic duty was, at this point, universal and unavoidable. While not all citizens required extended public schooling, primary education was now fundamental and, most important, conceived of as a state obligation.

However, one must not overstate the case. The Lepeletier plan took children entirely from their parents after the age of five but left them in the hands of their mothers until that point. Given the emphasis on the importance of early education, it is clear that even Lepeletier envisioned public education as a necessary addition to but not the entire foundation of public life. Additionally, while the Committee on Public Instruction, led by Robespierre, became increasingly radical, other deputies, less enamored of public control over moral education, continued to emphasize parental rights and obligations with respect to education. A Jacobin deputy from the Marne, Charles Delacroix, liked the idea of communal education but argued that mandating attendance and taking children away from their parents was not the right path to virtue.[41] Delacroix's primary concern was not the defense of paternal authority; a desire to protect fathers' rights did not provide the intellectual impetus for his opposition to the plan. In fact, if paternal authority had been the primary issue, the Lepeletier plan might more easily have passed muster with moderate Jacobins, for its provisions included the establishment of committees of local fathers to oversee individual schools.

While none of the deputies who opposed the Lepeletier plan believed that fathers' rights were negligible, the legislators who opposed compulsory attendance did so with reference to a Rousseauian understanding of nature and family education that included maternal nurturing. Jean Vignery has noted how Antoine-Clair Thibaudeau "denounced the [Lepeletier] project before the convention as contrary to nature and thus immoral," while citing "Rousseau's theory that the family is the natural character-building institution."[42] The Jacobin Jacques-Michel Coupé also published a number of pamphlets opposing compulsory instruction in late July 1793, after the widespread approval of the Lepeletier project.[43] In his writings, Coupé outlined the ways in which communal education diverged from the path that a virtuous society ought to take. He argued that mothers were the natural moral educators and that formal schooling could not take the place of parental guidance. Education in moral principles must remain the domain of the family and could not be synthesized into a universal attempt to educate and instruct in public schools.

Despite the fact that Robespierre still held to the belief that only the state had the right to educate the future citizens of France, in December 1793, the various deputies arrived at a middle ground between a desire for widespread education in revolutionary virtues and belief in the parents' "natural" right and obligation to control moral training.[44] The agreed-upon solution, known as the Bouquier Law on Primary Education, made schooling free and national. It emphasized local initiative and allowed all but criminals, counterrevolutionaries, and ardent Catholics to teach. Parents could also choose what school would best meet the needs of their children once they left the home. This law, legislators believed, was a compromise that would allow for the nation to guarantee appropriately republican upbringing of children, including physical education,

for both sexes.[45] The law went beyond Condorcet's or Talleyrand's instruction; no longer would teaching French be enough to move toward
national unity. R. R. Palmer has explained that this "law represented a
minimum on which members of the Convention could agree at the climax
of the Revolution: instruction for all in reading, writing, arithmetic, civic
training, and common morals, and participation by all in the adult education of political activity and national festivals."[46] However, under the
new law, public schools, despite being compulsory, were only a supple-
mental institution for civic training. The major educational portion of the
public mission would come from popular meetings, festivals, and the example of republican government. Parents still retained a great deal of control over their young children.

Education Returns to the Home

As with all earlier educational reforms, the Bouquier plan foundered
along with the political fortunes of its proponents. Implementation of the
Bouquier law ran into many obstacles, not the least of which was lack of
enforcement when parents disobeyed.[47] A sufficient supply of teachers
could not be found in most of the country, and even when there were
enough schools and instructors, parental reluctance to send their children
to state-run schools could not be simply legislated away. After the fall of
the Jacobins, the more extreme versions of political education, which had
sought to make moral education and instruction compulsory for both
boys and girls, gave way to less controversial plans that returned to separation by gender and allowed parents complete control over their children's moral—including physical—upbringing.

The Lakanal Law on Primary Education, adopted in November 1794
(27 Brumaire, an III), emerged as a practical compromise, consolidating
many of the instructional principles of the Revolution while abandoning
some of the most controversial, expensive, and difficult portions of earlier plans for education.[48] Under Lakanal's plan, teachers in state-run
schools would have their salaries paid for by the state, and juries of instruction (no longer called "bureaus of inspection") would oversee the
quality of teaching. While the government now facilitated "instruction"
in order to minimize differences in access to schooling, it also returned
primary responsibility for children's education to their parents. While
Lakanal, Romme, and others agitated for private schools to submit to the
same types of oversight legislated for public schools, in the end, the Convention gave discretion about schooling entirely to parents, making it neither compulsory nor state-controlled. The child's eventual incorporation

into public and civic life remained an obligation of the state, to be accomplished by the widespread use of festivals and other public displays. Much as Condorcet and Talleyrand had envisioned, domestic mothers would provide a prerational moral education and the government would later turn children into citizens and republicans.

In some sense, all of these plans and debates turned out to be, in practical terms, utopian. Once the financial crisis struck in full force, it became impossible either to attract teachers with the now worthless revolutionary money or to pay a living wage. The Republic was forced to abandon the idea of paying for state schools and teachers and instead retreated to a guarantee of paying for the lodging of these teachers. The goal was no longer to make schooling free and widely available. In fact, in 1795 when the Convention adopted the Daunou law to take the place of the Lakanal law, legislators all but abandoned previous goals for elementary education. While they expected each canton to have at least one primary school, the curriculum was severely pruned, with only reading, writing, arithmetic, and the most basic elements of republican dogma remaining.[49] After demolishing the *ancien régime* institutions, the revolutionary government essentially returned primary education entirely into the hands of parents and retreated from almost every demand for control of nonrational education.

Although, in hindsight, the Lakanal and Danou laws' failures might tempt one to see them as just two more choices in a constant stream of potential policies like those proposed by Condorcet, Romme, Bouquier, etc., this would be a mistake. Certainly, many of the stipulations sound similar to earlier proposals. The Lakanal Law gave the state responsibility for recruiting and paying the salaries of teachers. The curriculum of state-run schools was discussed at length and followed republican ideology: the Declaration of the Rights of Man and the Constitution were required reading material. History and geography provided a basis for understanding the liberty of France, and physical and moral education continued where mothers had left off. Yet, in a retreat from the most radical phase of the Revolution, parents again controlled their children's educational futures, not only in the choice of teachers, but in the choice of public, private, or no schooling at all. The state retreated from its demands to assert control over early education, and parents—especially mothers—remained the final arbiters of the moral education of their children.

Lakanal's and Daunou's laws demonstrate that the Revolution did not make widespread gains in the actual provision of schooling. However the debates over education make it equally clear that the philosophical tie between primary instruction and civic education had become a legislative reality. As Maurice Gontard explains,

Though it did not leave a strong network of national schools, the Revolution did leave a lasting product . . . [R]ecasting the ambitious views of Philosophers and Economists, removing yokes and shaking prejudices, substituting Reason for Faith, equality for privilege, it had deeply plowed the land of French schooling and planted the fertile seeds of principles that the republicans would no longer forget.[50]

Even though the initial plans were not implemented on any grand scale, the obligation of the state to create responsible citizens through instruction had become generally accepted and would faithfully appear in political debates about education in both the Napoleonic era and the Restoration. Equally important, the question of girls' participation figured prominently in many of these debates, marking the ways in which moral education might be one centerpiece for future demands of equality. Given the durability of the new strain of thought linking virtuous behavior and public instruction, the legislative impasse of the Revolution ought not to be seen as a failing entirely inherent in the various pieces of revolutionary legislation or the theories that underlay them, but one much more firmly rooted in the crises of these years. Isser Woloch claims that even when financial and political problems doomed the Lakanal law, among others, to legislative oblivion, the revolutionary ideas "guided the only sustained attempt to create and finance a national system of primary schooling, until the far more modest initiatives of Guizot in the 1830s,"[51] and they did so in terms that would have been increasingly acceptable not only to *philosophes* and revolutionaries but also to people who were not themselves particularly liberal.

Public Instruction in the Early Nineteenth Century

If a mother's nurturing was central to sending children into society, and only children with devoted mothers would be truly prepared for civic life, there was still the question of what, exactly, to do with children once they entered the schoolhouse. Rather than inquiring into the form and content of schooling in the first third of the nineteenth century, historians have generally focused on political inaction between the Revolution and 1833 to indicate that primary education remained relatively unimportant.[52] Most standard works on education in France claim that the passage of the Ferry Laws in 1883 was the watershed event in educational history as it seized schooling back from the grasping hands of reactionary clerical orders. More recent scholarship has emphasized the broader currents of agreement between religious and secular education over the course of the nineteenth century, but agrees that nineteenth-century education can be most easily summarized with reference to the period of expansion after 1833.[53] Certainly, Guizot's 1833 law requiring every commune to have a public school was the first major attempt to legislate instructional change since 1800 and was the most important legislative precursor to the modern educational system of the Ferry Laws. However, as the preceding chapters demonstrate, the years between 1799 and 1833 saw dramatic changes in domestic education and parental involvement, which in turn influenced legislative commitment to new ideals of instruction; without the social and cultural change of those years, the profound changes of the later nineteenth century would be unthinkable.

While histories of primary schooling in France often proceed directly from revolutionary legislation to the Guizot law without any discussion of the intervening years, politicians of that period were hardly silent on the question of instruction. Additionally, the fact that Church and State made tentative accords under Napoleon and then were closely aligned during the Restoration meant that practical problems that had frustrated legislators could begin to see resolution. Under Napoleon, the improving relationship between Church and State added the practical element of more teachers and schools to the legislation of the nineteenth century. Once clerical education had been fully reincorporated into the Restoration school system, generalized primary schooling in the provinces became a more realistic expectation. However, this also sparked tension between republicans and royalists when republicans perceived the Church to be infringing upon universal rights or promoting the superstition that many revolutionaries had tried to abolish. For that reason, the law of 1833 should be seen not only in the context of a growing influence of liberal thought but also as an attempt to provide a consistent enunciation of rights and responsibilities that steered away from personal moral education and instead focused on instruction and basic civic education, thereby avoiding the pitfalls of both republican and royalist educational practices. If Guizot's law was more modest than revolutionary laws such as Lakanal's, it was longer-lasting, which can be explained by reference not only to economic and political changes but also to lessons learned in the intervening years.

Revolutionary legislation remained officially unchanged throughout the Directory and Consulate, as the Daunou law that had replaced Lakanal remained in effect. However, in 1800, Napoleon's Minister of the Interior, Jean Chaptal, made an inquiry into the conditions of primary and secondary education.[54] Chaptal criticized the meager provisions for primary schooling, arguing, that "[i]n a representative government instruction is everywhere essential . . . Reading, writing, arithmetic and elementary ideas as to the social contract—this is the general education which the government owes to all alike. It is an absolute necessity for everyone and for that reason it is a public debt which society has the duty of discharging."[55] Chaptal claimed that primary education should be provided by the state, with salaries being covered half by municipalities and half by funds from state coffers. He would not have prescribed the exact form or content of teaching but wanted every teacher to take an oath of loyalty to the state before being allowed to teach, thereby guaranteeing that whatever he promoted would support government interests. Though Napoleon did not take action on Chaptal's report and left instruction up to the individual commune much as under the Daunou law, Chaptal's assumptions also fall in a direct line of development from revolutionary proposals, with limited early schooling as "an absolute necessity" and even "a public debt." Chaptal's report also continued in the same vein as the most prevalent strain of revolutionary thought. Reading, writing, and arithmetic—practical instruction—were the government's obligation, as was the communication of basic ideas that would integrate citizens into public life. Moral education in self-control and other personal characteristics was the parental foundation for education, not a public debt nor an obligation of the state.

Though Napoleon's legislative reforms of the secondary schooling system are legendary, his lack of action on Chaptal was representative of his general approach to primary instruction, since he neglected primary schooling almost entirely. Even so, the Napoleonic state's assumption of control of secondary education resulted in increased demands for governmental action at the primary level. As advanced training became a state commodity, parents and educators who had internalized the new educational norms voiced concerns that primary instruction ought to be developed as well.[56] While philosophies of education had made a distinction between domestic education, primary schooling, and later social training, both educators and parents claimed that truly national instruction needed to be attended to at the primary level.[57] Schooling should be national and comprehensive and had to begin at an early age in order to allow civic virtue—first taught at home—to be fully integrated into public life.

Given the similarity of the assumptions in the Napoleonic era to those during the revolutionary era, one might think that these demands were made only by former revolutionaries or liberals sympathetic to the changing ideals. If that were true, under the Restoration one would expect to find a return to the emphasis on Christian education and a call for the religious orders to focus on the spiritual training of youth and an emphasis on virtues like self-control. However, this was not the case. Pedagogical objectives continued on a secular trajectory even after Napoleon's fall; social expectations for education did not change drastically, even as political fortunes and prospects did.[58] While concessions to the Catholic church were related to the prevailing political winds, with fewer concessions in the liberal phases of the monarchy and greater concessions while the Ultras dominated politics, the community as a whole generally agreed that mothers would control general moral education and that this domestic education would provide the ideological foundation for the practical and civic instruction necessary for the advancement of society.

Despite political upheaval and ever-changing agendas from the Directory to Napoleon and the Restoration, the belief in national instruction still found a great degree of legislative continuity, which corresponded to a widespread belief, crossing political boundaries, in the power of foundational domestic education. King and citizen alike placed hope for the future in the proper training of citizens. The educational philosophies from Enlightenment to Restoration were, as a surprising result, more continuous than discontinuous and followed a line of generally increasing demand for schooling and institutional intervention in children's lives. Maurice Gontard has argued that, "in the most diverse milieus of opinion in 1815, people believed that ignorance was one of the greatest curses of contemporary society. Above all, [they thought that,] on the human plane, ignorance exhausts the mind, depraves the heart, delivers man over to his instincts, and engenders laziness and vice."[59] Even supporters of an ultra-royalist agenda could agitate for instructional change, such that the lower orders would be more productive and understand their proper roles in society.

In 1816, in response to the widespread demands for training that would provide literacy and support industry, the Restoration government ordered each commune to provide education to all children, even those who were unable to afford it. Pierre Royer-Collard, the regime's chief educationist, explained, "The day that the Charter was granted . . . universal instruction was promised because it was necessary."[60] In this sense, instruction was necessary not as the basis for defending one's natural rights, but for reeducation in social structures and practical training so that France would be able to compete on a world stage. Schooling would give children an understanding of traditional social duties and responsibilities even as it initiated them into the modern era. Much as the revolutionaries had envisioned, public instruction would be necessary, not for initial molding, but for guiding each child's transition into a new society.

The expected means for this desired transformation were not entirely clear. While the government believed it had a strong interest in providing universal popular education, the mere existence of a new royal ordinance commanding communes to provide primary education was by itself unlikely to insure practical access to education. However, in contrast to Napoleon's government, the Restoration government did include funds for primary education in the national budget and continued to increase the funding throughout the Restoration.[61] In fact, shortly before the Restoration government was overthrown in 1830, it announced that a portion of taxes would go to support primary education, especially for teacher salaries and student scholarships. This plan formed the basis for the declaration of Guizot's Law in 1833.

There was a clear commitment to schooling under the Restoration, but a great deal of confusion remained about the government's overall approach to primary education. The proposed taxes would hardly begin to cover buildings, salaries, and teacher training; would necessary costs be covered by municipalities or the national government? Would instruction be primarily by religious orders or secular teachers? What should the curriculum look like? Many reactionaries assumed that instruction ought to be religious in nature, and therefore secular educational institutions that had remained in place after the fall of Napoleon ought to be destroyed. In February 1816, the regime seemed to move toward this religious understanding as it adopted a policy of allying with religious authorities for the purpose of supervising primary education. However, the government did not give control over entirely to the Church, which indicated that instruction would be acceptable to the Church but would, first and foremost, serve practical state interests.[62]

Despite greater Church control after the Ultras took control in the 1820s, the attempts to blend state and religious concerns in the socialization of children resulted in policies that looked remarkably similar in practice to those of the revolutionary and Napoleonic eras.[63] The university remained in place and was ostensibly the center of educational control; local notables and clergy made decisions about primary instruction on the local level. There was a prevailing belief that schooling should inculcate civic responsibility, especially obedience to the government.[64] Local committees were to determine the best way to encourage these goals and also oversaw teacher's curriculums and teaching styles and had the power to revoke appointments. Teachers were required to have certificates of good conduct, which meant that official policy prevented anyone with improper political leanings from indoctrinating children. While reception of a certificate was now often contingent on having the proper monarchical inclinations, a record of supporting both King and Church, in practice primary schooling remained more similar to than different from what had gone before.[65]

The similarity in approach came with a recognizable set of problems. It had been difficult before and during the Revolution to find qualified applicants for the available positions; it was not much easier after the fall of Napoleon to find qualified candidates who were willing and able to teach. Liberals and conservatives alike initially found promise in the potential of the monitorial system or *éducation mutuelle*. With this method, known in England as the Lancaster method, but similar to the simultaneous instruction used by the Christian Brothers, one teacher could supervise the education of a number of children at one time. Previously, each student had approached the teacher individually for lessons, reciting or writing as directed, then returning to his appointed place. Under the new system, groups of children were divided by level of skill. Advanced students at each level monitored and facilitated the progress of students in their group. The teacher's contribution was to keep order and to instruct and direct the monitors at the beginning of each day. Students would advance from one level to the next as their accomplishments allowed. In this way, one well-trained teacher could educate a hundred or more students in educational fundamentals and more advanced students could systematically teach less advanced ones.[66]

Liberals approved of this idea for a number of reasons. The mutual method appeared to be scientific and objective; students who worked hard and did well would be recognized and would advance.[67] Conservatives harbored doubts about the suitability of this system (where the master was not firmly in control and hierarchy was unclear), but the idea that one teacher could instruct hundreds did appeal and the tie to the Christian Brothers made it less suspect, at least initially. All parties agreed that the system seemed to make good financial sense, given limited financial resources and parental pressure to reduce costs. In other words, though their political and thus educational agendas were radically different, both Ultras and revolutionaries wanted public instruction to be generally available. As liberal sponsorship of the idea became ever more prominent, even resulting in the founding of the Society for Elementary Instruction, conservatives eventually decided that this method was too risky—both in terms of its subversion of hierarchy and its ability to provide educational results—and began to campaign against it. While the Ultras came down entirely against *l'instruction mutuelle* when moderate royalists returned to power in 1827, the liberal regime made it a point to support this form of public education, claiming that "[p]rimary teaching appears to be the first necessity, from the political, economic, and social point of view. The King supports the Society for Elementary Instruction and recognizes it as an institution of public utility."[68] The Society for Elementary Instruction, which promoted mutual education, had, at least temporarily, won out over individual instruction.[69]

It is significant, however, that the questions across the political spectrum revolved around the debate over mutual schools, simultaneous schools, and schools of individual instruction, and not over a desire to provide moral education or whether society had an obligation to provide basic instruction at all. By the early nineteenth century, almost every vision of progress argued that properly schooled children were the key to the prosperity and success of society. As the Royal Academy of Nantes announced, "[n]o topic deserves to claim the attention of this assembly better than the progress of the popular education promised, at the expense of the state, to all French. Generous operation, it must dispense the necessary knowledge to all men in all classes, and thus add to our means of prosperity."[70] Instruction and practical training were necessary to further develop all young minds, training them in the ways of social life after mothers had nurtured their virtue and rationality.

Moving Toward Guizot's Law

When Guizot became the new Minister of Public Instruction in October 1832, he entered into a situation where nearly everyone, politicians and legislators included, could agree that public instruction of children was a key to constructing any particular social vision. The intersection of schooling and social behavior was now a "proven" political fact, the best way of training individuals to meet the needs of the state. Upheaval from the Revolution through the early Restoration had inspired legislators to aim for the stability they believed could come only from educating citizens in a fashion that integrated children into society and demanded respect for authority, both secular and religious. Historians have seen this education as "moral" in focus and intent.[71] As Barry Bergen explains, in the later nineteenth century, "to control the schools was to control minds, to unify the nation in the ideas of one's own 'morality.' Morality thus became a key word which signalled a whole range of opinions, and a general orientation to society and of society. Whether linked to or divorced from religion, 'morality' in education came to signal control over the minds of the young and thus over the future of the nation."[72] The goals of public instruction were fundamentally about social integration and the creation of a state that matched one's own civic vision.

However, this desire to inculcate "morality" primarily means that contemporary elites were in agreement that schooling should emphasize their own social priorities and norms, including the distinction between the lower and upper orders, and be relatively inexpensive. For that reason, the word "moral" obscures more than it clarifies, especially in the context of nineteenth-century expectations that domestic nurturing would first develop individual virtues such as self-control. When Guizot listed the obligations of the primary school teacher in a circular, he underlined principles of authority. He explained that the teacher's job was: "To preserve order and stability, to form good citizens, to develop faith in providence, the idea of the sacredness of duty, submission to paternal authority, and the respect due to the ruler, the law, and the rights of all."[73] While literacy and numeracy, not included in this list of obligations, were not irrelèvant, he was overt in emphasizing that his ultimate goal was the creation of citizens who would wholeheartedly join in and support a social order predicated on a view of principles such as "respect for order," "duty," etc.

While this might seem like moral education, it is more accurate to see it as civic education. Order, stability, citizenship, and social obligations were at the top of the list, not self-control or other personal virtues seen as the domain of the family. Significantly, Guizot himself recognized this distinction. He had opened discussion on his new law by saying, "Shall we ask the commune, which seems to participate in family and State life at the same time, to be the sole power behind primary instruction and its supervision, and as a consequence, its expenditures?"[74] The fact that Guizot offered no means for funding the required communal schools offers us an important hint to the answer for his rhetorical question. Governmental control of public instruction, even when necessary, could only offer half the picture. Rather than being displaced by schooling, family contributions, both financial and emotional, remained central to any larger understanding of education.

As William Connolly posits, democracy "requires the subject, capable of adjusting conduct to norms, willing to assume responsibility for commitments, and willing to take the common good into account in its public life when assured that others will too."[75] If that is true—and an examination of cultural and ideological change seems to indicate that early nineteenth-century legislators would have agreed with him that it was—then women's ability to demonstrate self-control and civic responsibility made them a central part of the new social vision. Rebecca Rogers explains how "educating for domesticity after the revolution involved from the beginning the breaking-down of simplistic divisions between public and private. The reconfigured family that emerged from the Revolutionary period played a central role in political debates about citizenship and formed the basis of a new social order."[76] Both Connolly and Rogers confirm that the interrelationship between domesticity and education thus helps to explain the shift from *l'éducation* to *l'instruction* and its meaning for the individual's relationship to society. Insofar as broad cultural currents reflected Rousseau's emphasis on gender differentiation, they also increasingly treated women as responsible individuals whose nurturing would help launch the child—both male and female—into life outside the home. In 1834, Louis-Aimé Martin explicitly linked the shift toward autonomous nurturing education to instructional change, when he explained:

The rod and starvation have ceased to be the moral powers of education, and the professors, who are now chosen from among fathers of families, no longer treat our children in the same way as criminals are treated in the public square. The source of these reforms springs altogether from the ameliorations in domestic life. In proportion as paternal severity has diminished, scholastic cruelties have ceased. Under our new *regime,* the tyrannical power of fathers has decreased, like that of kings, of which it was the image; but what we have lost in despotism we have regained in happiness.[77]

Overall political trends from the Revolution forward may have excluded women from complete participation in political life, and yet, as the debates surrounding education and family life indicate, politics hardly could contain the entire story of social change. As a result of a complex rhetoric about self-control, gender difference, and the ideal society, nineteenth-century conceptions of civic life had a strong domestic component. The relevance of the shift from many different forms of instruction to one general and universal need for schooling thus becomes clearest in a context where, rather than seeing the increasing public education of citizens as pushed by legislation or a growing demand for literacy in a modern world, we view the desired schoolhouse meeting of *l'instruction* and *l'éducation* as part of a greater assumption that maternal care served as the foundation of the early formation of a properly civic individual, while instruction would continue the process of incorporation that had been begun by a nurturing mother.

CONCLUSION

Autonomous Individuality, Self-Control, and Domesticity

Manners are the basis of government. —*American Museum* (1789)

You desire to restrict women to the mere management of their houses—you would only instruct them for that purpose; but you do not reflect that it is from the house of each citizen that the errors and the prejudices which prevail in the world, [sic] emanate.
—Louis-Aimé Martin, *The Education of Mothers*

Louis-Aimé Martin and Domestic Motherhood

*A*s the preceding chapters have demonstrated, the educational discourse that tied domestic child-rearing to civic virtue became increasingly widespread from the late eighteenth to the early nineteenth centuries. Not only did an emphasis on a domestic mother who could teach autonomy manifest itself in clothing for children, but it also resulted in entirely new genres of literature for women and children. The rhetoric that emphasized domestic education as the first and most important regenerative force also resulted in two new ideological constructs. First, as a stress on domestic education and autonomy, like that promoted by Rousseau's *Emile,* increased in prominence, it was accompanied by language that explained how maternal love was necessary to teach the crucial civic characteristic of self-control. Second, the highlighting of discrete gender roles and their links to social rejuvenation also resulted in an increased emphasis on the implications of women's actions as they affected both private and public life.

In 1834, just one year after the Saint-Simonian "Year of the Mother" and the passage of Guizot's law requiring every commune to have a public school, the first edition of Louis-Aimé Martin's *The Education of Mothers: or the Civilization of Mankind by Women* was published in Paris. This highly popular educational treatise incorporates all the characteristics that came from the cultural impact of Rousseauian rhetoric about maternal love and training in self-control. It lauded the role of the domestic mother as the central figure to nurture virtue and self-control in order to create truly free people. While no historians have done an in-depth study of Martin's work, this scholarly oversight should not diminish its importance. Martin's book, which devoted hundreds of pages to praising domestic motherhood, was exceedingly popular. The book was published in multiple French editions, both expensive and cheap, and was reprinted throughout the nineteenth century. It was also translated into English where it again went through many editions (more than twenty in the United States alone). Like Rousseau's *Emile,* Martin's work linked concern for education and an emphasis on self-control and domestic motherhood with demands for social change. Unlike Rousseau's work, however, which promoted domesticity as a new force, *The Education of Mothers* was published at a time when the ideal of domestic nurturing was ever more taken for granted. The publication numbers alone indicate that Martin was speaking to an already-receptive audience and had a wide popular appeal that went beyond disciples of Rousseau. Ideas that were nascent in 1762 had been widely embraced by 1834.

Even at first glance, it is relatively easy to see how Martin's language fit into an increased emphasis on domesticity. In *The Education of Mothers,* Martin resorted to the typical paeans of the era. He began, like Rousseau, with an address to women, who, he claimed, possessed the "voice whose sweet eloquence can penetrate the very depths of our soul" and can "impress upon the hearts of our children those divine truths which no resolution can overturn."[1] Readers could hardly miss the Rousseauian echo, nor could they think it accidental. Martin's entire work, as he himself explained, was inspired by Jean-Jacques. Martin outlined how Rousseau, in *Emile,* first pointed to the true path to social change:

One man, one man alone, at this juncture, thought of the future destinies of the country; and this man was not even a Frenchman, he was the son of a poor watchmaker of Geneva named Rousseau . . . His aim was to give citizens to the country, while he appeared only to think of giving mothers to our children! The mother's milk shall be the milk of liberty! Concealing the regeneration of France beneath the veil of an isolated education, he removes his pupil from the falsehoods of public education: in this plan, so vast, in which one saw merely the child and its tutor, the genius of Rousseau comprised all that might constitute a great people; he knew that ideas of individual liberty do not fail speedily to become ideas of national liberty. While educating a man, he thought of forming a nation.[2]

Martin was a Rousseauian through and through and, though he wrote seventy years after Rousseau, he emphasized Rousseau's own ideals, especially women's unique capacity to change the world through self-control and nurturing domesticity. He waxed eloquent concerning his mentor's relationship to female readers, saying that Rousseau did "not come as a severe moralist to impose sad and unfortunate duties" but that, instead,

> it is a family *fête* which he convokes; it is a mother which he presents to the adoration of the world, seated near the cradle, a beautiful child on her bosom, her countenance beaming with joy under the tender looks of her husband. A delightful picture, which revealed to woman a divine power, that of rendering us happy by virtue. Never did the human voice fulfil a more holy mission; at the voice of Rousseau each woman again becomes a mother, each mother again becomes a wife, each child will be a citizen.[3]

Martin assumed, with Rousseau and many intellectuals of the late eighteenth and early nineteenth centuries, that true change relied on women's power to inculcate virtue.

While Martin believed that he was continuing to promote the agenda set forth in *Emile*, and while his work was, like Rousseau's, ideologically prevalent, *The Education of Mothers* also demonstrated how radical an impact domestic ideals could have on cultural and intellectual trends. Louis-Aimé Martin was neither a conservative nor a reactionary. Martin considered himself a disciple of the pre-Romantic Bernardin de Saint-Pierre, and the Romantic poet and political activist Lamartine was a close friend. Like Lamartine, Martin's own ideology was firmly democratic, if politically idealistic. Martin promoted Rousseau's principles as the basis for an increasingly egalitarian society and applied Rousseauian ideals more generally than Rousseau himself did. Martin went much farther than the nurturing education of one boy; his work argued for advancement in the treatment of all people, especially women. While he admitted that Rousseau's writings did not go as far as Rousseau's social vision implied, Martin saw the educational mission of *Emile* as the first step toward women's liberation, with further developments relying on the changes begun after Rousseau. Martin's work thus demonstrates how men and women could see Rousseau and gendered domestic ideals best in the context of a revolution in the nation, a revolution directed by autonomous women. "There is in the heart of a woman something of republicanism which incites her to heroism and to self-sacrifice; and it is there that Rousseau looks for support: it is there, also, that he finds the power."[4] Without virtuous mothers, there could be no virtuous citizens.

The fact that motherhood had assumed a place of ideological prominence in the seventy-plus years between the publication of *Emile* and *The Education of Mothers* meant that this work could range farther afield than Rousseau had. If Rousseau's educational proposals were primarily theoretical, Martin's work appealed to a society that had already changed its relationship to women. While in 1762, Rousseau hoped to create a "good mother who knows how to think," by 1834, Martin believed that he was speaking to an already-formed audience of good mothers, and of husbands and fathers who might be persuaded to see their wives in a different light. As Martin explained, "[s]ince the period of Fénelon and Rousseau there has been progress among men, and the education of women has consequently improved. We now no longer discuss the question, whether they should be instructed, or the amount of the instruction which should be allowed them. We agree to develop their intelligence."[5] Martin thus wished to link the theoretical work of *Emile* with the new reader of the nineteenth century, who was likely to operate under very different assumptions than an eighteenth-century reader of Rousseau.

Martin demonstrated how far the ideas had come in seventy years insofar as he emphasized the education of all women in a new context, that of their liberation from men's tyranny and oppression, in order to improve all of society. As he explained, "[t]his is the essential point, or to express it better, it is the summary of the education of mothers of families. The object is, in fact, to cause women to emerge from the narrow circle to which society confines them, and to expand their thoughts over all the subjects which may make us better and happier."[6] He wished for a training that would "lead [women] to think with their own thoughts."[7] In "barbarous times women were slaves or servants," and at "the first glimmerings of civilization they became our housekeepers, then our companions," and still later, "they were less restricted to their houses, and were more closely united to the world by their agreeable talents, and to their husbands by the development of their intellect."[8] But he wished to see them take a leading role in the creation of a profoundly egalitarian society. In a better world, society, "having arrived at a more perfect state of civilization, without losing its courteous forms, recognized the rights of men, and woman assumed her position in the state; she was at once a housekeeper, a companion, and a citizen."[9] Martin wished to make certain that education would allow women to be fully free so that they would be part of a society that was also fully free. *The Education of Mothers* appeared in a context where a cultural and intellectual emphasis on nurturing education and the civic influence of mothers was increasingly taken for granted. This meant, Martin believed, that promotion of domestic ideals could take the next step forward, in order to emphasize the connection between the education and liberation of women and that of society as a whole. In brief, Martin used Rousseau, so often cited as an anti-feminist, as his model in order to advocate the freeing of women and the creation of an egalitarian society.

Domestic Education as the First Regenerative Force

Martin did not base his demands for a freer society on equal access to public instruction. While he had initially harbored great hope for the possibility of reform driven by changing instructional practices, he soon became disillusioned with this goal and realized, as had legislators in the French Revolution and the early nineteenth century, that "it is not from a law upon public instruction, even were it a good law, that we must seek the remedy for the evil [of social excesses]. This remedy will be found in the mixture of the two educations, private and public, it is there, and there only. This is the anchor of safety amidst the storm."[10] After all, "it is not the intellect which produces civilization."[11] Rather, his work argued that that the "maintenance of our liberties" relied on the existence of "mothers of our country" who would "train up good and faithful citizens."[12] Like Rousseau, Martin firmly placed private education ahead of public instruction and argued that only when the regeneration of the family had taken place could the regeneration of the nation begin.

The difference between private education and public instruction turned on virtue and self-control taught by a nurturing mother, exactly as the intellectual and cultural shifts after *Emile* had emphasized. Again, Martin built on the educational theory of the preceding century and made reference to a pervasive cultural construct when he insisted that children's domestic education was the most important. Since children's blank slates were written on by their first instructor, love and personal example were the most powerful sources of training. "[E]ducation belongs by right to women; they alone know how to smile upon childhood, they alone can seize by sympathy the first transports of a soul which is awakened by their caresses. We transfer this work to rhetoricians and to logicians, but they arrive too late."[13] However, the mother's special role was not merely as the first educator, otherwise, the solution would have been to send children out for ever-earlier instruction. In fact, Martin's work explicitly repudiated that notion, saying: "Let us, then, not seek out of the family for the governor of our children; the one which nature presents to us will relieve us from the necessity of inquiring further, and that one we shall every where find; in the cottage of the poor, as in the palace of the rich, every where endowed with the same prefect, and ready to make the same sacrifices."[14]

As the last quotation implies, the fact that almost all children had mothers to raise them inspired additional approval from Martin. If society was to become more egalitarian, then the methods of education would themselves have to be available to all. "Men only educate those who have gold; one may buy a tutor. Nature is more munificent, she gives one to each child. Leave, then, the child under the protection of its mother; it is not without design that Nature has confided it at its birth to the only love which is always faithful, to the only devotedness which terminates but with life."[15] Instruction remained unequal in its ideals, which limited the amount of social change that one could expect from it. However, motherhood was, at least in theory, natural and available to all. All families could benefit from, and in fact were in desperate need of, a mother's teaching.

The mother was uniquely gifted to develop the virtue and intellect, for only a mother "can teach us to prefer honour to fortune, to cherish our fellow-creatures, to relieve the unfortunate, to elevate our souls to the source of the beautiful and the infinite."[16] Mothers were, as the rhetoric of the years after *Emile* had established, the primary educators of their children and in a unique position to help their children develop the qualities that would make them good citizens. "Nature attaches them to your bosoms, awakens them by your caresses: she wills that they should owe every thing to you, so that after having received from you life and thought, these earthly angels await your inspirations, in order to believe and love."[17] Mothers, who combined nurturing love with early education, were universal teachers.

Maternal Love Leads to Self-Control

The fact that Martin emphasized the mother's role instead of that of the tutor demonstrates one concrete way in which *The Education of Mothers* drew not only on Rousseau but also retheorized self-control in light of the broader intellectual and cultural shifts that had followed the publication of *Emile*. Virtue and maternal influence were linked in an unbreakable bond, for only they would persuade the child to follow the teacher on the appropriate path toward self-control. A mother's job was to acquire "dominion over the soul" in order to "control the senses, and leave to time and nature the care of re-establishing harmony between them."[18] The mother would do far more than a tutor, as where "[a]n ordinary preceptor counsels and moralizes; that which he offers to our memory, a mother ingrafts in our hearts: she makes us love that which he can at most but make us believe, and it is by love that she leads us to virtue."[19] Martin expanded on the idea that children needed domestic education in order to be prepared for life beyond the home.

[C]hildren only understand what they see, and comprehend only what they feel—sentiment in them always precedes intelligence; therefore, to those who teach them to see, who awaken their tenderness, belong all the happiest influences. Virtue is not merely taught, it is inspired: the talent of women consists especially in the circumstance, that what they desire, they make us love—a delightful means of making us value it.[20]

Only mothers could perform the "mission of love," which was "to make us delight in virtue."[21] A mother's job was, as a result, far more than mere procreation to produce "an intelligent biped; it is a complete man which the world requires from them."[22] Mothers were the crucial link in creating whole men who could establish a properly virtuous nation.

When speaking of virtue, Martin did not refer to practical virtues such as temperance or generosity. Rather, his book emphasized that the most socially necessary virtue and the one most natural to maternal education was self-control. Mothers were the best teachers to lovingly mold children who could control their passions. This work thereby confirmed the ways in which domestic advice manuals and children's literature had noted that self-control was a quality that was developed prerationally, by loving mothers. Indeed, Martin echoed Rousseau's explanations about Emile's education when he explained that "[a]nimals enjoy the gifts of nature, but only within the limits of their faculties; when once satisfied they stop . . . Man's desires, on the other hand, are so exorbitant that nothing can satisfy them, and he soon perceives the necessity of restraining them within bounds."[23] The real difference between men and animals was not speaking or standing upright, but that man could "struggle with and conquer himself . . . The virtuous man is he in whom the will of the spiritual being is stronger than the will of the material being."[24] "To resist our passions, is to verify the existence in us of a will stronger than our passions."[25] And, in order to advance intellectually and socially, "[t]o make oneself a character for wisdom and virtue," one had to know how to "advance freely and resolutely against the torrent of our vice and of our passions . . . whence it results that the most powerful and free creature in the universe is he who knows how to submit to pain in obeying the dictates of virtue."[26] Freedom, both individually and socially, required a proper education in self-control. "Man is always free, but he is not always strong enough to make good use of his freedom; strong minds make the passions bend, other minds yield to them. Thus man enjoys true liberty only in strength and in enlightenment."[27] In this language, Martin gave a clear nod to Rousseau, who had explained, in *Emile*, that "[t]he man who is truly free only desires what he is capable of doing and only does what pleases him."[28] Only mothers could make truly free men.

Freer Men Require Freer Mothers

The idea that only a mother could provide her children with nurturing training in self-control and that no parents should seek to send their children outside the home for their initial education had some concrete repercussions for Martin's work. If only mothers could teach virtue through their unique attachment to children, then all mothers would need to be prepared to become nurturing parents who could foster freedom and self-control. That did not mean only the types of training that had been emphasized in literature after Rousseau, such as breast-feeding, physical freedom, and attention to children's desires. Since the exercise of virtue was a direct result of the mother's influence, and as contemporary ideology held, "[w]hatever be the customs or the laws of a country, it is the women who give the direction to its manners," then women, "be they our idols or our companions, courtesans, slaves, or beasts of burthen . . . will make us what they themselves are . . . Here then is a law of eternal justice; man cannot debase women without becoming himself degraded; he cannot elevate them without becoming better."[29] Martin explained that, historically, European women had not been treated as equals, with disastrous results.[30]

Our political and moral indifference, the ignorance of our interests and of our duties, the forgetfulness of our country, our petty vanities, our faults, our evils, all this is the work of women. Their character is become the national character. We have been obliged to receive from them what they had obtained from us. But let our mothers become citizens and all will be changed; instead of disputing, like nurses as to which has the prettiest and best dressed children, they would emulate each other as to which should best sow . . . the seeds of virtue in the soul, and of vigour in the mind.[31]

When women were slaves and unequal partners at home, then they would perpetuate slavery and inequality. The only way to achieve total social regeneration was to incorporate women as equals, as half of society.[32] As Martin emphatically complained, "[y]ou desire to restrict women to the mere management of their houses—you would only instruct them for that purpose; but you do not reflect that it is from the house of each citizen that the errors and the prejudices which prevail in the world, emanate."[33] Education in childcare and housekeeping would not solve the problem, for wives and mothers needed to be as enlightened as men in order to assist in the perfection of the nation.

It is here that Martin's argument needs a bit of fleshing out. He explained to his readers that "[t]o labour for [women's] education, is, then, to labour for our own. By giving them elevated and noble thoughts, we destroy at one blow our petty passions and our petty ambitions. We shall be so much the more worthy, in proportion as they become better; and they cannot render us better without becoming happier."[34] At first glance, this argument is persuasive. And yet, if self-control was the most important component in shaping a child into a future citizen, and women could demonstrate self-control at home, there is no obvious reason that children could not learn self-control from an oppressed housewife as well as, or perhaps better than, a citizen mother. But Martin was convinced that women's oppression was not autonomous self-control, but external control. If women had no choice and remained untrained and unequal to men, they could not make free civic choices. In order to raise children who would freely join in the new society, women had to model self-control as equals and demonstrate to their children how to choose freely a greater good. If the "most perfect and complete man" accepts his place in life "and far from killing the animal passions, regulates and deifies them by the sense of the beautiful, by reason and conscience,"[35] then it was surely no less important that women enter into society in similar ways. If they were to teach their children to use their self-control in order to remake their world, they too would have to be free enough to remake their worlds. While it was true that, in the process, a woman might need to sublimate her desires for a greater social cause, that was further proof of the value of that cause and was certainly not unlike what was expected of men in the political arena. As Elisabeth Colwill has pointed out: "Politics, in theory the ideal forum for the masculine self, in practice meant the voluntary subjection of the individual to the single will of Convention, Senate, or Emperor."[36]

None of this should suggest that Martin's work abandoned clear-cut gender roles. However, he was careful to note that women's work in a domestic realm, and women's importance in a realm for them alone, did not mean that women should be removed from the polity.

We know women as mothers, let us try to know them as lovers and as wives. In the age which has just passed away, they were nothing more than that, and yet they have reigned: in the age which is approaching, they will be something more, they will be citizens; and this title, which requires more enlightenment and reflection, promises to them a new empire."[37]

Both men and women were full members of society and, in fact, their self-control was best seen in its public context. "Sociability . . . is a condition of man's life, a second creation, which imparts to him all his value: for not only does it snatch him from these barbarities, but it discovers in him virtues and sentiments which would die without it." [38] In this context, as in many others, Martin explicitly used "men" to speak of a general imperative that he applied to "mankind." Both men and women needed to develop self-control. Both men and women needed to be integrated into society in order to be virtuous, and society as a whole needed free men and women in order to move forward. In the end, Louis-Aimé Martin offered his nineteenth-century readers a profoundly gendered and yet radically egalitarian look at domesticity, and he claimed that Rousseau was his inspiration.

Martin's work, which was immensely popular and drew on cultural and intellectual changes from *Emile* forward, ties together the currents of this work and demonstrates in some concrete ways how demands for maternal education and self-control could also lead to a broader acceptance of women's civic participation. Martin, who wrote after the promulgation of Guizot's law, distinguished between the goals of education and those of instruction. He did not ignore public instruction but, seeing it as secondary, chose to emphasize instead the foundational importance of the nurturing mother in the context of Rousseau's demands for self-control and social change. Despite, or perhaps because of, his agreement with Rousseau, his agitation for women's rights was part and parcel of his worldview. *The Education of Mothers* thus not only demonstrates the cultural force behind maternal education but also contextualizes it within demands for change, not for conservatism or the status quo.

Women Enter the World

An engraving from 1826, *The Prize for Wisdom,* reworks a similar revolutionary image and demonstrates the model that Martin took for granted when he wrote nearly ten years later (figure 16). In this engraving, a schoolteacher and her charge return to a young girl's home. The girl shows her mother the prize of a laurel wreath that she has been given for succeeding at her studies. The title of the engraving does not use words that imply that the daughter is being rewarded for intellectual achievements or technical skill but rather for "*sagesse,*" or wisdom and proper behavior.[39] Viewers understood that the girl had learned the most important lessons and, as a result, become mature and well-behaved, which was the true source of the approval. The girl's mother, her initial teacher and motivator, is in the center of the image and her kiss is one of the possible "prizes" that the girl received for wisdom. The father not only looks on from the sidelines but even exists entirely outside the main composition. The women in the engraving are central to the message, providing a laurel wreath, a kiss of approval, and even a promise of future responsibilities. Affection and nurturing are the motivating forces behind "wisdom," as we see a young woman who had been guided by her mother's love and as a result had herself begun to make wise decisions outside her home.

The symbolism of the painting confirms this impression. While the father and dog do not stand in any particular relationship to the medallions on the floor, all three women stand on the tiles in such a way that the lines that angle back and link the diamonds emphasize their locations. If one were to trace a line through the diamonds at the mother's feet and those that run through the schoolteacher's skirt, they form a triangle that cov-

Figure 16. The Prize for Wisdom. 1826. Bibliothèque nationale de France

ers the young girl.[40] Both mother and teacher are central to shaping her character. Additionally, and perhaps even more significantly, the placement and lighting of the three female figures forms a second triangle that draws the viewer's attention to the schoolteacher. In this sense, the *institutrice*, who oversees the touching return of the wise daughter to the home, occupies a position of more importance than either father or mother. In fact, according to standards of artistic composition from the era, the teacher's location at the apex indicates the *institutrice's* position as the true focal point of the image. The teacher does more than share in the glory of her successful student; she emphasizes the future of all wise girls and the relationship between family life and public responsibilities. A girl's primary influence on society could—and perhaps even should— be worked out in a context that included life outside the home.

Ultimately, this image offers us a vision of the ways in which a woman might use her skills in order to form the new society. The girl returns home with the laurel prize for proper behavior and is, we can assume, ready to take on adult responsibilities. Her mother, who provided the foundation for the daughter's proper behavior, recognizes and rewards her daughter's success, while the schoolteacher looks on approvingly. Both adults have passed on the necessary behavior so that the young girl will be prepared to act properly. And yet, the absence of other small children and the artistic centrality of the schoolteacher offer a more ambiguous message than we might initially discern from Rousseau, advice manuals, or didactic tales themselves. The young woman who internalized the gendered social lessons in self-control was now fit to become a mother, but the rhetoric also offered her a role as a nurturing presence outside the home, perhaps in a space such as a school. "Certainly the concept of public and private played an important role in pedagogical writing, but this rhetoric of separate spheres needs to be deconstructed . . . [w]omen adopted Rousseau's message concerning civic virtue and the family to forge a space for themselves within society." [41] Self-control continued to be the central and universal characteristic, and women's command of it allowed, and even encouraged, them to see themselves as part of society as a whole, not simply part of a nuclear family.

Why Study Domesticity?

For far too long, tales of education have focused on public instruction and political change and have assumed that domestic education was essentially irrelevant, a cipher in public life. While a great deal of work has been done on the history of public education, little historical work has been done on domestic education and child-rearing. More than the topic has been ignored. Sources produced in domestic contexts, such as children's literature and advice manuals, have also been routinely ignored or analyzed only within a limited context. Even as more recent historical works question the real distance between public and private and argue that domesticity was freeing in a limited sense, they have often continued to operate, both in their historical analysis and in their use of sources, as if "separate spheres" ideology has meant fundamentally the same thing from the eighteenth to the twentieth centuries, that is to say, social and political inequality between men and women and ever-increasing oppression based on gender difference.[42] Not surprisingly, then, most historical work has generally supported Carol Pateman's argument that the exclusion of women from political life clearly demonstrates how, "[i]n civil society, all men, not just fathers, can generate political life and political right. Political creativity belongs not to paternity but masculinity."[43] Gender distinctions in this view mean gender exclusion. As women's femaleness became emphasized, historians have insisted that it led, irrevocably, down the path of exclusion from civic life.

Schooling seemed to provide confirmation of this trend. Public education increased in importance, and yet this foundational form of public life was designed without consideration for girls. In general, boys were to become learned while girls could develop the skills of running a household by staying at home with their mothers. For boys, both public and private training was necessary and complementary. For girls, whose usefulness was expected to be as wives and mothers within the home, public schooling was not of paramount importance. Some, like Jacques Revel, have even dismissed women's private educational roles when they argued that the public school became necessary because "the family, under the authority of the father, was the place where a certain kind of education took place, but that by itself was no longer enough. Discipline was also needed, and the proper kind of discipline could be found only in the schools."[44] From multiple perspectives, women and family life have been seen as irrelevant to understanding civic life.

Despite this general consensus, there have been historians who hinted that domesticity's politics needed to be reexamined. In the American context, studies of republican motherhood have insisted that even women's indirect contributions were essential to understanding civic change. Linda Kerber, for example, argued that republican motherhood preserved traditional gender roles at the same time that it carved out a new, political role for women. She explains:

The ideology of Republican Motherhood also represented a stage in the process of women's political socialization. In recent years, we have become accustomed to thinking of political socialization as a *process* in which an individual develops a definition of self as related to the state. One of the intermediate stages in that process might be called the deferential citizen: the person who expects to influence the political system, but only to a limited extent. Deference represents not the negation of citizenship, but an approach to full participation in the civic culture.[45]

Jurgen Habermas also suggested the importance of domestic life for the public sphere. As Mary Ryan has explained, his analysis of public life relied on private education. "Without familial training in civility . . . the citizens of republics would be ill prepared to act rationally and unselfishly in behalf of the common good."[46] Despite these insights into the power of family formation, historians as well as political and literary theorists have often continued to see Rousseauian domesticity in particular as a way to exclude women from public life.[47] For example, Lynn Hunt has argued that "[d]omestic ideology only emerged in France because political and cultural leaders felt the need to justify in some systematic way the continuing exclusion of women from politics."[48]

Certainly, at first glance, Rousseau's domestic rhetoric, like that found in *Emile,* does not seem to be particularly forward-thinking. However, the documents demonstrate an increasing emphasis on maternal author-ity and on home life's ideological importance, long before a child would go to public school, in providing a discipline and training in self-control that would allow children to enter public life. When seen in the context of cultural and ideological changes in domesticity, this work may help put to rest the idea that domestic ideology and an increasing emphasis on gen-der have necessarily been retrograde and oppressive. Rather than seeing eighteenth- and nineteenth-century gender distinctions as the basis for women's exclusion from power, this work indicates how complex the process of liberation could be. Even if "gender inequality is a central and defining element of Enlightenment reason,"[49] the gender distinctions that Rousseau emphasized may not be the cause for women's exclusion from public responsibilities and instead may actually have enabled women to claim new forms of civic power.

Rather than accept that governmental intervention and political change were the only sources of power, this study has added nuance to the dis-tinction between public and private by demonstrating how politics and public life were not ideologically coterminous with civic participation. Early visions of nineteenth-century schooling operated on the assumption that the liberal "public" sphere existed because of its "private" counter-part, and that both were civic in nature. Rousseau's mother may not have intended to seize the political limelight or mount the rostrum, but her so-cial spaces were central to the public good, and to assert otherwise is to continue to prioritize political modes of thought and historical inequity. While some leaders may have used the rhetoric of domesticity in order to promote women's exclusion from politics, male and female educators, political, and public, women, as well as early feminists of all stripes also used domestic ideology "to endow woman's role with more competence, dignity, and consequence"[50] and demonstrated the ways in which women were now a central part of civic life. Eighteenth-century ideals, such as those found in Rousseau's *Emile,* demonstrate one way in which the rhet-oric of domesticity could contribute to the language of reform and liberal ideologies and, despite appearances, could be progressive, "criticizing, not celebrating the status quo."[51]

While the inscription of women within the home might seem to confirm the view that, at least in its initial impulses, modernity is anti-feminist, the evidence presented in this work—including clothing, advice manuals, and children's books—presents another image. Certainly much of the rheto-ric surrounding "separate spheres" is indeed misogynist and relies on a perception of women as inferior to men for its rhetorical success. And yet, the ideological authority wielded by domestic women tells a more posi-tive story. Rather than an outgrowth of the "sexual contract" where men exercised political power over women who were little more than domestic servants, the ideal of the domestic wife and mother could offer a sphere of autonomy within which a woman's work was powerful and valuable, even dominant, as the displaced father in *The Prize for Wisdom* might attest.

All of this also suggests that the picture of modernity as uniformly disciplining and ever more constraining may be unnecessarily bleak. While modern life is often coercive and nearly always requires a greater degree of self-control, these developments need not always be opposed to increasing freedom and equality. State-run educational systems did intend to train the individual and were more generally coercive than the more diffuse structures that had existed before. And yet, the fact is that, by the middle of the nineteenth century, national primary schooling flourished alongside a literature that gave domestic mothers authority and power over the household, argued that they were full participants in a new civic state, and advocated the preparation of children for their social duties, not by hanging them on hooks, but by loving and nurturing them and then slowly nudging them toward autonomy and the fulfillment of their modern obligations.

The cultural and intellectual history of this period thus makes it clear that ideas about individuality, gender, and self-control were formed not only in the salons of Enlightenment France but also at the skirts of the domestic mothers of the nineteenth century. The increasing valorization of motherhood and nurturing domesticity between 1762 and 1833 meant that there was a new emphasis on the formative experiences of childhood and the roles of mothers in guiding those experiences. Both mothers and children were to demonstrate virtuous self-control in order to be fully autonomous individuals. While women's social position was not yet founded on an egalitarian perspective for French society, the power of domestic rhetoric did not have to reside in its anti-feminism, but could equally exist in the world of possibilities that it offered, including full integration into civic life. Within the new ideologies, not only were women valued as unique individuals with foundational social roles, but also both women and men were expected to exhibit the same basic qualities of rationality and self-control. This meant that they were equally important in the formation of society and potentially shared similar responsibilities for maintaining social order. Changes from 1762 to 1833 led to the prominence of a cultural discourse in which women, like men, had real worth and natural rights, even if that worth and those rights were often enunciated in nonegalitarian ways. In the shift from a hierarchical society to one based on merit, increased differentiation may have focused on gender in a way that now seems problematic, but this focus need not imply a misogyny inherent in modernity.

Notes

Introduction. Enlightening Mothers: Gender and Self-Control in France
(pages 1–25)

1. Joan Landes, *Women and the Public Sphere in the Age of the French Revolution* (Ithaca, N.Y.: Cornell, University Press, 1988), 89.
2. Landes, *Women and the Public Sphere,* 226.
3. Lydia Lange, "Introduction," *Feminist Interpretations of Jean-Jacques Rousseau* (University Park: Pennsylvania State University Press, 2002), 1.
4. Susan Moller Okin, "Rousseau's Natural Woman," *Journal of Politics* 41 (May 1979): 395.
5. Robert Darnton ("Readers Respond to Rousseau," in *The Great Cat Massacre and Other Episodes in French Cultural History* [London: Lane, 1984], 215–56) has outlined some of the ways that women and men alike saw Rousseau's work as speaking directly to them and believed that it demanded a personal response. While Mary Seidman Trouille (*Sexual Politics in the Enlightenment: Women Writers Read Rousseau* [Albany: State University of New York Press, 1997]) has also demonstrated some of the ways that this response was hostile, her work demonstrates that even very educated and critical readers of Rousseau were often highly approving and enamored of his work.
6. Helena Rosenblatt, *Rousseau and Geneva: From the First Discourse to the Social Contract, 1749–1762* (New York: Cambridge University Press, 2007), and Lori Jo Marso, *(Un)Manly Citizens: Jean-Jacques Rousseau's and Germaine de Staël's Subversive Women* (Baltimore: Johns Hopkins University Press, 2001).
7. Joseph R. Reisert, *Jean-Jacques Rousseau: A Friend of Virtue* (Ithaca, N.Y.: Cornell University Press, 2003), ix.
8. See, for example, Victor Wexler, "'Made for Man's Delight': Rousseau as Antifeminist," *American Historical Review* 81 (April 1976). Helena Rosenblatt offers a solid historiography of this perspective—and takes clear issue with it—in "On the 'Misogyny' of Jean-Jacques Rousseau: The *Letter to d'Alembert* in Historical Context," *French Historical Studies* 25 (2002): 91–114.
9. Elizabeth Fox-Genovese, "Introduction," in *French Women and the Age of Enlightenment,* ed. Samia Spencer (Bloomington: Indiana University Press, 1984), 19.
10. The nature of the sources that remain from the eighteenth and nineteenth centuries necessarily limits this book to claims about cultural and intellectual, not social, change.

11. John Tosh, *A Man's Place: Masculinity and the Middle-Class Home in Victorian England* (New Haven: Yale University Press, 1999), p. 4.

12. Hugh Cunningham, *Children and Childhood in Western Society Since 1500* (New York: Longman, 1995), pp. 61ff.

13. Elizabeth Badinter, *Mother Love: Myth and Reality, Motherhood in Modern History* (New York: Macmillan, 1981); Ruth Bloch, "American Feminine Ideals in Transition: The Rise of the Moral Mother, 1785–1815," *Feminist Studies* 4 (1978); Isabelle Brouard-Arends, *Vies et images maternelles dans la littérature française du dix-huitième siècle*, Studies on Voltaire and the Eighteenth Century, vol. 291 (Oxford: Voltaire Foundation, 1991). This is not to argue that these mothers never loved their children or had intense emotional attachments to them but merely that their reproductive duties, not oversight of the day-to-day experiences or protection of their children, defined motherhood. One could be a "good" mother despite a lack of what we would today recognize as affection and nurturing concern. For example, the Empress Maria-Theresa evidenced a deep love for her husband that we would recognize as "modern," but was a "good mother" primarily in her ability to give birth to children and make solid political matches for them. Much of her correspondence with her offspring would, by present-day standards, be cold and calculating, concerned more with political gain than the personal happiness of the child.

14. Jean Jacques Rousseau, *Emile,* trans. Barbara Foxley, ed. Peter D. Jimack (London: Everyman, 1993), 10.

15. Rousseau, *Emile* (Jimack), 5.

16. Staël (1788), in Peter D. Jimack, "Editor's Introduction to Jean Jacques Rousseau," *Emile* (London: Everyman, 1993), xl.

17. See, for example, *The Archaeology of Knowledge and The Discourse on Language,* trans. A. M. Sheridan Smith (New York: Pantheon Books, 1982); *Discipline and Punish: The Birth of the Prison,* trans. Alan Sheridan (New York: Vintage Books, 1995); and *Madness and Civilization: A History of Insanity in the Age of Reason,* trans. Richard Howard (New York: Vintage Books, 1988).

18. Norbert Elias, *The Civilizing Process: The History of Manners and State Formation and Civilization,* trans. Edmund Jephcott (Cambridge: Blackwell, 1994), 151.

19. Elias, *Civilizing Process,* 182.

20. Landes, *Women and the Public Sphere,* 69.

21. Carole Pateman, *The Sexual Contract* (Stanford: Stanford University Press, 1988), 7. See also Zillah Eisenstein, *The Radical Future of Liberal Feminism* (Boston: Northeastern University Press, 1993); James Sterba, *Social and Political Philosophy: Classical Western Texts in Feminist and Multicultural Perspectives* (Belmont, Calif.: Wadsworth, 1998); and Andrea Nye, *Feminism and Modern Philosophy: An Introduction* (New York: Routledge, 2004).

22. Mira Morgenstern, *Rousseau and the Politics of Ambiguity: Self, Culture, and Society* (University Park: Pennsylvania State University Press, 1996).

23. Suzanne Desan, *The Family on Trial in Revolutionary France* (Berkeley: University of California Press, 2004), 10.

24. For example, Bonnie Smith, *Ladies of the Leisure Class: The Bourgeoises*

of Northern France in the Nineteenth Century (Princeton: Princeton University Press, 1981); Nancy Cott, *The Bonds of Womanhood: "Woman's Sphere" in New England, 1780–1835* (New Haven: Yale University Press, 1997); Leonore Davidoff and Catherine Hall, Family Fortunes: *Men and Women of the English Middle Class, 1780–1850* (Chicago: University of Chicago Press, 1991); and Laurel Thatcher Ulrich, *Good Wives: Image and Reality in the Lives of Women in Northern New England, 1650–1750* (New York: Oxford University Press, 1983).

25. See Jennifer Ngaire Heuer, *The Family and the Nation: Gender and Citizenship in Revolutionary France, 1789–1830* (Ithaca: Cornell University Press, 2005).

26. Work in the American context such as Linda Kerber's on the "Republican mother" ("The Republican Mother: Women and the Enlightenment—An American Perspective," *American Quarterly* 28:2 [1976]: 187–205) allows for the existence of a mother who performs a political function, however, it explicitly argues that the Rousseauian model of domesticity is an exclusive one, not one that is central to political socialization.

27. Desan, *Family on Trial*, 11.

28. Lydia Lange's *Feminist Interpretations* has a number of essays that confront these issues.

29. Jean Jacques Rousseau, *Discourse on the Origins and Foundations of Inequality Among Men* (New York: Penguin, 1984), 90.

30. Reisert, *Friend of Virtue*, 8.

31. Jean Jacques Rousseau, *Emile, or On Education*, trans. Allan Bloom (New York: Basic, 1979), 7.

32. Jeanne-Louise-Henriette Genest Campan. *De l'éducation* (Paris: Baudouin Frères, 1824), 2.

33. See, for example, R. R. Palmer, *The Improvement of Humanity: Education and the French Revolution* (Princeton: Princeton University Press, 1985); see also Jean Bloch, *Rousseauism and Education in Eighteenth-Century France,* Studies on Voltaire and the Eighteenth Century, vol. 325 (Oxford: Voltaire Foundation, 1995), 32–33; James Bowen, *A History of Western Education,* vol. 3, *The Modern West: Europe and the New World* (London: Methuen, 1981); C. A. Ottevanger, "From Subject to Citizen: The Evolution of French Educational Theory in the Eighteenth Century," *Transactions of the 7th International Congress on the Enlightenment,* Studies on Voltaire and the Eighteenth Century, vol. 264 (Oxford: Voltaire Foundation, 1989); and Edward J. Power, *A Legacy of Learning: A History of Western Education* (Albany: State University of New York Press, 1991).

34. David Hunt, *Parents and Children in History: The Psychology of Family Life in Early Modern France* (New York: Basic, 1970), 51.

35. Colin Heywood, *Childhood in Nineteenth-Century France: Work, Health, and Education Among the "Classes Populaires"* (New York: Cambridge University Press, 1988), 219.

36. This study does not intend to enter the debate about parental affection and concern except to argue that the terms of the debate itself are faulty. To our contemporary eye, it seems unlikely that parents who loved their children intensely would send them far away from home. However, just as this work argues

that freedom must be contextualized to be understood, it also accepts that judging the emotional expressions of the past with reference to modern norms of affection is unwise.

37. François Furet and Jacques Ozouf (*Lire et écrire : L'alphabétisation des Français de Calvin à Jules Ferry,* 2 vols. [Paris: Éditions de Minuit, 1977]) deal best with this distinction; see also Mary Jo Maynes, *Schooling in Western Europe: A Social History* (Albany: State University of New York Press, 1985), and Isser Woloch, *The New Regime: Transformations of the French Civic Order, 1789–1820s,* (New York: W. W. Norton, 1994).

38. For more discussion of the various contexts for schooling and literacy education, see also the essay collection edited by Donald N. Baker and Patrick J. Harrigan, *The Making of Frenchmen: Current Directions in the History of Education in France, 1679–1979* (Waterloo, Ont.: Historical Reflections Press, 1980).

39. Kerber, "Republican Mother," 187–205.

40. Annie Smart, "Bonnes Mères Qui Savent Penser": Motherhood and a Boy's Education in Rousseau's *Emile* and Epinay's *Lettres à Mon Fils,*" *New Perspectives on the Eighteenth Century* 3 (2006): 21–31.

41. Rousseau, *Emile* (Bloom), 46.

42. See, for example, Rebecca Rogers, *From the Salon to the Schoolroom: Educating Bourgeois Girls in Nineteenth-Century France* (University Park: Pennsylvania State University Press, 2005).

43. Jennifer M. Jones, *Sexing* La Mode: *Gender, Fashion and Commercial Culture in Old Regime France* (New York: Berg, 2004), xvii.

44. Karin Lee Fishbeck Calvert's *Children in the House: The Material Culture of Early Childhood, 1600–1900* (Boston: Northeastern University Press, 1992) offers a wonderfully detailed treatment of children's material culture in America. Unfortunately, there is no comparable work for the European context generally nor for France specifically.

45. A. V. Salguès, *L'Amie des mères des famille, ou Traité d'éducation physique et morale des enfans* (Paris: Dentu, 1810), frontispiece.

46. Campan, *De l'éducation,* 121.

47. Badinter, *Mother Love;* Brouard-Arends, *Vies et images maternelles;* Shari L. Thurer, *The Myths of Motherhood: How Culture Reinvents the Good Mother* (New York: Houghton Mifflin, 1994); Barbara Ehrenreich and Deirdre English, *For Her Own Good: 150 Years of the Experts' Advice to Women* (New York: Doubleday, 1978); Christina Hardyment, *Dream Babies: Three Centuries of Good Advice on Child Care* (New York: Harper and Row, 1983); and Henriette Marshall, "The Social Construction of Motherhood: An Analysis of Children and Parenting Manuals," in *Motherhood: Meanings, Practices, and Ideologies,* ed. Ann Phoenix, Anne Woollett, and Eva Lloyd (London: Sage, 1991), 66–86.

48. G. J. Barker-Benfield, *The Culture of Sensibility: Sex and Society in Eighteenth-Century Britain* (Chicago: University of Chicago Press, 1992) and Victoria de Grazia, ed., *The Sex of Things: Gender and Consumption in Historical Perspective* (Los Angeles: University of California Press, 1996).

49. Edward Shorter, *The Making of the Modern Family* (New York: Basic, 1975) and Bonnie Smith, *Ladies.*

50. Françoise Huguet, *Les livres pour l'enfance et la jeunesse de Gutenberg à*

Guizot (Paris: INRP, 1997); Anne Renonciat, Viviane Erzaty, and Geneviève Patte, ed., *Livres d'enfance, Livres de France* (Paris, Hachette, 1998).

51. Rogers, *Salon to the Schoolroom*, 36.

52. Laura Strumingher, *What Were Little Girls and Boys Made Of? Primary Education in Rural France 1830–1880* (Albany: State University of New York Press, 1983).

53. Mira Morgenstern, *Politics of Ambiguity*, 196.

54. Given the length of the period under discussion, a number of concrete plans or issues will be left out that might be dealt with in a history of education. The revolutionary legislation will be most central, for it sets up the debates over the meaning and importance of schooling in ways that later debates often replicate. For information about the specifics of plans and/or political machinations, Maurice Gontard (*L'Enseignement primaire en France de la Révolution à la loi Guizot [1789–1833]: des petite écoles de la monarchie d'ancien régime aux écoles primaires de la monarchie bourgeoise* [Paris: Belles-Lettres, 1959]), is one of the most comprehensive sources, though Furet and Ozouf's study is more generally accessible.

55. Betty Friedan, *The Feminine Mystique* (New York: Norton, 1997).

1. Lessons from Rousseau: Self-Control, Sexual Difference, and Changing Ideals (pages 26–51)

1. Lucio Colletti, "Rousseau as Critic of Civil Society," in *From Rousseau to Lenin: Studies in Ideology and Society*, trans. John Merrington and Judith White (New York: Monthly Review Press, 1972), 148. See also Jean Bloch, *Rousseauism and Education in Eighteenth-Century France*, Studies on Voltaire and the Eighteenth Century, vol. 325 (Oxford: Voltaire Foundation, 1995), 32–33; Jean Starobinski, "La mise en accusation de la société," *Jean-Jacques Rousseau* (Neuchâtel: Université de Neuchâtel, 1978). Contemporaries also read *Emile* in this light. For the outcry of the censors, see the *Censure de La Faculté de Théologie de Paris contre le Livre qui a pour titre*, Emile ou de l'Education (Paris: Le-Prieur, 1762). Another good example can be seen in Joseph de Maistre, *Against Rousseau*, ed. and trans. Richard A. Lebrun (Montreal: McGill-Queen's University Press, 1996).

2. Colletti, "Rousseau as Critic," 144.

3. Robert Derathé, in Colletti, 148. Ernst Cassirer has provided what is perhaps the clearest formulation of the theory of social transformation in his *The Question of Jean-Jacques Rousseau*, ed. and trans. Peter Gay (Bloomington: Indiana University Press, 1963), though for others such as Jean Dautry ("Le Revolution Bourgeoise et l'*Encyclopédie*," *La Pensée* 38 [1951]: 73–80), this concept informs their arguments about the role of Rousseauian thought in the French Revolution.

4. Rousseau, in Madeleine B. Ellis, *Rousseau's Socratic Aemilian Myths: A Literary Collation of* Emile *and the* Social Contract (Columbus: Ohio State University Press, 1977), 5.

5. Rousseau, in Ellis, 11–12.

6. Reisert, *Friend of Virtue*, 8.

7. John Rawls, *A Theory of Justice* (Cambridge: Harvard University Press, 1971), 11; Andrew Levine, *The Politics of Autonomy* (Amherst: University of Massachusetts Press, 1976), 48ff; and, for a general overview of the state of studies on Rousseau, the edited volume on *The Legacy of Rousseau* (Chicago: University of Chicago Press, 1997) provides an excellent introduction.

8. Mira Morgenstern, *Rousseau and the Politics of Ambiguity: Self, Culture, and Society* (University Park: Pennsylvania State University Press, 1996), 183–84.

9. Allan Bloom, "Translator's Introduction," Jean-Jacques Rousseau, *Emile, or On Education* (New York: Basic, 1979), 4.

10. Allan Bloom, "Translator's Introduction," 4.

11. *Censure de La Faculté;* and De Maistre, *Against Rousseau.* Mary Wollstonecraft also responded to Rousseau's conception of the individual in *A Vindication of the Rights of Woman.*

12. Morgenstern, *Politics of Ambiguity,* 183–84.

13. Colletti, "Rousseau as Critic," 148. See also Bloch, *Rousseauism and Education,* 32–33; Starobinski, "La mise en accusation."

14. Mary Hilton and Pam Hirsch, *Practical Visionaries: Women, Education and Social Progress 1790–1930* (New York: Longman, 2000), 3.

15. Victor Wexler, "'Made for Man's Delight': Rousseau as Antifeminist," *American Historical Review* 81 (April 1976): 266.

16. Linda Kerber, "The Republican Mother: Women and the Enlightenment—An American Perspective," *American Quarterly* 28: 2 (1976); 192.

17. Harvey Chisick (*The Limits of Reform in the Enlightenment: Attitudes Toward the Education of the Lower Classes in Eighteenth-Century France* [Princeton: Princeton University Press, 1981]), is perhaps the best-known author on this subject, though C. E. Elwell (*The Influence of the Enlightenment on the Catholic Theory of Religious Education in France, 1750–1850* [Cambridge: Harvard University Press, 1944]) is also useful, if dated.

18. See especially Peter Gay, ed., *John Locke on Education* (New York: Teacher's College, Columbia University, 1964); and Nina Reicyn, *La Pédagogie de John Locke* (Paris: Hermann,1941).

19. John Locke, *Some Thoughts Concerning Education,* ed. John W. and Jean S. Yolton (New York: Oxford University Press, 1989), 103.

20. Locke, *Some Thoughts,* 106.

21. Locke, *Some Thoughts,* 105–107.

22. W. M. Spellman, *John Locke* (New York: St. Martin's, 1997), 85–88.

23. Locke, *Some Thoughts,* 117 and 121.

24. Locke, *Some Thoughts,* 134.

25. Locke, *Some Thoughts,* 135: " . . . fill his Head with suitable Idea's, such as may make him in love with the present Business . . . For a Child will learn three times as much when he is *in tune,* as he will with double the Time and Pains, when he goes awkwardly, or is drag'd unwillingly to it." It is important to note that neither Locke nor Rousseau was revolutionary in advocating the amusement of the child. In his *Civilité puérile* of 1530, nearly 150 years before Locke, Erasmus had also suggested that adults use children's natural affinities for objects and experi-

ences to teach proper behavior. However, Locke's focus on sense experience and the development of a rational plan for the upbringing of children systematized thought about all children's needs and abilities in a way that the *Civilité puérile* could not.

26. See James Axtell, *The Educational Writings of John Locke: A Critical Edition with Introduction and Notes* (Cambridge: Cambridge University Press, 1968), and Peter Shouls, *Reasoned Freedom: John Locke and Enlightenment* (Ithaca: Cornell University Press, 1992).

27. Locke, *Some Thoughts*, 83.

28. While this chapter will discuss both physical and mental education, the importance of and meaning given to physical education is covered in much greater detail in chapter 2.

29. Shouls, *Reasoned Freedom*, 177–92.

30. Locke, "The Epistle Dedicatory," in *Some Thoughts*, 80.

31. Kerber, "An American Perspective," 189.

32. David Sehr, *Education for Public Democracy* (Albany: State University of New York Press, 1997).

33. Claude Adrien Helvétius, *A Treatise on Man; His Intellectual Faculties and His Education* (New York: B. Franklin, 1969), 322. See also Shouls, *Reasoned Freedom*, 68.

34. Jean le Rond d'Alembert, "College," in *The* Encyclopédie *of Diderot and D'Alembert* (Cambridge: Cambridge University Press, 1954); Helvétius, *Treatise on Man*, 73.

35. See Norman Hampson, "La Patrie," in *The French Revolution and the Creation of Modern Political Culture*, ed. Colin Lucas, vol 2. (Oxford: Pergamon Press, 1987), 125–37; and C. A. Ottevanger, "From Subject to Citizen: The Evolution of French Educational Theory in the Eighteenth Century," *Transactions of the 7th International Congress on the Enlightenment*, Studies on Voltaire and the Eighteenth Century, vol. 264 (Oxford: Voltaire Foundation, 1989), ii. 714–17.

36. Though this argument is certainly related to earlier natalist rhetoric, it differs insofar as it relies not only on the birth of more live children, but also on their general training in ways that are useful for society.

37. *Encyclopédie* in Jean-Pierre Costard, *L'Ami et le conservateur de l'enfance ou Le Guide des pères et des mères dans l'éducation des enfans; contenant la meilleure manière de les élever et de les instruire, tant par la pratique d'une infinité de petits soins toujours trop négligés jusqu'à présent, que par des moyens simples et naturels de leur rendre l'instruction aussi facile qu'agréable. Suivi de deux essais sur les avantages et l'utilité des promenades pour cette instruction, et sur l'usage des bonnes fêtes* (Paris: Galland, an 14 [1805]), 77–78.

Les enfans . . . doivent un jour former la société dans laquelle ils auront à vivre. Leur éducation est don—l'objet le plus intéressant: 1o pour eux-mêmes, que l'éducation doit rendre tels qu'ils soient utiles à cette même société, qu'ils y trouvent leur bien-être; 2o pour leurs facultés, qu'ils doivent soutenir et exercer; 3o pour l'État même, qui doit recueillir les fruits de la bonne éducation qui reçoivent les citoyens qui le composent . . .

38. Jean-Alexis Borrelly, *Système de législation, ou Moyens que la politique peut employer pour former à l'état des sujets utiles et vertueux* (Paris: Lacombe,

1768); Emile Durkheim, *The Evolution of Educational Thought: Lectures on the Formation and Development of Secondary Education in France,* trans. Peter Collins, (Boston: Routledge, 1977), 285–91; J. J. Garnier, *De l'Éducation civile* (Paris: N.p., 1765), 149–50; Père Jean Navarre, *De la Doctrine chrétienne, Discours qui a remporté le prix par le jugement de l'Académie des jeux floraux en l'année 1763, sur ces paroles: Quel serait en France le plan d'étude le plus avantageux* (N.p., n.d. 1763), 24.

39. See Chisick, *Limits of Reform.*

40. Gabriel Compayré, in his *History of Pedagogy,* trans. William Payne (Boston: Heath, 1886), 309, notes that the 25 years after 1762 saw twice as many books on education published as in the preceding 60 years. For the ferment over education in the period before *Emile,* see Bloch, "The pre-Revolutionary period: The fortunes of *Emile,*" in *Rousseauism and Education,* 19–27.

41. H. C. Barnard, *Education and the French Revolution* (Cambridge: Cambridge University Press, 1969), 29–30.

42. Louis-René de Caradeuc de la Chalotais, *Essai d'éducation nationale, ou, Plan d'études pour la jeunesse* (Geneva: Philibert, 1763).

43. R. R. Palmer, *The Improvement of Humanity: Education and the French Revolution* (Princeton: Princeton University Press, 1985); François de la Fontainerie, *French Liberalism and Education in the Eighteenth Century; the Writings of La Chalotais, Turgot, Diderot, Condorcet on National Education* (New York: McGraw-Hill, 1932), 4.

44. See, for example, Ross Hutchison, *Locke in France, 1688–1734,* Studies in Voltaire and the Eighteenth Century, vol. 290 (Oxford: Voltaire Foundation, 1991); Bernadette M. Baker, *In Perpetual Motion: Theories of Power, Educational History, and the Child* (New York: P. Lang, 2001); Frank Graves Pierrepont, *Great Educators of Three Centuries: Their Work and its Influence on Modern Education* (New York: AMS Press, 1971).

45. Jean Jacques Rousseau, *Emile,* trans. Barbara Foxley, ed. Peter D. Jimack (London: Everyman, 1993), 3.

46. John Charvet, *The Social Problem in the Philosophy of Rousseau* (Cambridge: Cambridge University Press, 1974), 145–46.

47. Morgenstern, *Politics of Ambiguity,* 182.

48. The word "man" is no accident. *Emile* focused on the education of the male citizen and devoted only one of its five books to the education of the ideal woman.

49. Morgenstern, *Politics of Ambiguity,* 182.

50. Rousseau, *Emile* (Foxley), 7–8.

51. Rousseau, *Emile* (Bloom), 85.

52. Rousseau, *Emile* (Foxley), 52.

53. Penny A. Weiss, "Sex, Freedom, and Equality in Rousseau's *Emile,*" *Polity* 22 (1990): 606.

54. Rousseau, *Emile* (Foxley), 11.

55. Rousseau, *Emile* (Bloom), 91.

56. Charvet, *Social Problem,* 47.

57. Rousseau, *Emile* (Bloom), 38.

58. Rousseau, *Emile* (Foxley), 189. While one never gets the sense that this

would be necessary, purchasing is rarely mentioned—and, after all, the very set-
ting of the story, with a tutor devoted to overseeing the development of one young
person, indicates a life of leisure—it is a frequent theme of Rousseau's rhetoric:
"O man! withdraw your existence into yourself, and you will no longer be miserable . . . Your liberty, your power extend no further than your natural capacities;
everything else is slavery, illusion, prestige."

59. Rousseau, *Emile* (Foxley), 189.

60. Rousseau, *Emile* (Foxley), 189.

61. Rousseau, *Emile* (Foxley), 190.

62. Rousseau, *Emile* (Foxley), 190.

63. Rousseau, *Emile* (Foxley), 192.

64. Rousseau, *Emile* (Foxley), 253.

65. Rousseau, *Emile* (Foxley), 10.

66. Rousseau, *Emile* (Foxley), 42.

67. Rousseau, *Emile* (Foxley), 178.

68. Rousseau, *Emile* (Foxley), 55–6.

69. Rousseau, *Emile* (Foxley), 59. Italics mine.

70. Rousseau, *Emile* (Foxley), 148.

71. Rousseau, *Emile* (Foxley), 363.

72. Rousseau, *Emile* (Foxley), 2.

73. Jean-Jacques Rousseau, *Discourse on the Origin of Inequality* (New
York: Washington Square Books, 967), 177.

74. Rousseau, *Emile* (Foxley), 69.

75. See Charvet, *Social Problem*; John William Chapman, *Rousseau — Totalitarian or Liberal?* (New York: Columbia University Press, 1956); Timothy O'Hagan, *Jean-Jacques Rousseau and the Sources of the Self* (Brookfield, Vermont:
Avebury, 1997); and Jacob Leib Talmon, *The Origins of Totalitarian Democracy*
(New York: Praeger, 1968).

76. Roger Barny, *Prélude idéologique à la Révolution française: le rousseauisme avant 1789* (Paris: Belles Lettres, 1985), and l'Eclatement révolutionnaire du
rousseauisme (Paris: Belles Lettres, 1988); and Lionel Sozzi, *Interprétations de
Rousseau pendant la Révolution*, Studies on Voltaire and the Eighteenth Century,
vol. 64 (Oxford: Voltaire Foundation, 1968). Interpretations that focus on obedience also miss the distinction, clearly outlined in *Emile*, between the "primitive
immediacy of sensation and feeling" and "the immediacy of the autonomous will
and reasonable intellect." This distinction is further explained in Jean Starobinski, *Jean Jacques Rousseau: Transparency and Obstruction*, trans. Arthur Goldhammer (Chicago: University of Chicago Press), 31.

77. Rousseau, *Emile* (Foxley), 68.

78. As just one point of comparison, when describing the second part of
Emile's education, Rousseau explains, "Deceit and falsehood are born along with
conventions and duties. As soon as we can do what we ought not to do, we try to
hide what we ought not to have done" (*Emile* [Foxley], 77). This is little different
from the Second Discourse where Rousseau writes: "It became to the interest of
men to appear what they really were not. To be and to seem became two very different things" (*Discourse on Inequality*, 224).

79. Rousseau, *Discourse on Inequality*, 177.

80. Rousseau, *Discourse on Inequality,* 177.

81. Jean-Jacques Rousseau, *Letter to D'Alembert on the Theatre,* in *Politics and the Arts,* trans. Allan Bloom (Ithaca: Cornell University Press, 1960), 6.

82. Rousseau, *Emile* (Foxley), 241.

83. Rousseau, *Emile* (Foxley), 117.

84. Rousseau, *Emile* (Foxley), 22.

85. Rousseau, *Emile* (Foxley), 64.

86. Rousseau, *Emile* (Foxley), 94

87. Rousseau, *Emile* (Foxley), 179.

88. Rousseau, *Emile* (Foxley), 312.

89. Peter Jimack, "Editor's Introduction to *Emile,*" xxxv.

90. Rousseau, *Emile* (Foxley), 253.

91. Rousseau, *Emile* (Foxley), 261.

92. Jimack, "Editor's Introduction," xxxv.

93. Rousseau, *Emile* (Foxley), 276–77.

94. Rousseau, *Emile* (Foxley), 107.

95. Rousseau, *Emile* (Foxley), 288. Italics mine.

96. Rousseau, *Emile* (Foxley), 170.

97. Rousseau, *Emile* (Foxley), 183–84.

98. Rousseau, *Emile* (Foxley), 153.

99. Rousseau, *Emile* (Foxley), 52.

100. Bloch, *Rousseauism and Education,* 2.

101. Lydia Lange, "Introduction," *Feminist Interpretations of Jean-Jacques Rousseau* (University Park: Pennsylvania State University Press, 2002), 2.

102. Rousseau, *Emile* (Bloom), 410.

103. Rousseau, *Emile* (Bloom), 410.

104. Rousseau, *Emile* (Bloom), 366.

105. Rousseau, *Emile* (Foxley), 6.

106. Rousseau, *Emile* (Bloom), 478.

107. Rousseau, *Emile* (Bloom), 33.

108. Rousseau, *Emile* (Bloom), 377. This description is less passive than it seems to modern eyes. One school of eighteenth-century optical theory believed that the viewing eye was an active and tangible agent that sent out rays and had its own sensation, closely linked to physical touch.

109. Rousseau, *Emile* (Bloom), 478.

110. Weiss, "Sex, Freedom, and Equality," 603.

111. Denise Schaeffer, "The Role of Sophie in Roussau's Emile," Polity 30 (1998): 607–26.

112. Schaeffer, "The Role of Sophie," 617.

113. Schaeffer, "The Role of Sophie," 617.

114. Rousseau, *Emile* (Bloom), 479.

115. Le Père [Cardinal] Gerdil B., *Réflexions sur la théorie, & la pratique de l'éducation contre les principes de M. Rousseau* (Genève: Em. Du Villard, 1764); Henri Griffet, *Lettre à M.D. sur le livre initulé* Emile, ou de l'éducation (Amsterdam: Grangé, 1762). "C'est don—à une égalité . . . que Rousseau voudrait réduire tous les hommes de quelque qualité & condition qu'ils soient" (36); Puget de Saint-Pierre, *Analyse des principes de M. J. J. Rousseau* (La Haye: N.p., 1763).

Puget corrects Rousseau's vision of the purpose of education, telling him that education ought to "de le raffermir dans le goût de son état" (68).

116. See Jean Henri Samuel Formey, *Anti-Emile* (Berlin: J. Pauli, 1763), and *Principes généraux pour servir à l'éducation des enfans, particulièrement de la noblesse françoise* (Amsterdam: Schneider, 1763).

117. Jean Bloch, "Rousseau's Reputation as an Authority on Childcare and Physical Education in France before the Revolution," *Paedagogica Historica* 14 (1974): 5–33; Peter Jimack, *The Defence of Educational Tradition in France, 1770–1789*, Studies on Voltaire and the Eighteenth Century, vol. 264 (Oxford: Voltaire Foundation, 1989), ii, 763–67, and *Some Eighteenth-Century Imitations of Rousseau's* Emile, Studies on Voltaire and the Eighteenth Century, vol. 284 (Oxford: Voltaire Foundation, 1991), 83–105.

118. Bloch, *Rousseauism and Education*, 61.

119. Alphonse de Serres de La Tour, *Du Bonheur* (Paris: N.p. 1767), 12: "Je conseille à toute mère sensible de lire Locke toute entier, & la première Partie d'Emile. On peut supposer même que je transcris ce dernier Ouvrage à la tête du mien, & que ce qui est de moi, est fait pour indiquer les choses sur lesquelles je pense différement que M. Rousseau."

120. Bloch, *Rousseauism and Education*, 52 ff.

121. Bloch, *Rousseauism and Education*, 56.

122. Bloch, *Rousseauism and Education*, 52ff.

123. These differences make it clear that there was still a fairly clear delineation between education and schooling. Parents might educate their children and the state or religious orders might school them, but the moral burdens and social connections between the two were not nearly as similar as they are now. If the state had an obligation to train its citizens to be rational and practical, parents were still the primary shapers of judgment. In general, only elite circles were demanding change from the existing instructional system, and this only at the secondary level, while parents were content to decide whether or not their children would attend school, not how the schools themselves should be run. According to Isser Woloch (*The New Regime: Transformations of the French Civic Order, 1789–1820s* [New York: W. W. Norton, 1994]), for example, only 1–3 percent of the *cahiers* spoke of primary education at all.

124. See especially Bronislaw Baczko, "Rousseau et la pédagogie révolutionnaire," *Rousseau and the Eighteenth Century: Essays in Memory of R. A. Leigh*, ed. Marian Hobson, J. T. A. Leigh, and Robert Wokler (Oxford: Oxford University Press, 1992): 407–20; Bloch, *Rousseauism and Education;* Celestin Hippeau, *L'Instruction publique en France pendant la Révolution: discours et rapports de Mirabeau, Talleyrand-Périgord, Condorcet, Lanthenas, Romme, Le Peletier, Saint-Fargeau, Calès, Lakanal, Daunou et Fourcroy* (Paris: Didier, 1881).

125. Ernest Hunter Wright, *The Meaning of Rousseau* (London: Oxford University Press, 1929).

126. Just a few of the primary sources are: Jacques Ballexserd, *Dissertation sur l'éducation physique des enfans, depuis leur naissance, jusqu'à l'âge de puberté* (Paris: Vallat La Chappelle, 1762); M. Cartier-Vinchon, *La parfaite demoiselle, recueil des règles, principes et maximes générales d'éducation et de bonne conduite, pour les demoiselles de tout âge; orné de gravures édifiantes: à l'usage*

des pensionnats de la France et de l'étranger, 2nd ed. (Paris: Alexis Eymery, 1825); M. Baron de Gérando, *Cours normal des instituteurs primaires ou Directions relatives à l'éducation physique, morale et intellectuelle dans les écoles primaires* (Paris: J. Renouard, 1832); A. V. Salguès, *L'amie des mères des famille, ou Traité d'éducation physique et morale des enfans* (Paris: Dentu, 1810). This trend is discussed at length in Maurice Gontard, *L'Enseignement primaire en France de la Révolution à la loi Guizot, 1789–1833* (Paris: Société d'édition, 1959). Barbara Maria Stafford (*Artful Science: Enlightenment Entertainment and the Eclipse of Visual Education* [Cambridge: MIT Press, 1994]) also agrees that Locke is crucial for understanding Enlightenment developments in education.

127. Jacqueline S. Reinier, *From Virtue to Character: American Childhood, 1775–1850* (New York: Twayne, 1996.)

128. See Gaspard Guillard de Beaurieu, *De l'allaitment et de la première éducation des enfans* (Geneva: n.p.,1782), Louis Philipon de La Madelaine, *Vues patriotiques sur l'éducation du peuple tant des villes que de la campagne: avec beaucoup de notes intéressantes: ouvrage qui peut être également utile aux autres classes de citoyens* (Lyon: Chez P. Bruyset-Ponthus, 1783).

129. Lange, *Feminist Interpretations,* 5–6.

130. Sehr, *Public Democracy,* 5.

131. Rousseau, *Emile* (Foxley), 397.

132. Rousseau, *Emile* (Foxley), 391.

133. Rousseau, *Emile* (Foxley), 384.

2. Freeing the Body, Educating the Mind: Childhood in Clothing and Toys
(pages 52–88)

1. In both Britain and France, the changes in children's styles were driven philosophically, not by the new textile boom. Styles began to change in Great Britain as early as the 1730s, long before the prodigious output of cotton cloth began. Additionally, while cotton outfits were more washable than those made out of silk fabric, the styles that emphasized freedom could have been made out of any fabric. Thus, if ideas about children had not changed, cotton still could have become the preferred fabric for producing constrictive clothing.

2. Alphonse Leroy, *Recherches sur les habillemens de femmes et des enfants, ou Examen de la manière dont il faut vêtir d'un et l'autre sexe* (Paris: Le Boucher, 1772), Avertissement. "Les vêtemens influent plus qu'on ne pense sur la santé & sur les moeurs. C'est sans doute pour cette raison que les Écrivains qui ont traité de l'éducation, ont préscrit quelques régles sur la manière d'habiller les enfans."

3. David Kuchta, *The Three Piece Suit and Modern Masculinity: Enlgand, 1550–1850* (Berkeley: University of California Press, 2002).

4. Philippe Perrot, *Fashioning the Bourgeoisie: A History of Clothing in the Nineteenth Century* (Princeton: Princeton University Press, 1994).

5. Susan Sontag, *A Barthes Reader* (New York: Hill and Wang, 1982), xxvi.

6. Daniel Roche, *La Culture des Apparances* (Paris: Fayard, 1989).

7. Charles Salmade, *Le Livre des mères et des nourrices, ou Instruction pra-*

tique sur la conservation des enfans (Paris: Merlin, an 9 [1801]), 11. "On couvre la tête de l'enfant avec un béguin dont on aura soin de ne pas trop serrer la bride. On met par-dessus le béguin, un bonnet de laine ou de coton, et l'on contient le tout, ou avec un ruban un peu large dont on entoure la tête, ou bien avec un mouchoir de toil ou de mousseline plié en triangle dont on noue les angles au-dessus du front."

8. Descriptive examples can be found in Jacques Ballexserd, *Dissertation sur l'éducation physique des enfans, depuis leur naissance, jusqu'à l'âge de puberté* (Paris: Vallat La Chappelle, 1762); Leroy, *Recherches sur les habillemens;* and Salmade, *Livre des mères.* As one might expect in keeping with its decreased importance in treatises after the turn of the century, detailed descriptions of this procedure became less common.

9. Jean-Charles Desessartz, *Traité de l'éducation corporelle des enfans en bas âge, ou Réflexions pratiques sur les moyens de procurer une meillures contitution aux citoyen* (Paris: T. J. Hérissant, 1760), 99. "Qu'on ne croie pas néanmois que notre intention est de bannir absolutment l'usage de maillot. Nous convenons qu'il est nécessaire dans les premiers temps de tenir l'enfant dans une situation assurée, de peur qu'en se tournant de côté & d'autre il ne se blesse."

10. Ballexserd, *Dissertation sur l'éducation physique,* 65.

11. Nicole Pellegrin, *Vêtements de la liberté: abécédaire des pratiques vestimentaires en France de 1780 à 1800* (Aix-en-Provence: Alinea, 1989), 77. "Quant à la raideur du corps emmailloté de l'enfant, elle n'a pas seulement pour finalité de rendre son portage plus aisé; elle est le fruit d'une conception ancienne et raisonnée de l'humanité comme stade ultime et toujours menacé de la bestialité: imposer la position droite grâce à un bandage serré, c'est accélérer un processus de développement, c'est proprement humaniser."

12. Johann Peter (JP) Frank, *Traité sur la Manière d'Élever sainement les enfans, fondé sur les principes de la médicine et de la physique, et desinté aux parens, particulièrement aux mères qui ont à coeur leur santé et celle de leurs enfans,* trans. Michel Boehrer (Paris: Crapelet, an 7), 103.

13. By the later eighteenth century, some writers even asserted that the bands should be changed at once (see Marie Angélique Anel le Rebours, *Avis aux mères qui veulent nourrir leurs enfans,* 3rd ed. [Paris: Théophile Barrois, 1783], 214); Salmade went even farther, writing that "il ne sera pas inutile d'ajouter ici qu'on doit changer les enfans de langes, toutes les fois qu'ils sont mouillés par les urines ou par les excrémens, et laver les parties sales avec de l'eau tiède, sans se contenter de les essuyer à sec" (13). Salmade and Rebours demonstrate the slow turn away from swaddling. The fact that Salmade still advocated changing the bands often, even as he claimed that this was a practice of previous periods and not the present, is a good indicator of how ingrained the custom was in popular practice.

14. Leroy, *Recherches sur les habillemens,* 36. "Les bras sont allongés des deux côtés de son corps, on presse ses genoux, & ses jambes s'étendent; on saisit cet instant pour l'enfermer entièrement dans le lange, & avec lui les excrémens qu'il peut rendre."

15. Medical treatises warned of the dangers of swaddling and straight pins, attributing colic, sleeplessness, and even seizures to misplaced pins.

16. Leroy, *Recherches sur les habillemens*, 177. "Ce vêtement représente la forme d'un cône, dont la base est en haut, & la pointe en en-bas, structure diamétralement opposée à celle de la poitrine, évasée du bas & étroite du haut."

17. The only hint that a small child might eventually occupy a different hierarchical position was to be found in the buttoning of the dress. If the dress buttoned up the front like a man's coat instead of up the back like a woman's dress, then it would have been clear to viewers that the child was male, though still entirely subordinate.

18. François Boucher, *Histoire du costume en occident de l'antiquité à nos jours* (Paris: Flammarion, 1965), 313: " . . . les garçons eux-mêmes portaient un corps baleiné qui de différait de celui des filles que parce qu'il était arrondi . . . il y avait même un modèle spécial pour 'garçon à sa première culotte.'"

19. Though Edward Shorter takes issue with the idea that corsets caused physical harm (*History of Women's Bodies* [New York: Basic, 1982], 28–34), there can be no doubt that such shaping was at best uncomfortable and often quite painful, whether or not it actively contributed to poor health.

20. Leroy, *Recherches sur les habillemens*, 195. "L'enfance n'est point, comme on le croit, environnée de pleurs; ne la conduisez que dans le chemin qu'a tracé la nature, la gaîté l'accompagnera toujours; laissez en liberté l'enfant qui vient de naître, après quelques jours ses yeux et ses lèvres annoncent que son ame s'ouvre au plaisir; il sourit à sa mère, déjà ses tendres mains s'élèvent pour la carresser."

21. Jean-Henri-Samuel Formey, *Traité d'Éducation Morale . . . Comment on doit gouverner l'esprit & le coeur d'un Enfant, pour le rendre heureux & utile. Auquel on a ajoûté quelques Pensées relatives à ce sujet* (Liège: Desoer, 1773), v. "Préface de l'Éditeur. Sur la nécessité & les avantages de l'Éducation, &c. L'homme naît sans connoissance & sujet au vice & à l'erreur. Si l'on veut perfectionner son esprit, il faut commencer à le former dès le berceau."

22. Costard, Jean-Pierre. *L'Ami et le conservateur de l'enfance ou le Guide des pères et des mères dans l'éducation des enfans; Contenant la meilleure manière de les élever et de les instruire, tant par la pratique d'une infinité de petits soins toujours trop négligés jusqu'à présent, que par des moyens simples et naturels de leur rendre l'instruction aussi facile qu'agréable. Suivi de deux essais sur les avantages et l'utilité des promenades pour cette instruction, et sur l'usage des bonnes fêtes* (Paris: Galland, an 14 [1805]; Bernard Christophe Faust Desessartz, *Sur un vêtement libre, uniforme & national, à l'usage des enfans ou réclamation solennelle des droits des enfants* (S.l., 1792); Théodore Léger, *Manuel des jeunes mères* (Paris, 1825); Antoine-François Prost de Royer, *Mémoire sur la conservation des enfants* (Lyon, 1778); A.V. Salguès, *L'amie des mères des famille, ou Traité d'éducation physique et morale des enfans* (Paris: Dentu, 1810).

23. Royer, *Mémoire sur la conservation*, 7. "Le maillot qui arrête le développement . . ."

24. J. P.Frank, *Traité sur la Manière d'Élever*, 114. "Mais aujourd'hui, les règles de la mode sont préférées aux loix et aux intentions de la nature. On débute, aussi-tôt que l'enfant est sorti de sa première demeure, par étendre son corps et ses membres; on l'emmaillotte, on le serre, on en forme une tige immobile . . ."

25. Leroy, *Recherches sur les habillemens*, 37. "Que l'enfant, lors de cette opération, ait la tête en vraie ou fausse position, peu importe, ce n'est pas pour lui, mais pour les autres qu'on l'arrange; c'est pour cela que sans distinguer si l'on est dans le mois d'Août ou de Décembre, on a la douce complaisance de le rouler dans un troisième lange ou petite couverture de laine, qui passant par-dessus sa tête en forme de capuchon, tient cette partie si roide & si assujettie, qu'il ne peut l'agiter."

26. Leroy, *Recherches sur les habillemens*, 43. "Les nourrices mercénaires ont adopté l'usage des maillots pour leur commodité . . . elles peuvent au moyen de ces liens, vanquer à leurs affaires, soit au dehors, soit à l'intrieur, sans craindre que leur indifférence mette en danger la vie de l'enfant . . ."

27. Louis-Sébastien Mercier, *Tableau de Paris* (Hamburg: Virchaux, 1781), II, 225.

28. Desessartz, *Traité de l'éducation corporelle*, 384.

29. M. Bailly, *Avis aux mères qui aiment leurs enfans et aux dames qui aiment leur taille* (Paris, 1786).

30. Salguès, *L'amie des mères*, 106; and Salmade, *Le Livre des mères*, 8.

31. Jeanne-Louise-Henriette Genest Campan, *Manuel de la jeune mère* (Paris: Baudoin Frères, 1828), 13, and Stephanie Félicité Ducrest de Saint Aubin, Comtesse de Genlis, *Le La Bruyère des Domestiques, précédé de considérations sur l'état de domesticité en général, et suivi d'une nouvelle*, 2 vols. (Paris: Thiercelin, 1828), 1:2.

32. Salmade, *Le Livre des mères*, 68–69.
Elles ne tiennent pas leurs membres à la gêne, comme cette mauvaise habitude de les suspendre par des lisières, qui, fortement attachées dessous les aisselles, soulèvent leurs épaules conjointement avec le poids du corps, au point que leur tête y est enfoncée. Cette position fatigante et désagréable à la vue, nuit à la conformation du corps et gêne la circulation; ce que l'on observe tous les jours par le gonflement et la rougeur du visage et des extémités supérieurs, chez ceux que l'on tient ainsi suspendus. Si pour remédier à ces inconvéniens, on attache au milieu du dos une sorte de lisière . . . cette manière sera encore plus dangereuse que l'autre. Elle comprime la poitrine, l'estomac, et empêche ces organes de faire leurs fonctions . . .

33. Jeanne-Louise-Henriette Genest Campan, *De l'Education* (Paris: Baudoin Frères, 1824), 23; Henri Louis Nicolas Duval (aka Cardelli), *Manuel de la Jeune Femme, contenant tout ce qu'il est utile de savoir pour diriger avec ordre, agrément et économie l'intérieur d'un ménage* (Paris: Charles-Béchet, 1826), 21; Mme Giost, *Avis aux bonnes mères sur la manière de soigner les enfans depuis leur naissance jusqu'à l'âge de puberté* (Paris: Chez l'auteur et Béchet, 1824), 6; Ballexsard, *Dissertation sur l'éducation physique*, 90.

34. *Journal des dames et des modes* [*Journal of Women and Fashion/JDD*] 7 (5 Brumaire, an 10): 51.
L'éducation doit former également aux deux sexes un bon tempérament, avec cette différence néanmoins que le tempérement de l'homme doit être préparé à de grands travaux, à de dures fatigues; celui de la femme à des souffrances plus frèquentes. Les exercices doivent cultiver dans l'un la force, et dans l'autre

dvelopper la grace . . . Dans l'homme qui a de plus grands hasards à courir, le courage physique doit être audacieux et intrépide. Dans la femme, qui a plus de maux à supporter qu'à braver, ce courage doit être calme et patient.

35. In this regard, however, it is both interesting and important to note that Rousseau was not in favor of the boys' fashions of the 1760s, especially the hussar outfit. He explained: "The best plan is to keep children in frocks as long as possible and then to provide them with loose clothes, without trying to define the shape which is only another way of distorting it. Their defects of body and mind may all be traced to the same source, the desire to make men of them before their time" (Jean Jacques Rousseau, *Emile* [Foxley], 108). He also thought girls should have more physical freedom than they had in paternal homes, where a girl "always pampered . . . seated within range of her mother's eyes . . . does not dare stand up, walk, speak, or breathe, and does not have a moment of freedom to play, jump, run, shout, or indulge in the petulance natural to her age" (Rousseau, *Emile* [Bloom], 366).

36. In fact, after outlining the need for moral clothing, the second section of Leroy's *Recherches sur les habillemens* outlines "[d]ifférences entre l'homme, la femme, & les enfans" in order to prescribe more accurately the proper attire and the changes necessary for an implementation of his ideas.

37. The broad collar was modeled after the collar of a sailor suit, but similar also to the wide scarves of women's outfits. This similarity to women's collars makes the transitional nature of the *matelot* more obvious.

38. The descriptions of the outfits are in *Cabinet des modes* [Closet of Fashions] (Février 1786): 41–43, (Octobre 1786): 177–80, (Juillet 1787): 188–89, (Septembre 1788): 254.

39. *Cabinet des modes* (Juillet 1787): 188. "Les petites filles suivent presque toujours les modes des femmes; mais les petits garçons, que l'on habille en matelots, en ont de particulières."

40. *JDD* 4 (5 Ventose, an 8): 324. "Quoique le costume des enfants soit moins sujet à changer que celui des femmes et même des hommes, il a cependant éprouvé quelques variations . . . Les pantalons de matelot ont été remplaces par les pantalons turcs . . ."

41. *JDD* 4 (25 Messidor, an 8): 477.
Rien n'habille joliment un petite garçon comme un costume à la grecque (moderne). Ce vaste pantalon de mousseline, qu'une coulisse fronce sur le soulier, donne à ses mouvemens une aisance, une grace enfantine qu'on ne lui trouve ni sous la robe féminine, ni sous l'étroit et gênant matelot. Aussi la mode qui réunit tous les âges sous son empire préscrit-elle aux enfans cet habillement aussi commode que distingué.

42. Nicole Pellegrin, *Vêtements de La Liberté*, 54.
Son abandon [general], préconcisé depuis les années 1750 par les médicins, est obtenu temporairement sous la Révolution; moins que le résultat de leur active propagande, c'est là le signe d'un désir collectif de liberté et peut-être egalité: la nation française régénérée n'a plus besoin de ses tuteurs politiques et vestementaires, corps constitués et . . . corsets à baleines! Un écrivain d'aujourd'hui n'a-t-il pas écrit: "La chute du corset est devenue l'équivalent vestimentaire de la prise de la Bastille."

43. For consumption, see especially bourgeois women's purchasing as described by Leora Auslander (*Taste and Power: Furnishing Modern France* [Berkeley: University of California Press, 1998]). Bonnie Smith (*Ladies of the Leisure Class: The Bourgeoises of Northern France in the Nineteenth Century* [Princeton: Princeton University Press, 1981]), Daniel Roche, and Nicole Pellegrin demonstrate an evolution that cuts across the revolutionary period for design and production.

44. Elizabeth Ewing, *History of Children's Costume* (London: Batsford, 1877), 65.

45. Ewing, *Children's Costume*, 65–66.

46. *JDD* 6 (15 Germinal, an 10): 306: ". . . consultez votre miroir, écoutez une vanité bien entendue, et songez qu'en perdant vos habits vous perdez vos grâces, aimables compagnes de la beauté."

47. The discussion of the development of a literature for children in chapter 4 contributes to this point. A faith in children's ability to reason for themselves, building on nurturing foundations and using the tools that their parents provided, was key to the success of this literature.

48. Barbara Maria Stafford, *Artful Science: Enlightenment Entertainment and the Eclipse of Visual Education* (Cambridge: MIT Press, 1994), 73–74.

49. Campan, *Jeune Mère*, 103. "Les balles, les raquettes, le cerceau, la corde, sont des jeux qui exigent une certaine adresse, et fortifient les enfans. Ils peuvent avoir lieu entre les filles et les garçons . . ."

50. Formey, *Traité d'éducation morale*, 45–48.
Il faut amuser les Enfants.
L'art des Mères, des Nourrices, & de ce qu'on nomme Femme d'enfant, se borne à prendre un Enfant sur les bras, lorsqu'il est inquiet & crie, à le promener de lieu en lieu, à le faire fautiller, & à lui frédonner quelques chansons. Tout cela n'est point ce que l'Enfant veut, ni ce qui lui convient. Il demand à être amusé; & personne ne l'entend, on ne veut l'entendre . . .
Asseyez-vous devant une table avec l'Enfant sur vos genoux, mettez sur cette table la moindre bagatelle, le plus mince jouet, & voyez faire l'Enfant. Il prendre ce jouet, le maniera en tout sens, & passera des heures entières avec une satisfaction, une gaité, dont son air ne permet pas de douter.

51. Rebours, *Avis aux mères*, 238. "Les laisser jouer, se fortifier, & profiter de seul tems de leur vie où ils puissent être heureux. . . . Si l'on veut se donner la peine de faire attention à leurs jeux, à leurs petits penchans, & de satisfaire leur curiosité naturelle, on sera étonné des occasions multipliées qu'on aura de leur faire prendre de bonnes habitudes, & de leur donner des idées exactes d'une infinité de choses . . ."

52. Campan, *Jeune Mère*, 100. "On remarque dans les jeux des enfans leurs constantes dispositions à imiter tout ce qu'ils voient faire aux gens formés; ils aiment les petits ménages dont toutes les pièces leur rétracent celui de leurs parens: un bâton transformé en cheval représente celui de leurs parens; ils sont ravis de faire claquer un fouet comme les postillons, et d'arroser comme le jardinier . . ."

53. *JDD* 25 (August 1821): 361.
A quinze ans, les garçons deviennennt les serviteurs des demoiselles: mais à sept ou huit ans, ils ne sont que leurs rivaux. Cette rivalité fait sentir aux Tui-

leries plus que partout ailleurs. A peine les petits messieurs eurent-ils des cerceux, que les petites filles s'en emparèrent. Ceux-ci mirent les cordes à la mode; celles-là commencèrent à sauter dès le lendemain. Il y a quelques jours, deux jolis enfans . . . se présenterent armés d'arcs et de flèches; ils triomphant déjà; mais les demoiselles témoignèrent la crainte d'être éborgnées et leur firent ôter leur nouveaux joujoux.

54. *JDD* 26 (10 May 1826): 202.

55. *JDD* 16 (10 August 1812): 345. "Tout le monde connoît à présent la forme du joujou à la mode, appelé le *diable* . . . Tel est le sujet de l'occupation et des études les plus réfléchies de nos jeunes gens des deux sexes . . ."

56. See "Les Etrennes," *JDD* 13 (31 December 1809): 576–79.

57. *JDD* 7 (10 Brumaire, an 11): 60. "Pour être un homme, il faut être long-tems un enfant: les fruits précoces sont desséchés quand la saison est venue: l'ar-bre qui pousse avant le tems des rejettons trompeurs, n'a plus de sève quand il est tems de produire."

58. This change is described most clearly by Philippe Ariès (*L'enfant et la vie familiale sous l'Ancien Régime* [Paris: Éditions de Seuil, 1973]) and Jacques Revel ("The Uses of Civility," in *A History of Private Life,* vol 3, ed. Roger Chartier, trans. Arthur Goldhammer [Cambridge, 1989]).

59. *Cabinet des Modes* (15 October 1786): 177–78.

Mesdames, avouez-le; tant que vos enfans sont assez petits . . . vous vous faites une gloire de les y montrer, parce que votre amour-propre jouit des éloges qu'on leur accord . . . alors vous voulez qu'ils soient habillés élégam-ment, avec goût, à la mode même; vous trouvez que c'est comme cela qu'à cet âge ils vous font honneur . . .

Vous ne meneriez pas avec plaisir des enfans d'un âge déjà un peu avancé, sur-tout parce qu'ils n'auroient plus cette gaité, cette vivacité, ce babil capable d'attirer tous les regards, & des les faire reporter sur vous.

60. *JDD* 12 (25 July 1808): 323–24.

Cette action enchanta toute l'assemblé et fut sur-tout remarquée par le vieux ami de M. de Merval. Il en parla à son fils, sur qui la conduite et la beauté de Julie avoient fait beaucoup d'impression, et huit jours après ils allèrent la de-mander en mariage. M. de Merval fut un peu piqué . . . mais il répondit . . . "Je crois que les demoiselles qui sortent de votre pensionnat dansent bien la gavotte, Mlle de Merval en est la preuve: mais je crois qu'une demoiselle élevée par sa mère, ajoute aux grâces de la danse le charme d'une bonne conduite et d'une bonne éducation, et j'ai épousé Mlle de Bonneval."

61. *JDD* 12 (15 August 1808); 363.

Non-seulement Justine avoit appris à être paresseuse et fière, mais elle avoit encore oublié l'art de se rendre utile. Ses mains douces et tendres ne pouvoient plus supporter l'action de feu ou la pression d'un aiguille, et elle avoit tant pe-fectionné ses jambes qu'elle ne savoit plus comment ill falloit tenir la plume avec sa main . . .

Nouvelle éducation: ma fille dut apprendre à redevenir bourgeoise . . .

62. Aileen Ribeiro, *The Art of Dress: Fashion in England and France, 1750 to 1820* (New Haven: Yale University Press, 1995), 3.

3. *"You will reign by means of love"*: *Advice Manuals and Domestic Motherhood (pages 89–111)*

1. Antoinette LeGroing-LaMaisonneuve, *Essai sur le Genre d'Instruction le plus analogue à la destination des femmes* (Paris: N.P., 1801). "Il me semble donc que les parens, ou à leur défault les institutrices, doivent cultiver l'esprit des jeunes personnes qui sont sous leur direction, perfectionner leur raison, les porter aussi loin que leur nature le permet mais en observant toujours soigneusement de préférer ce qui est nécessaire à ce qui n'est qu'avantageux."

2. Jean Jacques Rousseau, *Emile, or On Education*, trans. Allan Bloom (New York: Basic, 1979), 33.

3. Sean M. Quinlan has examined the medical discourse over self-control and gender in "Physical and Moral Regeneration After the Terror: Medical Culture, Sensibility and Family Politics in France, 1794–1804," *Social History* 29 (May 2004): 139–64. While he finds a similar emphasis on self-control, his work, which focuses entirely on literature after the French Revolution, does not explore the rhetoric before 1794.

4. Lydia Lange, "Introduction," *Feminist Interpretations of Jean-Jacques Rousseau* (University Park: Pennsylvania State University Press, 2002), 2.

5. Carole Duncan, "Happy Mothers and Other New Ideas in Eighteenth-Century Art," in *Feminism and Art History: Questioning the Litany*, ed. Norma Broude and Mary Garrard (New York: Harper and Row, 1982), 213. When referring to children, I will frequently use the masculine pronoun. This is not only for matters of agreement (in the original documents, the masculine pronoun is used to denote children of both sexes, where the feminine pronoun indicates only a girl child), but also for matters of simplicity, to differentiate easily between mother and child in places where the referent might otherwise be unclear.

6. Rousseau, *Emile* (Bloom), 37n.

7. See sections 2 and 3, *A History of Private Life*, vol. 4, *From the Fires of Revolution to the Great War*, ed. Michele Perrot, trans. Arthur Goldhammer (Cambridge: Belknap, 1990). Figure 12 (*La Mère à la mode*) gives a very good pictorial example of this change.

8. Rousseau, *Emile* (Bloom), 441.

9. Rousseau, *Emile* (Bloom), 37n.

10. Marie Angélique Anel le Rebours, *Avis aux mères qui veulent nourrir leurs enfans*, 3rd ed. (Paris: Théophile Barrois, 1783), 78–79.
Les enfans nourris par leurs mères peuvent y gagner autant pour le caractère que pour la santé, sur-tout s'il est vrai que le lait influe sur le caractère. La mère peut du moins tirer un grand avantage de la connoissance qu'elle a de son enfant pour sa première éducation. En nourrissant, on sait à point nommé, la cause des cris d'un enfant. On est à portée de le satisfaire, si c'est un besoin qui le fait crier, & de le refuser si c'est une fantaisie.

11. Jean-Marie Caillau, *Avis aux mères de famille* (N.p., 1769); Jean-Louis Fourcroy, *Les enfans élevés dan l'ordre de la nature, ou Abrége de l'histoire naturelle des enfans du premier âge. A l'usage des peres & meres de famille* (Liège: J. J. Tutot, 1781); André Théodore Brochard, *De l'allaitement maternel, étudié*

aux points de vue de la mère, de l'enfant et de la société (Paris: Maillet, 1868); William Buchan, *Le Conservateur de la santé des mères et des enfans, contenant: 10 La Conduite que les femmes doivent tenir avant le mariage pour conserver leur santé' 20 Le Régime et les précautions qu'elles doivent employer pendant et après leur grossesse; 30 L'Éducation qu'elles doivent donner à leurs enfans pour assurer leur santé, leur force et leur beauté,* trans. Thomas Duverne de Praîle (Paris: Métier, an 13 [1804]).

12. Historians have noted this shift of focus in advice manuals from men to women in other contexts as well. See, for example, Cissie Fairchilds, *Domestic Enemies: Servants and Their Masters in Old Regime France* (Baltimore: Johns Hopkins Press, 1984), and Sarah Maza, *Servants and Masters in Eighteenth-Century France: The Uses of Loyalty* (Princeton: Princeton University Press, 1983).

13. Gerda Lerner, *The Creation of Feminist Consciousness: From the Middle Ages to 1870* (New York: Oxford University Press, 1993), 135.

14. While some of this legislation dates from after 1762, the rhetoric surrounding motherhood became ever more intense. As with most of the cultural changes I discuss, it should be remembered that the periodization is approximate. Some intimations of "mother worship" were certainly evident before the publication of *Emile* in 1762, and writers continued to give great consideration to fathers and the patriarchal role in child-rearing well past the revolution. While fathers continued to exert force, both legally and socially, the change in perception that is described in this chapter is often credited to Rousseau's influence. Whether or not Rousseau's popularity initiated the shift or betokened *moeurs* that were already in flux, the fact remains that, by 1762, "mother love" and the demands for nurturing education were a recognizable trend.

15. Jean-Henri-Samuel, *Traité d'éducation morale . . . Comment on doit gouverner l'esprit et le coeur d'un enfant, pour le rendre heureux et utile. Auquel on a ajoûté quelques pensées relatives à ce sujet* (Liège: Desoer, 1773), 139: ". . . lorsque c'est un homme qui a lui même à peu près toutes les connoissances que l'on acquiert dans un cours suivi d'études."

16. Shari L. Thurer, *The Myths of Motherhood: How Culture Reinvents the Good Mother* (New York: Houghton Mifflin, 1994), 185. While John Tosh's work on later nineteenth-century Britain (*A Man's Place: Masculinity and the Middle-Class Home in Victorian England* [New Haven: Yale University Press, 1999]) demonstrates some concrete ways in which men still had clear roles to play in the household, his sources also demonstrate a trend toward a male role as provider and not organizer of the household.

17. The discussion of women's and children's clothing in chapter 2 provides a visual representation of this fact. Until the period under consideration, women and children of both sexes wore long skirts. As they were all inferior to men and subject to their authority, there appeared to be no need to differentiate between subordinates. As women began to command authority within the home and childhood assumed unique characteristics, more sartorial differences also developed.

18. Bonnie Smith (*Ladies of the Leisure Class: The Bourgeoises of Northern France in the Nineteenth Century* [Princeton: Princeton University Press, 1981]) astutely notes that we should analyze "domestic life as, in good measure, a female creation and as evidence of the continuing ingenuity of human agency" (17).

19. The discussion of figure 16 in the conclusion of this work is particularly telling as an example of this new emphasis on feminine centrality in opposition to masculine power.

20. Charles Salmade, *Le Livre des mères et des nourrices, ou Instruction pratique sur la conservation des enfans* (Paris: Merlin, an 9 [1801]), ix. "Pour que leur attention n'embrassât pas un sujet trop étendu, j'ai cru encore devoir limiter cette Instruction."

21. Thomas Duverne de Praîle, Translator's Introduction to Buchan, *Conservateur*, v–vi. "N'écrivant point pour les médicins, et sentant que, pour être véritablement utile, il falloit se faire comprendre par les femmes auxquelles son ouvrage est adressé, M. Buchan a dépouillé son style de tout appareil scientifique . . ."

22. J. M. Combes-Brassard, *L'ami des mères, ou Essai sur les maladies des enfans* (Paris: Méquignon, 1819), 1. "Il est douteux si les meilleurs livres de ce genre ont jamais été utiles aux personnes auxquelles ils étoient destinés, tandis qu'il est certain qu'il s ont tous fait un mal prodigieux à la société."

23. Théodore Léger, *Manuel des jeunes mères* (Paris: Chaboüillé, 1825), 8. Italics mine.

24. Claire Elisabeth Jeanne Gravier de Vergennes, Comtesse de Rémusat, *Essai sur l'éducation des Femmes* (Paris: L'advocat, 1824), 212. "La société d'un médicin éclairé, et il y en a beaucoup maintenat, serait fort avantageuse pour la mère de famille. Sa conversation, écoutée dans un intérêt pratique, la préserverait d'une foule d'erreurs et même de dangers qui suivent les minutes de l'ignorance. Elle s'instruirait pour le salut de tout ce qui l'entoure."

25. Mme Gacon-Dufour, *Manuel complet de la maîtresse de maison, et de la parfaite ménagère, ou Guide pratique pour la gestion d'une maison à la ville et à la campagne, contenant les moyens d'y maintenir le bon ordre et d'y établir l'abondance, de soigner les enfans, de conserver les substances alimentaires, etc.* (Paris: Roret, 1826), 4: ". . .j'ai dû prendre un style simple, afin de me faire mieux entendre de toutes celles que je désire instruire, et afin qu'elles soient dans le cas d'essayer ce que je dis de faire, sans être obligées d'aller demander l'explication du mot avant de s'occuper de la chose . . ."

26. Rebours, *Avis aux mères*, xiv–xxx; M. Bailly, *Avis aux mères qui aiment leurs enfans et aux dames qui aiment leur taille* (Paris, 1786), 30–31; Jean-Charles Desessartz, *Traité de l'éducation corporelle des enfans en bas âge, ou Réflexions pratiques sur les moyens de procurer une meillures contitution aux citoyen* (Paris: T. J. Hérissant, 1760), xxx, 383.

27. Costard, Jean-Pierre, *L'Ami et le conservateur de l'enfance ou le Guide des pères et des mères dans l'éducation des enfans; Contenant la meilleure manière de les élever et de les instruire, tant par la pratique d'une infinité de petits soins toujours trop négligés jusqu'à présent, que par des moyens simples et naturels de leur rendre l'instruction aussi facile qu'agréable. Suivi de deux essais sur les avantages et l'utilité des promenades pour cette instruction, et sur l'usage des bonnes fêtes* (Paris: Galland, an 14 [1805], 26. "On peut définir l'éducation: L'art de conserver, de fortifier et de perfectionner les facultés physique et morales que l'homme en naissant a reçues de la nature."

28. Rousseau, Rebours, Buchan, and Salmade all agree on this point.

29. A. V. Salguès, *L'amie des mères des famille, ou Traité d'éducation physique*

et morale des enfans (Paris: Dentu, 1810), vii–viii: "... la constitution d'un en-fant, sa santé, ses forces futures, son caractère moral, dépendant beaucoup plus qu'elles ne pensent, de leur manière de vivre pendant leur grossesse . . ."

30. Jeanne-Louise-Henriette Genest Campan, *De l'Education* (Paris: Bau-douin Frères, 1824), 20–21, 40. "La mère, qui n'a pas voulu que ses enfans puisassent leur nourriture dans le sein d'une étrangère, ne voudra pas que ces pre-mières idées, si durables, soient développées en eux par une femme sans éduca-tion: après avoir été la nourrice, elle sera la bonne de ses enfans . . . Les erreurs d'éducation ne sont point réparables, elles portent coup."

31. Isabelle Brouard-Arends, *Vies et images maternelles dans la littérature française du dix-huitième siècle,* Studies on Voltaire and the Eighteenth Century, vol. 291 (Oxford: Voltaire Foundation, 1991), 413. "Le mère n'est alors plus seulement *genetrix* mais garante de la société future."

32. Citoyenne Guerin-Albert, *Avis aux mères républicaines, ou Mes Reflex-ions sur l'éducation des jeunes citoyennes* (N.p., n.d.), 2: ". . . des vertus plus douces et moins éclatantes sont votre partage: c'est par leur exercise soutenu, que vous donnerez des héros au monde: car n'en doutez pas, c'est à vous que les hommes doivent tout ce qu'ils sont, leurs vices et leurs vertus sont votre ouvrage."

33. Gacon-Dufour, *Manuel complet,* 16. "La première éducation est celle qui importe le plus, et cette première éducation appartient incontestablement aux femmes . . ."

34. Gacon-Dufour, *Manuel complet,* 6–7.
La tendresse qu'elles portent à ces petits être intéressans, les rend attentives à leurs moindres mouvemens; elles cherchent à deviner dans leurs cris plaintifs ce qu'ils peuvent désirer, et ce qu'ils ne peuvent encore exprimer. Cette atten-tion empêche les enfans de se livrer à des impatiences, à des colères même, dont ils se ressentent toute leur vie. Je suis convaincue qu'un enfant nourri par sa mère n'a pas cette âcreté de caractère que l'on remarque quelquefois dans des enfans nourris loin de leurs parens, et qui reviennent à deux ou trois ans et sou-vent plus tard dans la maison paternelle.

35. Lucet, *Pensées de M. Rollin sur Plusieurs Points importans de Littérature, de Politique et de Réligion. Recueillies de son Histoire Ancienne et de son Traité des Études* (Paris: Frères Estienne, 1780), 377, "Éducation de la Jeunesse. *Son im-portance."* "L'éducation de la Jeunesse a toujours ét regardée par les plus grands Philosophes & par les plus fameux Législateurs, comme la source la plus certain du repos & du bonheur, non-seulement des Familles, mais des États même & des Empires."

36. Jean Pont Victor Lacoutz, l'abbé de Levizac, *Leçons de Fénélon, extraites de ses ouvrages pour l'éducation de l'enfance,* 2nd ed. (Paris: Gabriel Dufour, 1819), i. "Les premières impressions de l'enfance ne s'effacent presque jamais. Combien n'est-il donc pas essentiel de ne lui offrir que des objets faits pour développer et nourrir en elle des sentimens honntêtes, nobles, et élevés!"

37. This explicit linkage between moral conscience and social behavior high-lights an important difference between the literature intended for children and the literature about child-rearing. While advice about concrete activities or decisions will, over the course of time, show a change "in the direction of a gradual 'civi-

lization,' . . . only historical experience makes clearer what this word actually means. It shows, for example, the decisive role played in this civilizing process by a very specific change in the feelings of shame and delicacy" (Norbert Elias, *The Civilizing Process: The History of Manners and State Formation and Civilization*, trans. Edmund Jephcott [Cambridge: Blackwell, 1994], xii). In the advice manuals addressed to women, concrete linkages were made between daily behavior and moral instincts. While it is true that the analysis behind these manuals was firmly contemporary and not at all inclined to see moral education in the historical perspective, the explicit discussion of reason and moral development makes it easier to see the context behind the eighteenth and nineteenth centuries' meaning of "civilization."

38. Levizac, *Leçons de Fénélon*, i-ii. "Aurait-on jamais dû oublier que les enfans, étant l'espérance de la société dans laquelle ils sont nés, on ne peut, sans crime, négliger de prendre les moyens les plus propres à les en rendre un jour des membres utiles, soit par des connaissances solides, soit par les agréments de l'esprit, soit par les qualités du couer, ou enfin, ce qui est bien plus précieux, pas les trésors des moeurs?"

39. Rémusat, *l'éducation des Femmes*, 123, ch. 7, "De l'application des vrais principes de l'éducation."

Plus on aura laissé de latitude à l'exercice de la liberté des enfans, en leur abandonnant le choix du bien ou du mal pour leur enseigner l'un et l'autre par l'expérience, plus il sera importante de s'attacher de bonne heure à développer en eux cette notion du juste et de l'injuste, que nos portons tous au dedans de nos . . . La connaissance des devoirs est une suite de l'emploi de la raison, elle ne s'acquiert que peu à peu; mais il est utile qu'un enfant sache bientôt que tout créature a sur la terre des devoirs à remplir; et le sentiment de l'obligation morale, que l'éducation trouve et ne donne pas, rendra en peu de temps pour lui cette connaissance distincte et applicable.

40. Rémusat, *l'éducation des Femmes*, 243. "Nous naissons avec le sentiment du bien et du mal, c'est l'instinct moral: ne pourrait-on pas dire que le devoir de l'éducation est de transformer ce sentiment ou cet instinct en une connaissance raisonnée?"

41. Lucet, *Pensées de M. Rollin*, 466. "L'éducation est, à proprement parler, l'art de manier & de façonner les esprits. C'est de toutes les Sciences la plus difficile, la plus rare, & en même tems la plus importante."

42. Salguès, *L'amie des mères*, 264. "La raisonnement est la faculté qui réclame ici tous les soins d'un instituteur ou des parens . . . Les enfans n'ont point alors assez d'idées acquises, ils ont trop peut d'objets à rapprocher, à comparer, leur intelligence et resserrée dans des limites trop étroites, et leur sens moral est trop borné . . ."

43. Costard, *Conservateur de l'enfance*, 81 (italics in original): ". . . c'est d'ouvrir, d'éclairer, d'instruire *et de régler l'esprit des enfans* . . ."

44. Guerin-Albert, *Mères républicaines*, 1.

La vertu, voilà la base d'un gouvernement républicain; c'est par elle que les peuples recouvrent leur liberté, c'est par elles qu'ils la conservent; c'est une de ces vérités éternelles que les fastes du monde ont transmises à tous les peuples.

C'est donc à cette vertu régénératrice et conservatrice, que vous devez, mères de famille, former les jeunes coeurs que la nature a confiés à vos soins.

45. Levizac, *Leçons de Fénélon,* 268, ch. 23, "Que la vrai liberté est fondée sur la crainte des dieux." "Le plus libre de tous les hommes est celui qui peut-être libre dans l'esclavage même. En quelque pays et en quelque condition qu'on soit, on est très-libre pourvu qu'on craigne les dieux, et qu'on ne craigne qu'eux. En un mot, l'homme véritablement libre est celui qui, dégagé de toute crainte et de toute désir, n'est soumis qu'aux dieux et à la raison."

46. Guerin-Albert, *Mères républicaines,* 5–6. "Jusqu'à six ans . . . je ne mettrais acune différence dans ma manière de soigner les deux sexes. Perhaps this is why Rousseau himself did not encourage the use of separate forms of clothing for children before they had reached the age of reason."

47. Johann Peter (JP) Frank (*Traité sur la Manière d'Élever sainement les enfans, fondé sur les principes de la médecine et de la physique, et desinté aux parens, particulièrement aux mères qui ont à coeur leur santé et celle de leurs enfans,* trans. Michel Boehrer [Paris: Crapelet, an 7], 103) defined the terms "enfance" and "adolescence" for the readers of his book, saying, "[l]e mot enfance, suivant sa signification usitée, s'étend jusqu'à l'âge de sept ans, et les sept années suivantes, sont celles de l'adolescence" (1). These were newly evolving concepts, so while some advice manuals refer to "enfance" to cover the entire period from birth to maturity, the age distinctions that Frank made between the time under a mother's care ("enfance") and the time in school or apprenticeship ("adolesencc") can be applied to other authors' use of similar terms.

48. Dr. Jean-François Verdier-Huertin, *Discours et essai aphoristique sur l'allaitement et l'éducation des enfans et Dissertation sur un foetus trouvé dans le corps d'un enfant male* (Paris: Chez l'auteur, an 12 [1804]), 72. "Mères, c'est à vous que je m'addresse particulièrement; c'est vous que je veux initier dans des secrets importans; c'est vous dont je veux guider les pas incertains. Tout ce qu'il vous sera utile de savoir, et possible d'apprendre pour votre conservation et celle de vos enfans, je le dirai . . ."

49. Antoine Caillot, *Tableau des exercises et de l'enseignement en usage dans un pensionnat de jeunes demoiselles dirigé par une sage institutrice; Accompagné de récits historiques relatifs aux sujets dont il est composé. À l'usage des jeunes personnes, et même des dames chargées de leur instruction. Avec figures* (Paris: Brunot-L'Abbe, 1816), 1:vii. "Ainsi que les garçons, les filles ont un coeur qu'il faut former à la vertu, cet unique principe de notre bonheur."

50. Campan, *De l'éducation,* 44. "C'est jusqu'à l'âge de sept ans qu'un jeune garçon peut être guidé par les mains maternelles; plus tard, il faut l'en éloigner: l'austérité des études, la violence des jeux, celle des exercices, tout ce qu'il faut faire enfin dans l'éducation des hommes, pour tremper fortement leurs âmes, viendraient sans cesse heurter l'exquise sensibilité d'une mère."

51. Rollin, *Traité des Etudes,* in Campan, *De l'éducation,* 43. "Le soin d'éducation des enfans jusqu'à l'âge dont vous parlez (six à sept ans) roule principalement sur elles, et fait partie de ce petit empire domestique que la Providence leur a spécialement assigné."

52. Costard, *Conservateur de l'enfance,* 54–55: "de la patience surtout . . . jamais d'ordres, jamais de sévrité ni de rigeur, qui mettent le coeur de l'enfant

comme en état de siége et de défense perpétuel; toujours le langage de la nature et de la bonté . . ."

53. Campan, *De l'éducation,* 56–57. "C'est le moyen de séparer l'idée de la contrainte de celle de l'obéissance; mais dans tous les cas, agréable ou sévère, que l'ordre soit irrévocable."

54. Rémusat, *L'éducation des Femmes,* 215, ch. 13, "De l'autorité dans l'éducation" "Bien éléver un enfant dans le sens moral, c'est lui faire contracter le goût et l'habitude des volonté vertueuses. Mais est-ce lui en donner la raison? L'éducation doit-elle lui dicter d'avance le formulaire de tous les devoirs, ou mettre son âme en état de les discerner, de les connaître et de les vouloir dans l'occasion?"

55. Costard, *Conservateur de l'enfance,* 13–14. (See also Guerin-Albert, *Mères républicaines,* 8–11.) ". . . on ne doit jamais perdre de vue celui de se rappeler la faiblesse de cet âge. Il ne nous arrive que trop souvent de juger les enfans comme s'ils étaient hommes, comme s'ils avaient notre force, nos facultés . . . nous interprétons très-faussement les intentions, les discours et les actions de nos enfans."

56. Introduction to Campan, *De l'éducation,* x (italics in original): ". . . une mère *attentive, laborieuse, et patiente* reçoit toujours le prix de ses soins. Elle a raison de remarquer encore qu'il faut que la conduite soit toujours d'accord avec la leçon . . . Un mot, un gest, un regard, rien ne leur échappe; ils ont bientôt remarqué s'il existe une distinction entre ce qu'on fait et ce qu'on dit . . ."

57. Guerin-Albert, *Mères républicaines,* 15–16. "Ma fille sera sobre, parce que je lui donnerai l'exemple de cette vertu . . . elle sera courageuse, parce que je ne me laisserai point abattre par la douleur physique ou morale; elle saura de bonne heure que la maladie et les chagrins sont inséparables de la condition d'homme, et qu'on se révolterait en vain contre des choses qui tiennent absolument à notre essence . . ."

58. Guerin-Albert, *Mères républicaines,* 16. "Je ne dis pas que ma fille sera sage et modeste, parce qu'il est impossible qu'une jeune personne élevée dans les principes que j'ai données à la mienne, ne le soit point."

59. *Journal des dames et des modes* [*Journal of Women and Fashion*/*JDD*] 6 (5 Brumaire, an 10), 52. "L'homme peut se parer de ses avantages; la femme ne doit faire valoir les siens que par la modestie."

60. I use the word "interiorization" to mean a complex of issues, all of which focus on women's role within the home. This is more than separate sphere ideology, because it specifically involves the idea that women ought to remain within the walls of their home, always available to their children and spouse, not the notion that men and women have separate worlds and separate responsibilities.

61. Guerin-Albert, *Mères républicaines,* 15. "Ma fille sera accoutumée à s'occuper des petits ouvrages de son sexe; pendant qu'elle travaillera je lui lirai des ouvrages utiles, soit relatifs à ceux des peuples qui nous ont précédés dans la carrière de la liberté: ce n'est pas tout d'observer les loix par lesquelles on est régi, il faut les aimer . . ."

62. Caillot, *Tableau des exercices,* 1:63. "Il leur importe donc, pour répondre au voeu de la nature et à celui de la société, de contracter de bonne heure l'habitude des occupations domestiques."

63. Gacon-Dufour, *Manuel complet,* i. "Tout maîtresse de maison a sans doute son régime d'administration. Il n'est pas de jeune femme entrant en ménage

qui ne se forme un plan de conduite, qui ne se dites: Je réglerai ma maison de telle manière; si j'ai le bonheur d'être mère, je gouvernerai telle éducation; je dirigerai de telle sorte mon intérieur; je mettrai mes domestiques sur tel pied."

64. Campan, *De l'éducation*, 150. "Les femmes sont destinées à la vie sédentaire: c'est chez soi qu'on trouve le vrai bonheur . . ."

65. Rémusat, *L'éducation des Femmes*, xv–xvi. "Ma mère avait connu le monde, la cour, la retraite . . . La vie en se prolongeant l'avait conduite à ces convictions pleines et pures qu'on abandonne ordinairement . . . à l'enthousiasme d'une imprudent jeunesse. Plus elle a connu la société, plus elle est rentrée en elle-même . . . la vie la quittait, la vérité s'emparait d'elle . . ."

66. Campan, *De l'éducation*, 138. "Tout Française vertueuse éprouve cette attrait exclusif [sic] qu'une femme doit avoir pour son intérieur, et s'en éloigne bien plus difficilement que les dames anglaises ne quittent leur *dear home*."

67. Caillot, *Tableau des exercices*, 2:285. "Dieu n'a pas limité l'enceinte que l'homme doit parcourir; mais il a déterminé celle de la femme aux murs de sa maison."

68. Campan, *De l'éducation*, 145. "Il faut en convenir, les devoirs de la société sont d'une nature fort opposée à ceux d'une mère qui veut élever ses filles. *Les Veillées du Château, les Enfans du Vieux Château,* ces titres d'ouvrages estimés prouvent que les auteurs de ces plans d'éducation maternelle, pour éviter d'avoir à combattre les entraînements du monde, ont pris le parti de les fuir . . ."

69. Louis Nicolas Duval (aka Cardelli), *Manuel de la Jeune Femme, contenant tout ce qu'il est utile de savoir pour diriger avec ordre, agrément et économie l'intérieur d'un ménage* (Paris: Charles-Béchet, 1826), 15.

Que vos amis, même les plus chers, ne soient point les confidens des petits chagrins qui sont inévitables dans un ménage: que trop souvent une simple pîquire s'envenime par les conseils pernicieux des étrangers et devient une blessure profonde que rien ne peut guérir! Méfiez-vous des personnes qui vous donneront raison, et tort à votre mari; qui, sous le prétexte spécieux de vous plaindre, exagéreront ses défauts; qui vous présenteront ses procédés envers vous, comme ne méritant pas votre affection . . .

70. Cardelli, *Manuel de la Jeune Femme*, 13. "Une des choses qui contribuent le plus au bonheur d'une femme, dans l'intérieur de son ménage, c'est sa conduite envers son mari: j'entends par ce mot, ses manières, les soins qu'elle prend de lui, etc."

71. Campan, *De l'éducation*, iv–v. "Une femme doit être, dans sa jeunesse, la compagne et l'amie de celle qui lui a donné le jour; plus tard, ses soins ne sauraient avoir d'autre objet que le bonheur de son mari et l'éducation de ses enfans . . . Tous ses devoirs de fille, d'épouse et de mère sont renfermés dans le cercle étroit et fortuné de la famille."

72. Campan, *De l'éducation*, iv–v. "Il est bien permis d'être aimable pour être heureuse, et d'obtenir à la fois l'amour et l'estime. Le respect de ceux qui l'approchent est sa plus douce récompense; la plus chère comme la plus constante et la plus honorable occupation de sa vie doit être d'élever des filles qui lui ressemblement."

73. Caillot, *Tableau des exercices*, 2:285. "Une femme jette d'autant plus d'éclat, qu'elle passe sa vie dans une plus grande obscurité."

74. *JDD* 6 (5 Brumaire, an 10), 51–52.
L'éducation doit former également aux deux sexes un bon tempérament . . .
avec cette différence néanmoins que le tempérament de l'homme doit être préparé à de grands travaux, à de dures fatigues; celui de la femme à des souffrances plus frèquentes . . . Dans l'homme qui a de plus grands hasards à
courir, le courage physique doit être audacieux et intrépide . . . Dans la femme,
qui a plus de maux à supporter qu'à braver, ce courage doit être calme et patient . . . Le courage moral, entr'eux, doit avoir le même différence: la fermeté
et la fierté sont le partage de l'homme; la plainte et la résignation conviennent
à la femme.

75. *JDD* 8 (5 Frimaire, an 12), 104 (Italics in original). "La réserve est l'arma-
ture des femmes . . . C'est pour les femmes sur-tout, comme le dit Mad. de Lambert, que *la principale prudence consiste à se défier de soi-même plus que des
autres.* C'est dans le respect qu'elles ont pour elles-mêmes, que consiste aussi leur
véritable modestie. *Il faut vivre respecteursement avec soi . . .*"

76. While works on feminism in the nineteenth century often indicate that
later nineteenth-century feminism seized separate spheres ideology in a compen-
satory fashion (Claire Goldberg Moses, *French Feminism in the Nineteenth Century* [Albany: State University of New York, 1984], and Karen Offen, *European
Feminisms: 1700–1950: A Political History* [Stanford: Stanford University Press,
2000]), the later eighteenth- and early nineteenth-century rhetoric has no such
tone and came to the fore before the Napoleonic Code inscribed political gender
exclusion into law.

77. *JDD* 6 (25 Floreal, an 10), 375; Caillot, *Tableau des exercises,* 2:128–29.

78. Denise Schaeffer, "The Role of Sophie in Roussau's *Emile,*" *Polity* 30
(1998): 618.

79. Brouard-Arends, *Vies et images maternelles,* 418–27.

80. Buchan, *Conservateur,* 224.

81. Rebours, *Avis aux mères,* viii–ix: ". . . ces mères injustes qui sacrifient à
un vil intérêt, dont elles font rarement un bon usage, la vie ou la santé de leurs enfans . . ."

82. I. Girouard, *Avis aux mères et aux nourrices, ou Conseils aux femmes,
pour les préserver des maladies du sein, ou les en guérir lorsqu'elles en sont attaquées. Avec des refléxions sur les maladies prétendues laiteuses* (Paris: Chez l'auteur et Martinet, an 12), 3. "On ne voit pas les sauvages donner leurs enfans à
nourrir à des autres sauvages; ce n'est que par la civilisation, le luxe et la dépra-
vation des moeurs, que des mères ne veulent pas donner à teter à leurs enfans: les
unes pour éviter les gênes et les soins, qui ne sont rien en comparaison des avantages et du bonheur de la maternité; les autres pour conserver certains agrémens
très-frivoles et passagers . . ."

83. Elizabeth Badinter, *Mother Love: Myth and Reality, Motherhood in Modern History* (New York, Macmillan, 1981), ch. 5; Brouard-Arends, *Vies et images
maternelles;* and Edward Shorter, *The Making of the Modern Family* (New York:
Basic, 1975).

84. Cardelli, *Manuel de la Jeune Femme,* 17–18. "Les soins qu'une bonne
mère prend de ses enfans, sont une preuve véritable de sa tendresse pour eux . . .
laissent ces jeunes êtres aux soins de ces bonnes qui laissent l'enfant seule pour

aller causer chez le portier, ou font venir leurs amoureux . . . [sont] indignes du nom de mère . . . Que de maux cruels pour les malheureux enfans n'ont-ils pas été la suite d'une négligence criminelle et d'une indifférence impardonnable!"

85. Georges Louis Leclerc Buffon in Jacques Ballexserd, *Dissertation sur l'éducation physique des enfans, depuis leur naissance, jusqu'à l'âge de puberté* (Paris: Vallat La Chappelle, 1762), 53: ". . . sont assez cruelles pour n'être pas touchées de leurs gémissemens; alors ces petits infortunés entrent dans une sorte de désespoir, ils font tous les efforts dont ils sont capables, ils poussent des cris qui durent autant que leurs force; enfin ces excès leur causent des maladies."

86. *JDD* 6 (5 Thermidor, an 10), 481; *JDD* 7 (20 Fructidor, an 11), 561–63.

87. Louis Dubroca, *Le Livre des pères et des mères, pendant la première éducation de leurs enfans, où l'on montre quels sont les dangers d'une tendresse malentendue et d'une conduite inconsidérée de la part des parens, pendant cette première éducation, et en même temps, de quelle manière et par quelles méprises on peut, sans s'en doûter, gâter le meilleur naturel des enfans, et leur imprimer des vices et des travers qui pour parent leur malheur et celui de leurs familles*, vol. 1 (Paris: Dubroca, Delaunay, and Mongie, 1823), 33–35.

88. *JDD* 5 (5 Fructidor, an 9), 531.

89. J. P. Frank, *Traité sur la Manière d'Élever*, 13.

90. Dubroca, *Livre des pères et des mères*, 1:184. "Il entra donc dans le monde tel que sa fabile mère l'avait formé, absolu dans ses volontés, capricieux, insociable, ignorant, plein de travers; en un mot, tel qu'un enfant gâté y entrera toujours, si la providence ne vient pas l'arrêter sur le bord de l'abime où ses parens l'ont poussé."

91. Salguès, *L'amie des mères*, i–iii. Pourquoi les efforts des philosophes et de plusieurs grands médecins, sont-ils restés en partie sans résultats heureux? Il faut d'abord en accuser le peu d'instruction d'un grand nombre de femmes, la paresse ou l'insouciance des unes, la routine habituelle des autres. Mais il est encore une autre cause bien plus puissante . . . les ouvrages mêmes des philosophes ou des médecins n'est revêtu de la forme ou du style convenables, et propres à donner une instruction claire et familière.

92. Campan, *Jeune Mère*, 6.

93. *JDD* 5 (25 Germinal, an 9), 322, extrait du *Journalde Paris*. "A peine connoissoient-ils les auteurs de leurs jours: aussi les parens et les enfans n'étoient unis que par des convenances, et les doux sentimens de piété filiale et de tendresse paternelle ne leur étoient guères connus que par ce qu'ils en avoient ou lu ou entendu dire."

94. Dubroca, *Livre des pères et des mères*, 1:7. "Quoi! pour de si vains motifs, elle sacrifiera le plaisir toujours si pur de presser chaque jour dans ses bras son enfant, de faire couler dans ses veines sa propre vie, d'assister aux développement successifs de son organisation, de recevoir son premier sourire et d'entendre la première les accens de sa voix filiale!"

95. Cardelli, *Manuel de la Jeune Femme*, 16–19; Mme Giost, *Avis aux bonnes mères sur la manière de soigner les enfans depuis leur naissance jusqu'à l'âge de puberté* (Paris: Chez l'auteur et Béchet, 1824), 15–25.

96. Costard, *Conservateur de l'enfance*, 7. "Faites donc, ô mères, faites donc tout votre possible pour que votre enfant reçoive vos services comme des bienfaits. Qu'il apprenne, qu'il sache de vous-mêmes que les auteurs de ses jours sont ses premiers, ses meilleurs amis; qu'il sache aussi qu'ils ne doivent jamais être ses esclaves!"

97. Rebours, *Avis aux mères*, 9–10 (see also Salmade, *Livre des mères*, 21). "D'autres femmes disent qu'elles sont trop délicates. Eh bien! qu'elles nourrissent pour rétablir leur santé. C'est justement là le meilleur remèd qu'elles puissent employer, L'enfant sera leur médicin."

98. Rebours, *Avis aux mères*, vii. "Les soins que les Mères qui nourissent prennent de leurs enfans, rendent leur caractère plus aimable: l'intérêt que l'on prend naturellement à leur conservation devient plus général, & leur Père s'en occupe davantage; en vous rendant plus Mères, vous rendez tous les coeurs plus humains."

99. Buchan, *Conservateur*, 1. "La bonne mère, la mère raisonnable n'écoutera pas, j'en suis sûr, sans un tendre intérêt, la voix de celui qui veut lui enseigner les moyens certains de conserver sa propre santé, de s'assurer de l'attachement constant du mari qui lui est cher, et d'élever des enfans beaux, sains, et robustes."

100. Verdier-Huertin, *Sur l'allaitement et l'éducation*, frontispiece.

101. *JDD* 4 (20 Messidor, an 8), 473, extrait du *Journal des Arts*. "C'est dans la vie de famille que les femmes reprennent cet ascendant qu'elle perdent dans le monde; c'est-là qu'elles sont ce qu'elles doivent être . . ."

102. Jean Jacques Rousseau, *Emile*, trans. Barbara Foxley, ed. Peter D. Jimack (London: Everyman, 1993), 10.

103. Rousseau, *Emile* (Foxley), 69.

104. Linda Kerber, "The Republican Mother: Women and the Enlightenment—An American Perspective," *American Quarterly* 28:2 (1976): 200.

105. *JDD* 6 (20 Frimaire, an 10), 123. "Rousseau accorde tant aux femmes, qu'on ne peut être faché de ce qu'il leur refuse."

4. *"To Amuse and Instruct"*: Self-Control, Adult Expectations, and Children's Literature (pages 112–39)

1. Rebecca Rogers, *From the Salon to the Schoolroom: Educating Bourgeois Girls in Nineteenth-Century France* (University Park: Pennsylvania State University Press, 2005), 36.

2. Norbert Elias, *The Civilizing Process: The History of Manners and State Formation and Civilization*, trans. Edmund Jephcott (Cambridge: Blackwell, 1994), 67.

3. Rogers, *Salon to the Schoolroom*, 35–38.

4. Most of the books were published in $\frac{1}{16}$ or $\frac{1}{32}$ format and printed on inexpensive paper, with slightly thicker paper for the cover pages. They could have anywhere from six to twenty different tales.

5. Geoffrey Summerfield, *Fantasy and Reason: Children's Literature in the Eighteenth Century* (Athens: University of Georgia Press, 1985), 76 and 188.

6. Paul Hazard, *Books, Children and Men*, trans. Marguerite Mitchell (Boston: Horn Books, 1944), 3.

7. Elias, *Civilizing Process*, 67.

8. Isabelle Havelange, *La Littérature à l'usage des demoiselles, 1750–1830* (Thèse de 3ème cycle, EHESS, 1984).

9. Elaine Showalter, in Mitzi Myers, "Impeccable Governesses, Rational Dames, and Moral Mothers: Mary Wollstonecraft and the Female Tradition in Georgian Children's Books," *Children's Literature* 14 (1986): 32–33.

10. Mary V. Jackson, *Engines of Instruction, Mischief, and Magic: Children's Literature in England from Its Beginnings to 1839* (Lincoln: University of Nebraska Press, 1989), xvii. See also Patricia Demers, *Heaven upon Earth: The Form of Moral and Religious Literature, to 1850* (Knoxville: University of Tennessee Press, 1993); Bette P. Goldstone, *Lessons to Be Learned: A Study of Eighteenth-Century English Didactic Literature* (New York: Lang, 1984); and Peter Hunt, *An Introduction to Children's Literature* (Oxford: Oxford University Press, 1994).

11. Of these, the best-known are likely F. J. Harvey Darton, *Children's Books in England: Five Centuries of Social Life*, 3rd ed., rev. Brian Alderson (Cambridge: Cambridge University Press, 1982); and John Rowe Townsend, *Written for Children: An Outline of English-Language Children's Literature*, 3rd ed. (New York: Lippincott, 1987).

12. Henri Lemaire, *Guide de la jeunesse à son entrée dans le monde, ou le retour des anciennes vertus. Leçons d'un oncle à ses neveux et à sa nièce; appuyées d'exemples et de morceaux de morale puisés dans la vie des personnages et dans les ouvrages des Auteurs les plus célèbres* (Paris: Belin-Leprieur, 1818), 5.

13. Paul Hazard's *Books, Children and Men* argues that the difference in output and quality can be related to the difference between the pedagogy of Protestant and Catholic countries and the different intellectual interests of national types (125–28). Isabelle Jan (*On Children's Literature* [New York: Schocken, 1974]) recaps this view and ties it to the different literary traditions in Britain and France. More persuasively, Rosemary Lloyd's *The Land of Lost Content: Children and Childhood in Nineteenth-Century French Literature* (Oxford: Clarendon Press, 1992) argues that children and children's literature are also culturally important in France, simply in a different context.

14. Isabelle Havelange, *Le Magasin des Enfants: La Litterature pour la Jeunesse, 1750–1830* (Montreuil: Bibliothèque Robert-Desnos, 1988), 9.

15. Jean-Noël Luc, *L'invention du jeune enfant au XIX siècle, de la sale d'asile à l'école maternelle* (Paris: Bellin, 1997).

16. Jeanne-Louise-Henriette Genest Campan, *Conseils aux jeunes filles, d'un théâtre pour les jeunes personnes et de quelques essais de morale* (Paris: Baudouin Frères, 1825), 1. "J'ai lu bien des ouvrages écrits pour la jeunesse; presque tous traitent de l'éducation des enfans qui appartiennent aux classes aisées de la société."

17. Demers, *Heaven upon Earth*, 6–7.

18. Peter Hunt, *Introduction*, 5.

19. W. B. Carnochan, "The Child Is Father of the Man," in *A Distant Prospect: Eighteenth-Century Views of Childhood* (Los Angeles: Clark Library, 1982), 27–28.

20. Demers, *Heaven upon Earth*, and Samuel F. Pickering Jr., *Moral Instruction and Fiction for Children, 1749–1820* (Athens: University of Georgia Press, 1993).

21. Geneviève Bollème, *La Bibliothèque bleue, la littérature en France du XVI siècle au XIX siècle* (Paris: Julliard, 1971), and Jan, *On children's Literature*, 16.

22. Ségolène Le Men, *Les Abécédaires Français Illustrés du XIX Siècle* (Paris: Promodis, 1984), 13–14.

23. *Le Gros A,B,C pour instruire la jeunesse chrétienne & catholique, à l'usage des écoles du diocèse de Châlons* (Châlons: Mercier, 1783), is a good example of this type of *abécédaire*.

24. *Abécédaire joujou, contenant dans un étui élégamment cartonné, un alphabet et un joujou pour récréer l'enfant après la lecture* (Paris: Eugène Balland, 1827) and *L'Alphabet mis en jeu* (Paris: Favre, s.d.).

25. *L'Alphabet mis en jeu* (Paris: Favre, s.d.). "Cet ouvrage, destiné à instruir les Enfants en les amusant . . ."

26. *Élémens du jeune républicain. Alphabet composé par un instituteur père de famille, d'après le projet de décret présenté à la Convention Nationale, pour honorer l'être Suprème, pour célébrer les vertus républicaines et les fêtes décadaires, etc.* (Paris: Fantelin, n.d.), no pagination: ". . . ad-mi-re la jus-ti-ce et la bon-té de l'ê-tre Su-prê-me."

27. *Abécédaire de l'histoire de France, contenant, soixante-dix leçons, extraites des règnes de ses rois, depuis Pharamond jusqu'à Charles X, accompagné de petites phrases pour apprendre à lire aux enfans, et leur donner le goût de la lecture. Orné de neuf planches gravées, reprsentant un grand nombre de portraits des rois de France* (Paris: Ancelle, 1827), 12, "Mots composés de plusieurs syllabes." "Ad-ju-di-ca-ti-on . . . Bé-a-ti-fi-cat-ti-on . . . Fla-gel-la-ti-on . . ."

28. *Élémens du jeune républicain*, no pagination: "ad-mi-re la jus-ti-ce et la bon-té de l'ê-tre Su-prê-me."

29. *Abécédaire de l'histoire de France*, 12, "Mots composés de plusieurs syllabes." "Ad-ju-di-ca-ti-on . . . Bé-a-ti-fi-cat-ti-on . . . Fla-gel-la-ti-on . . ."

30. Basset, *Explication morale des proverbes populaires français* (Paris: Louis Colas, 1826), 1:1–2. "Si, après avoir reçu, étant jeune, les élémens que personne ne devrait ignorer, il a oussé la négligence ou l'insousiance jusqu'à les oublier entirèment, on n'a pas de lui une meilleure opinion, et on dit: qu'il faut le renvoyer à l'A, B, C. Ce reproche est humiliant, car on ne va pas volontiers à l'école quand on est jeune; il est bien tard pour y aller quand le temps de l'enfance est passé . . ."

31. Le Men, *Abécédaires Français*, 12: ". . . la culture enfantine se dévoile à travers les abécédaires . . . La transmission des valeurs de la société se fait à partir d'un répertoire de textes de la littérature adulte 'adaptés' pour l'enfant destinataire et illustrés de gravures où domine la tradition de l'imagerie populaire bien que des emprunts à la culture savante . . ."

32. *Abécédaire nouveau, ou Méthode amusante pour apprendre à lire aux enfans* (Paris: Delion, an 11 (1802). "Aux mères tendres."

33. Hubert Wandelaincourt, *Cours d'éducation Pour les écoles du premier âge* (Paris: Ancelle, an 10 [1801]), avis de l'éditeur. "La méthode . . . ne demande, du côté de l'écolier, que de faire usage de l'attachement qu'il doit avoir . . . et une attention assez commune à écouter ce qu'il dit."

34. *Abécédaire nouveau,* frontispiece. "Ma petite Maman, embrasse ton enfant, il sera bien gentil . . . Ce n'est pas tout d'être gentil, il faut encore apprendre à lire."

35. Goldstone, *Lessons to Be Learned,* 75–77; Summerfield, *Fantasy and Reason,* 3–8; Kenneth MacLean, *John Locke and English Literature of the Eighteenth Century* (New York: Garland, 1984).

36. The prerational emphasis explains the fact that *abécédaires* were generally intended for the use of children of both sexes. Just as a mother could educate both boys and girls in a similar fashion until the boys reached the age of reason, so too could these books teach both at the same time.

37. Cadmus, *A, B, C, Syllabaire nouveau, conforme au principe adopté par l'institute National. Orné d'un frontispice, et de vingt-quatre figure d'animaux, par ordre alphabétique, gravées en taille-douce, avec leurs explications, quelques Fables de la Fontaine, Contes et Dialogues moraux* (Paris: Bonneville, an 7), avertissement. "De tous les Abécédaires et Syllabaires, le plus utile et le plus agréable pour les enfans, est sans contredit, celui qui présente à leurs yeux l'idée de quelque objet existant."

38. Pickering, *Moral Instruction and Fiction,* 9.

39. *Élémens du Jeune Républicain,* préface. "Pour faciliter les progrès de mon élève, j'ai simplifié toutes mes expressions, particularisé toutes mes idées, donné, de la manière la plus courte et la plus claire, toutes les définitions nécessaires, afin de l'amuser et l'instruisant."

40. Hazard, *Books, Children and Men,* 19.

41. Eric Rabkin, *Fantastic Worlds* (New York: Oxford University Press, 1979), 167.

42. Abbé Gaultier, *Jeu de fables, faisant partie du cours complet d'études élémentaires* (Paris: L. Colas, 1816), iii. "Nous leur fournissons en outre les moyens non seulement d'exercer leurs élèves à s'exprimer et à développer leurs idées naissantes, mais encore d'appliquer les règles de l'orthographe en les obligeant à écrire leurs réponses."

43. M. l'Abbé Gaultier, *Amusing and Instructive Conversations for Children of Five Years* (New York: Johnson Reprint Corporation, 1970 [1800]), viii.

44. L'Abbé Aubert, *Fables nouvelles, accompagnées de notes, et suivies du discours sur la manière de lire les fables ou de les reciter,* 4th ed. (Paris: Moutard, 1773), 256. "Je doute qu'à la première lecture, il en comprenne tout-à-fait le commencement . . . C'est un ouvrage pour l'esprit d'un enfant, que de démêler cela. Il faut qu'on lui en donne au moins une explication légère."

45. Harvey Chisick, *The Limits of Reform in the Enlightenment: Attitudes Toward the Education of the Lower Classes in Eighteenth-Century France* (Princeton: Princeton University Press, 1981), 39–40.

46. Jean Jacques Rousseau, *Emile, or On Education,* trans. Barbara Foxley, ed. Peter D. Jimack (London: Everyman, 1993), 91.

47. Rousseau, *Emile* (Foxley), 94.

48. Rousseau, *Emile* (Foxley), 91.

49. Louis Chambaud, *Fables Choisies, à l'usage des Enfans et des autres personnes qui commencent à apprendre la langue françoise* (Londres: Nourse, 1786), preface.

50. Some examples from throughout this period are: *Le Fablier des Enfans, choix des fables Analogues aux goûts du premier age, avec des notes grammaticales, Mythologiques, et Historiques* (Paris: Devaux, an 8); Abbé Gaultier, *Jeu de Fable;* Laurent de Jussieu, *Fables et Contes en Vers* (Paris: Louis Colas, 1829).

51. Gaultier, *Jeu de Fables,* xiii. "*A qui peut-on comparer cette cigale?* A ceux qui préfèrent le plaisir du moment à leur bonheur à venir. (1 jeton) *A qui peut-on comparer la fourmi?* Aux gens prévoyants qui prennent toutes les mesure pour ne jamais tomber dans l'indigence. (2 jetons) *Excusez-vous le refus peu charitable de cette fourmi?* Oui, parce-qu'on ne fait pas volontiers du bien à ceux qui sont malheureux par leur faute. (3 jetons.)"

52. *Fablier des Enfans,* 36. "Note: L'auteur, en terminant par cette moralité [Vous chantiez! . . . Hé bien, dansez maintenant!], n'a envisagé que le but de sa fable, qui était de prouver aux fainéans la nécessité du travail; mais en lisant ses autres fables, on se convaincra qu'il était loin de sa pensée d'insulter aux misérables, lors même que l'indigence est une suite de leur oisiveté."

53. Jussieu, *Fables et Contes en Vers,* 49–50. "Que feriez-vous, je vous prie, / Si, comme vous, aujourd'hui / J'étais insensible et fière; / Si j'allais vous inviter / A promener ou chanter? / Mais rassurez-vous, ma chère; / Entrez, mangez à loisir, / Usez-en comme du vôtre, / Et surtout, pour l'avenir, / Apprenez à compter / A la misère d'une autre."

54. *Fablier des Enfans,* 9. "Quand il a bien joué, Cola dit: C'est mon tour. / Mais Fanfan n'était plus son frère; / Fanfan le trouva téméraire; / Fanfan le repoussa d'un air fier et mutin./ Perette alors prend Colas par la main./ Viens, lui-dit-elle avec tristesse,/ Voilà Fanfan devenu grand seigneur; / Viens, mon fils, tu n'as plu son coeur. / L'amité disparaît oûl'égalité cesse."

55. *Fablier des Enfans,* 11–12. "Colas, vous méprisiez mon fils et votre mèe; / Vous traitiez durement tous ceux que la misère, / Pour subsister, obliger de servir: / Vous allez apprendre à les plaindre. / Vous voyez qu'au sein du bonheur, / La retours du sort sont à craindre . . ."

56. *Fablier des Enfans,* 51–52. "Lui donna ce conseil de morale commune / Mais bien conforme au sort qu'il avait éprouvé: / Souvenez-ous, dit-il, si jamais la fortune / Vous place en un poste élevé, / Du petit accident dont vous voilà sauvé."

57. *Fablier des Enfans,* 45. "Note: Nous ne connaissons pas en France cette condition malheureuse, qui met un homme dans la puissance absolue d'un autre homme."

58. Goldstone, *Lessons to Be Learned,* 175.

59. Sophie Renneville, *Correspondance de deux petites filles, ouvrage propre à former de bonne heure les enfans au style épistolaire* (Paris: Belin, 1811), 18. "Madame Hortense ne veut pas nous faire apprendrons les *Fables de La Fontaine;* elle dit que cette lecture ne convient qu'aux grandes personnes, et que les enfans n'y entendent rien."

60. Renneville, *Deux petites filles,* 81. "Je t'écris pour te dire que je t'aime, et que je vais devenir savant. Je sais déjà par coeur plusieurs fables de Phèdre."

61. Alida Savignac, "La Mère Courageuse," in *Encouragemens donnés à la jeunesse industrieuse* (Paris: Louis Colas, 1828), 1; Antoine de Saint Gervais, "Favart, ou le Petit Patissier," in *Les petits artisans devenus hommes célèbres, ouvrage fait pour inspirer des sentimes d'élévation aux jeunes gens des deux*

sexes, même dans les classes les plus inférieures de la Société (Parïs: F. Denn, 1829), 19.

62. Renneville, *Deux petites filles*, 4–8. "Tu sais pourquoi je suis ici; cela ne me fait pas honneur: si j'étais douce et sage comme toi, maman m'aimerait et me garderait chez elle."

63. Etienne-François Bazot, "La Jeune Pédante," *Historiettes et Contes à ma petite fille et à mon petit garçon, ornés de douze gravures coloriées* (Paris: L'écrivain, 1821), 110. "Il fallut obéir et se corriger, à moins de s'exposer à passer toute sa vie dans une retraite. Elvire se corrigea donc: D'abord par nécessité, puis en profitant des conseils maternels, de la lecture de bons livres, et de l'expérience."

64. Rogers, *Salon to the Schoolroom*, 34.

65. Hubert Wandelaincourt, *Cours d'Education Pour les Ecoles du Second Age, ou des Adolescents* (Paris: Ancelle, an 10 [1802]) 1:146.

Pourquoi les hommes, qui sont associés à leur félicité, les laisseraient-ils s'avilir elles-mêmes, vivre sans aucune bonne idée, sans aucuns grands principes sur les sciences, pas même sur la morale, er borner tout leur mérite et leurs forces à quelques attraits passagers, qui bientôt flétris, ne leur laissent que l'impuissance de contribuer à la réformation des moeurs, au bonheur et à la gloire des familles? Ne devons-nous pas plutôt leur fournir les secours propres à les perfectionner et nécessaires à leur bonheur et au nôtre. Si nos les abandonnions à elles-mêmes, pourrions-nous nous plaindre des maux, suite inévitable de cet abandon?

66. Renneville, *Deux petites filles*, 92: "...car il n'est pas naturel que tu fasses tes volontés à ton âge, avec une mauvaise tête comme celle que tu as, et chez des personnes qui ont ordonner de veiller sur tes actions et de réprimer la pétulance de ton caractère ..."

67. Etienne-François Bazot, "Alphonsine, la jeune colère," *Historiettes et Contes à ma petite fille et à mon petit garçon, ornés de douze gravures coloriées* (Paris: L'écrivain, 1821), 100. "Les femmes, ma nièce, ne sont intéressantes, aimées, et respectés qu'autant que leurs actions, leurs paroles et leurs gestes sont en harmonie avec la délicatesse de leurs traits, la douceur naturelle de leur sexe. Les femmes bien nées ne se doivent jamais départir de la timidité et de la pudeur, leur séduisant partage."

68. C. Deleyre, *Contes dans un nouveau genre pour les enfans qui commencent à lire* (Paris: Gabriel Dufour, 1807), vi. "Que le dénouement de ce Conte serve seulement de morale, par le plaisir ou la peine qe doivent éprouver le héros ou l'héroïnes ... selon qu'ils ont obéi ou désobéi à leurs parens!"

69. Mme Van der Bruck, *Contes et Conseils à mes jeunes enfans, convenables à la première enfance pour les deux sexes* (Paris: Ledentu, 1819), iv. "Tous les exemples, au moins vraisemblables, offrent le tableau du vice puni souvent par lui-même, et la vertu récompensée."

70. Sophie Renneville, *Les Deux éducations ou le pouvoir de l'exemple* (Paris: Alexis Eymery, 1813), 1–2. "J'ai essayé de prouver, par cette *ébauche* sur l'éducation, que les jouissances trompeuses de l'orgueil ne sont pas le bonheur, et que la prudence, que les dédaigne, qui les proscrit, peut seul attirer l'estime des honnêtes gens et fixer la fortune."

71. Claudine Coeurderoy, *Dialogues d'une mère avec sa fille* (Paris: Rondo-

neau, an 10), 314–15. "Mon enfant, l'instruction est utile, je n'en fais aucun doute; mais tout ce qu'elle peut faire de mieux pour les femmes, c'est de les occuper dans leur moment de retraite; il est si rare qu'elle nous serve en société; ce n'est que dans l'intimité que nous pouvons la faire paraître; mais la douceur, cette vertu aimable et touchante, qui nous fait éviter de blesser personne, par nos paroles & nos procédés; qui nous fait supporter les défauts moraux & physiques des autres; & qui, par-là, nous fait chérir dans la société. Ha! mon enfant, quelle différence!"

72. Renneville, *Deux éducations*, 156. "Depuis que j'ai élévé Mélanie l'éducation d'une fille n'a plus rien qui m'effraie; je dirai aux mères: Réglez vos moeurs; vos filles seront vertueuses; formez leur caractère sur le vôtre; connaissez le pouvoir de l'exemple . . ."

73. Philippe-Antoine-Ascension Garros, ed., *Esprit de la Morale Universelle ou Manuel de Tous les Ages, traduit d'un ancien manuscrit indien, dédié à la jeunesse, et mis en concordance avec l'Ecriture-Sainte* (Paris: Renard, s.d.), 103–104. "Elle forme l'esprit de ses enfans à la sagesse, et son exemple y grave les bonnes moeurs. Ses paroles sont la loi de leur jeunesse; un seul de ses regards est un ordre pour leur obéissance."

74. A. Antoine, *Les Soirées de l'adolescence ou Aventures Amusantes, racontées par une société de jeunes enfans de deux sexes* (Paris, Lechard, 1823), 37–81.

75. Antoine, *Soirées de l'adolescence*, 1–37.

76. Elisabeth Celnart, *Les Soirées du Dimanche, ou le Curé de Village: Leçons de Morale Pratique. Ouvrage Couronné par la Société pour l'instruction élémentaire* (Paris: L. Colas, 1827), 11. "Malgré une si fâcheuse éducation, j'appris à lire, à écrire, un peu a compter. Je lus beaucoup d'histoires morales, où, par des exemples vifs et naturels, l'auteur prouvait que malgré toutes sortes de traverses on pouvait toujours se faire un sort heureux avec la patience, le courage, et la confiance en Dieu. Ce sont sans doute ces bonnes lectures qui m'ont soutenu dans toutes les épreuves de ma vie."

77. Celnart, *Curée de Village*, 17. "Le jeune homme devint avocat comme son père; la demoiselle épousa M. de Vesselmond, magistrat riche et considéré . . ."

78. Van der Bruck, *Contes et Conseils*, iii.

5. Education and Politics: Schooling, Revolution, and Rousseau
(pages 140–64)

1. H.C. Barnard, *Education and the French Revolution* (Cambridge: Cambridge University Press, 1969), 2–3. This is not to conclude necessarily that the pre-1789 schools were fundamentally unsound, just that the state was not especially concerned with primary education. While much nineteenth-century thought on education argues that the legislative agenda from 1790 to 1800 is proof that the pre-revolutionary system was deeply flawed and untenable, with or without revolution, most modern historians say that this is incorrect. Of these, some of the most important works are: François Furet and Jacques Ozouf (*Lire et écrire: L'alphabétisation des Français de Calvin à Jules Ferry,* 2 vols. (Paris: Éditions de Minuit, 1977); Dominique Julia, Roger Chartier, and Marie Madeleine Compère,

L'éducation en France du 16e au 18e siècle (Paris: Société d'édition d'enseigne-ment supérieur, 1976); R. R. Palmer, *The Improvement of Humanity: Education and the French Revolution* (Princeton: Princeton University Press, 1985); and Isser Woloch, *The New Regime: Transformations of the French Civic Order, 1789–1820s* (New York: W. W. Norton, 1994).

2. See for example, Palmer, *Improvement*; Woloch, *New Regime*; and Furet and Ozouf, *Lire et écrire*.

3. See, for example, Antoinette LeGroing-LaMaisonneuve, *Essai sur le Genre d'Instruction le plus analogue à la destination des femmes* (Paris: N.P., 1801), 5.

4. Mira Morgenstern, *Rousseau and the Politics of Ambiguity: Self, Culture, and Society* (University Park: Pennsylvania State University Press, 1996), 183n.

5. Louis-Aimé Martin, *The Education of Mothers; or, The Civilization of Mankind by Women*, trans. Edwin Lee (Philadelphia: Lea and Blanchard, 1843), 40.

6. Lynn Hunt, *The Family Romance of the French Revolution* (Berkeley: University of California Press, 1993), 171.

7. Barnard, *Education and the French Revolution*, 2–3.

8. Palmer, *Improvement*, 7. Palmer identified four general trends in educational thought from the pre-revolutionary period to the rise of Napoleon: nationalization (pre-revolutionary), politicization (1789–1792), democratization (1792–1794), and modernization (1795–1799). While a close examination of each stage is not necessary for an understanding of the general development of educational theories, an awareness of these divisions has informed my discussion of revolutionary and post-revolutionary education.

9. Palmer, *Improvement*, 7.

10. James Guillaume, *Procès-Verbaux du Comité d'Instruction Publique de l'Assemblée Législative* (Paris: Imprimerie Nationale, 1889), Constituent Assembly notes for September 3–4, 1791.

11. Jean Verdier, *Discours sur l'éducation nationale, physique et morale des deux sexes, pour servir de prospectus des ouvrages d'éducation et d'économie* (Paris: Chez l'auteur, 1792), 2.

La Nation elle-même doit en faire tracer dans sa législation, le *Plan National . . . Ces . . . éducations [domestique et méthodique] doivent se réunir, pour conduire uniformément tous les élèves de la patrie vers le bonheur commun et individuel:* mais leur confusion, leur imperfection, leurs vices et leur oppostion ne leur ont guères fait produire jusqu'à ce jour, que des fruits sauvages, peu nombreux et souvent empoisonnés . . . [latter emphasis mine].

12. Robert J. Vignery, *French Revolution and the Schools: The Educational Politics of the Mountain, 1792–1794* (Madison: State Historical Society, 1965), 4.

13. Jean Jacques Rousseau, *Considérations sur le gouvernment de Pologne.* "Tout vrai républicain suça avec le lait de sa mère l'amour de sa patrie, c'est-à-dire des lois et de la liberté."

14. The Talleyrand report is reprinted in its entirety in Célestin Hippeau, *Instruction publique en France pendant la révolution: discours et rapports de Mirabeau, Talleyrand-Périgord, Condorcet, Lanthenas, Romme, Le Peletier, Saint-Fargeau, Calès, Lakanal, Daunou et Fourcroy* (Paris: Didier, 1881), 1: 33–184.

15. August Vallet de Viriville, *Histoire de l'instruction publique en Europe et*

principalement en France depuis le christianisme jusqu'à nos jours: universités, colléges, écoles des deux sexes, académies, bibliothèques publiques, etc. (Paris: Administration du moyen age et la renaissance, 1849), 265–67.

16. Barnard, *Education and the French Revolution,* 69–71; Woloch, *New Regime,* 178; Palmer, *Improvement,* 82.

17. Condorcet's plan is reprinted in its entirety in Guillaume, *Assemblée Législative,* 188–226. Of course, Guillaume's collection was not itself without ideological design. For the best discussion of Guillaume's project and its intent, see Charles Coutel, "République et instruction publique chez Condorcet. Autour d'un jugement de James Guillaume," and Josiane Boulad-Ayoub, "Les processus d'idéologisation et l'action symbolique. Le Cas Guillaume et les procès-verbaux des Comités d'instruction publique," both found in Josiane Boulad-Ayoub, ed., *Former un nouveau peuple? Pouvoir, éducation, révolution* (Paris: Harmattan, 1996).

18. Condorcet, in Guillaume, *Assemblée Legislative,* 190. Note the distinction between the education of "enfance" and the schooling that never was. "La loi m'assurait une entière égalité des droits, mais on me refuse les moyens de les connaitre. Je ne dois dépendre que de la loi, mais mon ignorance me rend dépendant de tout ce qui m'entoure."

19. Condorcet, in Guillaume, *Assemblée Legislative,* 190. "On m'a bien appris dans mon enfance que j'avais besoin de savoir; mais, forcé de travailler pour vivre, ces premières notions se sont bientôt effacées, et il ne m'en reste que la douleur de sentir dans mon ignorance non la volonté de la nature, mais l'injustice de la société."

20. Condorcet, in Guillaume, *Assemblée Legislative,* 195.

21. Guillaume, *Assemblée Legislative,* 192 ff.

22. Condorcet, in Guillaume, *Assemblée Legislative,* 219–21.

23. Condorcet, in Guillaume, *Assemblée Legislative,* 220.
. . . si l'on observe que, dans les familles peu riches, la partie domestique de l'éducation des enfants est presque uniquement abandonnée à leurs mères; si l'on songe que sur vingt-cinq familles livrées à l'agriculture, au commerce, aux arts, une au moins a une veuve pour son chef, on sentira combien cette portion du travail qui nous a été confié est importante et pour la prospérité commune, et pour le progrès général des lumières.

24. Vignery, *French Revolution and the Schools,* 26.

25. See especially Guillaume, *Assemblée Legislative,* 202–205.

26. Guillaume, *Assemblée Legislative,* 223.

27. See the discussion about necessary inequalities in talent in Guillaume, *Assemblée Legislative,* 202–205.

28. Olwen Hufton, *Women and the Limits of Citizenship in the French Revolution* (Toronto: University of Toronto Press, 1992), goes into detail about the problems of teaching orders and the disarray of education.

29. Many explain the lack of legislative action by reference to the fact that Condorcet and many of the deputies on the Committee for Public Instruction were Girondins. See, for example, Palmer, *Improvement;* and Maurice Gontard, *L'Enseignement primaire en France de la Révolution à la loi Guizot, 1789–1833* (Paris: Société d'édition, 1959), 99–113. It is true that, at the culmination of the

Montagnard-Girondin conflict, there was little room for compromise on issues of public education. That only serves as a partial answer, however.

30. Massuyer, *Discours sur l'éducation publique* (Paris, 1795).

31. Vignery, *French Revolution and the Schools,* 31.

32. Jean Bloch, *Rousseauism and Education in Eighteenth-Century France,* Studies on Voltaire and the Eighteenth Century, vol. 325 (Oxford: Voltaire Foundation, 1995); Mona Ozouf, *Festivals and the French Revolution* (Cambridge: Harvard University Press, 1991); James Guillaume, *Procès-Verbeaux du Comité d'instruction publique de la Convention Nationale* (Paris: Hachette, 191–92) 1: 231, 507–16.

33. See, for example, Julia et al., *L'éducation en France,* and Woloch, *New Regime.* Vignery is an exception to this rule, though his work does not concern itself at all with a broader context for moral education but focuses only on what the schools could provide.

34. Guillaume, *Convention,* 1: xvii, 124–26, 143, 191, 216, 252; See also Keith Baker, *Condorcet: From National Philosophy to Social Mathematics* (Chicago: University of Chicago Press, 1975), 293–320; Roger Hahn, *The Anatomy of a Scientific Institution: The Paris Academy of Sciences* (Berkeley: University of California Press, 1971), 159–225.

35. Albert Babeau, *L'école de village pendant la Révolution* (Paris: Didier, 1881), ch. 2; and Julien Tiersot, *Les fêtes et les chants de la Révolution française* (Pais: Hachette, 1908). For example, the Jacobin Joseph-Marie Lequinio proposed, like Condorcet, to leave moral education in the hands of the family and to promote instruction in the schools.

36. Gilbert Romme, *Rapport dur l'instruction publique, consideérée dans son ensemble, suivi d'un projet de décret sur le princpales bases du plan général, présenté à la Convention Nationale au nom du comité d'Instruction publique* (Paris, 1793), 7–9.

37. André Jeanbon Saint-André, *Sur l'éducation nationale* (Paris: N.p., n.d.).

38. Lepeletier's plan is in Guillaume, *Convention,* 2:34–61. Palmer argues that Lepeletier's acceptance of most of Condorcet's plan was also an acceptance of distinctions in equality. While this may be true, the idea of compulsory boarding schools so that all might have equal opportunity seems to counter this argument and adds to the perception of this plan as more extreme than moderate in its leanings.

39. Lepeletier, in Woloch, *New Regime,* 179.

40. Guillaume, *Convention,* 2: 56,163.

41. Charles Delacroix, *Projet de loi sur l'éducation commune, part Ch. Delacroix, député de la Marne à la Convention nationale* (Paris, n.d.), 2–7.

42. Vignery, *French Revolution and the Schools,* 88.

43. Jacques-Michel Coupé, *Suite de l'instruction publique, par J. M. Coupé, député du département de l'Oise* (Paris, n.d.).

44. *Réimpression de l'ancien Moniteur: seule histoire authentique et inaltérée de la Révolution française depuis la réunion des Etats-Généraux juqu'au consulat (mai 1789–novembre 1799), avec des notes explicatives,* 31 vols. (Paris: 1858–63) 20:409.

45. Text and details are in Guillaume, *Convention,* 3: 56–62, 191–96. Incisive

commentary and criticisms can be found in Jean Louis Crémieux-Brilhac, ed., *L'éducation nationale: le Ministère; l'administration centrale; les services* (Paris: Presses universitaires de France, 1965), 17; Gontard, *De la Révolution,* 116–20.

46. Palmer, *Improvement,* 181.

47. Palmer, *Improvement,* 181–83; Vignery, *French Revolution and the Schools;* Woloch, *New Regime,* 179–81.

48. Text and discussion can be found in Guillaume, *Convention,* 5: 142–51, 177–85, and 223–38.

49. The debate over Daunou's compromise is in Guillaume, *Convention,* 6: 336–37, 580, 793–94, 869–70.

50. Gontard, *De la Révolution,* 188.
A défaut d'un réseau solide d'écoles nationales, la Révolution laissait pourtant une oeuvre durable. D'abord ses idées: reprenant les vues ambitieuses des Philosophes et des Economistes, secouant jougs et préjugés, substituant la Raison à la Foi, l'égalité au privilège, elle avait profondément labouré le terrain scolaire français, enfoncé dans son soi les semences fécondes de principes que les républicains n'oublieront plus.

51. Woloch, *New Regime,* 183.

52. Colin Heywood, *Childhood in Nineteenth-Century France: Work, Health, and Education Among the "Classes Populaires"* (New York: Cambridge University Press, 1988); Woloch, *New Regime;* Robert Gildea, *Education in Provincial France, 1800–1914* (Oxford: Clarendon Press, 1983); Joseph N. Moody, *French Education Since Napoleon* (Syracuse: Syracuse University Press, 1978); and Felix Ponteil, *Histoire de l'enseignement en France: Les Grandes étapes, 1789–1964* (Paris: Sirey, 1966).

53. See Barry Herman Bergen, "Molding Citizens: Ideology, Class, and Primary Education in Nineteenth-Century France," Ph.D. diss, University of Pennsylvania, 1987, and Sarah A. Curtis, *Educating the Faithful: Religion, Schooling and Society* (DeKalb: Northern Illinois University Press, 2000).

54. The report is published in its entirety in *Le Moniteur Universal,* an 9 (November 1800), no. 19.

55. Chaptal, in Barnard, *Education and the French Revolution,* 200–201.

56. Furet and Ozouf, *Lire et écrire,* 116–19.

57. François Guizot, *Essai sur l'histoire et sur l'état actuel de l'instruction publique en France* (Paris: Chez Maradon, 1816), 57–59.

58. Moody, *Education Since Napoleon,* 3.

59. Gontard, *De la Révolution,* 267. "En effet, dans les milieux les plus divers de l'opinion de 1815, on se prend à considérer l'ignorance comme un des grands fléaux de la société contemporaine. D'abord, sur le plan humain, l'ignorance abrutit l'esprit, déprave le coeur, livre l'homme aux instinct, engendre paresse et vice."

60. Woloch, *New Regime,* 217.

61. Moody, *Education Since Napoleon,* 21.

62. Gontard, *De la Révolution,* 267–359.

63. Antoine Prost, *Histoire de l'Enseignement en France, 1800–1967* (Paris: A. Colin, 1968), 155–68.

64. Bergen, Curtis, and Gildea all confirm this idea.

65. Woloch, *New Regime*, 222–23.

66. Ambroise Rendu, *Essai sur l'instruction publique et particulièrement sur l'instruction primaire*, 3 vols. (Paris: n.p., 1819); Guillaume de Bertier de Sauvigny, *The Bourbon Restoration* (Philadelphia: University of Pennsylvania Press, 1966), ch. 17.

67. Alexis Léaud and Emile Glay, *L'école primaire en France ses origins, ses différents aspects au cours des siècles, ses luttes, ses victoires, sa mission dans la démocratie*, preface by Edouard Herriot (Paris: La Cité française, 1934), 1:231.

68. Ponteil, *Grandes étapes*, 197. "L'enseignement primaire paraît de première nécessité, au point de vue politique, économique, et social. Le roi soutient la *Société pour l'instruction élémentaire*, qui est reconnue comme établissment d'utilité publique (ordonnance du 29 avril 1831)."

69. This is not to argue that mutual and simultaneous instruction were more widespread than individual instruction but to make a point about official expectations and desires. Furet and Ozouf note that, "[i]n January 1829, four-fifths of the teaching profession were still using [individual instruction], as a ministerial circular notes with regret" (115). Though it is not central to this study, which focuses generally on the intersection between familial and state control of education, a study of the rhetoric surrounding individual versus mutal instruction might be a promising place to begin a different kind of study on the relationship of the individual to public education.

70. J. A. Dubochet, *Discours sur l'Éducation Populaire, prononcé à la séance publique de la Société Royale Académique de Nantes, le 25 Novembre 1832* (Nantes: N.p., 1833), 3. "Aucun sujet ne mérite mieux de fixer l'attention de cette assemblée que le progrès de l'éducation populaire promise, aux frais de l'état, à tous les Français. Opération généreuse, qui doit répandre dans toutes les classes les connaissances nécessaires aux hommes, et ajouter à nos moyens de prospérité."

71. Robert David Anderson, *Education in France 1848–1870* (Oxford: Clarendon Press, 1975), 15; Gontard, *De la Révolution*, 501.

72. Bergen, "Molding Citizens," 33.

73. Bergen, "Molding Citizens," 27.

74. Guizot, *Exposé des Motifs*, 2. "Demanderons-nous à la commune, qui semble participier à la fois de la famille et de l'Etat, de se charger seule de l'instruction primaire, de la surveillance, et par conséquent, aussi des dépenses?"

75. William Connolly, *The Terms of Political Discourse* (Princeton: Princeton University Press, 1984), 241.

76. Rebecca Rogers, *From the Salon to the Schoolroom: Educating Bourgeois Girls in Nineteenth-Century France* (University Park: Pennsylvania State University Press, 2005), 4.

77. Martin, *Education of Mothers*, 83.

Conclusion. Autonomous Individuality, Self-Control, and Domesticity
(pages 165–179)

1. Louis-Aimé Martin, *The Education of Mothers; or, The Civilization of*

Mankind by Women, trans. Edwin Lee (Philadelphia: Lea and Blanchard, 1843), xxxii.

2. Martin, *Education of Mothers,* 34.
3. Martin, *Education of Mothers,* 34–35.
4. Martin, *Education of Mothers,* 34.
5. Martin, *Education of Mothers,* 56–57.
6. Martin, *Education of Mothers,* 70.
7. Martin, *Education of Mothers,* 56–57.
8. Martin, *Education of Mothers,* 61.
9. Martin, *Education of Mothers,* 61.
10. Martin, *Education of Mothers,* 92.
11. Martin, *Education of Mothers,* 117.
12. Edwin Lee, translator's preface to Martin, *Education of Mothers,* xxxii.
13. Martin, *Education of Mothers,* 159.
14. Martin, *Education of Mothers,* 41.
15. Martin, *Education of Mothers,* 35.
16. Martin, *Education of Mothers,* 37.
17. Martin, *Education of Mothers,* 171.
18. Martin, *Education of Mothers,* 162.
19. Martin, *Education of Mothers,* 37.
20. Martin, *Education of Mothers,* 37.
21. Martin, *Education of Mothers,* 300–301.
22. Martin, *Education of Mothers,* 231.
23. Martin, *Education of Mothers,* 119–20.
24. Martin, *Education of Mothers,* 132.
25. Martin, *Education of Mothers,* 136.
26. Martin, *Education of Mothers,* 137.
27. Martin, *Education of Mothers,* 136.
28. Jean Jacques Rousseau, *Emile,* trans. Barbara Foxley, ed. Peter D. Jimack (London: Everyman, 1993), 69.
29. Martin, *Education of Mothers,* 42.
30. Martin, *Education of Mothers,* 50.
31. Martin, *Education of Mothers,* 55.
32. Martin, *Education of Mothers,* 43–44.
33. Martin, *Education of Mothers,* 47.
34. Martin, *Education of Mothers,* 56.
35. Martin, *Education of Mothers,* 150–51.
36. Colwill, Elisabeth, "Women's Empire and the Sovereignty of Man in *La Décade Philosophique,*" *Eighteenth-Century Studies* 29 (1996): 277.
37. Martin, *Education of Mothers,* 41.
38. Martin, *Education of Mothers,* 219.
39. To give one concrete example, footnote 62 of ch. 4 demonstrates this in Caroline's claim that "si j'étais douce et sage comme toi, maman m'aimerait et me garderait chez elle." The same sense of "sage" is captured in the French phrase "sage comme une image," which can be roughly translated by the English phrase "as good as gold."
40. Many thanks to Michelle Rhoades, who noted the tiles on the floor, and

others who commented on this image at the annual meeting of the WSFH in Albuquerque, N.M., 2007.

41. Rebecca Rogers, *From the Salon to the Schoolroom: Educating Bourgeois Girls in Nineteenth-Century France* (University Park: Pennsylvania State University Press, 2005), 43.

42. Suzanne Desan has a good overview of this tendency in her introduction to *The Family on Trial in Revolutionary France* (Berkeley: University of California Press, 2004), notes 13 to 17.

43. Carole Pateman, *The Sexual Contract* (Stanford: Stanford University Press, 1988), 36.

44. Jacques Revel, "The Uses of Civility," in *A History of Private Life*, vol III, ed. Roger Chartier, trans. Arthur Goldhammer (Cambridge, UK: 1989), 174.

45. Linda Kerber, "The Republican Mother: Women and the Enlightenment—An American Perspective," *American Quarterly* 28: 2 (1976): 187–205.

46. Mary P. Ryan, "The Public and the Private Good: Across the Great Divide in Women's History," *Journal of Women's History* 15 (2003), 19.

47. For example, Rosemarie Zagarri ("Morals, Manners, and the Republican Mother," *American Quarterly* 44 [1992]), suggests that the civil jurisprudential school of the Scottish Enlightenment—not Rousseauian domesticity—is the source of Republican motherhood.

48. Lynn Hunt, *The Family Romance of the French Revolution* (Berkeley: University of California Press, 1993), 203.

49. Lori J. Marso, "The Stories of Citizens: Rousseau, Montesquieu, and de Staël Challenge Enlightenment Reason," *Polity* 30 (1998): 436.

50. Mitzi Myers, "Reform or Ruin: 'A Revolution in Female Manners,'" in *Studies in Eighteenth-Century Culture*, vol. 11, ed. Harry C. Payne (Madison: University of Wisconsin Press, 1982), 201.

51. Myers, "Revolution in Female Manners," 203.

Bibliography

Primary Sources

A. B. C. *Instructif, pour apprendre aux enfans les élémens de la langue françoise. Corrigé et augmenté par un ami des enfans.* Amsterdam: J. R. Poster, 1812.

L'A.B.C. national, dédeé aux républicains, par un royaliste. Paris: N.p., 1793.

Abécédaire à l'usage des écoles régimentaires. Strasbourg: Eck, 1818.

Abécédaire complet, instructif et amusan, pour tous les âges, dans lequel se trouvent des fables, des morceaux d'histoire naturelle, et les premiers élémens de la grammaire, de l'orthographe et de l'arithmétique. Paris: L'Écrivain, 1815.

Abécédaire de La Cour de France, contenant les détails de la rentrée dans le royaume de S.M. Louis XVIII, dit Le Désiré, et des princes et princesses de la famille royale; précédé d'un précis historique sur les malheurs de Louis XVI et de sa famille; avec des anecdotes propres à inspirer aux enfans, dès leur jeune âge, l'attachement pour les augustes personnages de la branche régnante, et leur donner la connoissance des traits de bonté et de bienfaisance dont cette illustre maison a présenté de si nombreux exemples. Paris: Ancelle, 1814.

Abécédaire des arts et métiers, pour apprendre à lire aux enfans, et leur donner la connoissance des inventions les plus connues et les plus utiles; orné de vingt-six gravures. Paris: Ancelle, 1813.

Abécédaire des petites demoiselles, avec des leçons tirées de leurs jeux et de leurs occupations ordinaires; et orné de jolies gravures. Paris: P. Blanchard, 1811.

Abécédaire des petits enfans, orné de 25 gravures. Nouvelle édition. Lille: Bloquel, n.d.

Abécédaire des petits garçons, ou petits tableaux des principaux jeux de l'enfance. Paris: P. Blanchard, 1811.

Abécédaire d'histoire naturelle, contenant vingt-cinq leçons par ordre alphabétique extraites de l'histoire aturelle des quadrupèdes; accompagné de petites phrases et de fables amusantes pour apprendre lire aux enfans. Orné de huit planches en taille-douce représentant un grand nombre d'animaux et suivi de caractères d'écriture. Paris: Ancelle, 1813.

Abécédaire de l'histoire de France, contenant, soixante-dix leçons, extraites des règnes de ses rois, depuis Pharamond jusqu'à Charles X, accompagné de petites phrases pour apprendre à lire aux enfans, et leur donner le goût de la lecture. Orné de neuf planches gravées, reprsentant un grand nombre de portraits des Rois de France. Paris: Ancelle, 1827.

Abécédaire du petit naturaliste, contenant tout ce qu'il est nécessaire d'apprendre aux enfans, et un petit abrégé de l'histoire des animaux fort intéressant, et orné de 24 figures. Paris: Saintin, 1812.

Abécédaire et prières. Beauvais: Desjardins, an 7 (1803).

Abécédaire Français, à l'usage des enfans et des étrangers; d'après la nouvelle méthode simple et facile d'épellation et de prononciation. Ouvrage orné de quatre-vingt-une gravures en taille-douce représentant autant de sujets, parfaitement terminés au burin. 2nd ed. Paris: Capelle et Renand, 1807.

Abécédaire joujou, contenant dans un étui élégamment cartonné, un alphabet et un joujou pour récréer l'enfant après la lecture. Paris: Eugene Balland, 1827.

Abécédaire nouveau, ou Méthode amusante pour apprendre à lire aux enfans. Paris: Delion, an 11 (1802).

Abécédaire républicain, nouvelle méthode d'enseigner l'A-B-C et l'épeler aux enfants en les amusant par des figures agréables et propres à leur faire des progres dans la lecture. Paris: N.p., an 2.

Abrégé de toutes les sciences à l'usage des enfants. Lyon: Aimable Leroy, 1799.

Adry, Jean Félicissime. *Dictionnaire des jeux de l'enfance et de la jeunesse chez tous les peuples.* Paris: H. Barbou, 1807.

Aikin, John and Anna Letitia. *Les soirées au logis ou l'ouverture du portefeuil de la jeunesse, renfermant un mélange de pièces diverses pour l'instruction des jeunes personnes, traduites de l'anglais.* Paris: Maradan, 1797.

Alletz, Pons-Augustin. *Magasin des adolescents, ou Entretien d'un gouverneur avec son élève.* Paris: Guillyn, 1765.

Almanach du santé, ou Étrennes d'Hygie, aux gens du monde. Paris: N.p., 1811.

Alphabet Impérial mililtaire, contenant: 1° L'art d'apprendre lire en écrivant. 2° Quelques notions des premiers elémens qui composent une armée de terre et de mer. 3° Valeur des nombres arabes et romains. 4° Nouveaux poids et mesures, etc. 5° Les principes d'arithmétique. Paris: Lebel et Guitel, 1810.

Alphabet initiatif par Pompée instituteur à Vesoul. Sons articules, articulations ou consonnes. Paris: Selves fils, 1822.

Alphabet initiatif par Pompée instituteur à Vesoul. Sons vocaux, voix, ou voyelles. Paris: Selves fils, 1822.

L'Alphabet mis en jeu. Paris: Favre, n.d.

Alphabet national, pour apprendre facilement à lire, en françois, en très peu de temps, dans lequel on a runit tout ce qui peut former le coeur à la pratique de la religion, à l'amour de la vertu et de la Patrie; ensemble de maximes conformes aux principes de la Constitution françoise, suivies de la déclaration des droits de l'homme et du citoyen. Paris: Nyon jeune, 1791.

L'Amie des jeunes citoyennes, suive d'un choix des actions héroïques et civiques qui ont distingué les femmes depuis la révolution, et de maximes morales tirées des meilleurs auterus. Ouvrage propre à former le coeur et l'esprit. Paris: Millet, 1795.

Antoine, A. de Saint Gervais. *Les petits artisans devenus hommes célèbres, ouvrage fait pour inspirer des sentimes d'élévation aux jeunes gens des deux sexes, même dans les classes les plus inférieures de la société.* Paris: F. Denn, 1829.

———. *Les Soirées de l'adolescence ou Aventures amusantes, racontées par une société de jeunes enfans de deux sexes.* Paris: Lechard, 1823.

Appay, Abbé. *Abécédaire propre à applanir toutes les difficultés de la lecture françoise, offert aux écoles primaires.* Orange: Jh. Bouchony, 1816.

Archives Nationales, Paris, France. Series AD VIII 21–32: Public Instruction and general instruction (1789–1874); AD XIX H 1: The Committee on Public Instruction (1791–1792); AF I 16: Register and Reports from the Committee on Public Instruction (1791–1792); AF * I 17: Meeting proceedings, Committee on Public Instruction (1791–an 2); AF II 30–33: Decrees, proceedings, etc., Committee on Public Instruction (An 2–an 4); AF II 67: Directory of Public Instruction; AF * II 91–93: Registration of correspondence with the Committee on Public Instruction; AF II 106 (791): Proceedings of the Committee on National Instruction; AF IV 1049, 1050: Reports from the Minister of the Interior regarding letters, arts, sciences, and public instruction; F 17 1547–48: Commission for the examination of elementary books, meeting proceedings (1829–1833); F 17 1556: Commission for the examination of elementary schoolbooks (1829–1833); F 17 1557–58: Commission for the revision of elementary school books; F 17 2503 $^{1-4}$: Laws relating to primary and secondary instruction, 1790–1833; F 17 2504: Laws, decrees, and announcements concerning public education, 1793–1814; F 17 2782: Proceedings and reports on the elementary schoolbooks under consideration (1829–1833)

d'Argé, Auguste-Philibert Chaalons. *Contes à ma soeur.* Paris: Peytieux, 1822.

Arnaud, F. H. *Abécédaire du premier âge, contenant des détails curieux sur l'histoire naturelle. Livre instructif, amusant et propre à inspirer le goût de la lecture.* Orné de 21 figures gravée en taille-douce. Paris: Arnaud, 1814.

Arnault. *Principes de lecture mis à la portée de la première enfance des deux sexes, précédée d'une méthode très-utile aux pères et mères, aux instituteurs et institutrices, et suivis de notions sur la vie sociale, la géographie, la physique, et l'histoire naturelle, nouvelle éditions, corrigée et approuvée des meilleurs grammairiens.* Paris: Chez l'auteur, 1798.

Aubert, L'Abbé Jean-Louis. *Fables nouvelles, accompagnées de notes, et suivies du discours sur la manière de lire les fables ou de les réciter.* 4th ed. Paris: Moutard, 1773.

———. *Fables nouvelles, divisées en six livres, avec des notes. Et un discours sur la manière de lire les fables, ou de les réciter.* Paris: Desaint et Saillant, Duchesne, and Langlois Fils, 1761.

L'Avantcoureur, feuille hebdomadaire, ou Gazette et avant-coureur de littérature, des sciences et des arts. Paris: Michel Lambert, 1760–1773.

Averin. *Méthode de lecture, contenant huit leçons, une idée de l'univers à la portée des enfants, quelques fables de Phèdre; le tout mis sous un nouvel ordre.* Paris: Clousier, 1801.

Babeau, Albert. *L'école de village pendant la Révolution.* Paris: Didier, 1881.

Bailly, M [Tailleur de Corps pour Femmes]. *Avis aux mères qui aiment leurs enfans et aux dames qui aiment leur tailles.* Paris: Chez l'auteur, 1786.

Bajolet. *Nouvelle méthode d'enseigner à lire, très-simple et très facile, au moyen de laquelle les enfans font des progrès incomparablement plus rapides et plus assurés, qu'ils n'en pourroient faire en suivante toute autre méthode.* Paris: Chez l'auteur, 1772.

Balland, Eugene Amédée. *Les animaux industrieux, ouvrage instructif et amusant, destiné à la jeunesse des deux sexes.* 2nd ed. Paris: Pierre Blanchard, 1824.

———. *Fablier de l'enfance et de la jeunesse, ou choix des meilleurs fables Françaises, extraites de LaFontaine, Florian, Lamotte, Aubert, Boisard, Richer, Lemonnier, Dorat, Imbert, Ginguené, Dutramblay, Lebailly, Vitallis, Gosse, Arnault, Hoffman, Jauffret, Stassart, Chabanon, Naudet, etc.* Paris: Eugene Balland, 1827.

Ballexserd, Jacques. *Dissertation sur l'éducation physique des enfans, depuis leur naissance, jusqu'à l'âge de puberté.* Paris: Vallat La Chappelle, 1762.

Banier, Abbé Antoine. *Explication historique des fables.* 2 vols. Paris: Barrois aîné, 1785.

Basset, César-Auguste. *Explication morale des proverbes populaires Français.* Vol. I. Paris: Louis Colas, 1826.

Bazot, Etienne-François. *Historiettes et contes à ma petite fille et à mon petit garçon, ornés de douze gravures coloriées.* Paris: L'écrivain, 1821.

Beaurieu, Gaspard Guillard de. *De l'allaitment et de la première éducation des enfans.* Geneva: N.p., 1782.

Belair, M. de. *Petit savant de société, ouvrage dédié à la jeunesse des deux sexes, contenant tous les jeux dont on s'amuse en société, et le pénitences qui s'y ordonnent, avec la manière de s'y conformer en les exécutent. Recueil extrait des manuscrits de M. Enfantin.* Paris: Caillot, 1818.

Berneaud, Arsenne Thiébault de. *Annuaire de l'industrie française, ou Recueil par ordre alphabetique des inventions, dcouvertes et perfectionemens dans les arts utiles et agréables.* N.p., 1811–1812.

Berquin, Arnaud. *L'ami des enfants et des adolescents, nouvelle édition.* Paris: Didier, 1857.

———. *Contes et historiette: tirés de L'ami des enfans. Nouv. éd.* Paris: Ledentu, 1821.

———. *Œuvres complètes . . . précedée . . . de la vie de l'auteur; augmentées de la Bibliothèque des villages, de plusieurs idylles et romances inédites jusqu à présent.* 10 vols. Paris: N.p., 1802.

———. *Pièces choisies de l'Ami des enfans, à l'usage des écoles.* 5th ed. London: N.p., 1806.

Berthaud, M. l'Abbé. *Le Quadrille des enfans, avec lequel, par le moyen de quatre-vingt-quatre figures, et sans épeler, ils peuvent, à l'âge de quatre ou cinq ans, et au-dessous, être mis en état de lire à l'ouverture de toutes sortes de livres, en trois ou quatre mois, même plutôt, selon leurs dispositions.* Paris: Coururier, 1783.

Bertuch, Friedrich Justin, ed. *Portefeuille des enfants: Mélanges intéresants d'animaux, plantes, fleurs, fruits, minéraux, costumes, antiquités et autres objets instructifs et amusants pour la jeunesse; choisis et gravés sur les meillerus originaux; avec de courtes explications scientifiques et proportionnées à l'entendement d'un Enfant.* 10 vols. Weimar: Bureau de l'Industrie, 1796.

———. *Porte feuille instructif et amusant pour la jeunesse: Mélange intéressant*

*d'animaux, plantes, fleurs, fruits, minéraux,costumes, antiquités et autres ob-
jets instructifs et amusants pour la jeunesse; choisis et gravés sur les meilleurs
originaux, avec de courtes explications scientifiques et proportionnées à l'entendement de la jeunesse.* Avienne: Antoine Pichler, 1807.

*Bibliothèque des enfans de la campagne divisée en huit chapitres, contentant 1°
Des Notices sur différens sujets; 2° Le Petit dictionnaire; 3° La Géographie
universelle; 4° Les Connoissances humaines; 5° Cours complet d'arithmétique;
6° Notice sur le commerce, etc. 7° Maximes pour diriger une maison; 8° Lettres sur différens sujets, etc. Ouvrage utile à toutes sortes de personnes.* Paris:
Veuve Hérissant, 1783.

Blanchard, Pierre. *Premières leçons de l'histoire de France, ou précis de cette histoire.* Paris: Blanchard, 1830.

[Bleton, Jean-François.] *Des Devoirs des serviteurs, des maîtres, des enfants, des
parens, de tous les homme envers l'Eglise et l'État.* Lyon: François Guyot,
1830.

Blocquel, Simon, a.k.a. Buqcellos. *La Morale de l'ouvrier, ou Choix d'anecdotes
réunies pour consacrer les belles actions des artisans, et les encourager à en re-
nouveler les exemples.* Paris: Delarue, 1827.

[Boinvilliers, Jean-Etienne-Judith Forstier]. *Le Code de morale et de politique, mis
à la portée des jeunes républicains par demande et par réponses.* Paris: Cailleau, an 2.

Borrelly, Jean Alexis. *Système de législation, ou Moyens que la politique peut employer pour former à l'état des sujets utiles et vertueux.* Paris: Lacombe, 1768.

Bouilly, Jean-Nicolas. *La Portefeuille de la jeunesse, ou La Morale et l'histoire en-
seignées par des exemples; précédé d'un discours dur l'ensemble de l'ouvrage.*
Vol. 15. "Récréations." Paris: Moutardier, 1830.

de Bouissoudy, B. *Contes et fables, pour l'instruction et l'amusement de la jeunesse suivis de lettres d'un père à ses filles sur la manière de se conduire dans
la maison paternelle.* Gien: Pellisson, 1830.

Le bouquet des enfans: Alphabet instructif et amusant. Paris: Alexis Eymery,
1815.

Bradi, Agathe-Pauline Cazeac de Ceylon, Comtesse de. *Un Nouvelle par mois ou
lectures pour la jeunesse depuis l'âge de dix à seize ans.* 2 vols. Paris: F. Louis,
1828.

Brès, Jean Pierre. *Contes de Robert mon oncle.* Paris: Louis Janet, 1829.

———. *Les Jeudis dans le chateau de ma tante.* 8 vols. Paris: Lefuel, c.1826.

Brochard, André Théodore. *De l'allaitement maternel, étudié aux points de vue
de la mère, de l'enfant et de la société.* Paris: Maillet, 1868.

Brougham, Henry. *Observations pratiques sur l'éducation du peuple.* Traduit de
l'anglais. Paris: Bossange, 1826.

Buchan, William. *Le Conservatuer de la santé des mères et des enfans, contenant:
1° la conduite que les femmes doivent tenir avant le mariage pour conserver
leur santé' 2° Le Régime et les précautions qu'elles doivent employer pendant
et après leur grossesse; 3° L'Éducation qu'elles doivent donner à leurs enfans
pour assurer leur santé, leur force et leur beauté.* Trans. Thomas Duverne de
Praîle. Paris: Métier, an 13 (1804).

Burtel, Mme. *Du goût et de son influence sur l'éducation.* Paris: A. Guerin, 1830.

Butet, Pierre Roland François. *Cours pratique d'instruction élémentaire.* Paris: Éverat, 1818.

———. *Cours théorique d'instruction élémentaire.* Paris: Éverat, 1818.

Cabinet des modes, ou les Modes nouvelles, décrites d'une manire claire et précise, et représentées par des planches gravées. Paris: N.p., 1786–1788.

Cadmus. *A, B, C, syllabaire nouveau, conforme au principe adopté par l'Institut National. Orné d'un frontispice, et de vingt-quatre figure d'animaux, par ordre alphabétique, gravées en taille-douce, avec leurs explications, quelques fables de la Fontaine, contes et dialogues moraux.* Paris: Bonneville, an 7.

Cahier de dessin, représentant les jeux de l'enfance et de la jeunesse avec une explication et une devise morale. 2 vols. "Jeux de Jeunes Garçons." Paris: N. Schenker, n.d. (before 1848).

Caillau, Jean-Marie. *Avis aux mères de famille.* N.p., 1769.

Caillot, Antoine. *Histore d'un pensionnat de jeunes demoiselles.* 2 vols. Paris: N.p., 1808.

———.*Tableau des exercices et de l'enseignement en usage dans un pensionnat de jeunes demoiselles dirigé par une sage institutrice; accompagné de récits hisotriques relatifs aux sujets dont il est composé. À l'usage des jeunes personnes, et même des dames chargées de leur instruction. Avec figures.* 2 vols. Paris: Brunot-L'Abbe, 1816.

Campan, Jeanne-Louise-Henriette Genest. *Conseils aux jeunes filles, d'un théâtre pour les jeunes personnes et de quelques essais de morale.* Paris: Baudouin Frères, 1825.

———. *Conseils aux jeunes filles.* Paris: Hippolyte Baudouin et Bigot, 1830.

———. *De l'Education.* Paris: Baudouin Frères, 1824.

———. *Manuel de la jeune mère.* Paris: Baudoin Frères, 1828.

Campe, Joachim Heinrich. *Bibliothèque géographique et instructive des jeunes gens, ou Recueil de voyages intéressants dans toutes les parties du monde, pour l'instruction et l'amusement de la jeunesse.* Paris: J. E. G. Dufour, 1802.

Cartier-Vinchon, M. *La parfaite demoiselle, recueil des règles, principes et maximes générales d'éducation et de bonne conduite, pour les demoiselles de tout âge; orné de gravures édifiantes: À l'usage des pensionnats de la France et de l'étranger.* 2nd ed. Paris: Alexis Eymery, 1825.

Celnart, Elisabeth Félicité Bayle-Mouillard, Mme de. *Manuel des demoiselles, ou Arts et métiers qui leur conviennent, et dont elles peuvent s'occuper avec agrément, tels que la couture, la broderie, le tricoter, la dentelle, la tapisserie, les bourses, les ouvrages en filets, en chenille, en ganse, en perles, en cheveux, etc., etc.* Paris: Roret, 1826.

———. *Les Soirées du dimanche, ou le Curé de village: Leçons de morale pratique. Ouvrage couronné par la société pour l'instruction élémentaire.* Paris: L. Colas, 1827.

———. *Les Veillées de la Salle Saint-Roch, ou Les Leçons d'économie.* Paris: L. Colas, 1828.

Censure de la faculté de théologie de Paris contre le livre qui a pour titre, Émile ou de l'Éducation. Paris: LePrieur, 1762.

Chalotais, Louis-René de Caradeuc de la. *Essai d'éducation nationale, ou, Plan d'études pour la jeunesse.* Geneva: Philibert, 1763.

Chambaud, Louis. *Fables choisies, à l'usage des enfans et des autres personnes qui commencent à apprendre la langue françoise.* Londres: Nourse, 1786.

Chamousset, Claude-Humbert Piarron de. "Mémoires politique sur les enfans." In *Ouevres complètes de M. de Chamousset, contenant ses projets d'humanité, de bienfaisance et de patriotismes: précédées de son éloge.* 2nd ed. Paris: Pierres, 1787.

Chanvalon, Abbé de. *Manuel des champs, ou, Recueil choisi, instructif et amusant de tout ce qui est le plus nécessaire et le plus utile pour vivre à la campagne avec aisance et agrément. Nouvelle édition, revue, corrigée et considérablement augmentée.* Paris: Aux dépens de Lottin le jeune, 1765.

Chastanier, Bénédict. *Le Livre de la nature ou le Vrai sens des choses, expliqué et mis à la portée des enfans. Traduit librement de l'Anglois.* Londres: Bénédict Chastanier, 1788.

Chastel, François Thomas. *Petit Recueil de fables, contes et petits drames, avec une table alphabétique des mots, termes et expressions contenus sans ce livre, et les remarques nécessaires de syntaxe et sur le génie de la langue.* Giessen, Marbourg: Krieger Jeune, 1785.

Child, Maria L. *The Girl's Own Book.* 1834. Reprint, Bedford, Mass.: Applewood Books, 1992.

La Civilité honnête, en laquelle est mise la manière d'apprendre à bien lire, prononcer et écrire, et mise en meilleur ordre qu'auparavant. Rouen: Mégard, 1822.

La Civilité puérile pour l'instruction des enfans, précédé de la manière d'apprendre à bien lire, prononcer et écrire; dressée par un missionaire; suivie des préceptes et instruction pour apprendre à la jeunesse à se bien conduire dans les compagnies. Nouvelle édition, augmentée d'un traité d'orthographe, et d'une table de multiplication. Paris: Moronval, 1833.

Clemendot, N. S. *Cours de lecture, ou Nouveau syllabaire Français, contenant les principes de la lecture, mis à la portée des enfans.* Paris: Bernard et Devaux, an 5 (1797).

Coeurderoy, Claudine. *Dialogues d'une mère avec sa fille.* Paris: Rondoneau, an 10.

Combes-Brassard, Jean Michel. *L'Ami des mères, ou Essai sur les maladies des enfans.* Paris: Méquigon, 1819.

Conseils maternels, ou Manuel pour les jeunes filles, les épouses, les mères et les maîtresses de maison. Extrait et traduction libre d'un ouvrage allemand de feu J. L. Ewald. Paris: Paschoud, 1825.

Le Conteur amusant et instructif de la jeunesse. Paris: N.p., 1809.

Le Conteur des petits enfans, ou Choix d'historiettes, de contes moraux, d'anecdotes et traits caractéristiques de l'enfance, par Florian, Berquin, Campe, etc. Paris: Alexis Eymery, 1816.

Costard, Jean-Pierre. *L'Ami et le conservateur de l'enfance ou le Guide des pères et des mères dans l'éducation des enfans; Contenant la meilleure manière de les élever et de les instruire, tant par la pratique d'une infinité de petits soins toujours trop négligés jusqu'à présent, que par des moyens simples et naturels de leur rendre l'instruction aussi facile qu'agréable. Suivi de deux essais sur les avantages et l'utilité des promenades pour cette instruction, et sur l'usage des bonnes fêtes.* Paris: Galland, An 14 (1805).

Costumes d'enfants. N.p., c. 1808.

Coupé, Jacques-Michel. Suite de l'instruction publique, par J. M. Coupé, député du département de l'Oise. Paris, n.d.

Couplets, chantés au nom de la jeunesse, le jour de la Fête de l'Etre-Suprême, 20 Prairial, 2eme année de la République une et indivisible, par de jeunes élèves de la pension du Citoyen Audet. Caen: G. le Roy, n.d.

Creton, Nicolas-Joseph. *Le Bonheur domestique.* Paris: Brissot-Thivars, 1826.

Culant, René Alexandre de. *Morale enjouée, ou Recueil de fables, contes, epigrammes, pièces fugitives, et pensées diverses.* 2nd ed. Cologne: Pierre Marteau, 1783.

D***, Mme. *Les Jeux des quatre saisons, ou les Amusemens du jeune âge.* Paris: Eymery, 1812.

Dalloz. *Le Joujou instructif des enfans, avec lequel on peut apprendre à lire, en moins de quatre mois, dès l'âge de quatre à cinq ans. Ouvrage utile aux pères de familles.* Paris: Gouriet, an 3 (1796).

Danbri, A. [Pierre-César Briand]. *La Petite morale en exemples, anecdotes, contes, et fables propres à corriger l'enfance de ses défauts.* Paris: Masson Libraire, 1825.

Delacroix, Charles. *Projet de loi sur l'éducation commune, par Ch. Delacroix, député de la Marne à la Convention nationale.* Paris, n.d.

Delafaye-Bréhier, Julie. *Les Petits Béarnais ou Leçons de morale convenables à la jeunesse.* 4 vols. Paris: Alexis Eymery, 1816.

Deleyre, C. *Contes dans un nouveau genre, pour les enfans qui commencent à lire.* Paris: Gabriel Dufour, 1807.

DeMaistre, Joseph. *Against Rousseau.* Ed. and trans. Richard A. Lebrun. Montreal: McGill-Queen's University Press, 1996.

Depping, Georges-Bernard. *Les Soirées d'hiver, ouvrage amusant et instructif dédié à la jeunesse.* Paris: Villet, s.d.

Desessartz, Bernard Christophe Faust. *Sur un vêtement libre, uniforme & national, à l'usage des enfans ou réclamation solennelle des droits des enfants.* S.l., 1792.

Desessartz, Jean-Charles. *Traité de l'éducation corporelle des enfans en bas âge, ou Réflexions pratiques sur les moyens de procurer une meillures contitution aux citoyens.* Paris: T. J. Hérissant, 1760.

Diderot, Denis, and Jean le Rond D'Alembert. *The* Encyclopédie *of Diderot and D'Alembert: Selected Articles.* Ed. John Lough. Cambridge: Cambridge University Press, 1954.

Discours sur l'éducation des femmes, prononcés dans un pensionnat de demoiselles, à Paris, et Plan d'éducation pour une jeune princesse. Paris: Lebel et Guitel, 1810.

Dubochet, J. A. *Discours sur l'éducation populaire, prononcé à la séance publique de la Société Royale Académique de Nantes, le 25 Novembre 1832.* Nantes: Mellinet, 1833.

Dubroca, Louis. *Le Livre des pères et des mères, pendant la première éducation de leurs enfans, où l'on montre quels sont les dangers d'une tendresse malentendue et d'une conduite inconsidérée de la part des parens, pendant cette première éducation, et en même temps, de quelle manière et par quelles méprises on peut, sans s'en doûter, gâter le meilleur naturel des enfans, et leur imprimer des vices et des travers qui pr parent leur malheur et celui de leurs familles.* 2 vols. Paris: Dubroca, Delaunay, and Mongie, 1823.

Ducray-Duminil, François Guillaume. *Lolotte et Fanfan, ou les Aventures de deux enfans abandonnées dans une île déserte, rédigées sur des manuscrits anglais.* Paris: Maradan, 1789.

Dufrénoy, Adélaide-Gilette Billet. *Etrennes à ma fille, ou Soirées amusantes de la jeunesse.* Paris: Alexis Eymery, 1816.

———. *Petite Encyclopédie de l'enfance, ou Leçons élémentaires de grammaire, de géographie, de mythologie, d'histoire ancienne et moderne, d'histoire des religions, d'arithmétique et de mathématique, de physique, d'histoire naturelle, des arts et métiers, etc. Ouvrage propre à donner aux enfans les notions premières les plus indispensibles, et orné de plus de cent sujets de jolies gravures en taille douce.* 2 vols. Paris: Alexis Eymery, 1817.

Dufresne, Abel. *Contes à Henri.* 2nd ed. Paris: Pierre Blanchard, 1828.

———. *Contes à Henriette, pour les enfans de 4 à 5 ans.* Paris: Pierre Blanchard, 1822.

———. *Leçons de morale pratique à l'usage des classes industrielles.* Paris: L. Colas, 1826.

Dupont, A. B. *Abécédaire méthodique, ou L'art d'apprendre à lire et à prononcer correctement le française, divisé en plusieurs volumes à l'usage des Écoles.* Paris: Ribemont aîné, 1831.

Duval, Henri Louis Nicolas, a.k.a. Cardelli. *Manuel de la jeune femme, contenant tout ce qu'il est utile de savoir pour diriger avec ordre, agrément et économie l'intérieur d'un ménage.* Paris: Charles-Béchet, 1826.

E***, M. *Promenades instructives et amusantes d'un père avec ses enfans, dans Paris et ses environs.* Paris: Guillaume, 1817.

Ecrits populaires de Franklin, choisis et appropriés aux lecteurs Français par le compagnon de Simon de Mantua. Paris: Louis Colas, 1829.

Edgeworth, Maria. *Éducation familère.* Trans. Louis S.W.-Belloc. Paris: Alexandre Mesnier, 1829.

———. *The Little Dog Trusty; The Orange Man; and The Cherry Orchard: Being the Tenth Part of Early Lessons.* 1801. Augustan Reprint Society, Publication Numbers 263–264. Los Angeles: William Andrews Clark Memorial Library, 1990.

Élémens du jeune républicain. Alphabet composé par un instituteur père de famille, d'après le projet de décret présenté à la Convention Nationale, pour honorer l'être Suprême, pour célébrer les vertus républicaines et les Fêtes Décadaires, etc. Paris: Fantelin, n.d.

Emma, ou L'enfant du malheur. Traduit de l'anglois sur la seconde édition. Paris: Buisson, 1788.

Enfantin, M. *Le Petit savant de société, ouvrage dédié à la jeunesse des deux sexes, contenant la manière de jouer tous les jeux innocens dont on s'amuse en société, et les pénitances qui s'y ordonnent, avec la manière de s'y conformer en les exécutant.* 4 vols. Paris: Caillot, 1818.

d'Epinay, Louise Florence Petronille Tardieu D'Esclavelles, Marquise. *L'amitié de deux jolies femmes: Suivie de un rêve de mademoiselle Clairon.* Paris: Librairie des Bibliophiles, 1885.

———. *Conversations d'Emilie, ou, Entretiens instructifs et amusants d'une mere avec sa fille.* Paris: Belin, 1782.

———. *Etrennes aux enfans, ou Petit théâtre de la jeunesse.* Paris: Mericot, 1792.

Erasmus, Desiderius. *La Civilité puérile.* Paris: I. Liseux, 1877.

Ewalde, Louis. *Manuel de l'instituteur primaire.* Liège: N.p., 1824.

Le Fablier de flore, ou Choix de fables sur les fleurs; dédié aux dames. Paris: F. Louis, 1828.

Le Fablier des enfans, choix de fables analogues aux goûts du premier age, avec des notes grammaticales, mythologiques, et historiques. Paris: Devaux, an 8.

Faust, Bernard Christophe. *Sur un vêtement libre, uniforme et national, à l'usage des enfans ou réclamation solemnelle des droits des enfants.* Paris, aux dépense de l'auteur, 1792.

Fénélon des Demoiselles. Paris: Louis Janet, 1824.

Fénelon, François de Salignac de La Mothe. *Education des filles de Fénelon.* Ed. Oct. Gréard. Paris: Librairie des Bibliophiles, 1890.

———. *Fénelon on education: A translation of the 'Traité de l'éducation des filles' and other documents illustrating Fénelon's educational theories and practice.* Trans. and ed. H. C. Barnard. Cambridge: Cambridge University Press, 1966.

Flammerang, Comtesse de [a.k.a. Comtesse de Flamarang and Flesselles]. *De l'Influence des femmes dans la société et de l'importance de leur éducation.* Paris: Guerin, 1826.

Fordyce, James. *Discours sur l'éducation des jeunes dames et jeunes demoiselles. Traduit de l'anglois.* Yverdon: N.p., 1779.

Formey, Jean-Henri-Samuel. *Anti-Emile.* Berlin: J. Pauli, 1763.

———. *Principes généraux pour servir à l'éducation des enfans, particulièrement de la noblesse françoise.* Amsterdam: Schneider, 1763.

———. *Traité d'éducation morale . . . Comment on doit gouverner l'esprit et le coeur d'un enfant, pour le rendre heureux et utile. Auquel on a ajoûté quelques pensées relatives à ce sujet.* Liège: Desoer, 1773.

Fouqueau de Pussy, J. J. *Le Grand-Père: Livre de lecture à l'usage des écoles primaires.* Paris: Firmin Didot, 1832.

Fourcroy, Jean-Louis. *Les Enfans élevés dan l'ordre de la nature, ou Abrége de l'histoire naturelle des enfans du premier âge. À l'usage des pères et mères de famille.* Liège: J. J. Tutot, 1781.

Frank, Johann Peter. *Traité sur la manière d'élever sainement les enfans, fondé sur les principes de la médicine et de la physique, et destiné aux parens, particulièrement aux mères qui ont à coeur leur santé et celle de leurs enfans.* Trans. Michel Boehrer. Paris: Crapelet, an 7.

Fréderic, ou Les Effets de la désobéissance. Paris: Didot le Jeune, 1817.

Fresneau, Pierre. *Petit abrégé des fables d'Ésope, avec des figures analogues à chacque fable: Supplement à la première partie, nouvelle édition, de l'ABC, ou du jeu des lettres de l'Académie des enfans, et du recueil de leurs études.* Paris: Veuve Hérissant, 1784.

Fréville, Anne François Joachim. *Correspondance de My Lady Cécile, avec ses enfans, ou Recueil de lettres relatives au jeux et aux études dee la jeunesse, pour la former aux vertus morales, à la narration et au style épistolaire.* 2nd ed. 2 vols. Paris: Genets Jeune, an XI.

G***, Madame la Comtesse Clémence de. *Manuel de la jeune femme, contenant* *tout ce qui'il est utile de savoir pour diriger l'intérieur d'un ménage.* Paris: Charles Béchet, n.d.

Gacon-Dufour, Mme. *Manuel complet de la maîtresse de maison, et de la parfaite ménagère, ou Guide pratique pour la gestion d'une maison à la ville et à la campagne, contenant les moyens d'y maintenir le bon ordre et d'y établir l'abondance, de soigner les enfans, de conserver les substances alimentaires, etc.* Paris: Roret, 1826.

Garnier, J. J. *De l'Éducation civile.* Paris: S.l., 1765.

Garros, Philippe-Antoine-Ascension, ed. *Esprit de la morale universelle ou Manuel de tous les ages, traduit d'un ancien manuscrit indien, dédié à la jeunesse, et mis en concordance avec l'Ecriture-Sainte.* Paris: Renard, n.d.

Gasc, J. P. *Discours sur l'éducation des femmes, prononcés dans un pensionnat de demoiselles, à Paris, et Plan d'éducation pour une jeune Princesse.* Paris: Lebel et Guitel, 1810.

———. *Éducation rationelle, discours su la réforme universitaire et sur la liberté d'enseignement, suivi de notes et jugemens divers en faveur de l'éducation rationnelle.* Paris: Paulin, 1833.

Gaultier, l'Abbé Aloisius Edouard Camille. *Amusing and Instructive Conversations for Children of Five Years.* New York: Johnson Reprint Corporation, 1970 [1800].

———. *Jeu de fables, faisant partie du cours complet d'études élémentaires.* Paris: L. Colas, 1816.

Genlis, Stephanie Félicité Ducrest de Saint-Aubin, Comtesse de. *Le La Bruyère des domestiques, précédé de considérations sur l'état de domesticité en général, et suivi d'une nouvelle.* 2 vols. Paris: Thiercelin, 1828.

———. *Les Jeux champêtres des enfans et de l'ile des monstres, conte de fées pour faire suite aux veillées du château.* Paris: Marc, 1822.

———. *Géographie historique des dames.* N.p., n.d.

———. *Théatre d'éducation: À l'usage de la jeunesse.* New ed., rev. and corr. Paris: Didier, 1860.

Gérando, Joseph Marie, baron de. *Cours normal des instituteurs primaires ou directions relatives à l'éducation physique, morale et intellectuelle dans les écoles primaires.* Paris: J. Renouard, 1832.

Gerdil, le Père [Cardinal]. *Réflexions sur la théorie, & la pratique de l'éducation contre les principes de M. Rousseau.* Genève: Em. Du Villard, 1764.

Giost, Mme. *Avis aux bonnes mères sur la manière de soigner les enfans depuis leur naissance jusqu'à l'âge de puberté.* Paris: Chez l'auteur et Béchet, 1824.

Girouard, I. *Avis aux mères et aux nourrices, ou Conseils aux femmes, pour les préserver des maladies du sein, ou les en guerir lorsqu'elles en sont attaquées. Avec des refléxions sur les maladies prétendues laiteuses.* Paris: Chez l'auteur et Martinet, an 12.

Griffet, Henri. *Lettre à M.D. sur le livre initulé* Emile, ou de l'éducation. Amsterdam: Grangé, 1762.

Le Gros A,B,C pour instruire la jeunesse Chrétienne et Catholique. À l'usage des écoles du diocèse de Châlons. Chalons: Mercier, 1783.

Guerin-Albert, Citoyenne. *Avis aux mères républicaines, ou Mes Reflexions sur l'éducation des jeunes citoyennes.* (N.p., n.d.)

Guillaume, James. *Note sur l'instruction publique de 1789 à 1818, suivie du cata-*

logue des documents originaux existant au musée pedagogique et relatifs à l'histoire de l'instruction publique en France durant cette période. Paris: Musée Pédagogique, 1888.

———. *Procès-Verbaux du Comité d'Instruction Publique de l'Assemblée Législative.* Paris: Imprimerie Nationale, 1889.

———. *Procès-Verbaux du Comité d'instruction publique de la Convention Nationale.* 6 Vols. Paris: Hachette, 1891–1892.

Guimps, Mme le Baronne de. *L'Histoire mise à la portée des enfans, contenant ce qu'ils doivent connaître de l'histoire ancienne, de celle des Romains et du Bas-Empire.* Paris: L. Colas, 1819.

Guizot, Elisabeth Charlotte Pauline de Meulan, Mme de. *Conseils de morale, ou Essais sur l'homme, les moeurs, les caractères, le monde, les femmes, l'éducation, etc.* Paris: Pichon et Didier, 1828.

Guizot, François. *Essai sur l'histoire et l'état actuel de l'instruction publique en France.* Paris: Chez Maradon, 1816.

Haüy, Valentin. *Nouveau syllabaire.* Paris: Institut National des Aveugles-Travailleurs, an 8.

Hélène, ou L'enfant gâté et corrigé. Paris: Delaunay, 1818.

Helvétius, Claude Adrien. *A Treatise on Man; His Intellectual Faculties and His Education.* New York: B. Franklin, 1969.

Henriquez, L. M. *Morale républicaine en conseils, et en exemples, pour toutes les décades de l'année. À l'usage des jeunes sans-culottes, présentés à la Convention Nationale.* Paris: Cailleau, an 3.

Hippeau, Célestin. *L'Instruction publique en France pendant la révolution: Débats législatifs publiés.* Paris: Didier, 1883.

———. *Instruction publique en France pendant la révolution: Discours et rapports de Mirabeau, Talleyrand-Périgord, Condorcet, Lanthenas, Romme, Le Peletier, Saint-Fargeau, Calès, Lakanal, Daunou et Fourcroy.* Paris: Didier, 1881.

Jauffret, Louis-François. *Petite école des arts et métiers, contenant des notions simples et familière sur tout ce que les arts et métiers offrent d'utile et de remarquable, ouvrage destiné à l'instruction de la jeunesse et orné de cent vingt-cinq gravures.* 4 vols. Paris: Alexis Eymery, 1816.

Jeu de l'histoire d'Angleterre. Paris: Aug. Ant. Renouard, 1808.

Jeu des hommes illustrés anciens et modernes. Dédié à la Jeunesse. Paris: Chez Susse, n.d.

Jeux d'enfans. N.p., c. 1839.

Jeux des jeunes filles de tous les pays, représentés en vingt-cinq lithographies; d'après ou par MM. Xavier le Prince, Colin et Noel, offrant des costumes de toutes les nations; Avec l'explication détaillée des règles de chacque jeu; accompagnés de fables nouvelles par Mme. Le Franc, Naudaet, Armand-Gouffé, etc. Et suivis d'anecdotes relatives à chacque jeu. Paris: Nepveu et Giroux, 1823.

"J'Instruis en amusant." Jeu de lettres pour enseigner aux enfans à former leurs noms et leur donner le moyen de composer toutes les parties du discourse, dans plume ni crayon seulement en les placant sur un table. N.p., n.d. [between 1820–1839].

Jomard, Edme-François. *Abrégé de la méthode des écoles élémentaires.* Paris: Colas, 1816.

Jouey, V. E. *Jeu de cartes géographiques.* N.p., n.d.

———. *Jeu de fables, pour faire suite au jeu de lecture.* Paris: Doumerc et Ponthieu, 1827.

———. *Neuvième jeu de cartes instructives, contenant un abrégé de l'histoire des animaux avec des gravures. Ouvrage destiné à l'instruction de la jeunesse des deux sexes.* Paris: Chez Ant. Aug. Renouard, 1808.

Julietta, ou Le coeur et l'esprit font plus que la beauté; ouvrage propre à l'instruction et à l'amusement des jeunes demoiselles. Traduit de l'anglais. 2nd ed. Paris: F. Louis, 1819.

Jussieu, Laurent de. *Fables et contes en vers.* Paris: Louis Colas, 1829.

Kappelhoff, A. *Nouvel abécédaire et syllabaire pour des petits enfans.* Amsterdam: Brave, 1812.

Laborde, A. *Plan d'éducation pour les enfants pauvres d'après les deux méthodes combinées du Dr. Bell et de M. Lancastre.* Paris: N.p., 1816.

Labouïsse-Rochefort, Jean Pierre Jacques Auguste de. *Pensées et réflexions morales, littéraires, et philosophiques.* Paris: Michaud and Delaunay, 1810.

Lacombe. "Jeu." In *Dictionnaire des jeux* in the *Encyclopédie méthodique mathématiques.* Vol. 3. Paris: Plomteux, 1792.

de Ladoucette, Jean-Charles-François. *Nouvelles, contes, apologues et mélanges.* 3 vols. Paris: Fantin, 1822.

Lambert, Anne-Thérèse de Marguenat de Courcelle, Marquise de. *Avis d'une mère à son fils, suivis du Traité de l'Amitié.* Paris: F. Louis, 1811.

LaMésangère, Pierre, ed. *Collection de meubles et objets de goût, comprenant tout ce qui a rapport à l'ameublement, tel que vases, tripieds, candelabres, canalettes.* Paris: Journal des Dames et des Modes, 1801–1835.

———. *Costumes des femmes françaises du XIIe au XVIIIe siècle.* Paris: Librairie Charles Tallandier, 1900.

———. *Le Journal des dames et des modes.* Paris, 1797–1839.

———. *Modes et manières du jour à Paris à la fin du 18 siècle et au commencement du 19ème. Collection de 52 Gravures Coloriées.* Paris: Bureau du Journal des Dames, n.d.

La Salle, Jean-Baptiste de. *Les Règles de la bienséance et de la civilité chrétienne, divisées en deux parties, à l'usage des écoles chrétiennes.* Tours: Chez Mame, 1827.

Les Leçons maternelles. Paris: Marcilly fils aîné, 1827.

Legat, A. J. *Abécédaire extrait des leçons élémentaires de la langue françoise.* Paris: Mérigot, an 7.

LeGay, M. *Récréations de l'enfance.* 3 vols. Paris: Caillot, 1817.

Léger, Théodore. *Manuel des jeunes mères.* Paris: Chaboüillé, 1825.

LeGroing-LaMaisonneuve, Antoinette. *Essai sur le Genre d'Instruction le plus analogue à la destination des femmes.* Paris: N.P., 1801.

Lemaire, Henri. *Les exemples célèbres; ou, Nouveau choix de faits historiques et d'anecdotes propres a orner la mémoire de la jeunesse, et a lui inspirer l'amour de toutes les vertus qui peuvent faire le bonheur el la gloire de l'homme en société.* 3rd ed. Paris: Ledentu, 1823.

————. *Guide de la jeunesse à son entrée dans le monde, ou Le retour des anciennes vertus. Leçons d'un Oncle à ses Neveux et à sa Nièce; appuyées d'exemples et de morceaux de morale puisés dans la vie des personnages et dans les ouvrages des Auteurs les plus célèbres.* Paris: Belin-Leprieur, 1818.

Leprince de Beaumont, Marie. *Encyclopédie des jeunes demoiselles, ou Choix des conversations instructives sur diférens sujets.* Paris: Bargeas, 1822.

————. *Instructions pour les jeunes dames qui entrent das le monde, se marient, leurs devoirs dans cet état, et envers leurs enfans. Pour servir de suite au Magasin des Adolescentes.* 4 vols. Paris: Desaint et Saillant, 1764.

————. *Magasin des adolescentes, ou Dialogues d'une sage gouvernante avec ses élèves de la première distinction. Pour servir de suite au Magsin des Enfants.* 5th ed. 4 vols. Lyon: Jacquenod et Rusand, 1768.

————. *Magasin des enfants, ou Dialogues d'une sage gouvernante avec ses élèves de première distinction; dans lesquels on fait penser, parler, agir les jeunes gens suivant le génie, le tempérament et les inclinations de chacun. On y représente les défauts de leur âge, l'on y montre de quelle manière on peut les en corriger; on s'applique autant à leur former le coeur, qu'à leur éclairer l'esprit.* 5th ed. 2 vols. Lyon: Jacquenod et Rusand, 1768.

Le Rebours, Marie Angélique Anel de. *Avis aux mères qui veulent nourrir leurs enfans.* 3rd ed. Paris: Théophile Barrois, 1783.

Leroy, Alphonse. *Recherches sur les habillemens de femmes et des enfants, ou Examen de la manière dont il faut vêtir d'un et l'autre sexe.* Paris: Le Boucher, 1772.

Lestrange, l'Abbé. *Conversations de Dom Augustin.* Paris: LeClerc, 1798 (an 6).

Lettre sur l'éducation, ou Extraite d'une letter écrite à un père de famille. Paris: Perisse, 1789.

Levizac, Jean Pont Victor Lacoutz, l'abbé de. *Leçons de Fénélon, extraites de ses ouvrages pour l'éducation de l'enfance.* 2nd ed. Paris: Gabriel Dufour, 1819.

Leymerie, Jean. *Conseils aux mères de famille. Dissertation sur la fernère découverte de Jenner Tendent à prévenir les varioles qui surviennent après la vaccine.* Paris: Chez Leymeyrie, 1830.

Le Livre des enfans. Paris: Louis Janet, 1827.

Livre pour une petite fille bien sage en trente caractères; Depuis les plus gros et les plus simples, jusqu'aux plus petits et aux plus compliqués, ornée de douze estampes coloriées. Ouvrage spécialement consacré à perfectionner les enfants dans la lecture en à leur inspirer le goût du dessin. Paris: Nepveu, 1824.

Locke, John. *Some Thoughts Concerning Education.* Ed. John W. and Jean S. Yolton. New York: Oxford University Press, 1989.

Lucet, Jean-Claude. *Pensées de M. Rollin sur plusieurs points importans de littérature, de politique et de réligion. Recueillïes de son* Histoire ancienne *et de son* Traité des études. Paris: Frères Estienne, 1780.

Madelaine, Louis Philipon de la. *Vues patriotiques sur l'éducation du peuple tant des villes que de la campagne; avec beaucoup de notes intéressantes: ouvrage qui peut être également utile aux autres classes de citoyens.* Lyon: Chez P. Bruyset-Ponthus, 1783.

Malo, Charles. *L'Ami des jeunes demoiselles.* Paris: Louis Janet, 1822.

Manuel, B. E. *Abécédaire contenant, avec le figure des objets les plus communs, et leur nom inscrit au milieu, l'histoire naturelle des animaux domestiques ou les plus connus, moralisée, et mis à la portée de l'enfance. Ouvrage destiné pour les pères et les mères qui veulent donner à leurs enfans, de l'un et de l'autre sexe, le premier aliment, d'une lecture utile et d'une instruction intéressante, ainsi que pour les Instituteurs et les Institutrices des Écoles primaires.* Paris: Dufart, an 3.

Manuel de l'instituteur primaire ou Principes généraux de pédagogie. Paris: Levrault, 1831.

Martin, Louis-Aimé. *The Education of Mothers; or, The Civilization of Mankind by Women.* Trans. Edwin Lee. Philadelphia: Lea and Blanchard, 1843.

Massuyer. *Discours sur l'éducation publique.* Paris, 1795.

Mercier, Louis-Sébastien. *Tableau de Paris.* Hamburg: Virchaux, 1781.

Michaud, M. *Abécédaire et préceptes de morale et de civilité, pour les enfans de l'un et de l'autre sexe. Suivis par un petit traité sur l'écriture, des noms des différens cris des animaux les plus connus, et d'un tableau propre à apprendre à connaître et nommer les divers chiffres.* Aurillac: Ternat, 1819.

Millevoye, Charles. *L'Amour maternel, poëme.* Paris: Crapelet, an 13 (1805).

Le Morale en exemples. Paris: Louis Janet, n.d.

Morceaux choisis de Fénélon, Fleury, Rollin, Dupuy, Halifax et Mme de Lamber, pour servir à l'éducation des jeunes personnes; auxquels on a ajouté l'ouvrage intitulé: Instructions d'un père à ses filles. Paris: Laurens Jeune, 1810.

Navarre, Père Jean, de la Doctrine chrétienne. *Discours qui a remporté le prix par le jugement de l'Académie des jeux floraux en l'année 1763, sur ces paroles: Quel serait en France le plan d'étude le plus avantageux.* S.l., s.d., 1763.

Naville, François-Marie-Louis. *L'Education publique considérée dans ses rapports avec le développement des facultés, la marche progressive de la civilisation et le besoins actuels de la France.* Paris: Audin, 1832.

Noël, Alexis. *Les Jeux de la poupée, ou Les étrennes des Demoiselles, composés de 7 gravures en taille-douce, avec une explication en vers français.* Paris: Chez A. Noël, éditeur, 1806.

Noël, Jeune. *Cahier de dessin réprésentant les jeux de l'enfance et de la jeunesse avec une explication et une devise morale. Cahier Jeux des jeunes garçons.* Paris: Chez A. Noël jeune, graveur, 1807.

Noël, Louis-Joseph. *Syllabaire simplifié.* Paris: Barret, an 7.

Norton, Mme. *Etrennes aux enfans qui savent bien lire ou contes moraux.* Trans. Delannoy. Paris: Chez Delannoy, 1789.

Nouveau magasin des enfans, contenant des historiettes morales. Paris: Devaux, an 10.

Nouveau syllabaire instructif et amusant. Paris: Caillot, 1816.

Patot, Eimée. *Essai sur l'art d'apprendre à lire, suivi d'une nouvelle méthode de lecture au moyen de laquelle on abrège considérablement le temps consacré d'ordinaire à cette première étude de l'enfance.* Paris: Brunot-Labbe, 1829.

Pestalozzi, Johann Heinrich. *Léonard et Gertrude; ou, Les mœurs villageoises telles qu'on les retrouve à la ville et à la cour.* Lausanne: G. Decombaz, 1784.

———. *Manuel des mères.* Geneva: J. J. Paschoud, 1821.

La Petite prisonnière du Fort Saint-Elm ou L'Enfant perdue et retrouvée. Ouvrage dédié à l'enfance, traduit de l'anglais. 2 vols. Paris: Vernarel et Tenon, 1824.

Les Petites moralistes; choix de nouvelles morales pour les enfans. Paris: Louis Janet, 1825.

Petit Tableau des arts et métiers, ou, Notions sur les principaux travaux des hommes: Ouvrage instructif et amusant, a l'usage de la jeunesse de l'un et l'autre sexe. 3rd ed. Paris: Pierre Blanchard, 1825.

Pluche, Noël Antoine. *Concorde de la géographie des différens âges.* Paris: Frères Estienne, 1792.

————. *Le Spectacle de la nature, ou Entretiens sur les particularités de l'histoire naturelle: Qui ont paru les plus propres à rendre les Jeunes Gent curieux, et à leur former l'esprit.* Nouvelle ed. 4 vols. Utrecht: Chez Etienne Neaulme, 1736.

Pottier. *Abécédaire récréatif orné de vingt-six gravures propres à piquer la curiosité des enfants, ou Méthode amusante pour enseigner l'A, B, C.* 37th ed. Paris: Devaux, 1802 (an 10).

Principes de J. J. Rousseau, sur l'éducation des enfants, ou Instruction sur le conservation des enfans, et sur leur éducation physique et morale, depuis leur naissance, jusqu'à l'époque de leur entrée dans les écoles nationales. Paris: Aubry, an 2.

Prost de Royer, Antoine-François. *Mémoire sur la conservation des enfants.* Lyon: Aîné de la Roche, 1778.

Recréation de l'enfance, ou Recueil de gravures amusantes, dédié aux petite demoiselles. Paris: Blanchard and Eymery, n.d.

Réimpression de l'ancien Moniteur: Seule histoire authentique et inaltérée de la Révolution française depuis la réunion des Etats-Généraux juqu'au consulat (mai 1789–novembre 1799), avec des notes explicatives. 31 vols. Paris: 1858–1863.

Rémusat, Charles de. *De la Jeunesse dans passé et présent.* 2 vols. Paris: Ladrango, 1847.

Rémusat, Claire Elisabeth Jeanne Gravier de Vergennes, Comtesse de. *Essai sur l'éducation des femmes.* Paris: Ladvocat, 1824.

Rendu, Ambroise. *Essai sur l'instruction publique et particulièrement sur l'instruction primaire.* 3 vols. Paris: N.p, 1819.

Renneville, Sophie de Senterre, Mme de. *Les Bons petits enfants, contes et dialogues pour le jeune âge* Limoges: Ardant, 1882.

————. *Contes à ma petite fille et à mon petit garçon: Pour les amuser, leur former un bon coeur, et les corriger des petits défauts de leur age.* 4th ed. Paris: Saintin, 1817.

————. *Contes pour les enfans de cinq à six ans.* 6th ed. Paris: Blanchard, 1829.

————. *Correspondance de deux petites filles, ouvrage propre à former de bonne heure les enfans au style épistolaire.* Paris: Belin, 1811.

————. *Les Deux éducations ou Le pouvoir de l'exemple.* Paris: Alexis Eymery, 1813.

————. *L'Éducation de la poupée, ou Petits dialogues instructifs et moraux, à la portée du jeune âge.* Paris: A. Eymery, 1822.

————. *La Fée bienfaisante, ou, La Mère ingénieuse.* Paris: A. Eymery, 1814.

————. *Galerie des jeunes vièrges, ou, Modèle des vertus qui assurent le bonheur des femmes . . . : Ouvrage destiné aux jeunes personnes de tous les états: Où l'on prouve, par des exemples, qu'un cœur pur est le premier des biens: Qu'il est le garant de toutes les vertus chrétiennes et des qualités sociales: Que l'inno-*

cence de mœurs appelée sagesse fait la bonne fille, l'épouse respectable, ainsi que la bonne mère: Qu'enfin, elle assure aux femmes des jours heureux jusque dans la vieillesse la plus avancée. 3rd ed. Paris: Chez Thiérot et Belin, 1824.

———. *Lettres d'Octavie, jeune pensionnaire de la maison de Saint-Clair, ou Essai sur l'éducation des demoiselles.* Paris: Leprieur, 1806.

———. *Lettres d'Octavie, jeune pensionnaire de la maison de Saint-Clair, ou Essai sur l'éducation des demoiselles.* 2nd ed. Paris: Villet, 1818.

———. *La Mère gouvernante, ou Principes de politesse fondés sur les qualités du coeur.* Paris: Berlin-LePrieur, 1828.

———. *Les récréations d'Eugénie, contes propres á former le coeur et à dévelop-per la raison des enfans.* Paris: Genets jeune, 1815.

Richard, Thomas. *La Science enseignée par les jeux, ou Théories scientifiques des jeux les plus usuels, accompagnées de recherches historiques sur leur origine, servant d'introduction à l'étude de la mécanique, de la physique, etc., imité de l'anglais.* 2 vols. Paris: Roret, 1830.

Romain, Bernard. *Abécédaire graphiamalégique, ou principes de lecture. Extraits de la graphiamalégie, ou l'Art d'apprendre tout la fois à lire et à écrire en très-peu de temps.* Avignon: Chaillot, 1830.

Romme, Gilbert. *Rapport sur l'instruction publique, considéree dans son ensemble, suivi d'un projet de décret sur le principales bases du plan général, présenté à la Convention Nationale au nom du comité d'Instruction publique.* Paris, 1793.

Roullé, Jh. *Premiers élémens de la grammaire françoise où l'on fait des observa-tions sur l'orthographe et où l'on donne une manière d'apprendre à lire.* Paris: Chez l'auteur et Favre, an 8 (1800).

Rousseau, Jean-Jacques. *Considérations sur le gouvernment de Pologne.*

———. *Discourse on the Origin and Foundation of Inequality Among Mankind.* New York: Penguin, 1984.

———. *Emile, or On Education.* Trans. Allan Bloom. New York: Basic, 1979.

———. *Emile, or On Education.* Trans. Barbara Foxley, ed. Peter D. Jimack. London: Everyman, 1993.

———. *Politics and the Arts: Letter to M. D'Alembert on the Theatre.* Trans. Allan Bloom. Cornell: Cornell University Press, 1960.

———. *The Social Contract.* New York: Penguin, 1968.

———. The Social Contract *and* Discourse on the Origin and Foundation of In-equality Among Mankind. New York: Washington Square Books, 1967.

Saint-André, André Jeanbon. *Sur l'éducation nationale.* Paris: N.p., n.d.

Saint-Ouen, Laure de Boen de. *Histoire de France.* Paris: Colas, 1827.

Saint-Paul, François-Marie Mayeur de. *Tableau du nouveau Palais-Royal.* 2 vols. Paris: Maradan, 1788.

Saint-Pierre, Puget de. *Analyse des principes de M. J. J. Rousseau.* La Haye: S.l., 1763.

Saint-Sernin, Mlle. *Les Jeux des jeunes demoiselles, représenté en estampes d'après les dessin de J. Degourc, dessinateur de la chambre du roi, ou Histori-ettes morales, relatives des jeux de l'enfance et de l'adolesence.* Paris: Chez Nepveu, 1820.

Salguès, A. V. *L'Amie des mères des famille, ou Traité d'éducation physique et morale des enfans.* Paris: Dentu, 1810.

Salmade, Mathieu-Antoine. *Le Livre des mères et des nourrices, ou Instruction pratique sur la conservation des enfans.* Paris: Merlin, an 9 (1801).

Savignac, Alida. *Encouragemens donnés à la jeunesse industrieuse.* Paris: Louis Colas, 1828.

Schmid, Joahnn Cristopher von. *Comment le jeune Henri apprit à connaitre Dieu: Histoire morale et amusante composée pour les enfans, et traduite de l'allemand.* Trans. M. Lambert. Paris: P. Blanchard, 1820.

Sicard, Roch Ambroise. *Manuel de l'enfance, contenant des élémens de lecture et des dialogues intructifs et moraux: Dédié aux mères et à toutes les personnes chargées de l'éducation de la première enfance.* Paris: Le Clerc, an 5 (1797).

Stella, Jacques. *Jeux et plaisris [sic] de l'enfance.* Engr. Claudine Stella. Paris: Jacques Stella, 1657.

———. *Les Jeux et Plaisirs de L'Enfance.* Engr. Alexandre Charponnier. Paris: Chaise Jeune, n.d. [eighteenth century].

Texier de La Pommeraye, Arnaud. *Lecteur français, amusant et instructif, propre aux jeunes étudians qui ont déjà acquis une certaine connaissance de la langue française.* [Philadelphia]: J. F. Hurtel, 1826.

Tour, Alphonse de Serres de la. *Du Bonheur.* Paris: N.p. 1767.

Van der Bruck, Mme. *Contes et conseils à mes jeunes enfans, convenables à la première enfance pour les deux sexes.* Paris: Ledentu, 1819.

Verdier, Jean. *Discours sur l'éducation nationale, physique et morale des deux sexes.* Paris: Onfronoy, 1792.

Verdier-Huertin, Dr. Jean-François. *Discours et essai aphoristique sur l'allaitement et l'éducation des enfans et Dissertation sur un foetus trouvé dans le corps d'un enfant male.* Paris: Chez l'auteur, an 12 (1804).

Vernhes aîné. *Abécédaire nouveau, fondé sur le mécanisme du langage. Indiqué par la nature; suivi d'un traité d'orthographe et de tous les homonymes français; terminé par des exemples servant d'application aux règles d'orthographe et aux homonymes.* Beziers: Fuzier, 1824.

Viel-Castel, Horace. *Costumes, armes, et meubles pour servir à l'histoire de France depuis le commencement du cinqième siècle jusqu'à nos jours.* Vol. 4 (1774–1811). Paris: Chez l'auteur et Caillault, 1845.

Villeterque, Alexandre-Louis de. "Sur les livres nouveaux à l'usage des enfans." *Journal de Paris,* 8 Pluviose, an 7.

Wandelaincourt, Hubert. *Cours d'éducation pour les écoles du premier âge.* 2 vols. Paris: Ancelle, an 10 (1801).

———. *Cours d'éducation pour les écoles du second âge, ou des Adolescents.* 2 vols. Paris: Ancelle, an 10 (1802).

Wollstonecraft, Mary. *A Vindication of the Rights of Woman.* 2nd ed . New York: W.W. Norton, 1988.

Secondary Sources

Adamson, John William. *A Short History of Education.* Cambridge: Cambridge University Press, 1919.

Adhémar, Jean. "L'éducation visuelle des fils de France et l'origine du Musée de Versailles." *La Revue des Arts* (Paris) 6 (1956): 29–34.

L'âge d'or du petit portrait. Exhibition Catalogue for Bordeaux, Geneva, and Paris, 1995–1996. Paris: Seuil, 1995.

Allain, Ernst. *L'Instruction primaire en France avant la Révolution.* Paris: Tardieu, 1881.

Allemagne, Henry-René d'. *Histoire des jouets.* Paris: Hachette, c. 1900.

———. *Le noble jeu de l'Oie en France de 1640 à 1950.* Paris: Grund, 1950.

Anchor, Robert. "History and Play: Johann Huizinga and his Critics." *History and Theory, Studies in the Philosophy of History* 28 (1978): 63–93.

Anderson, Robert David. *Education in France 1848–1870.* Oxford: Clarendon Press, 1975.

Ariès, Philippe. *Centuries of Childhood: A Social History of Family Life.* Trans. Robert Baldick. London: J. Cape, 1962.

———. *L'enfant et la vie familiale sous l'Ancien Régime.* Paris: Éditions de Seuil, 1973.

Armengaud, André. *La Famille et l'enfant en France et en Angleterre du XVI au XVIII Siècle.* Paris: CDU et SEDES, 1975.

Armstrong, Nancy. *Desire and Domestic Fiction: A Political History of the Novel.* New York: Oxford University Press, 1987.

Auslander, Leora. *Taste and Power: Furnishing Modern France.* Berkeley: University of California Press, 1998.

Averill, Esther Holden. *Political Propaganda in Children's Books of the French Revolution.* New York: N.p., 1935.

Avery, Gillian. *Childhood's Pattern: A Study of the Heroes and Heroines of Children's Fiction 1770–1950.* London: Hodder and Stoughton, 1975.

Axtell, James. *The Educational Writings of John Locke: A Critical Edition with Introduction and Notes.* Cambridge: Cambridge University Press, 1968.

Baczko, Bronislaw. "Rousseau et la pédagogie révolutionnaire." In *Rousseau and the Eighteenth Century: Essays in Memory of R. A. Leigh,* ed. Marian Hobson, J. T. A. Leigh, and Robert Wokler. Oxford: Oxford University Press, 1992.

Badinter, Elisabeth. *Mother Love: Myth and Reality, Motherhood in Modern History.* New York, Macmillan, 1981.

Baker, Bernadette M. *In Perpetual Motion: Theories of Power, Educational History, and the Child.* New York: P. Lang, 2001.

Baker, Donald N., and Patrick J. Harrigan. *The Making of Frenchmen: Current Directions in the History of Education in France, 1679–1979.* Waterloo, Ont.: Historical Reflections Press, 1980.

Baker, Keith. *Condorcet: From National Philosophy to Social Mathematics.* Chicago: University of Chicago Press, 1975.

Barker-Benfield, G. J. *The Culture of Sensibility: Sex and Society in Eighteenth-Century Britain.* Chicago: University of Chicago Press, 1992.

Barnard, H. C. *Education and the French Revolution.* Cambridge: Cambridge University Press, 1969.

Barny, Roger. *L'Eclatement révolutionnaire du rousseauisme.* Paris: Belles Lettres, 1988.

———. *Prélude idéologique à la Révolution française: Le rousseauisme avant 1789.* Paris: Belles Lettres, 1985.

Bederman, Gail. *Manliness and Civilization: A Cultural History of Gender and Race in the United States, 1880–1917*. Chicago: University of Chicago Press, 1995.

Berg, Maxine, and Elizabeth Eger, ed. *Luxury in the Eighteenth Century: Debates, Desires, and Delectable Goods*. New York: Palgrave, 2003.

Bergen, Barry Herman. "Molding Citizens: Ideology, Class, and Primary Education in Nineteenth-Century France." Ph.D. diss., University of Pennsylvania, 1987.

Bertaud, Jules. "Madame de Genlis, éducatrice." *Revue des deux mondes* 68 (1942): 54–71.

Bertier de Sauvigny, Guillaume de. *The Bourbon Restoration*. Philadelphia: University of Pennsylvania Press, 1966.

Billot, Claudine. "Le rôle de l'image dans la littérature enfantine jusqu'à la Restauration." *Gazette des Beaux-Arts* 6 (1972): 165–72.

Bloch, Jean. *Rousseauism and Education in Eighteenth-Century France*. Vol. 325. Studies on Voltaire and the Eighteenth Century. Oxford: Voltaire Foundation, 1995.

———. "Rousseau's Reputation as an Authority on Childcare and Physical Education in France before the Revolution." *Paedagogica Historica* 14 (1974): 5–33.

Bloch, Ruth. "American Feminine Ideals in Transition: The Rise of the Moral Mother, 1785–1815." *Feminist Studies* 4: 2 (1978): 100–26.

Bollème, Geneviève. *La Bibliothèque bleue, la littérature en France du XVI siècle au XIX siècle*. Paris: Julliard, 1971.

Bonnefont, G. *Les Jeux et les récréations de la jeunesse*. Paris: M. Dreyfus, c. 1888.

Bonno, Gabriel Dominique Bonno. "Locke et son traducteur français Pierre Coste." *Revue de littérature comparée* 33 (1959): 161–79.

———. *Les Relations intellectuelles de Locke avec la France. D'après des documents inédits*. Berkeley: University of California Press, 1955.

Borch-Jacobsen, Mikkel. *The Emotional Tie: Psychoanalysis, Mimesis, and Affect*. Stanford: Stanford University Press, 1992.

Boucher, François. *Histoire du costume en occident de l'antiquité à nos jours*. Paris: Flammarion, 1965.

Bouilly 1761–1845: Un Grand peintre français de la Révolution à la Restauration. Expostion Catalogue: Musée des Beaux-Arts de Lille, 23 October 1988 to 9 Janvier 1989. Lille: Morel et Corduant, 1988.

Boulad-Ayoub, Josiane, ed. *Former un nouveau peuple? Pouvoir, éducation, révolution*. Paris: Harmattan, 1996.

Bourdieu, Pierre. *Distinction: A Social Critique of the Judgement of Taste*. Trans. Richard Nice. Cambridge: Harvard University Press, 1984.

Bowen, James. *A History of Western Education.* Vol. 3. *The Modern West: Europe and the New World*. London: Methuen 1981.

Bravo-Villasante, C. "Le Vice et la vertu: L'enfant bon et l'enfant méchant dans l'oeuvre de Berquin." In *The Portrayal of the Child*. ed. Denis Escarpit. Munich: Saur, 1985.

Brouard-Arends, Isabelle. *Vies et images maternelles dans la littérature française du dix-huitième siècle.* Vol. 291. Studies on Voltaire and the Eighteenth Century. Oxford: Voltaire Foundation, 1991.

Brown, Marilyn. *Picturing Children: Constructions of Childhood between Rousseau and Freud.* Burlington, Ver.: Ashgate, 2002.

Buck, Anne. *Clothes and the Child: A Handbook of Children's Dress in England, 1500–1900.* New York: Holmes and Meier, 1996.

Buisson, F., ed. *Dictionnaire de pédagogie et d'instruction primaire.* Paris: Hachette, 1882.

Caillois, Roger. *Les Jeux et les hommes: Le masque et le vertige.* Paris, 1958.

Calvert, Karin Lee Fishbeck. *Children in the House: The Material Culture of Early Childhood, 1600–1900.* Boston: Northeastern University Press, 1992.

Caradec, François. *Histoire de la littérature enfantine en France.* Paris: Albin-Michel, 1977.

Carnochan, W. B. "The Child is Father of the Man." In *A Distant Prospect: Eighteenth-Century Views of Childhood.* Los Angeles: Clark Library, 1982.

Caspard, Pierre. *La Presse de l'éducation et d'enseignement, XVIIIè siècle—1940.* 3 vols. Paris: INRP et CNRS, 1988–1991.

Cass, Walter J. *A Primer in Philosophy of Education.* Dubuque, Iowa: Kendall and Hunt, 1974.

Cassirer, Ernst. *The Question of Jean-Jacques Rousseau.* Ed. and trans. Peter Gay. Bloomington: Indiana University Press, 1963.

Chabaud, Louis. *Les Précursors du féminisme: Mmes de Maintenon, de Genlis et Campan, leur rôle dans l'éducation chrétienne de la femme.* Paris: Plon-Nourrit et Cie, 1901.

Chambert de Lauwe, M. J. "La Répresentation de l'enfant dans la littérature d'enfance et de jeunesse." In *The Portrayal of the Child,* ed. D. Escarpit. Munich: Saur, 1985.

Chapman, John William. *Rousseau—Totalitarian or Liberal?* New York: Columbia University Press, 1956.

Chartier, Roger. "Forms of Privatization." In *The History of Private Life,* ed. Roger Chartier. Vol. 3. *Passions of the Renaissance,* trans. Arthur Goldhammer, series ed. Philippe Ariès and Georges Duby. Cambridge, Mass.: Belknap Press, 1989.

Charvet, John. *The Social Problem in the Philosophy of Rousseau.* Cambridge: Cambridge University Press, 1974.

Chevalier, Alexis. *Les Frères des écoles chrétiennes et l'enseignement primaire après La Révolution, 1797–1830.* Paris: Poussielgue frères, 1887.

Chevalier, Louis. *Classes laborieuses et classes dangereuses à Paris pendant la première moitié du dix-neuvième siècle.* Paris: Plon, 1958.

Chisick, Harvey. *The Limits of Reform in the Enlightenment: Attitudes Toward the Education of the Lower Classes in Eighteenth-Century France.* Princeton: Princeton University Press, 1981.

Clancy, Patricia A. "Mme Le Prince de Beaumont: A Founder of Children's Literature in France." *Australian Journal of French Studies* 16 (January–April 1979): 187–281.

Claretie, Léo. "L'Industrie des jouets en France." *Revue de Paris* 6 (1900): 891–906.

———. *Les Jouets de France, leur histoire, leur avenir.* Paris: Delagrave, 1920.

Coe, Richard N. "Reminiscences of Childhood." *Proceedings of the Leeds Philosophical Society* 19 (1984): 227–321.

Coleman, Patrick. "Characterizing Rousseau's *Emile.*" *MLN* 92 (1977): 761–78.

Colletti, Lucio. "Rousseau as Critic of Civil Society." In *From Rousseau to Lenin: Studies in Ideology and Society,* trans. John Merrington and Judith White. New York: Monthly Review Press, 1972.

Collomp, Alain. *La Maison du père, famille et village en Haute-Provence aux XVIIe et XVIIIe siècles.* Paris: Presses universitaires de France, 1983.

Colwill, Elisabeth. "Women's Empire and the Sovereignty of Man in *La Décade Philosophique.*" *Eighteenth-Century Studies* 29 (1996): 265–89.

Compayré, Gabriel. *Histoire critique des doctrines de l'éducation en France depuis le XVIè siècle.* 5th ed. Paris: Hachette, 1885.

———. *History of Pedagogy.* Trans, William Payne. Boston: Heath, 1886.

Compère, Marie Madeleine. *L'éducation en France du 16ᵉ au 18ᵉ siècle.* Paris: Société d'édition d'enseignement supérieur, 1976.

Connolly, William. *The Terms of Political Discourse.* Princeton: Princeton University Press, 1984.

Cott, Nancy. *The Bonds of Womanhood: "Woman's Sphere" in New England, 1780–1835.* New Haven: Yale, 1997.

Crémieux-Brilhac, Jean-Louis, ed. *L'Education nationale: Le Ministère; l'administration centrale; les services.* Paris: Presses universitaires de France, 1965.

Crubellier, Maurice. *L'Enfance et la jeunesse dans la société française, 1800–1950.* Paris: Armand Colin, 1979.

Cunningham, Hugh. *Children and Childhood in Western Society Since 1500.* New York: Longman, 1995.

Curtis, Sarah A. *Educating the Faithful: Religion, Schooling and Society.* DeKalb: Northern Illinois University Press, 2000.

Damamme, Jeanne, Michel Manson, and Florence Poisson. *Jouets et poupées dans les musées français.* Paris: Jouve, 1983.

Darton, Frederick Joseph Harvey. *Children's Books in England: Five Centuries of Social Life.* 3rd ed. Rev. by Brian Alderson. Cambridge: Cambridge University Press, 1982.

Darnton, Robert. *The Great Cat Massacre and Other Episodes in French Cultural History.* New York: Vintage, 1985.

Dautry, Jean. "La Revolution bourgeoise et *l'Encyclopédie.*" *La Pensée* 38 (1951): 73–80.

Davidoff, Leonore, and Catherine Hall. *Family Fortunes: Men and Women of the English Middle Class, 1780–1850.* Chicago: University of Chicago Press, 1991.

Davidson, Cathy N. *Revolution and the Word: The Rise of the Novel in America.* New York: Oxford University Press, 1986.

Delpierre, Madeleine. *Le Costume: Consulat-Empire.* Paris: Flammarion, 1990.

Delumeau, Jean, and Daniel Roche, ed. *Histoire des pères et de la paternité.* Paris: Larousse, 1990.

Delzons, L. *La Famille française et son évolution.* Paris: Colin, 1913.

DeMause, Lloyd. *The History of Childhood.* New York: Psychohistory Press, 1974.

Demers, Patricia. *Heaven upon Earth: The Form of Moral and Religious Literature, to 1850.* Knoxville: University of Tennessee Press, 1993.

Deniel, Raymond. *Une Image de la famille et de la société sous la Restauration.* Paris: Les Editions ouvrières, 1985.

Desan, Suzanne. *The Family on Trial in Revolutionary France.* Berkeley: University of California Press, 2004.

Deschamps, J. G. *The History of French Children's Books, 1750–1900.* Boston: The Bookshop for Boys and Girls, Women's Educational and Industrial Union, 1934.

Dijkstra, Bram. *Idols of Perversity: Fantasies of Feminine Evil in Fin-de-Siècle Culture.* New York: Oxford University Press, 1986.

Dixon-Fyle, Joyce. *Female Writers' Struggle for Rights and Education for Women in France (1848–1871).* New York: Peter Lang, 2006.

Donzolot, Jacques. *The Policing of Families.* Trans. Robert Hurley. New York: Pantheon, 1979.

Dumont, Jean-Marie. *La Vie et l'oeuvre de Jean-Charles Pellerin, 1756–1836.* Epinal: L'Imagerie Pellerin, 1956.

Duncan, Carole. "Happy Mothers and Other New Ideas in Eighteenth-Century Art." In *Feminism and Art History: Questioning the Litany,* ed. Norma Broude and Mary Garrard. New York: Harper and Row, 1982.

DuPasquier, Jacqueline. *Pierre-Edouard Dagoty 1775–1871 et la miniature bordelaise au XIXe siècle.* Chartres: Jacques Laget, 1974.

Durel, Pétrus. "Les Jouets et leur origine." *La Nouvelle Révue* 13 (1901): 607–16.

Durkheim, Emile. *The Evolution of Educational Thought: Lectures on the Formation and Development of Secondary Education in France.* Trans. Peter Collins. Boston: Routledge, 1977.

Ehrenreich, Barbara, and Deirdre English. *For Her Own Good: 150 Years of the Experts' Advice to Women.* New York: Doubleday, 1978.

Eisenstein Zillah. *The Radical Future of Liberal Feminism.* Boston: Northeastern University Press, 1993.

Elias, Norbert. *The Civilizing Process: The History of Manners and State Formation and Civilization.* Trans. Edmund Jephcott. Cambridge: Blackwell, 1994.

Ellis, Madeleine B. *Rousseau's Socratic Aemilian Myths: A Literary Collation of* Emile *and the* Social Contract. Columbus: Ohio State University Press, 1977.

Elwell, C. E. *The Influence of the Enlightenment on the Catholic Theory of Religious Education in France, 1750–1850.* Cambridge: Harvard University Press, 1944.

Escarpit, Denise. *Les Exigences de l'image dans le livre de la première enfance.* Paris: Magnard, 1973.

———. *La Littérature d'enfance et de jeunesse en Europe, panorama historique.* Paris: Presses Universitaires de France, 1981.

Les Enfans: Leurs portraits et leurs jouets, 1789–1900. Exposition Organisée par la Société Nationale des Beaux-Arts dans les Palais du Domaine de Bagatelle, du 14 mai au 15 juillet 1910. Paris: Jourdan, 1910.

L'Enfant dans les collections de la Ville de Paris. Expostion organisée par la délégation à l'action artistique de la ville de paris. 30 mars–3 décembre 1979.

Enfants d'autrefois: L'enfant dans l'art, la vie et le livre français du dix-septième au milieu du dix-neuvième siècle. Exhibition at the Bibliothèque de Versailles, Mai–Juin 1931. Préface de Edmond Pilion. Paris: E. Durand, 1931.

Erikson, Erik. *Childhood and Society.* New York: Norton, 1950.

———. *Young Man Luther.* New York: Norton, 1958.

Evans, Sara. *Personal Politics: The Roots of Women's Liberation in the Civil Rights Movement and the New Left.* New York: Vintage, 1980.

Ewing, Elizabeth. *History of Children's Costume.* London: Batsford, 1877.

Fairchilds, Cissie. *Domestic Enemies: Servants and Their Masters in Old Regime France.* Baltimore: Johns Hopkins Press, 1984.

Fontainerie, François de la. *French Liberalism and Education in the Eighteenth Century: The Writings of La Chalotais, Turgot, Diderot, Condorcet on National Education.* New York: McGraw-Hill, 1932.

Foucault, Michel. *The Archaeology of Knowledge and the Discourse on Language.* Trans. A. M. Sheridan Smith. New York: Pantheon, 1982.

———. *Madness and Civilization: A History of Insanity in the Age of Reason.* Trans. Richard Howard. New York: Vintage Books, 1988.

———. *Power/Knowledge: Selected Interviews and Other Writings.* Ed. Colin Gordon. New York: Pantheon, 1980.

Fournier, Louis Edouard. *Histoire des jouets et des jeux d'enfants.* Paris: E. Dentu, 1889.

Fox-Genovese, Elizabeth. "Introduction." In *French Women and the Age of Enlightenment,* ed. Samia Spencer. Bloomington: Indiana University Press, 1984.

Franklin, Alfred. *La Vie privée d'autrefois. Arts et métiers, modes moeurs, usages des Parisiens du XIIe au XVIIIe siècle, d'après des documents originaux ou inédits.* Vol. 10. Écoles et Collèges. Paris: Plon, 1891.

———. *La Vie privée d'autrefois. Arts et métiers, modes moeurs, usages des Parisiens du XIIe au XVIIIe siècle, d'après des documents originaux ou inédits.* Volume 15. Les Magasins de Nouveautés, part 1. Paris: Plon, 1894.

———. *La Vie privée d'autrefois. Arts et métiers, modes moeurs, usages des Parisiens du XIIe au XVIIIe siècle, d'après des documents originaux ou inédits.* Volume 17. L'enfant, part 1. La Naissance–Le Baptême. Paris: Plon, 1895.

———. *La Vie privée d'autrefois. Arts et métiers, modes moeurs, usages des Parisiens du XIIe au XVIIIe siècle, d'après des documents originaux ou inédits.* Volume 19. L'enfant, part 2. La Layette–La Nourrice–La Vie de famille–Les Jouets et les Jeux. Paris: Plon, 1896.

Freidan, Betty. *The Feminine Mystique.* New York: Norton, 1997.

Furet, François, and Jacques Ozouf. *Lire et écrire: L'alphabetisation des Français de Calvin à Jules Ferry.* Paris: Editions de Minuit, 1977.

———. *Reading and Writing: Literacy in France from Calvin to Jules Ferry.* Cambridge: Cambridge University Press, 1982.

Garnier, Adrien. *Au Temps de l'empire et de la Restauration. L'Eglise et l'éducation du peuple.* Paris: De Gigord, 1933.

Gavault, Paul. "Preface." In *Les Livres de l'enfance du quinzième au dix-neuvième siècles.* Vol. 1. "Texte." Paris: Gumuchian, n.d. (before 1940).

Gay, Peter, ed. *John Locke on Education.* New York: Teacher's College, Columbia University, 1964.

Gélis, Jacques. "The Child: From Anonymity to Individuality." In *A History of Private Life.* Vol 3. *Passions of the Renaissance,* ed. Roger Chartier, trans. Arthur Goldhammer, series ed. Philippe Ariès and Georges Duby. Cambridge, Mass.: Belknap Press, 1989.

Gerin, Elisabeth. *Tout sur la presse enfantin.* Paris: Maison de la Bonne Press, 1953.

Glénisson, Jean, and Ségolène le Men. *Le Livre d'enfance et de jeunesse en France.* Bordeaux: Société des bibliophiles de Guyenne, 1994.

Goldstein, Jan. *Console and Classify: The French Psychiatric Profession in the Nineteenth Century.* New York: Cambridge University Press, 1987.

Goldstone, Bette P. *Lessons to Be Learned: A Study of Eighteenth-Century English Didactic Literature.* New York: Lang, 1984.

Gontard, Maurice. *L'Enseignement primaire en France de la Révolution à la loi Guizot (1789–1833): Des petite écoles de la monarchie d'ancien régime aux écoles primaires de la monarchie bourgeoise.* Paris: Belles-Lettres, 1959.

Grand-Carteret, John. *Dix-neuvième Siècle en France. Classes, moeurs, usages, costumes, inventions.* Paris: Firmin Didot, 1893.

de Grazia, Victoria, ed. *The Sex of Things: Gender and Consumption in Historical Perspective.* Berkeley and Los Angeles: University of California Press, 1996.

Grenédan, Joachim du Plessis de. *Histoire de l'autorité paternelle et de la société familiale en France avant 1789: Les origines, l'époque franque, le moyen-âge, et les temps modernes.* Paris: A. Rousseau, 1900.

Gumuchain. *Les Livres de l'enfance du cinqième au dix-neuvième siècles.* Préface de Paul Gavault. 2 vols. Paris: Gumuchian et Cie, c. 1930.

Hahn, Roger. *The Anatomy of a Scientific Institution: The Paris Academy of Sciences.* Berkeley and Los Angeles: University of California Press, 1971.

Halttunen, Karen. *Confidence Men and Painted Women: A Study of Middle-Class Culture in America, 1830–1870.* New Haven: Yale University Press, 1982.

Hampson, Norman. "La Patrie." In *The French Revolution and the Creation of Modern Political Culture,* ed. Colin Lucas. Vol. 2. Oxford: Pergamon Press, 1987.

Hardyment, Christina. *Dream Babies: Three Centuries of Good Advice on Child Care.* New York: Harper and Row, 1983.

Havelange, Isabelle. *La Littérature à l'usage des demoiselles, 1750–1830.* These de 3ème cycle, EHESS, 1984.

———. *Le Magasin des enfants: La littérature pour la jeunesse, 1750–1830.* Montreuil: Bibliothèque Robert-Desnos, 1988.

Hazard, Paul. *Books, Children and Men.* Trans. Marguerite Mitchell. Boston: Horn Books, 1944.

———. *Les Livres, les enfants, les hommes.* Paris: Flammarion, 1932.

Henriot, Jacques. *Le Jeu.* Paris: N.p., 1969.

Heuer, Jennifer Ngaire. *The Family and the Nation: Gender and Citizenship in Revolutionary France, 1789–1830.* Ithaca: Cornell University Press, 2005.

Heywood, Colin. *Childhood in Nineteenth-Century France: Work, Health, and Education Among the "Classes Populaires."* New York: Cambridge University Press, 1988.

————. *Growing Up in France: From the Ancien Régime to the Third Republic.* New York: Cambridge University Press, 2007.

Higonnet, Margaret. "Diffusion et débats du féminisme," In *Écriture féminine et littérature de jeunesse,* ed. Jean Perrot and Véronique Hadengue. Actes du colloque d'Eaubonne (March 1994). Paris: La Nacelle, 1995.

Hilton, Mary, and Pam Hirsch, ed. *Practical Visionaries: Women, Education and Social Progress 1790–1930.* New York: Longman, 2000.

Hoffman, Lois Wadis. "Cross-Cultural Differences in Childrearing Goals." In *Parental Behavior in Diverse Societies,* ed. Robert A. LeVine, Patrice Miller, and Mary Maxwell West. San Francisco: Jossey-Bass, 1988.

Hollis, Martin. "A Remarkable Change in Man." In *Jean-Jacques Rousseau and the Sources of the Self,* ed. Timothy O'Hagan. Brookfield, Ver: Avebury Books, 1997.

Homer, Herbert. *A Brief History of Toy Books, Exemplified in a Series of Characters with Figures to Dress and Undress, 1810–1830.* South Lancaster, Mass.: John Green Chandler Museum, 1954.

Hufton, Olwen. *Women and the Limits of Citizenship in the French Revolution.* Toronto: University of Toronto Press, 1992.

Huguet, Françoise. *Les Livres pour l'enfance et la jeunesse de Gutenberg à Guizot.* Les Collections de la Bibliothèque de l'Institut National de Recherche Pedagogique. Paris: INRP, 1997.

Hunt, David. *Parents and Children in History: The Psychology of Family Life in Early Modern France.* New York: Basic, 1970.

Hunt, Lynn. *The Family Romance of the French Revolution.* Berkeley: University of California Press, 1993.

Hunt, Peter. *Criticism, Theory, and Children's Literature.* London: Blackwell, 1991.

————. *An Introduction to Children's Literature.* Oxford: Oxford University Press, 1994.

————. *Understanding Children's Literature.* New York: Routledge, 1998.

Hutchison, Ross. *Locke in France, 1688–1734.* Vol. 290. Studies in Voltaire and the Eighteenth Century. Oxford: Voltaire Foundation, 1991.

Jackson, Mary. *Engines of Instruction, Mischief, and Magic: Children's Literature in England from Its Beginnings to 1839.* Lincoln: University of Nebraska Press, 1989.

Jan, Isabelle. *On Children's Literature.* New York: Schocken, 1974.

Jeux et travaux de l'enfance. Exposition at the INRP, from the Musée National de l'Éducation, Rouen (1990). Paris: INRP, 1990.

Jimack, Peter D. *The Defence of Educational Tradition in France, 1770–1789.* Vol. 264. Studies on Voltaire and the Eighteenth Century. Oxford: Voltaire Foundation, 1989.

————. *La Genèse et la rédaction de l'*Emile *de Jean J.-J. Rousseau.* Ed. Theodore Besterman. Vol. 13. Studies on Voltaire and the Eighteenth Century. Geneva: Institute et Musée Voltaire, 1960.

————. *Some Eighteenth-Century Imitations of Rousseau's* Emile. Vol. 284. Studies on Voltaire and the Eighteenth Century. Oxford: Voltaire Foundation, 1991.

Johansson, S. Ryan. "Centuries of Childhood/Centuries of Parenting: Ariès and the Modernization of Privileged Infancy." *Journal of Family History* 12 (1987): 343–65.

Jones, Jennifer. *Sexing La Mode: Gender, Fashion and Commercial Culture in Old Regime France*. New York: Berg, 2004.

Julia, Dominique, Roger Chartier, and Marie Madeleine Compère. *L'éducation en France du 16ᵉ au 18ᵉ siècle*. Paris: Société d'édition d'enseignement supérieur, 1976.

Kates, Gary. *The Cercle Social, the Girondins, and the French Revolution*. Princeton: Princeton University Press, 1985.

———. *Monsieur d'Eon Is a Woman: A Tale of Political Intrigue and Sexual Masquerade*. New York: Basic, 1995.

Kegan, Robert. *The Evolving Self*. Cambridge: Harvard University Press, 1982.

Kerber, Linda. *No Constitutional Right to Be Ladies: Women and the Obligations of Citizenship*. New York: Hill and Wang, 1998.

———. "The Republican Mother: Women and the Enlightenment—An American Perspective." *American Quarterly* 28:2 (1976): 187–205.

———. *Toward an Intellectual History of Women: Essays by Linda K. Kerber*. Chapel Hill: University of North Carolina Press, 1997.

———. *Women of the Republic: Intellect and Ideology in Revolutionary America*. Chapel Hill: University of North Carolina Press, 1980.

Kessen, William. "The American Child and other Cultural Inventions." In *The Child and Other Cultural Inventions*, ed. Frank S. Kessel and Alexander W. Siegel. New York: Praeger, 1983.

Knottnerus, J. David, and Frédérique Van de Poel-Knottnerus. *The Social Worlds of Male and Female Children in the Nineteenth-Century French Educational System: Youth, Rituals, and Elites*. Lewiston, N.Y.: E. Mellen Press, 1999.

Kramnick, Isaac. "Children's Literature and Bourgeois Ideology: Observations on Culture and Industrial Capitalism in the Later Eighteenth Century." In *Culture and Politics from Puritanism to the Enlightenment*, ed. Perez Zagorin. Berkeley: University of California Press, 1980.

Kuchta, David. *The Three-Piece Suit and Modern Masculinity: England, 1550–1850*. Berkeley: University of California Press, 2002.

La Mode en France, 1715–1815: De Louis XV à Napoléon Ier. Paris: Bibliothèque des Arts, 1990.

La Mode et les Poupées du XVIIIe siècle à nos jours. Exposition au Musee de la mode et du costume, 15 décembre 1981–18 avril 1982. Paris: Le Musée, 1982.

Lallemand, Paul. *Histoire de l'éducation dans l'ancien Oratoire de la France*. Paris: E. Thorin, 1888.

Landes, Joan. *Women and the Public Sphere in the Age of the French Revolution*. Ithaca: Cornell University Press, 1988.

Lange, Lydia. "Introduction." in *Feminist Interpretations of Jean-Jacques Rousseau*. ed. Lydia Lange. University Park: Pennsylvania State University Press, 2002.

Latzarus, Marie Thérèse. *La Littérature enfantine en France dans la seconde moitié du XIX siècle: Etude précédée d'un rapide aperçu des lectures des enfants en France avant 1860*. Paris: Presses Universitaires de la France, 1923.

Léaud, Alexis, and Emile Glay. *L'École primaire en France: Histoire pittoresque, documentaire, anecdotique de l'école, des maîtres, des écoliers depuis les origines jusqu'à nos jours*. Préface de Edouard Herriot. Vol. 1. *Des Origines à la fin du Second Empire*. Paris: La Cité française, 1934.

Leloir, Maurice. *Histoire du costume de l'Antiquité à 1914*. Vol. 11: *1725 à 1774*. Paris: Ernst, 1938.

———. *Histoire du costume de l'Antiquité à 1914*. Vol. 12: *1775 à 1795*. Paris: Ernst, 1949.

LeMen, Ségolène. *Les Abécédeaires français illustrés du dix-neuvième siècle*. Paris: Promodis, 1984.

———. "Les Images de l'enfant dans la littérature enfantine." In *L'Enfant, la famille et la Révolution française*, ed. M. F. Lévy. Paris: Orban, 1990.

Lerner, Gerda. *The Creation of Feminist Consciousness: From the Middle Ages to 1870*. New York: Oxford University Press, 1993.

Leteinturier, Christine. "La Littérature pour enfants." In *Histoire littéraire de la France*, ed. Pierre Abraham and Roland Desne. Paris: Éditions Sociales, 1977.

Levi, Giovanni, and Jean-Claude Schmitt. *Histoire des Jeunes en Occident*. Vol. 2. *L'époque contemporaine*. Paris: Seuil, 1996.

Levine, Andrew. *The Politics of Autonomy*. Amherst: University of Massachusets Press, 1976.

Levine, Lawrence W. *Highbrow, Lowbrow: The Emergence of Cultural Hierarchy in America*. Cambridge: Harvard University Press, 1988.

LeVine, Robert A. "Human Parental Care: Universal Goals, Cultural Strategies, Individual Behavior." In *Parental Behavior in Diverse Societies*, ed. Robert A. LeVine, Patrice Miller, and Mary Maxwell West. San Francisco: Jossey-Bass, 1988.

Lherete, Annie. "L'Enfant, son livre, son éducation à la fin du dix-neuvième siècle." Stanford French Review 3 (1979): 243–60.

Lloyd, Rosemary. *The Land of Lost Content: Children and Childhood in Nineteenth-Century French Literature*. Oxford: Clarendon Press, 1992.

Luc, Jean-Noël. *L'Invention du jeune enfant au XIXè siècle: De la salle d'asile à l'école maternelle*. Paris: Belin, 1997.

Lynch, Katherine A. *Family, Class, and Ideology in Early Industrial France: Social Policy and the Working-Class Family, 1825–1848*. Madison: University of Wisconsin Press, 1988.

Lyotard, Jean-François. *The Postmodern Condition: A Report on Knowledge*. Trans. Geoff Bennington and Brian Massumi. Minneapolis: University of Minnesota Press, 1993.

MacLean, Kenneth. *John Locke and English Literature of the Eighteenth Century*. New York: Garland, 1984.

Manson, Michel. "*L'Album d'A. Noël (1806) sur* Les Jeux de la poupée et ses avatars au XIX siècle." In *Jeux graphiques dans l'album pour la jueness*, ed. Jean Perrot. Paris: Idéalia, 1991.

———. "Continuités et ruptures dans l'édition du livre pour la jeunesse à Rouen de 1700 à 1900." *Revue française d'histoire du livre* 82–83 (1994): 93–125.

———. "L'Histoire des jouets devient sérieuse. . . ." In *Jouets et Poupées Dans les Musées Français*, ed. Jeanne Damamme, Michel Manson, and Florence Poisson. Paris: Jouve, 1983.

———. "La Librarie d'éducation dans le premier tiers du XIX siècle." In *La Commerce de la Librairie en France au XIXe Siècle 1789–1914,* ed. Jean-Yves Mollier. Paris: IMEC Éditions, Éditions de la Maison des Science de l'Homme, 1998.

———. "La Littérature enfantine française de 1750 à 1850 comme source de l'histoire du jouet. Rémarques méthodologiques." In *Jouet et jeu dans l'histoire de l'éducation de la petite enfance* (Colloque 1986). Paris: Université René Descartes, 1987.

———. *Les Livres pour l'enfance et la jeunesse publiés en Français de 1789 à 1799.* Paris: INRP, 1989.

———. "Madame d'Aulnoy, les contes et le jouet." In *Tricentenaire Charles Perrault, les grands contes du XVIIe siècle et leur fortune littéraire,* ed. Jean Perrot. Paris: InPress, 1998.

———. *Rouen, le livre et l'enfant, 1700–1900: La production Rouennaise de manuels et de livres pour l'enfance et la jeunesse.* Paris: INRP, 1993.

———. "La Traduction culturelle des gestes du jeu: L'exemple du jeu de la poupée vu par les éducatuers français de la fin du XVIIe siècle au milieu du XIX siècle." In *Maîtrise du geste et pouvoirs de la main chez l'enfant.* Colloque International UNICEF (Paris-UNESCO, 2–24 Novembre 1984). Paris: Flammarion, 1985.

Mara, Gerald M. "Rousseau's Two Models of Political Obligation." *The Western Political Quarterly* 33 (1980): 536–49.

Marcus, Leonard S. *An Epinal Album: Popular Prints from Nineteenth-Century France.* Boston: David R. Godine, 1984.

Marks, Jonathan. "The Savage Pattern: The Unity of Rousseau's Thought Revisited." *Polity* 31 (1998): 75–105.

Marshall, Henriette. "The Social Construction of Motherhood: An Analysis of Children and Parenting Manuals." In *Motherhood: Meanings, Practices, and Ideologies,* ed. Ann Phoenix, Anne Woollett, and Eva Lloyd. London: Sage, 1991.

Marso, Lori J. "The Stories of Citizens: Rousseau, Montesquieu, and de Staël Challenge Enlightenment Reason." *Polity* 30: 3 (1998).

———. *(Un)Manly Citizens: Jean-Jacques Rousseau's and Germaine de Staël's Subversive Women.* Baltimore: Johns Hopkins University Press, 2001.

Martin, Angus. "Notes sur l'*Ami des enfants* de Berquin et la littérature enfantine en France aux alentours de 1780." *XVIIIème siècle* 6 (1974): 299–308.

Martin, Henri Jean, and Roger Chartier. *Histoire de l'édition française.* Vol. 2. *Le Livre triomphant: 1660–1830.* Paris: Promodis, 1984.

———. *Histoire de l'édition française.* Vol. 3. *Le Temps des éditeurs: Du Romantisme à la Belle Epoque.* Paris: Promodis, 1985.

Masseau, Didier. "La Littérature enfantine et la Révolution: Rupture ou continuité." In *L'enfant, la famille et la Révolution française,* ed. Marie Françoise Lévy. Paris: Orban, 1990.

Maza. Sarah. *The Myth of the French Bourgeoisie: An Essay on the Social Imaginary.* Cambridge: Harvard University Press, 2003.

———. *Private Lives and Public Affairs: The Causes Célèbres of Prerevolutionary France.* Berkeley: University of California Press, 1993.

———. *Servants and Masters in Eighteenth-Century France: The Uses of Loyalty.* Princeton: Princeton University Press, 1983.

Maynes, Mary Jo. *Schooling for the People*. New York: Holmes and Meier, 1985.
———. *Schooling in Western Europe: A Social History*. Albany: State University of New York Press, 1985.
Maynes, Mary Jo, Birgitte Soland, and Christina Benninghaus, ed. *Secret Gardens, Satanic Mills: Placing Girls in European History, 1750–1960*. Bloomington: Indiana University Press, 2005.
Mead, Margaret. *Coming of Age in Samoa: A Psychological Study of Primitive Youth for Western Civilisation*. Kolkata, India: Quill, 1973.
Meckel, Richard Alan. "Childhood and the Historians: A Review Essay." *Journal of Family History* 9: 4 (1984): 415–24.
Mercier, Roger. *L'Enfant dans la société du dix-huitième siècle: Avant Emile*. Paris: Dakar, 1961.
Miller, Daniel. *Material Culture and Mass Consumption*. Oxford: Basil Blackwell, 1987.
Modes Enfantines: 1750–1950. Exposition au Musee de la mode et du costume, juin–novembre 1979. Paris: Musée de la mode et du costume, 1979.
Mollier, Jean-Yves, ed. *La Commerce de la librairie en France au XIXe siècle 1789–1914*. Paris: IMEC Editions, Editions de la Maison des Science de l'Homme, 1998.
Moody, Joseph. *French Education Since Napoleon*. Syracuse, N.Y.: Syracuse University Press, 1978.
Morgenstern, Mira. *Rousseau and the Politics of Ambiguity: Self, Culture, and Society*. University Park: Pennsylvania State University Press, 1996.
Moses, Claire Goldberg. *French Feminism in the Nineteenth Century*. Albany: State University of New York Press, 1984.
Myers, Mitzi. "Impeccable Governesses, Rational Dames, and Moral Mothers: Mary Wollenstonecraft and the Female Tradition in Georgian Children's Books." *Children's Literature* 14 (1986): 31–59.
———. "Reform or Ruin: 'A Revolution in Female Manners.'" In *Studies in Eighteenth-Century Culture*, vol. 11, ed. Harry C. Payne. Madison: University of Wisconsin Press, 1982.
Niestroj, Brigitte H. E. "Some Recent German Literature on Socialization and Childhood in Past Times." *Continuity and Change* 2 (1989): 339–57.
Nikliborc, Anna. *La Littérature française pour la jeunesse au siècle des lumières*. Wroclaw: Zaklad Narodowy, 1975.
Nodelman, Perry. "Children's Literature as Women's Writing." *Children's Literature Association Quarterly* 13 (1988): 31–34.
Nye, Andrea. *Feminism and Modern Philosophy: An Introduction*. New York: Routledge, 2004.
Offen, Karen. *European Feminisms: 1700–1950: A Political History*. Stanford: Stanford University Press, 2000.
Ogbu, John U. "Cultural Influences on Plasticity in Human Development." In *The Malleability of Children*, ed. James Gallagher and Craig Ramey. Baltimore: P. H. Brookes 1987.
O'Hagan, Timothy. *Jean-Jacques Rousseau and the Sources of the Self*. Brookfield, Ver.: Avebury, 1997.
Okin, Susan Moller. "Rousseau's Natural Woman." *Journal of Politics* 41: 2 (1979): 393–416.

Orwin, Clifford, and Nathan Tarcov. *The Legacy of Rousseau.* Chicago: University of Chicago Press, 1997.

Ottevanger, C. A. "From Subject to Citizen: The Evolution of French Educational Theory in the Eighteenth Century." In *Transactions of the 7th International Congress on the Enlightenment.* Vol. 264. Studies on Voltaire and the Eighteenth Century. Oxford: Voltaire Foundation, 1989.

Ozouf, Mona. *Festivals and the French Revolution.* Cambridge: Harvard University Press, 1991.

Palmer, R. R. *The Improvement of Humanity: Education and the French Revolution.* Princeton: Princeton University Press, 1985.

Parker, Alice A., and Elizabeth A Meese. *Feminist Critical Negotiations.* Philadelphia: John Benjamin Publishing Co., 1992.

Pateman, Carole. *The Sexual Contract.* Stanford: Stanford University Press, 1988.

Patterson, Sylvia. *Rousseau's Emile and Early Children's Literature.* Metuchen, N.J.: Scarecrow Press, 1978.

Paul, Lissa. "Enigma Variations: What Feminist Theory Knows about Children's Literature." In *Children's Literature: The Development of Criticism,* ed. Peter Hunt. London: Routledge, 1990.

Pellegrin, Nicole. *Les Vêtements de la liberté: Abécédaire des pratiques vestimentaires en France de 1780 à 1800.* Aix-en-Provence: Alinéa, 1989.

Perrot, Jean. *Du Jeu, des enfants et des livres.* Paris: Editions du Cercle, 1987.

Perrot, Jean, and Véronique Hadengue. *Ecriture féminine et littérature de jeunesse.* Actes du colloque d'Eaubonne (1994). Paris: La Nacelle, 1995.

Perrot, Michelle, ed. *A History of Private Life.* Vol. 4. *From the Fires of Revolution to the Great War,* trans. Arthur Goldhammer. Cambridge, Mass.: Belknap, 1990.

Perrot, Philippe. *Fashioning the Bourgeoisie: A History of Clothing in the Nineteenth Century.* Princeton: Princeton University Press, 1994.

Pichard, J. *Les Images éducatifs et leur utilisation dans l'enseignment au XIXième siècle.* Paris: Centre Audio-Visuel, 1961.

Pickering, Samuel F. Jr. "The Evolution of a Genre: Fictional Biographies for Children in the Eighteenth Century." *Journal of Narrative Technique* 7 (Winter 1977): 1–23.

———. *Moral Instruction and Fiction for Children, 1749–1820.* Athens: University of Georgia Press, 1993.

Pierrepont, Frank Graves. *Great Educators of Three Centuries: Their Work and Its Influence on Modern Education.* New York: AMS Press, 1971.

Plumb, J. H. "The First Flourishing of Children's Books." In *Early Children's Books and Their Illustration.* ed. J. H. Plumb. Boston: David R. Godine, 1975.

———. "The New World of Children in Eighteenth-Century England." *Past and Present* 67 (1975): 64–83.

Ponteil, Felix. *Histoire de l'enseignement en France: Les grandes étapes, 1789–1964.* Paris: Sirey, 1966.

Power, Edward J. *A Legacy of Learning: A History of Western Education.* Albany: State University of New York Press, 1991.

Préaud, Maxime, Pierre Casselle, Marianne Grivel, and Corinne Le Bitouzé. *Dictionnaire des éditeurs d'estampes à Paris sous l'ancien régime.* Paris: Promodis, 1987.

Prost, Antoine. *Histoire de l'enseignement en France, 1800–1967*. Paris: A. Colin, 1968.

Quinlan, Sean M. "Physical and Moral Regeneration after the Terror: Medical Culture, Sensibility and Family Politics in France, 1794–1804." *Social History* 29 (May 2004): 139–64.

Rabecq-Maillard, Marie Madeleine. *Histoire des jeux éducatifs*. Paris: F. Nathan, 1969.

———. *Histoire du jouet*. Paris: Hachette, 1962.

Rabkin, Eric. *Fantastic Worlds*. New York: Oxford University Press, 1979.

Rawls, John. *A Theory of Justice*. Cambridge: Harvard University Press, 1971.

Reed-Danahy, Deborah. *Education and Identity in Rural France: The Politics of Schooling*. Cambridge: Cambridge University Press, 1996.

Reicyn, Nina. *La Pédagogie de John Locke*. Paris: Hermann, 1941.

Reinier, Jacqueline S. *From Virtue to Character: American Childhood, 1775–1850*. New York: Twayne, 1996.

Reisert, Joseph R. "Authenticity, Justice, and Virtue in Taylor and Rousseau." *Polity* 33: 2 (2000): 305–30.

———. *Jean-Jacques Rousseau: A Friend of Virtue*. Ithaca: Cornell University Press, 2003.

Renault, Alain. *The Era of the Individual: A Contribution to the History of Subjectivity*. Trans. M. B. DeBevoise and Franklin Philip. Princeton: Princeton University Press, 1997.

Renonciat, Anne, ed., with Vivane Ezratty and Geneviève Patte. *Livres d'enfance, livres de France*. Paris: Hachette, 1998.

Revel, Jacques. "The Uses of Civility." In *A History of Private Life*, vol 3, ed. Roger Chartier, trans. Arthur Goldhammer. Cambridge, U.K.: 1989.

Reyniès, Nicole de. *Inventaire générale des monuments et des richesses artistiques de la France. Principes d'analyse scientifique*. Vol. 1. *Le Mobilier domestique*. Paris: Imprimerie Nationale, 1987.

Ribeiro, Aileen. *The Art of Dress: Fashion in England and France, 1750 to 1820*. New Haven: Yale University Press, 1995.

Richman, Amy L., et al. "Maternal Behavior to Infants in Five Cultures." In *Parental Behavior in Diverse Societies*, ed. Robert A. LeVine, Patrice Miller, and Mary Maxwell West. San Francisco: Jossey-Bass, 1988.

Ritvo, Harriet. "Learning from Animals: Natural History for Children in the Eighteenth and Nineteenth Centuries." *Children's Literature: Annual of the Modern Language Association Division on Children's Literature and the Children's Literature Association*. 13 (1985): 72–93.

Roach, Mary Ellen, and Kathleen Ehle Musa, ed. *New Perspectives on the History of Western Dress*. New York: NutriGuides, 1980.

Roche, Daniel. *The Culture of Clothing*. Trans. Jean Birrell. Cambridge: Cambridge University Press, 1996.

Rogers, Rebecca. *From the Salon to the Schoolroom: Educating Bourgeois Girls in Nineteenth-Century France*. University Park: Pennsylvania State University Press, 2005.

Rojek, Chris. "Problems of Involvement and Detachment in the Writings of Norbert Elias." *The British Journal of Sociology* 37 (1986): 584–96.

Rose, Jacqueline. *The Case of Peter Pan, or the Impossibility of Children's Fiction.* London: Routledge, 1984.

Rosenblatt, Helena. "On the 'Misogyny' of Jean-Jacques Rousseau: The *Letter to d'Alembert* in Historical Context." *French Historical Studies* 25: 1 (2002): 91–114.

———. *Rousseau and Geneva: From the First Discourse to The Social Contract, 1749–1762.* New York: Cambridge University Press, 2007.

Ryan, Mary P. "The Public and the Private Good: Across the Great Divide in Women's History," *Journal of Women's History* 15: 1 (2003): 10–27.

Salisbury, Joyce. *The Beast Within: Animals in the Middle Ages.* New York: Routledge, 1994.

Sanciaud, Anne. "L'evolution du costume enfantin au dix-huitième siècle: Un enjeu politique et social." Unpublished paper presented at the 2nd European Social Science History Conference, Amsterdam, The Netherlands, March 1997.

Schaeffer, Denise. "Reconsidering the Role of Sophie in Rousseau's *Emile.*" *Polity* 30 (1998): 607–26.

Sebbar-Pignon, Leila. "Mlle Lili ou l'ordre des poupées." *Les Temps Modernes* 31 (1976): 1796–1828.

See, Raymond. *Le Costume de la révolution à nos jours.* Preface by Gérard d'Houville. Paris: Éditions de la Gazette des Beaux-Arts, 1929.

Sehr, David T. *Education for Public Democracy.* Albany: State University of New York Press, 1997.

Sevrin, Raphaël. *Histoire de l'enseignement primaire en France sous la Révolution, le Consulat et l'empire.* Berlin: A. Clement, 1932.

———. *Histoire de l'enseignement primaire en France. La Restauration, 1815–1830.* Berlin: A. Clement, 1933.

Shorter, Edward. *History of Women's Bodies.* New York: Basic, 1982.

———. *The Making of the Modern Family.* New York: Basic, 1975.

Shouls, Peter. *Reasoned Freedom: John Locke and Enlightenment.* Ithaca: Cornell University Press, 1992.

Un Siècle d'enseignement à travers la caricature et l'image, 1805–1905. Exposition, Musée de l'enseignement (musée pedagogique). Préface de Marie Madeleine Kahain-Rabecq et L. Cros. Catalog par Jean Adhemar et Melle Hanote. Paris: Imprimerie Nationale, 1952.

Simon, Julia. *Mass Enlightenment: Critical Studies in Rousseau and Diderot.* Albany: State University of New York Press, 1995.

Smart, Annie. "'Bonnes Mères Qui Savent Penser': Motherhood and a Boy's Education in Rousseau's *Emile* and Epinay's *Lettres à Mon Fils.*" *New Perspectives on the Eighteenth Century* 3 (2006): 21–31.

Smith, Bonnie. *The Gender of History: Men, Women, and Historical Practice.* Cambridge: Harvard University Press, 1998.

———. *Ladies of the Leisure Class: The Bourgeoises of Northern France in the Nineteenth Century.* Princeton: Princeton University Press, 1981.

Smith, Teresa Ann. *The Emerging Female Citizen: Gender and Enlightenment in Spain.* Berkeley: University of California Press, 2006.

Sontag, Susan. *A Barthes Reader.* New York: Hill and Wang, 1982.

Soriano, Marc. "Histoire littéraire et folklore: La source oubliée de deux Fables de La Fontaine." *Revue d'histoire littéraire de la France* 70 (1970): 836–60.

———. "La Naissance du livre pour enfants." In *Bulletin des Bibliothèques de France* 11 (1966): 401–16.

Sozzi, Lionel. *Interprétations de Rousseau pendant la Révolution.* Vol. 64. Studies on Voltaire and the Eighteenth Century. Oxford: Voltaire Foundation, 1968.

Spacks, Patricia Meyer. "'Always at Variance': Politics of Eighteenth-Century Adolescence." In *A Distant Prospect: Eighteenth-Century Views of Childhood.* Los Angeles: Clark Library, 1982.

Spellman, W. M. *John Locke.* New York: St. Martin's, 1997.

Sperling, Liz. *Women, Political Philosophy and Politics.* Edinburgh: Edinburgh University Press, 2001.

Sroufe, L. Alan. "The Role of Infant-Caregiver Attachment in Development." In *Clinical Implications of Attachment,* ed. Jay Belsky and Teresa Nezworski. Hillsdale, N.J.: L. Erlbaum Assoc., 1988.

Stafford, Barbara Maria. *Artful Science: Enlightenment Entertainment and the Eclipse of Visual Education.* Cambridge: MIT Press, 1994.

Starobinski, Jean. *1789, The Emblems of Reason.* Charlottesville: University Press of Virginia, 1982.

———. *Jean-Jacques Rousseau: La transparence et l'obstacle suivi de sept essais sur Rousseau.* Paris: Gallimard, 1991.

———. *Jean-Jacques Rousseau, Transparency and Obstruction.* Trans. Arthur Goldhammer. Chicago: University of Chicago Press, 1988.

———. "La Mise en accusation de la société." *Jean-Jacques Rousseau.* Neuchâtel: Université de Neuchâtel, 1978.

Steele, Philip. *A History of Fashion and Costume.* Volume 7: *The Nineteenth Century.* New York: Facts On File, 2005.

Sterba, James. *Social and Political Philosophy: Classical Western Texts in Feminist and Multicultural Perspectives.* Belmont, Calif.: Wadsworth, 1998.

Stock-Morton, Phyllis. *Moral Education for a Secular Society: The Development of Morale Laique in Nineteenth Century France.* Albany: State University of New York, Albany, Press, 1988.

Stone, Lawrence. *The Family, Sex, and Marriage in England, 1500–1800.* New York: Harper and Row, 1979.

Strumingher, Laura. *What Were Little Girls and Boys Made of? Primary Education in Rural France, 1830–1880.* Albany: State University of New York, Albany, Press, 1983.

Summerfield, Geoffrey. *Fantasy and Reason: Children's Literature in the Eighteenth Century.* Athens: University of Georgia Press, 1985.

Talmon, Jacob Leib. *The Origins of Totalitarian Democracy.* New York: Praeger, 1968.

Taylor, Charles. *Sources of the Self: The Making of Modern Identity.* Cambridge: Harvard University Press, 1989.

Thirion, Christine. *La Presse pour les jeunes de 1815 à 1848.* Paris: Bulletin des Bibliothèques de France, 1972.

Thurer, Shari L. *The Myths of Motherhood: How Culture Reinvents the Good Mother.* New York: Houghton Mifflin, 1994.

Tiersot, Julien. *Les Fêtes et les chants de la Révolution française.* Paris: Hachette, 1908.

Tilly, Charles. "Population and Pedagogy in France." *History of Education Quarterly* 13 (1973): 113–28.

Todorov, Tzvetan. *Frail Happiness: An Essay on Rousseau.* Trans. Joan Scott and Robert Zaretsky. University Park: Pennsylvania State University Press, 2001.

Toledano, A. D. *La Vie de famille sous la Restauration et la Monarchie de Juillet.* Paris: Albin Michel, 1943.

Tosh, John. *A Man's Place: Masculinity and the Middle-Class Home in Victorian England.* New Haven: Yale University Press, 1999.

Townsend, John Rowe. *Written for Children: An Outline of English-Language Children's Literature.* 3rd ed. New York: Lippincott, 1987.

Trésors d'enfances au musée national de l'éducation: Education, école et jeux en France de 1500 à 1914. Exhibition at the Musée National de l'Education (Rouen/Mont Saint Aignan), 1991–1992. Paris: INRP, 1991.

Trigon, Jean de. *Histoire de la littérature enfantine. De ma Mère l'Oye au Roi Babar.* Paris: Hachette, 1950.

Trouille, Mary Seidman. *Sexual Politics in the Enlightenment: Women Writers Read Rousseau.* Albany: State University of New York, Albany, Press, 1997.

Ulrich, Laurel Thatcher. *Good Wives: Image and Reality in the Lives of Women in Northern New England, 1650–1750.* New York: Oxford University Press, 1983.

Vignery, John Robert. *The French Revolution and the Schools: The Educational Politics of the Mountain,1792–1794.* Madison: State Historical Society of Wisconsin for the Department of History, University of Wisconsin, 1965.

Vincent, Patrick H. *The Romantic Poetess: European Culture, Politics, and Gender, 1820–1840.* Durham: University of New Hampshire Press, 2004.

Viriville, August Vallet de. *Histoire de l'instruction publique en Europe et principalement en France depuis le christianisme jusqu'à nos jours: Universités, colléges, écoles des deux sexes, académies, bibliothèques publiques, etc.* Paris: Administration du moyen age et la renaissance, 1849.

Vulbeau, Alain. *Du Gouvernement des enfants.* Lonrai: Ateliers de Normandie, 1993.

Weiner, Martin J. "Treating Historical Sources as Literary Texts: Literary Historicism and Modern British History." *Journal of Modern History* 70 (September 1998): 619–38.

Weiss, Penny A. *Gendered Community: Rousseau, Sex, and Politics.* New York: New York University Press, 1993.

———. "Sex, Freedom, & Equality in Rousseau's *Emile.*" *Polity* 22 (1990): 603–25.

Wexler, Victor. "'Made for Man's Delight': Rousseau as Antifeminist." *American Historical Review* 81: 2 (April 1976): 266–91.

Wilkins, Kay S. *Children's Literature in Eighteenth-Century France.* Vol. 176. Studies on Voltaire and the Eighteenth Century. Oxford: Voltaire Foundation, 1978.

Wilson, Adrian. "The Infancy of the History of Childhood: An Appraisal of Philippe Ariès." *History and Theory* 19 (1980): 138–41.

Woloch, Isser. *The New Regime: Transformations of the French Civic Order, 1789–1820s.* New York: W. W. Norton, 1994.

Wright, Ernest Hunter. *The Meaning of Rousseau.* London: Oxford University Press, 1929.

Wyndham, Violet. *The Greatest Enchantress: Madame de Genlis.* London: André Deutsch, 1958.

Wyngaard, Amy S. *From Savage to Citizen: The Invention of the Peasant in the French Enlightenment.* Newark, N.J.: University of Delaware Press, 2004.

Yonge, Charlotte M. "Children's Literature of the Last Century." *Macmillan's Magazine* 20 (July 1869): 229–37; (August 1869): 310–20; (September 1869): 448–56.

Zagarri, Rosemarie. "Morals, Manners, and the Republican Mother." *American Quarterly* 44: 2 (1992): 192–215.

Index